# THE X FILES™

## VOLUME 3



GROUP

Library of Congress Cataloging-in-Publication Data

Rozum, John.
  The X-files / written by John Rozum and Gordon Purcell
   p. cm.
  "X-files created by Chris Carter."
  "Originally published by Topps Comics."
  ISBN 1-933160-39-X (alk. paper)
  I. Rozum, John. II. Purcell, Gordon. III. Carter, Chris, 1957- IV. Title.
  PN6727.P4685X2 2005
  741.5'973--dc22

                                        2005003802

"We work in the dark. We do what we can to battle the evil that would otherwise destroy us. But if a man's character is his fate, it's not a choice but a calling. Sometimes the weight of this burden causes us to falter, breaching the fragile fortress of our mind. Allowing the monster without to turn within. We are left alone staring into the abyss. Into the laughing face of madness. "
                        - Special Agent Fox Mulder

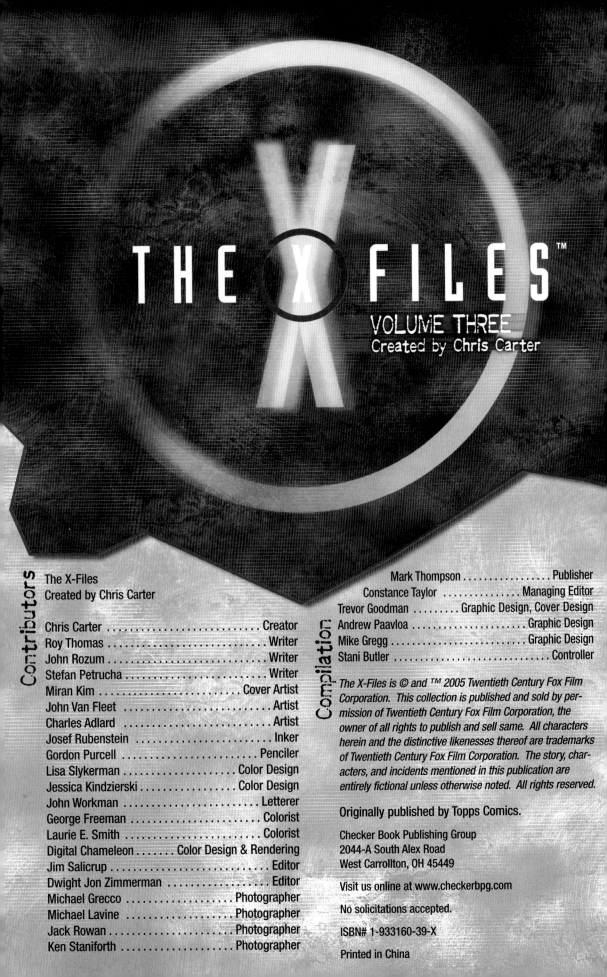

# THE X FILES™

## VOLUME THREE
### Created by Chris Carter

**Contributors**

The X-Files
Created by Chris Carter

Chris Carter . . . . . . . . . . . . . . . . . . . . . . . . . Creator
Roy Thomas . . . . . . . . . . . . . . . . . . . . . . . . . . Writer
John Rozum . . . . . . . . . . . . . . . . . . . . . . . . . . Writer
Stefan Petrucha . . . . . . . . . . . . . . . . . . . . . . . Writer
Miran Kim . . . . . . . . . . . . . . . . . . . . . Cover Artist
John Van Fleet . . . . . . . . . . . . . . . . . . . . . . . . Artist
Charles Adlard . . . . . . . . . . . . . . . . . . . . . . . . Artist
Josef Rubenstein . . . . . . . . . . . . . . . . . . . . . Inker
Gordon Purcell . . . . . . . . . . . . . . . . . . . . . Penciler
Lisa Slykerman . . . . . . . . . . . . . . . . . . Color Design
Jessica Kindzierski . . . . . . . . . . . . . . . Color Design
John Workman . . . . . . . . . . . . . . . . . . . . . Letterer
George Freeman . . . . . . . . . . . . . . . . . . . . Colorist
Laurie E. Smith . . . . . . . . . . . . . . . . . . . . Colorist
Digital Chameleon . . . . . . . Color Design & Rendering
Jim Salicrup . . . . . . . . . . . . . . . . . . . . . . . . . Editor
Dwight Jon Zimmerman . . . . . . . . . . . . . . . . Editor
Michael Grecco . . . . . . . . . . . . . . . . . . Photographer
Michael Lavine . . . . . . . . . . . . . . . . . . Photographer
Jack Rowan . . . . . . . . . . . . . . . . . . . . Photographer
Ken Staniforth . . . . . . . . . . . . . . . . . . Photographer

**Compilation**

Mark Thompson . . . . . . . . . . . . . . . . . Publisher
Constance Taylor . . . . . . . . . . . . . . Managing Editor
Trevor Goodman . . . . . . . . . Graphic Design, Cover Design
Andrew Paavloa . . . . . . . . . . . . . . . . . . Graphic Design
Mike Gregg . . . . . . . . . . . . . . . . . . . . . Graphic Design
Stani Butler . . . . . . . . . . . . . . . . . . . . . . . Controller

Originally published by Topps Comics.

Checker Book Publishing Group
2044-A South Alex Road
West Carrollton, OH 45449

Visit us online at www.checkerbpg.com

No solicitations accepted.

ISBN# 1-933160-39-X

Printed in China

## Table of Contents

## Trust vs. Skepticism

I miss the X-Files. Even watching it ten years after it was on the air, it still holds up, like good entertainment should. The comics are no exception… writers with all types of backgrounds converged to tell their own stories of the unexplained. From Bigfoot to vengeful organ donors back from the grave, the variety of the paranormal activity in the comics is definitely up to par with the television show.

In lots of the X-Files stories, whether the mystery turns out to be of paranormal origin or not, the overriding theme seems to be about confronting the "monsters" underneath society's collective bed. Right now we've got the media barking at us about terrorism, school shootings, war, global warming, pollution… the list goes on and on. I'm not saying that these aren't legitimate problems. Of course they are. But where did all these problems come from? Unfortunately, about 99% came directly from us. And by that I mean humanity's maddening propensity to not take any social responsibility, for not opening our eyes to see greater possibilities, for continuing to make (instead of learning from) the same mistakes and blunders we've made for thousands of years. The damage we're doing is becoming more and more irreversible, because now we have toxic waste, nuclear bombs, and other such lovely things… and yet we still focus on eradicating symptoms instead of causes, since we refuse to learn how to make things better. Since we refuse to learn our own truth. We're putting out fires while everyone ignores the kid in the corner with the matches and newspapers.

Don't we wish that our fears stemmed from something as exotic and mysterious as a soul-sucking overcoat or a homicidal pyrokinetic? While the X-Files has antagonists like these in spades, they'll occasionally blindside us with a story like "Be Prepared", in which we're reminded that so many of our fears and problems come from the very human tendency to get caught up in popular superstition (which could be anything from urban legends to government propaganda) and ignore the root of the problem. It is up to us, of course, to sort fact from fiction, to dig beyond what we're told to find the truth. Forget angels and demons on our shoulders… what we need are little Mulders and Scullys whispering at us.

Constance Taylor
Managing Editor
Checker Book Publishing Group

# DONOR

STORY: John Rozum
ART: Charles Adlard

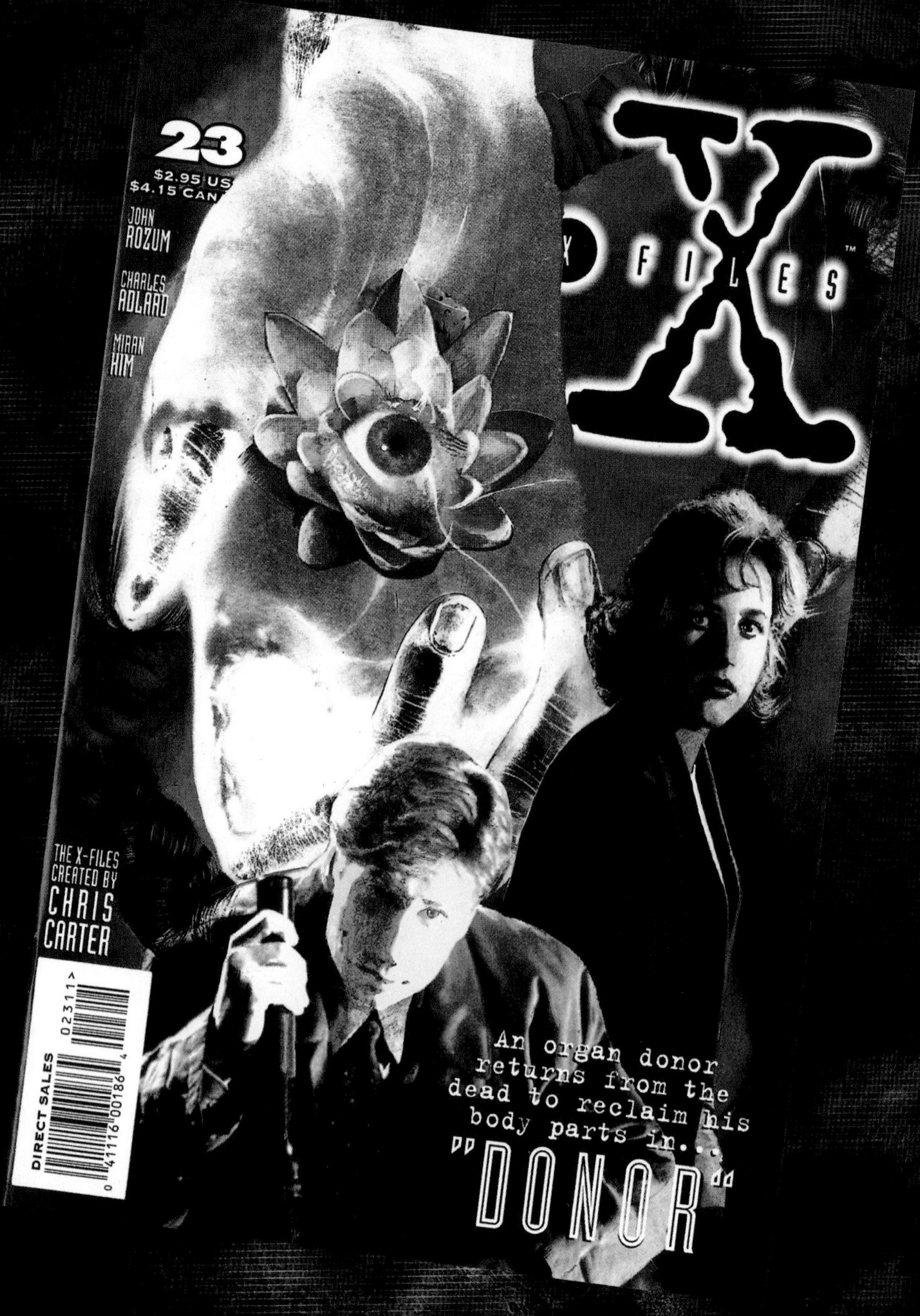
23
$2.95 US
$4.15 CAN
JOHN ROZUM
CHARLES ADLARD
MIRAN KIM
X FILES
THE X-FILES CREATED BY CHRIS CARTER
DIRECT SALES
An organ donor returns from the dead to reclaim his body parts in...
"DONOR"

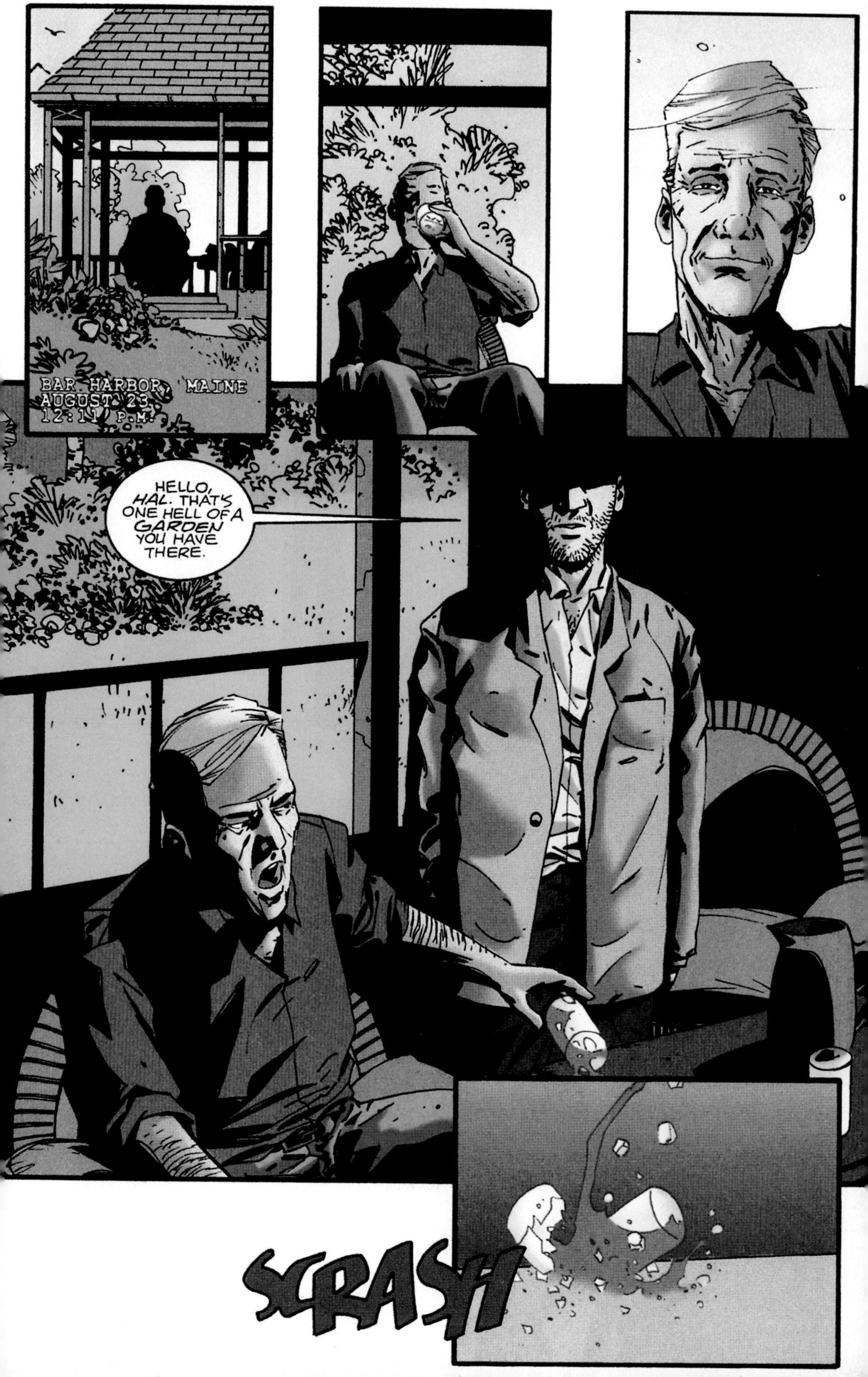
BAR HARBOR, MAINE
AUGUST 23
12:11 P.M.
HELLO, HAL. THAT'S ONE HELL OF A GARDEN YOU HAVE THERE.
SCRASH

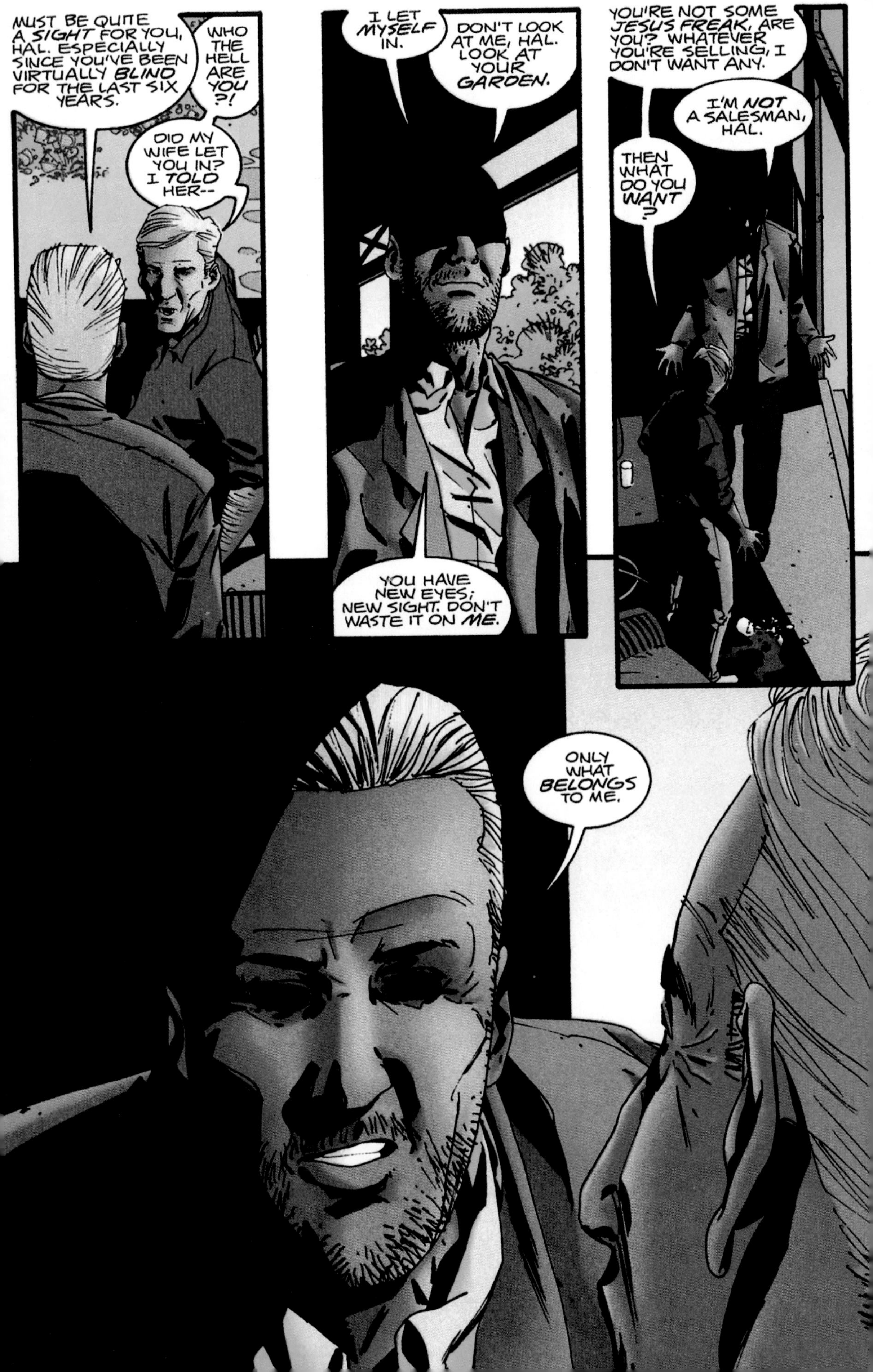
MUST BE QUITE A SIGHT FOR YOU, HAL. ESPECIALLY SINCE YOU'VE BEEN VIRTUALLY BLIND FOR THE LAST SIX YEARS.
WHO THE HELL ARE YOU ?!
DID MY WIFE LET YOU IN? I TOLD HER--
I LET MYSELF IN.
DON'T LOOK AT ME, HAL. LOOK AT YOUR GARDEN.
YOU HAVE NEW EYES; NEW SIGHT. DON'T WASTE IT ON ME.
YOU'RE NOT SOME JESUS FREAK, ARE YOU? WHATEVER YOU'RE SELLING, I DON'T WANT ANY.
I'M NOT A SALESMAN, HAL.
THEN WHAT DO YOU WANT ?
ONLY WHAT BELONGS TO ME.

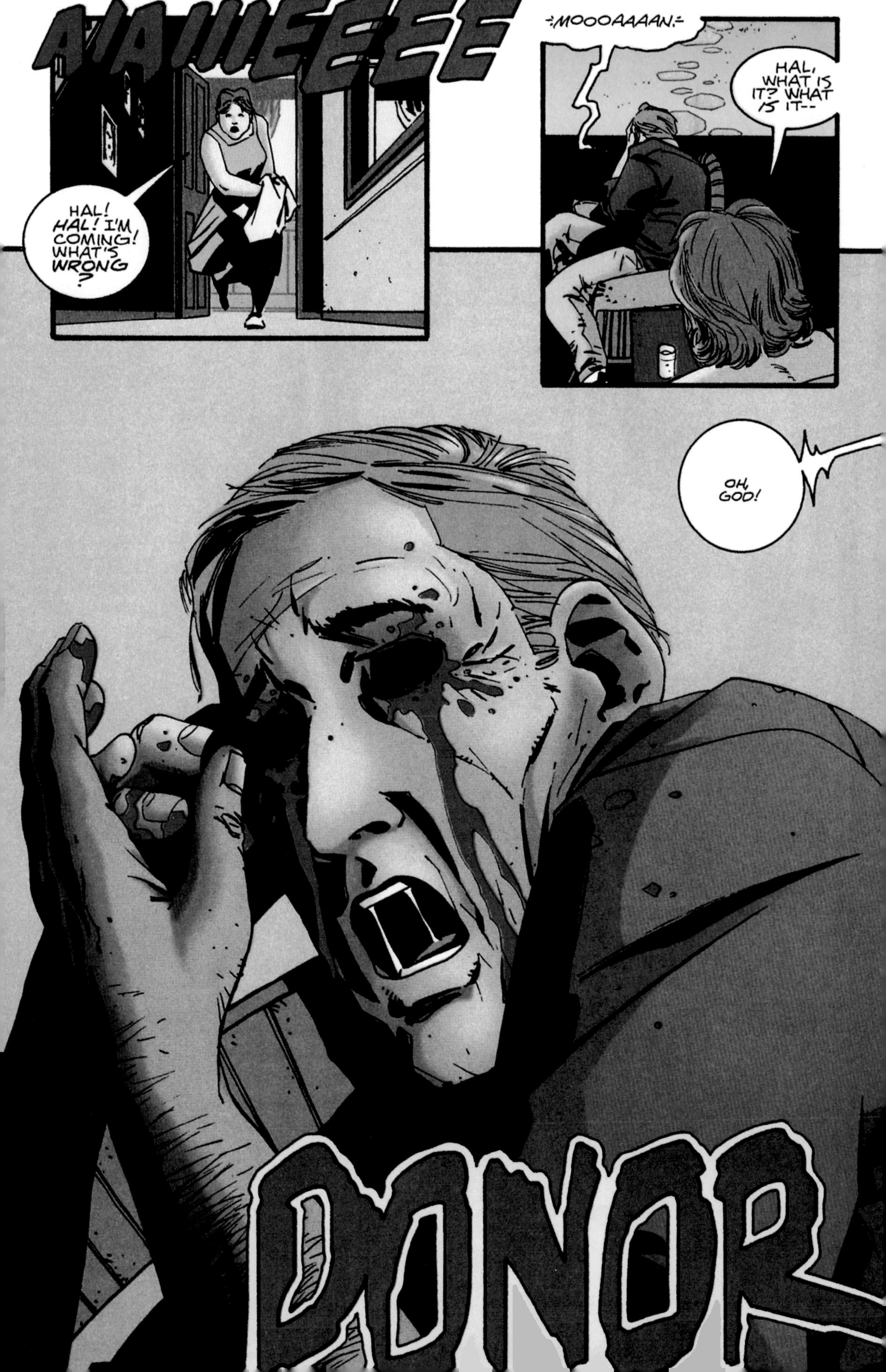
AIAIIIEEEEE
HAL! HAL! I'M COMING! WHAT'S WRONG?
MOOOAAAAN
HAL, WHAT IS IT? WHAT IS IT--
OH, GOD!
DDNOR

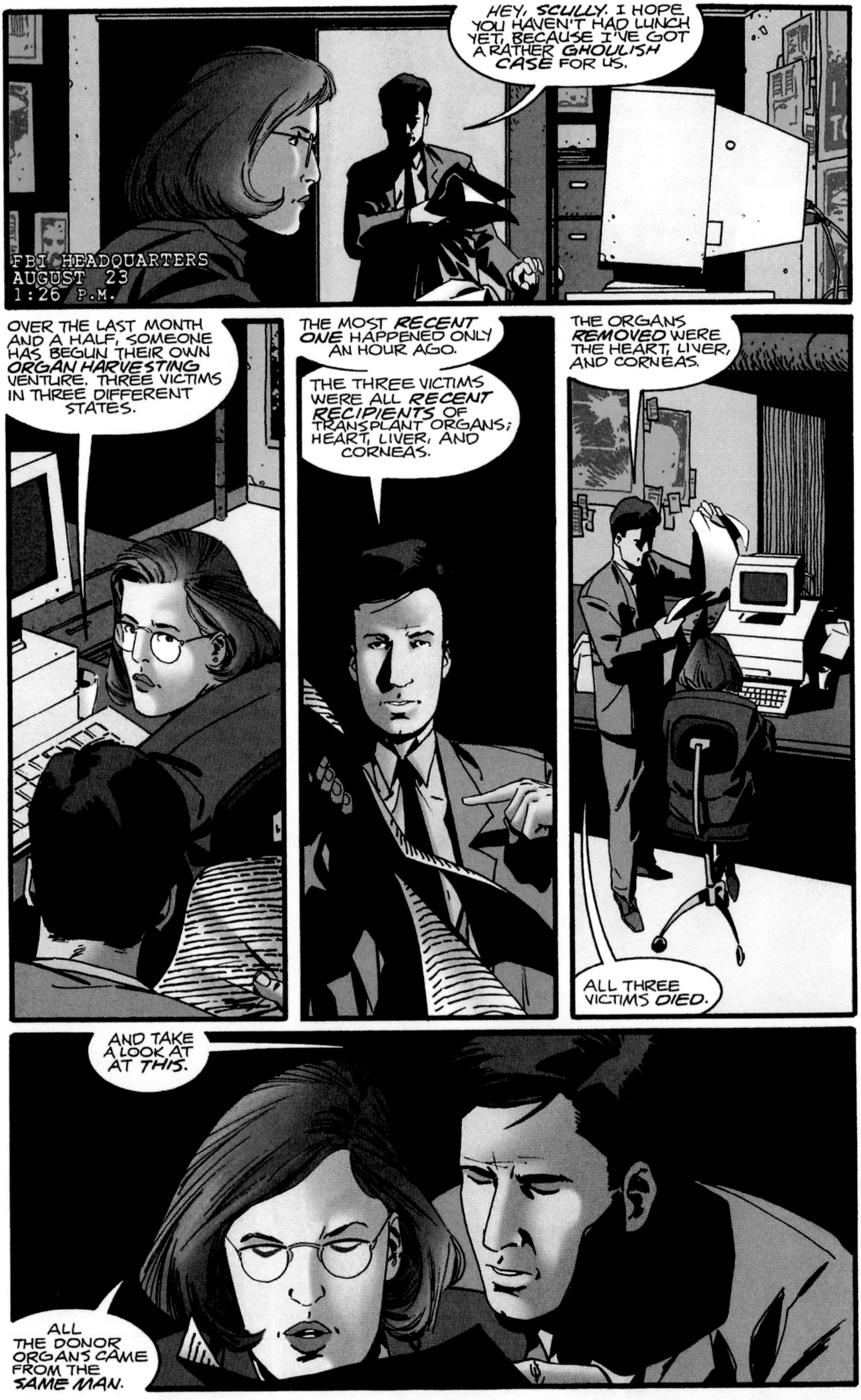
HEY, SCULLY. I HOPE YOU HAVEN'T HAD LUNCH YET, BECAUSE I'VE GOT A RATHER GHOULISH CASE FOR US.
FBI HEADQUARTERS AUGUST 23 1:26 P.M.
OVER THE LAST MONTH AND A HALF, SOMEONE HAS BEGUN THEIR OWN ORGAN HARVESTING VENTURE. THREE VICTIMS IN THREE DIFFERENT STATES.
THE MOST RECENT ONE HAPPENED ONLY AN HOUR AGO.
THE THREE VICTIMS WERE ALL RECENT RECIPIENTS OF TRANSPLANT ORGANS; HEART, LIVER, AND CORNEAS.
THE ORGANS REMOVED WERE THE HEART, LIVER, AND CORNEAS.
ALL THREE VICTIMS DIED.
AND TAKE A LOOK AT AT THIS.
ALL THE DONOR ORGANS CAME FROM THE SAME MAN.

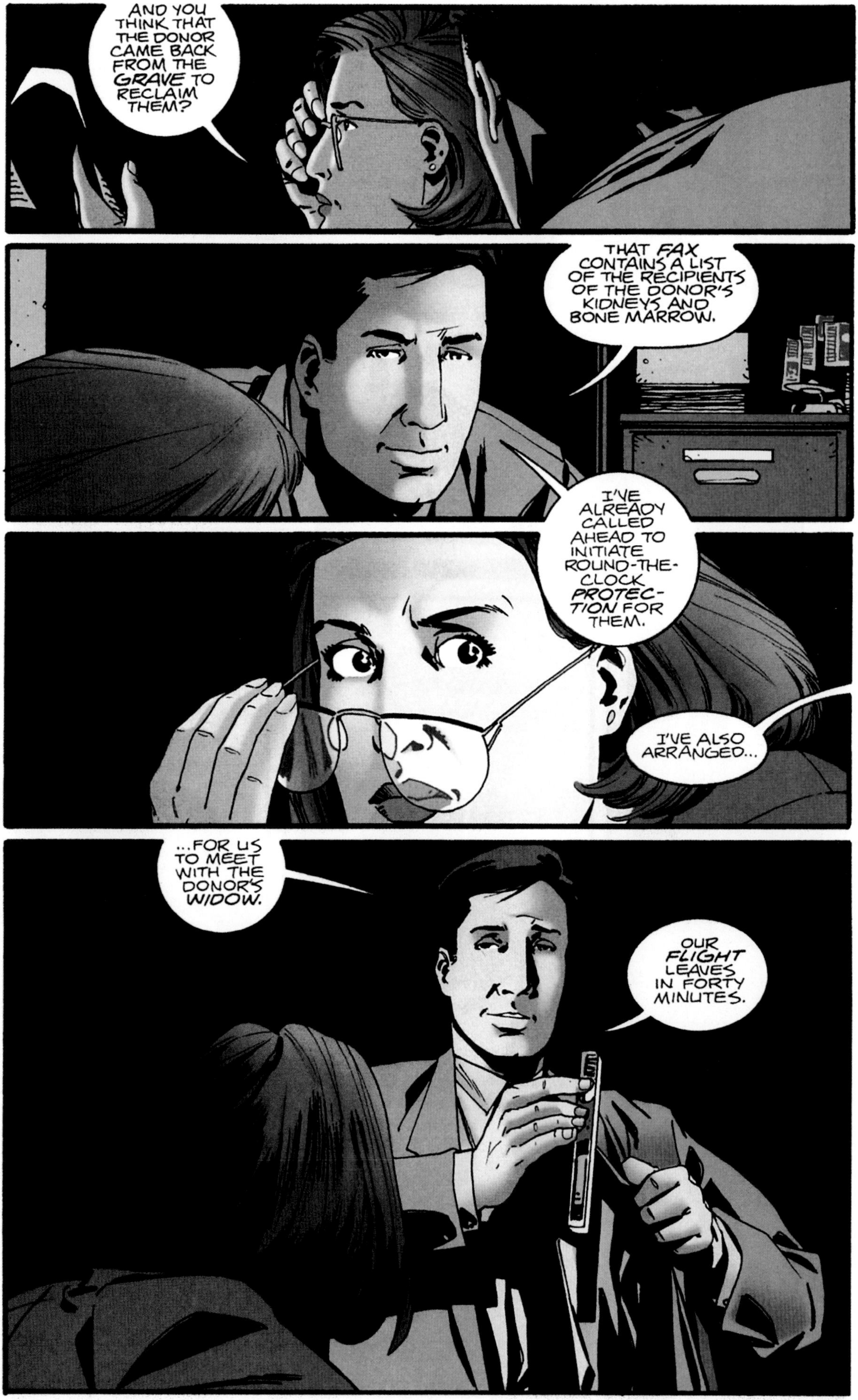
AND YOU THINK THAT THE DONOR CAME BACK FROM THE GRAVE TO RECLAIM THEM?
THAT FAX CONTAINS A LIST OF THE RECIPIENTS OF THE DONOR'S KIDNEYS AND BONE MARROW.
I'VE ALREADY CALLED AHEAD TO INITIATE ROUND-THE-CLOCK PROTECTION FOR THEM.
I'VE ALSO ARRANGED...
...FOR US TO MEET WITH THE DONOR'S WIDOW.
OUR FLIGHT LEAVES IN FORTY MINUTES.

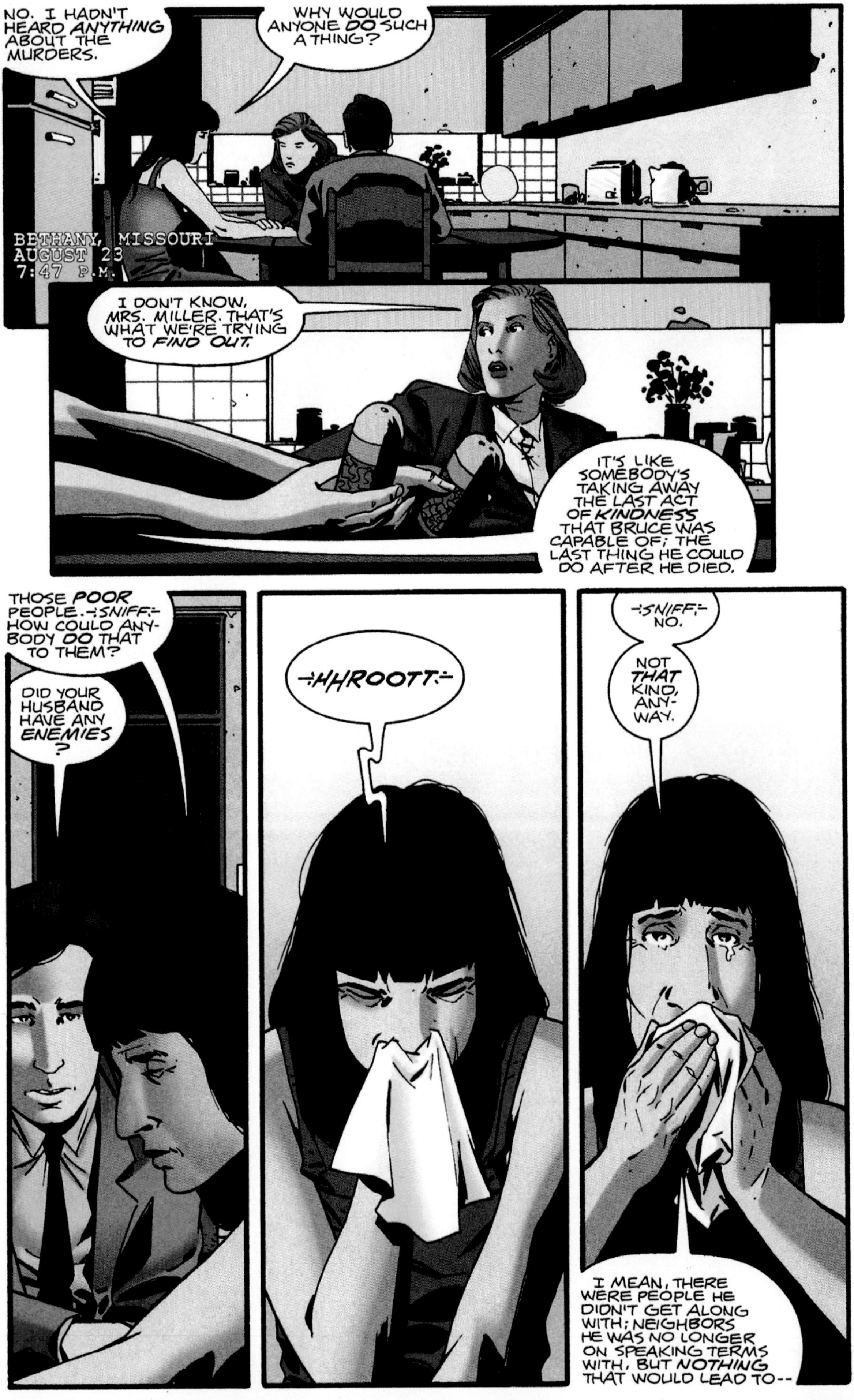
NO. I HADN'T HEARD ANYTHING ABOUT THE MURDERS.
WHY WOULD ANYONE DO SUCH A THING?
BETHANY, MISSOURI AUGUST 23 7:47 P.M.
I DON'T KNOW, MRS. MILLER. THAT'S WHAT WE'RE TRYING TO FIND OUT.
IT'S LIKE SOMEBODY'S TAKING AWAY THE LAST ACT OF KINDNESS THAT BRUCE WAS CAPABLE OF; THE LAST THING HE COULD DO AFTER HE DIED.
THOSE POOR PEOPLE. -SNIFF- HOW COULD ANYBODY DO THAT TO THEM?
DID YOUR HUSBAND HAVE ANY ENEMIES?
-HHROOTT-
-SNIFF- NO.
NOT THAT KIND, ANYWAY.
I MEAN, THERE WERE PEOPLE HE DIDN'T GET ALONG WITH; NEIGHBORS HE WAS NO LONGER ON SPEAKING TERMS WITH, BUT NOTHING THAT WOULD LEAD TO--

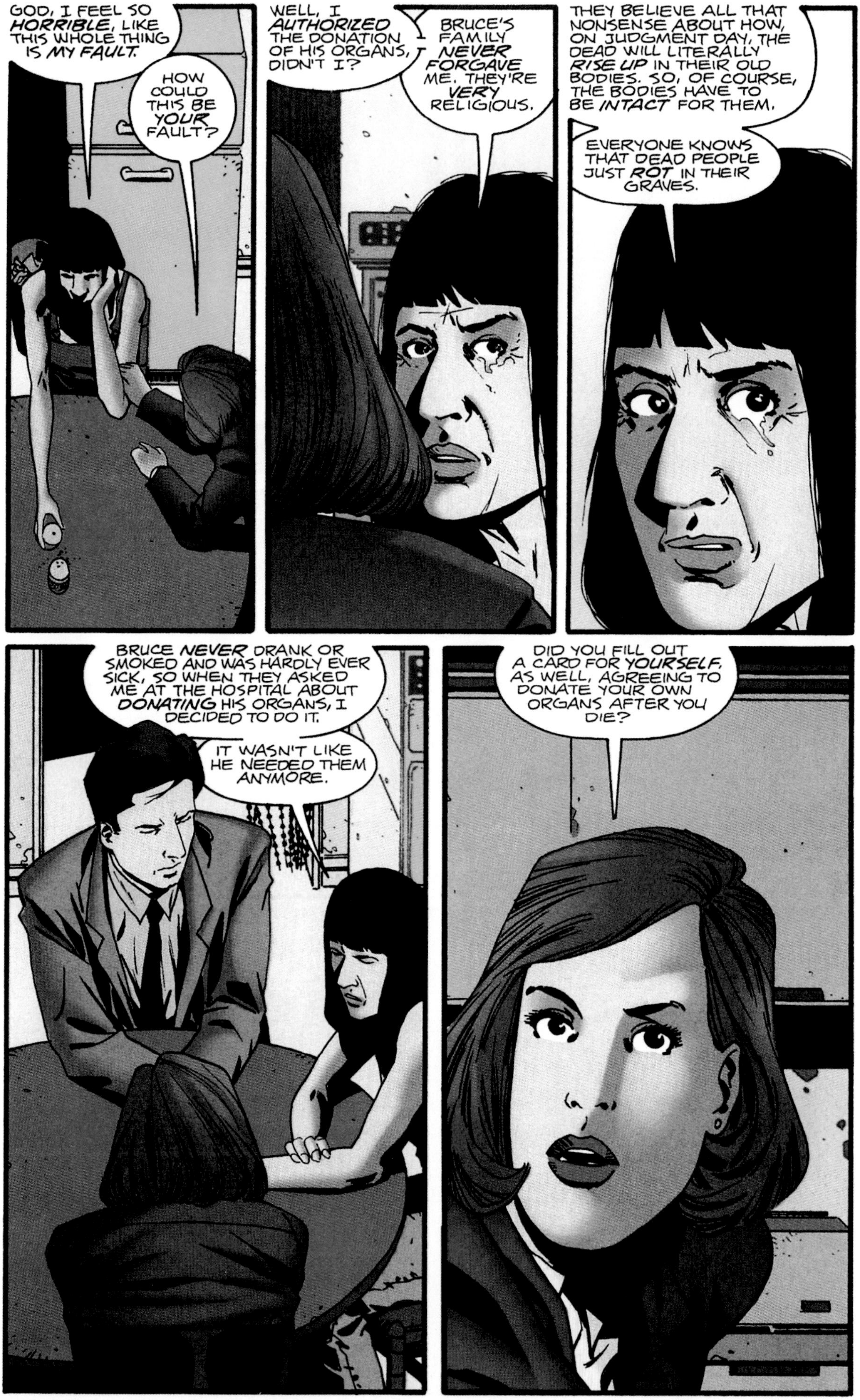
GOD, I FEEL SO *HORRIBLE*, LIKE THIS WHOLE THING IS *MY FAULT*.
HOW COULD THIS BE *YOUR* FAULT?
WELL, I *AUTHORIZED* THE DONATION OF HIS ORGANS, DIDN'T I?
BRUCE'S FAMILY *NEVER FORGAVE* ME. THEY'RE *VERY* RELIGIOUS.
THEY BELIEVE ALL THAT NONSENSE ABOUT HOW, ON JUDGMENT DAY, THE DEAD WILL LITERALLY *RISE UP* IN THEIR OLD BODIES. SO, OF COURSE, THE BODIES HAVE TO BE *INTACT* FOR THEM.
EVERYONE KNOWS THAT DEAD PEOPLE JUST *ROT* IN THEIR GRAVES.
BRUCE *NEVER* DRANK OR SMOKED AND WAS HARDLY EVER SICK, SO WHEN THEY ASKED ME AT THE HOSPITAL ABOUT *DONATING* HIS ORGANS, I DECIDED TO DO IT.
IT WASN'T LIKE HE NEEDED THEM ANYMORE.
DID YOU FILL OUT A CARD FOR *YOURSELF*, AS WELL, AGREEING TO DONATE YOUR OWN ORGANS AFTER YOU DIE?

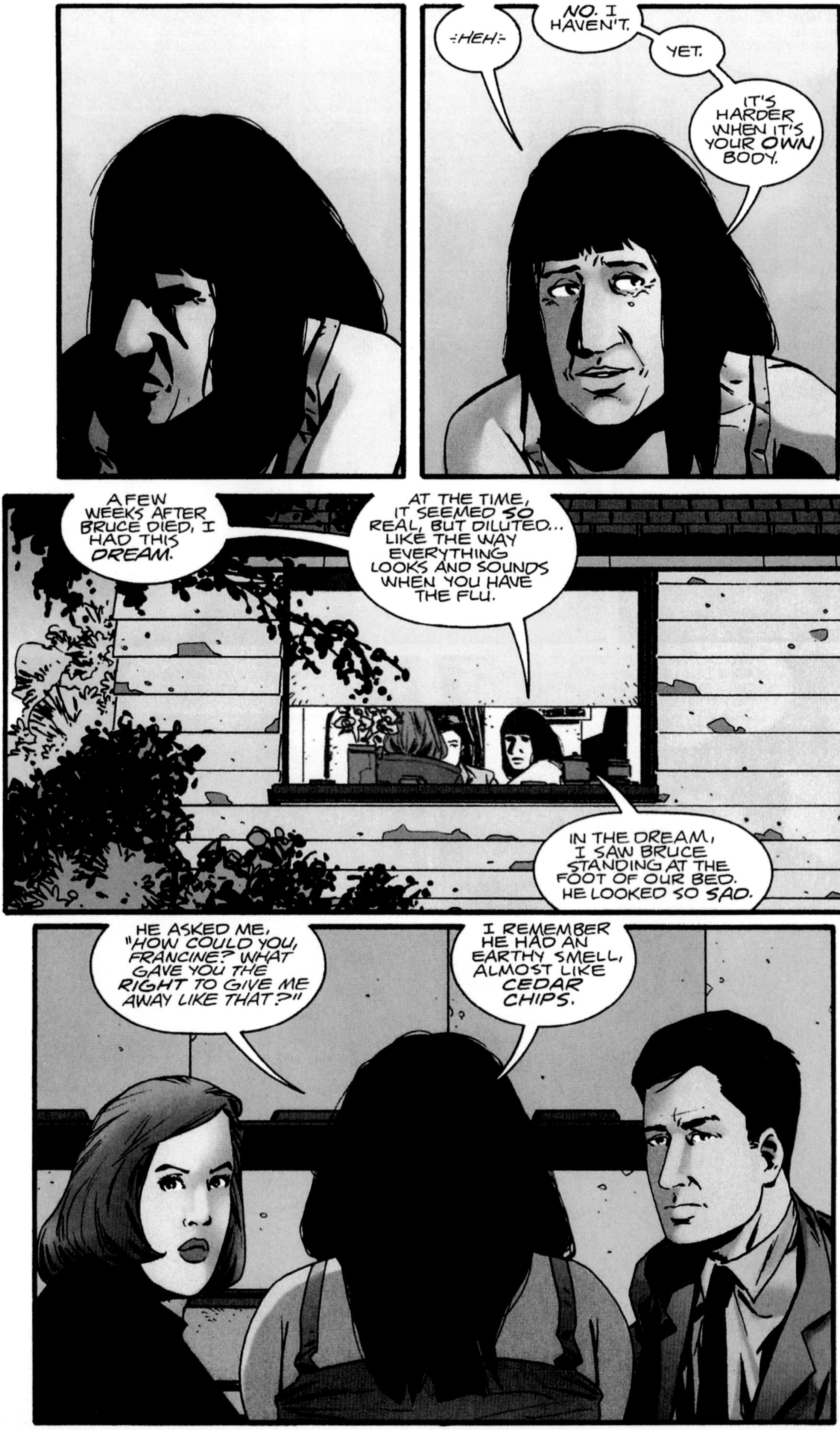

HEH
NO. I HAVEN'T.
YET.
IT'S HARDER WHEN IT'S YOUR OWN BODY.
A FEW WEEKS AFTER BRUCE DIED, I HAD THIS DREAM.
AT THE TIME, IT SEEMED SO REAL, BUT DILUTED... LIKE THE WAY EVERYTHING LOOKS AND SOUNDS WHEN YOU HAVE THE FLU.
IN THE DREAM, I SAW BRUCE STANDING AT THE FOOT OF OUR BED. HE LOOKED SO SAD.
HE ASKED ME, "HOW COULD YOU, FRANCINE? WHAT GAVE YOU THE RIGHT TO GIVE ME AWAY LIKE THAT?"
I REMEMBER HE HAD AN EARTHY SMELL, ALMOST LIKE CEDAR CHIPS.

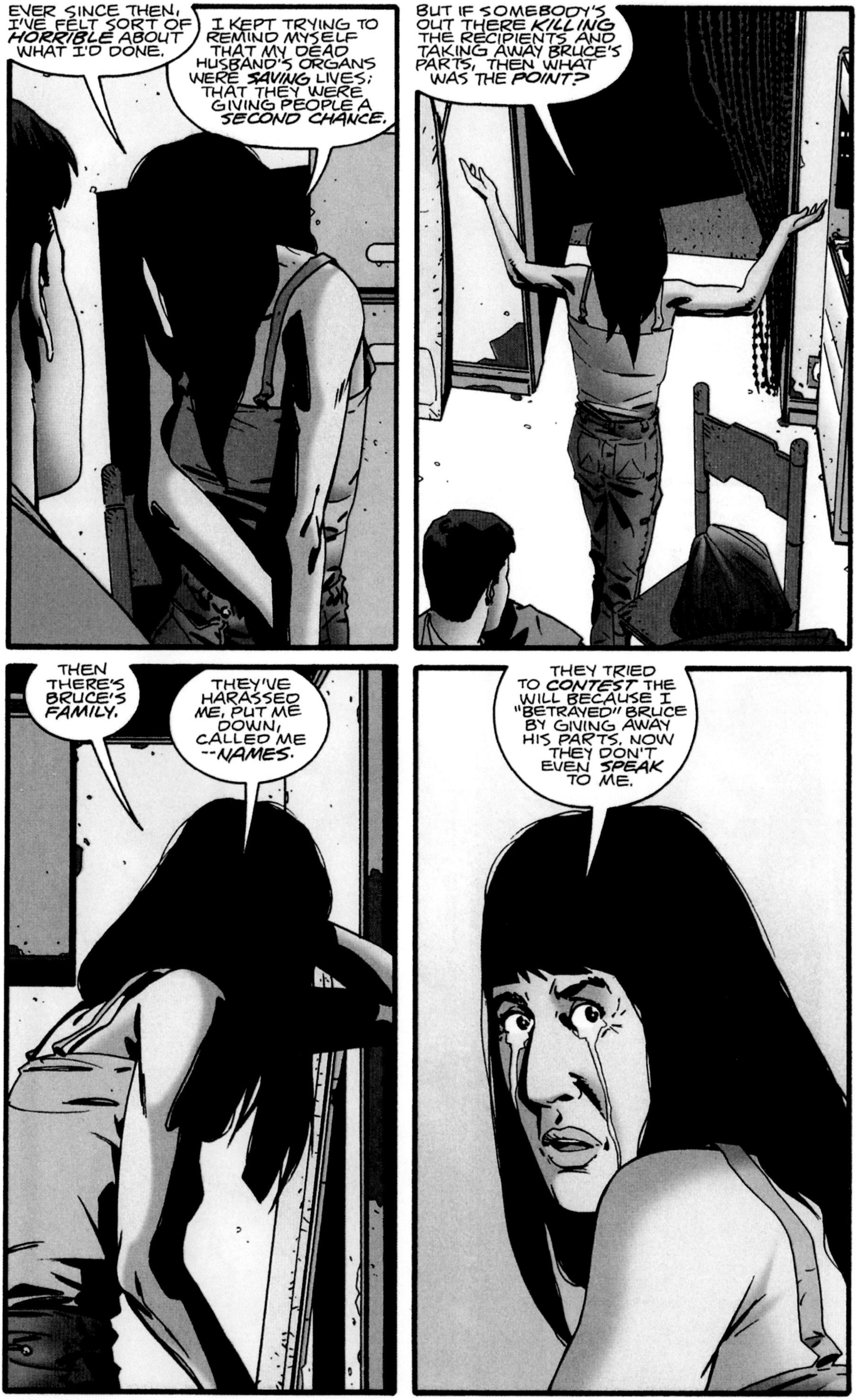
EVER SINCE THEN, I'VE FELT SORT OF HORRIBLE ABOUT WHAT I'D DONE.
I KEPT TRYING TO REMIND MYSELF THAT MY DEAD HUSBAND'S ORGANS WERE SAVING LIVES; THAT THEY WERE GIVING PEOPLE A SECOND CHANCE.
BUT IF SOMEBODY'S OUT THERE KILLING THE RECIPIENTS AND TAKING AWAY BRUCE'S PARTS, THEN WHAT WAS THE POINT?
THEN THERE'S BRUCE'S FAMILY.
THEY'VE HARASSED ME, PUT ME DOWN, CALLED ME --NAMES.
THEY TRIED TO CONTEST THE WILL BECAUSE I "BETRAYED" BRUCE BY GIVING AWAY HIS PARTS. NOW THEY DON'T EVEN SPEAK TO ME.

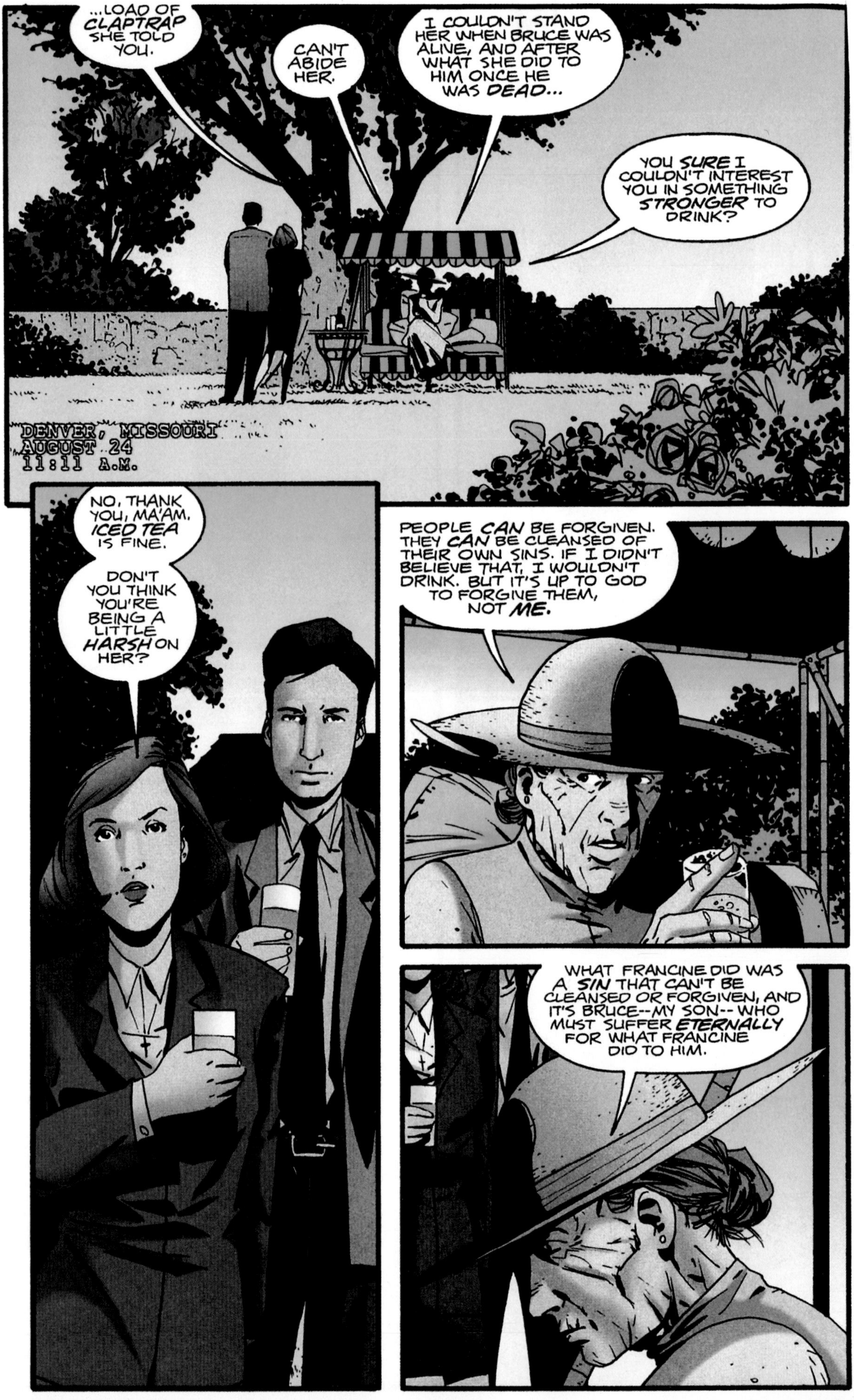
...LOAD OF CLAPTRAP SHE TOLD YOU.
CAN'T ABIDE HER.
I COULDN'T STAND HER WHEN BRUCE WAS ALIVE, AND AFTER WHAT SHE DID TO HIM ONCE HE WAS DEAD...
YOU SURE I COULDN'T INTEREST YOU IN SOMETHING STRONGER TO DRINK?
DENVER, MISSOURI
AUGUST 24
11:11 A.M.
NO, THANK YOU, MA'AM. ICED TEA IS FINE.
DON'T YOU THINK YOU'RE BEING A LITTLE HARSH ON HER?
PEOPLE CAN BE FORGIVEN. THEY CAN BE CLEANSED OF THEIR OWN SINS. IF I DIDN'T BELIEVE THAT, I WOULDN'T DRINK. BUT IT'S UP TO GOD TO FORGIVE THEM, NOT ME.
WHAT FRANCINE DID WAS A SIN THAT CAN'T BE CLEANSED OR FORGIVEN, AND IT'S BRUCE--MY SON--WHO MUST SUFFER ETERNALLY FOR WHAT FRANCINE DID TO HIM.

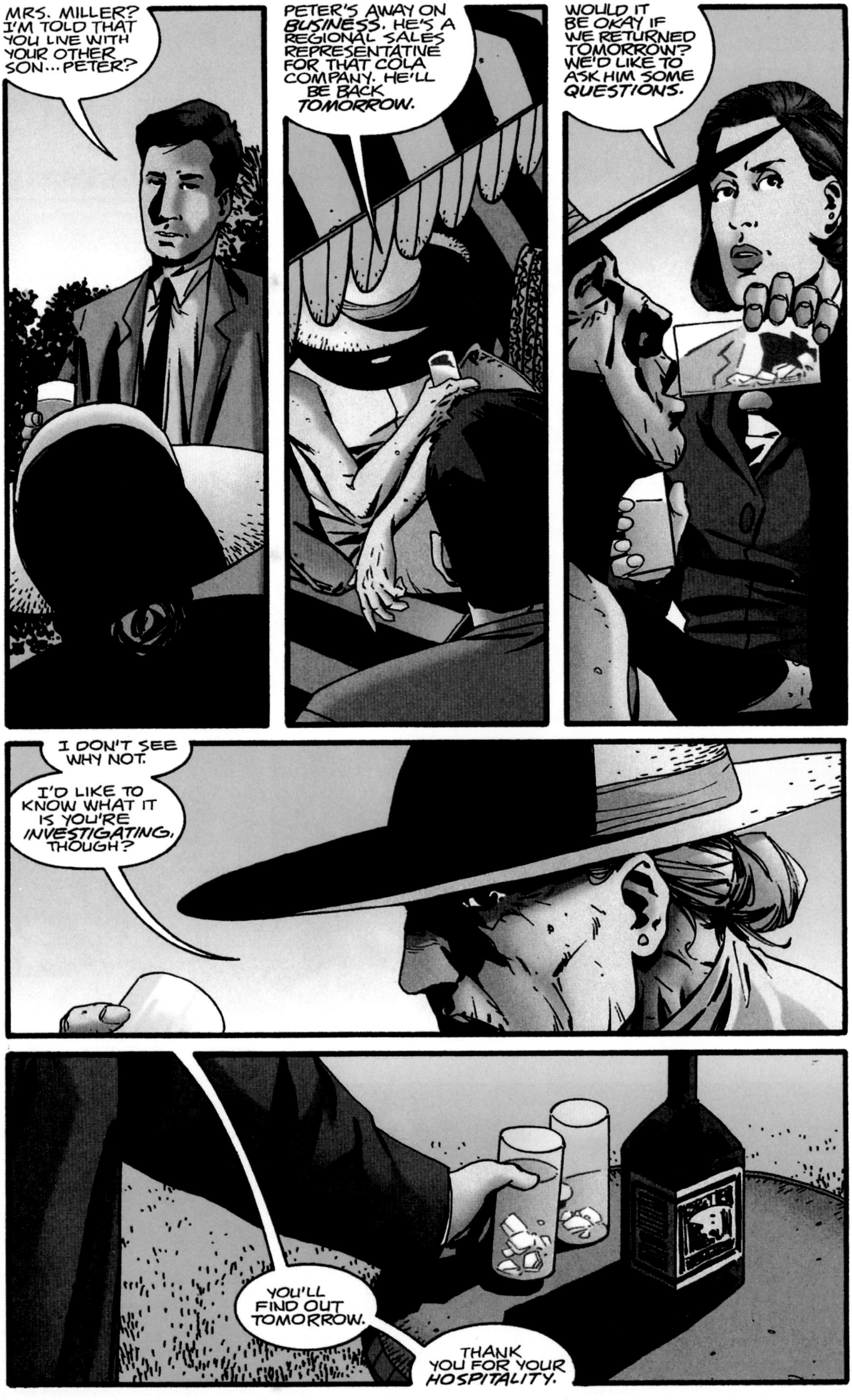
MRS. MILLER? I'M TOLD THAT YOU LIVE WITH YOUR OTHER SON... PETER?
PETER'S AWAY ON BUSINESS. HE'S A REGIONAL SALES REPRESENTATIVE FOR THAT COLA COMPANY. HE'LL BE BACK TOMORROW.
WOULD IT BE OKAY IF WE RETURNED TOMORROW? WE'D LIKE TO ASK HIM SOME QUESTIONS.
I DON'T SEE WHY NOT.
I'D LIKE TO KNOW WHAT IT IS YOU'RE INVESTIGATING, THOUGH?
YOU'LL FIND OUT TOMORROW.
THANK YOU FOR YOUR HOSPITALITY.

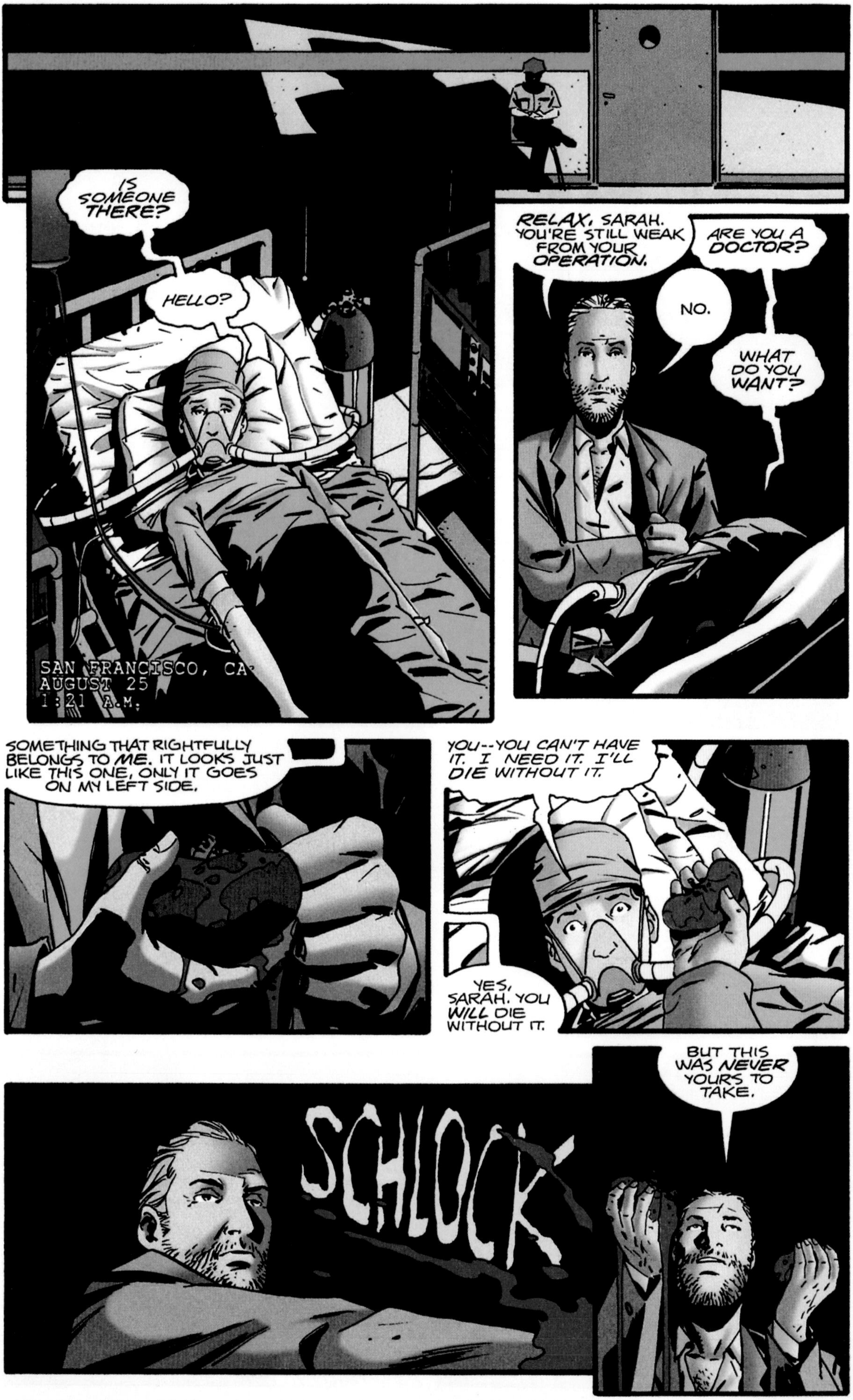
IS SOMEONE THERE?
HELLO?
SAN FRANCISCO, CA
AUGUST 25
1:21 A.M.
RELAX, SARAH. YOU'RE STILL WEAK FROM YOUR OPERATION.
ARE YOU A DOCTOR?
NO.
WHAT DO YOU WANT?
SOMETHING THAT RIGHTFULLY BELONGS TO ME. IT LOOKS JUST LIKE THIS ONE, ONLY IT GOES ON MY LEFT SIDE.
YOU--YOU CAN'T HAVE IT. I NEED IT. I'LL DIE WITHOUT IT.
YES, SARAH. YOU WILL DIE WITHOUT IT.
SCHLOCK
BUT THIS WAS NEVER YOURS TO TAKE.

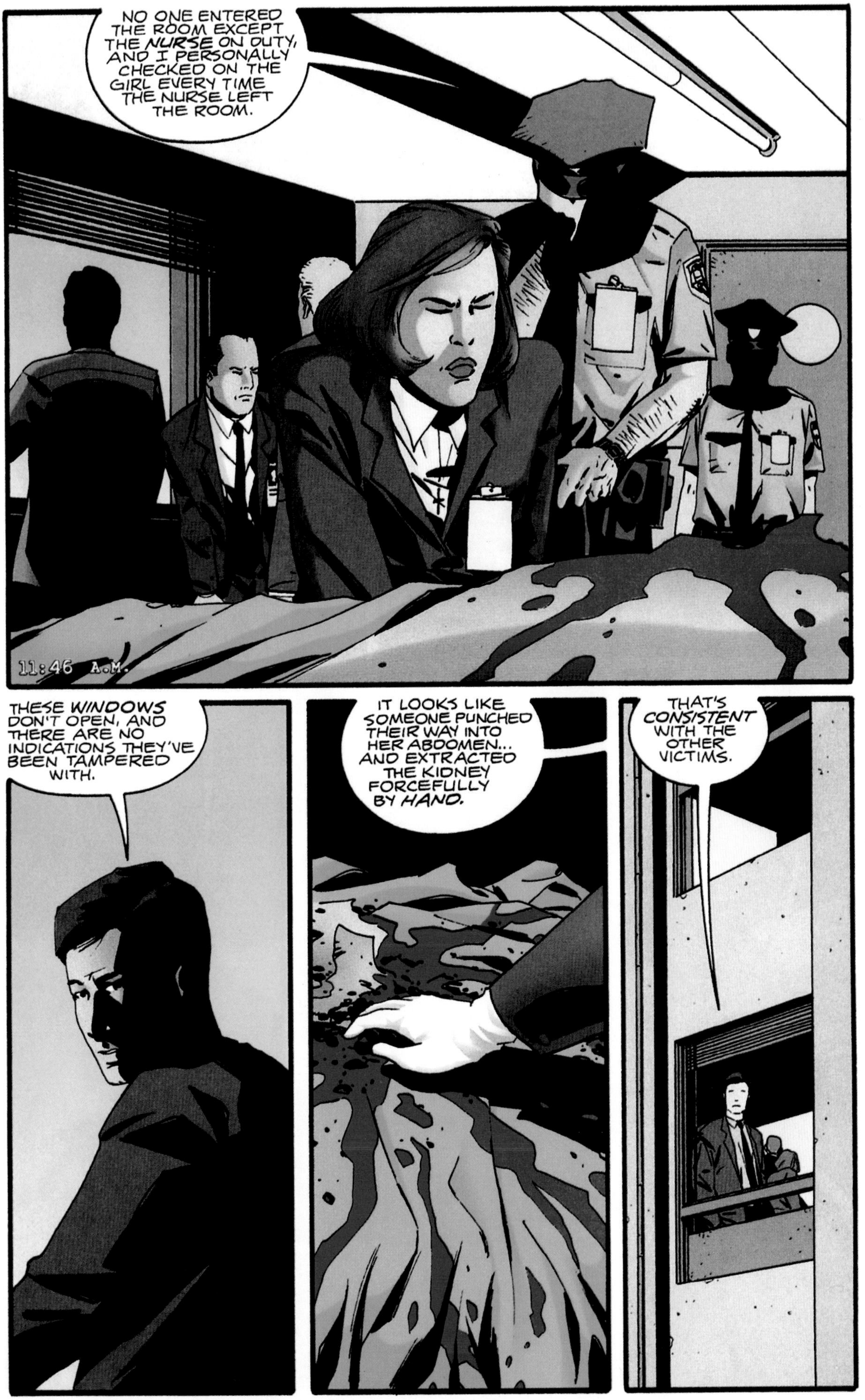
NO ONE ENTERED THE ROOM EXCEPT THE NURSE ON DUTY, AND I PERSONALLY CHECKED ON THE GIRL EVERY TIME THE NURSE LEFT THE ROOM.
11:46 A.M.
THESE WINDOWS DON'T OPEN, AND THERE ARE NO INDICATIONS THEY'VE BEEN TAMPERED WITH.
IT LOOKS LIKE SOMEONE PUNCHED THEIR WAY INTO HER ABDOMEN... AND EXTRACTED THE KIDNEY FORCEFULLY BY HAND.
THAT'S CONSISTENT WITH THE OTHER VICTIMS.

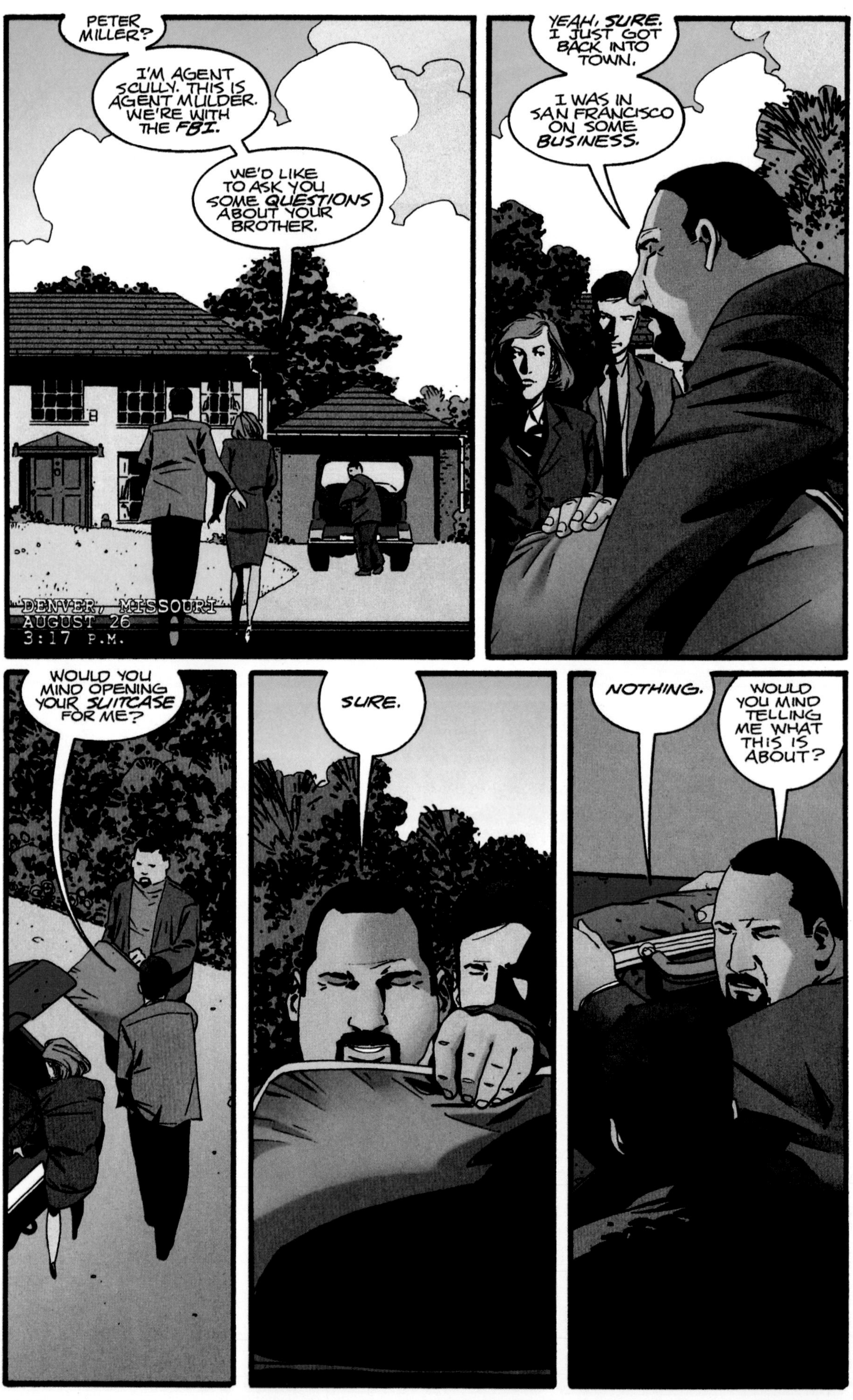
PETER MILLER?
I'M AGENT SCULLY. THIS IS AGENT MULDER. WE'RE WITH THE FBI.
WE'D LIKE TO ASK YOU SOME QUESTIONS ABOUT YOUR BROTHER.
DENVER, MISSOURI
AUGUST 26
3:17 P.M.
YEAH, SURE. I JUST GOT BACK INTO TOWN.
I WAS IN SAN FRANCISCO ON SOME BUSINESS.
WOULD YOU MIND OPENING YOUR SUITCASE FOR ME?
SURE.
NOTHING.
WOULD YOU MIND TELLING ME WHAT THIS IS ABOUT?

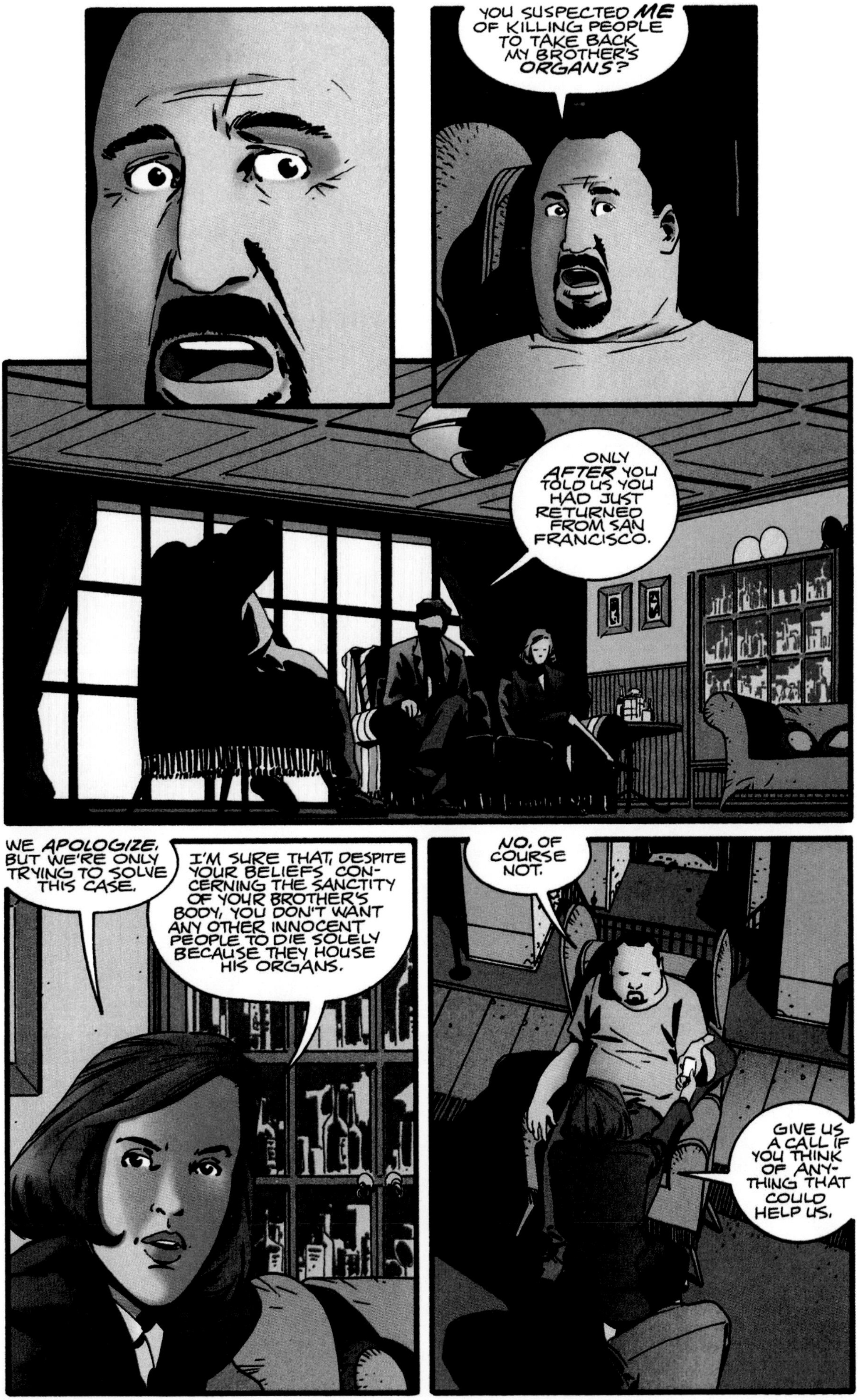
YOU SUSPECTED ME OF KILLING PEOPLE TO TAKE BACK MY BROTHER'S ORGANS?
ONLY AFTER YOU TOLD US YOU HAD JUST RETURNED FROM SAN FRANCISCO.
WE APOLOGIZE, BUT WE'RE ONLY TRYING TO SOLVE THIS CASE.
I'M SURE THAT, DESPITE YOUR BELIEFS CONCERNING THE SANCTITY OF YOUR BROTHER'S BODY, YOU DON'T WANT ANY OTHER INNOCENT PEOPLE TO DIE SOLELY BECAUSE THEY HOUSE HIS ORGANS.
NO. OF COURSE NOT.
GIVE US A CALL IF YOU THINK OF ANYTHING THAT COULD HELP US.

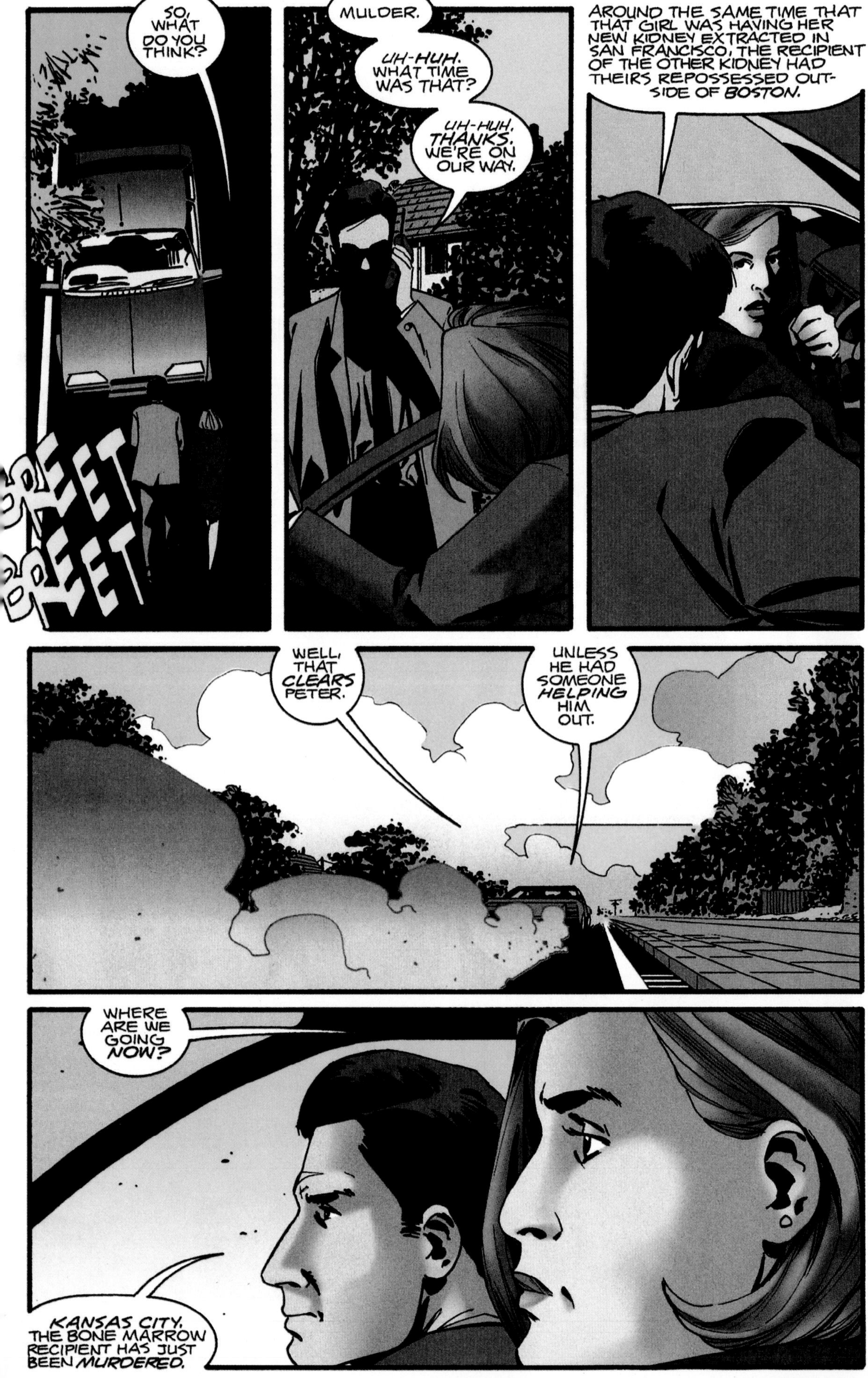
SO, WHAT DO YOU THINK?
BREET BREET
MULDER.
UH-HUH. WHAT TIME WAS THAT?
UH-HUH. THANKS. WE'RE ON OUR WAY.
AROUND THE SAME TIME THAT THAT GIRL WAS HAVING HER NEW KIDNEY EXTRACTED IN SAN FRANCISCO, THE RECIPIENT OF THE OTHER KIDNEY HAD THEIRS REPOSSESSED OUT-SIDE OF BOSTON.
WELL, THAT CLEARS PETER.
UNLESS HE HAD SOMEONE HELPING HIM OUT.
WHERE ARE WE GOING NOW?
KANSAS CITY. THE BONE MARROW RECIPIENT HAS JUST BEEN MURDERED.

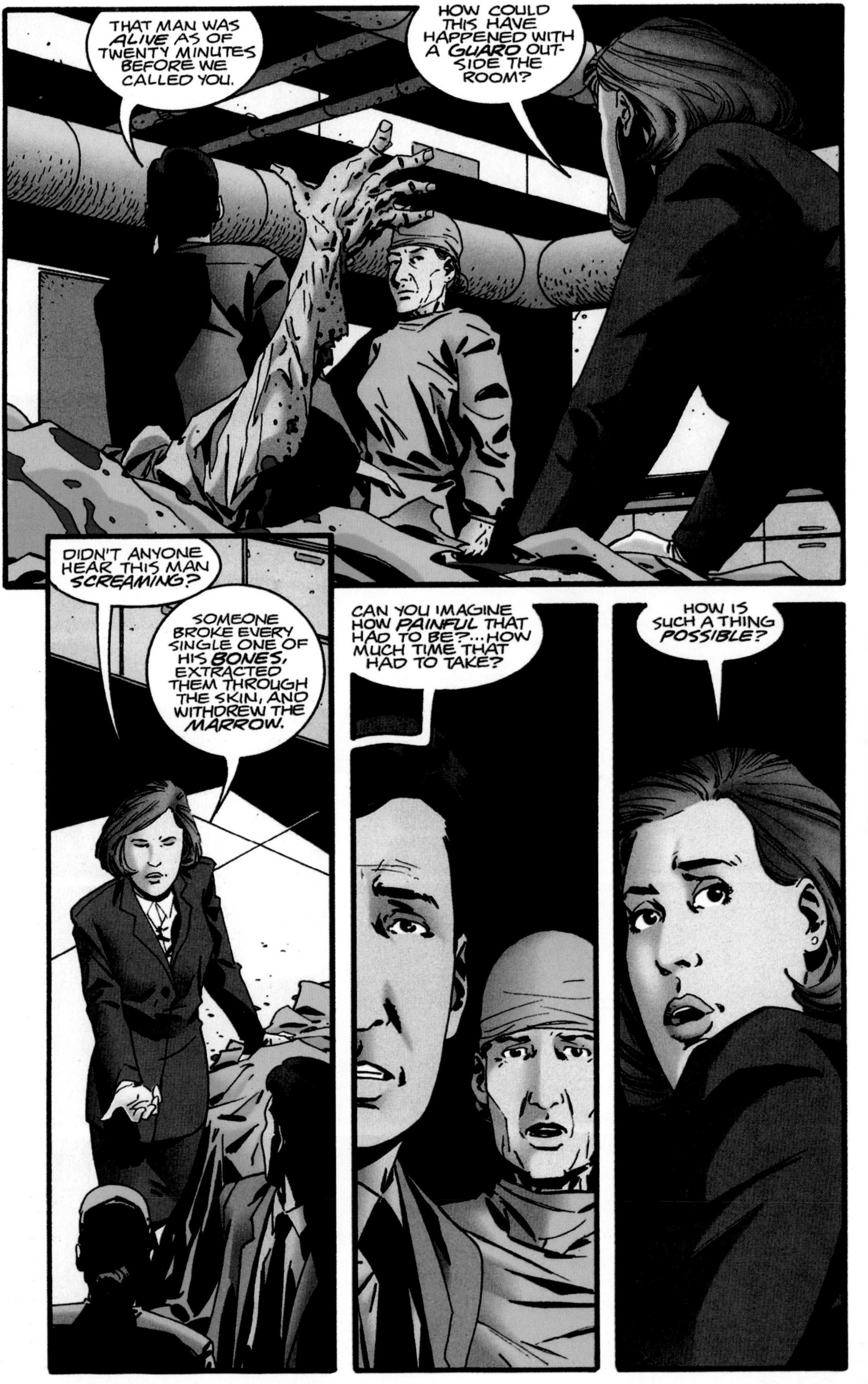
THAT MAN WAS ALIVE AS OF TWENTY MINUTES BEFORE WE CALLED YOU.
HOW COULD THIS HAVE HAPPENED WITH A GUARD OUT-SIDE THE ROOM?
DIDN'T ANYONE HEAR THIS MAN SCREAMING?
SOMEONE BROKE EVERY SINGLE ONE OF HIS BONES, EXTRACTED THEM THROUGH THE SKIN, AND WITHDREW THE MARROW.
CAN YOU IMAGINE HOW PAINFUL THAT HAD TO BE?...HOW MUCH TIME THAT HAD TO TAKE?
HOW IS SUCH A THING POSSIBLE?

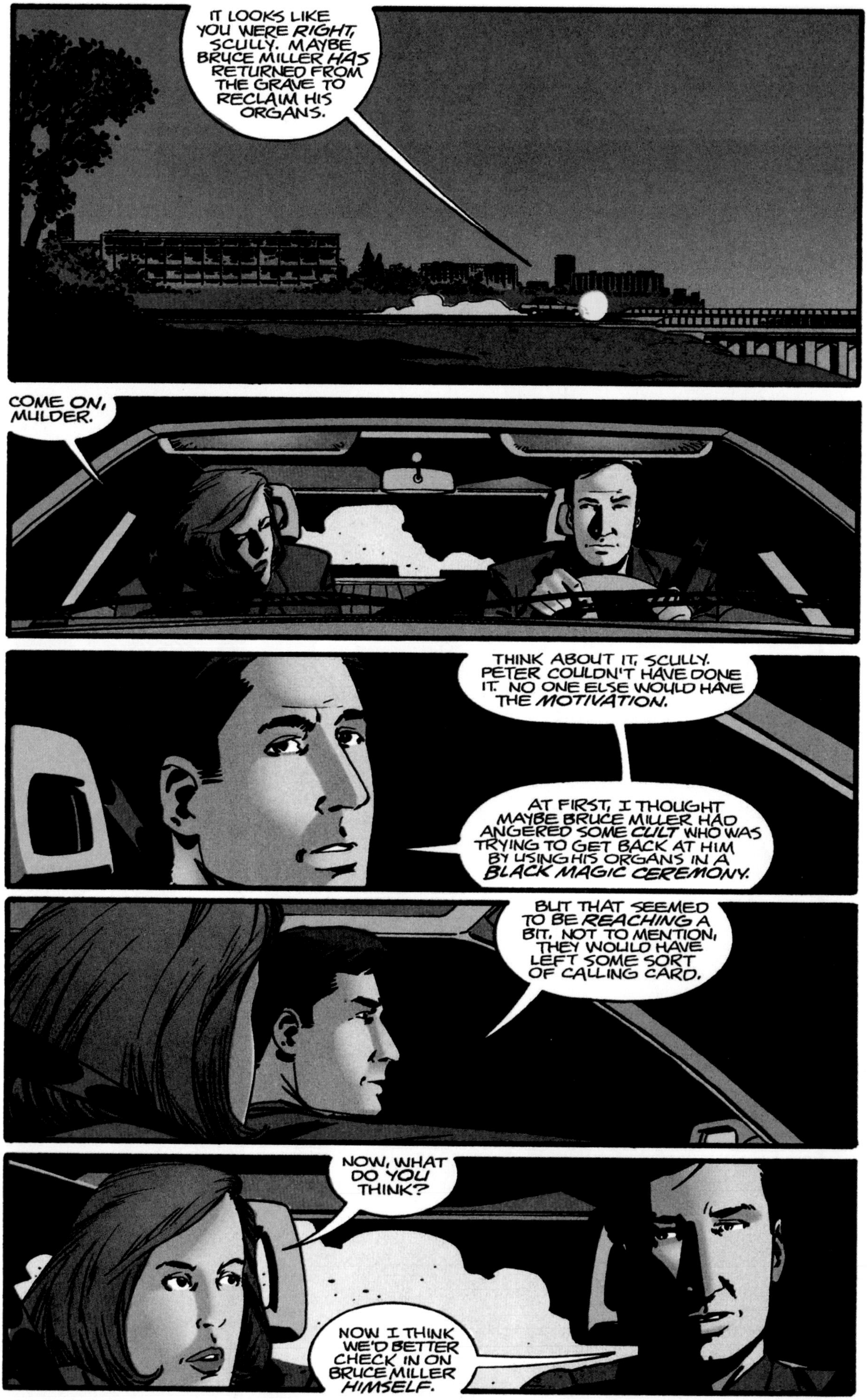
IT LOOKS LIKE YOU WERE *RIGHT*, SCULLY. MAYBE BRUCE MILLER *HAS* RETURNED FROM THE GRAVE TO RECLAIM HIS ORGANS.
COME ON, MULDER.
THINK ABOUT IT, SCULLY. PETER COULDN'T HAVE DONE IT. NO ONE ELSE WOULD HAVE THE *MOTIVATION*.
AT FIRST, I THOUGHT MAYBE BRUCE MILLER HAD ANGERED SOME *CULT* WHO WAS TRYING TO GET BACK AT HIM BY USING HIS ORGANS IN A *BLACK MAGIC CEREMONY*.
BUT THAT SEEMED TO BE *REACHING* A BIT. NOT TO MENTION, THEY WOULD HAVE LEFT SOME SORT OF CALLING CARD.
NOW, WHAT DO *YOU* THINK?
NOW I THINK WE'D BETTER CHECK IN ON BRUCE MILLER *HIMSELF*.

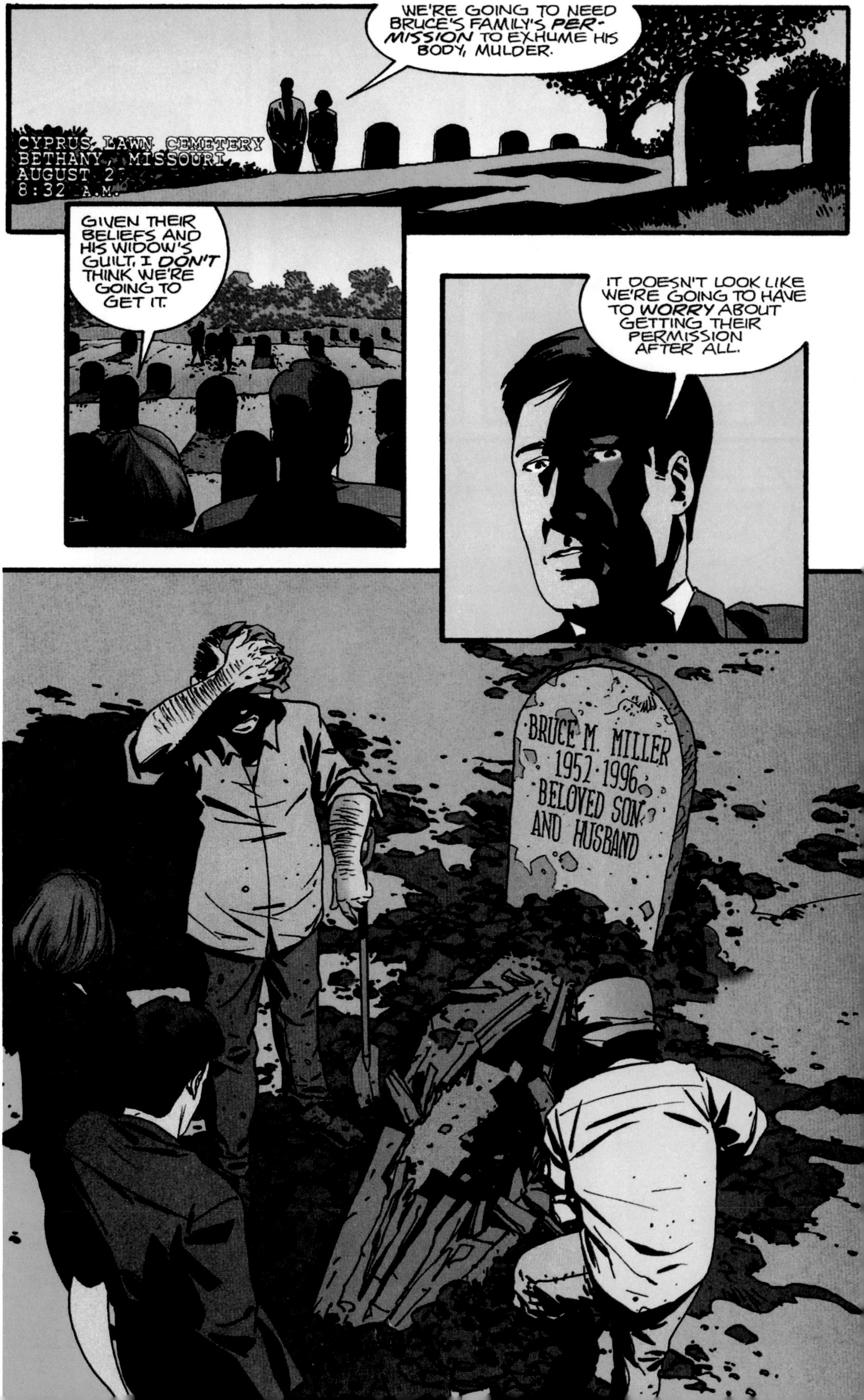
CYPRUS LAWN CEMETERY
BETHANY, MISSOURI
AUGUST 27
8:32 A.M.
WE'RE GOING TO NEED BRUCE'S FAMILY'S PERMISSION TO EXHUME HIS BODY, MULDER.
GIVEN THEIR BELIEFS AND HIS WIDOW'S GUILT, I DON'T THINK WE'RE GOING TO GET IT.
IT DOESN'T LOOK LIKE WE'RE GOING TO HAVE TO WORRY ABOUT GETTING THEIR PERMISSION AFTER ALL.
BRUCE M. MILLER
1952-1996
BELOVED SON AND HUSBAND

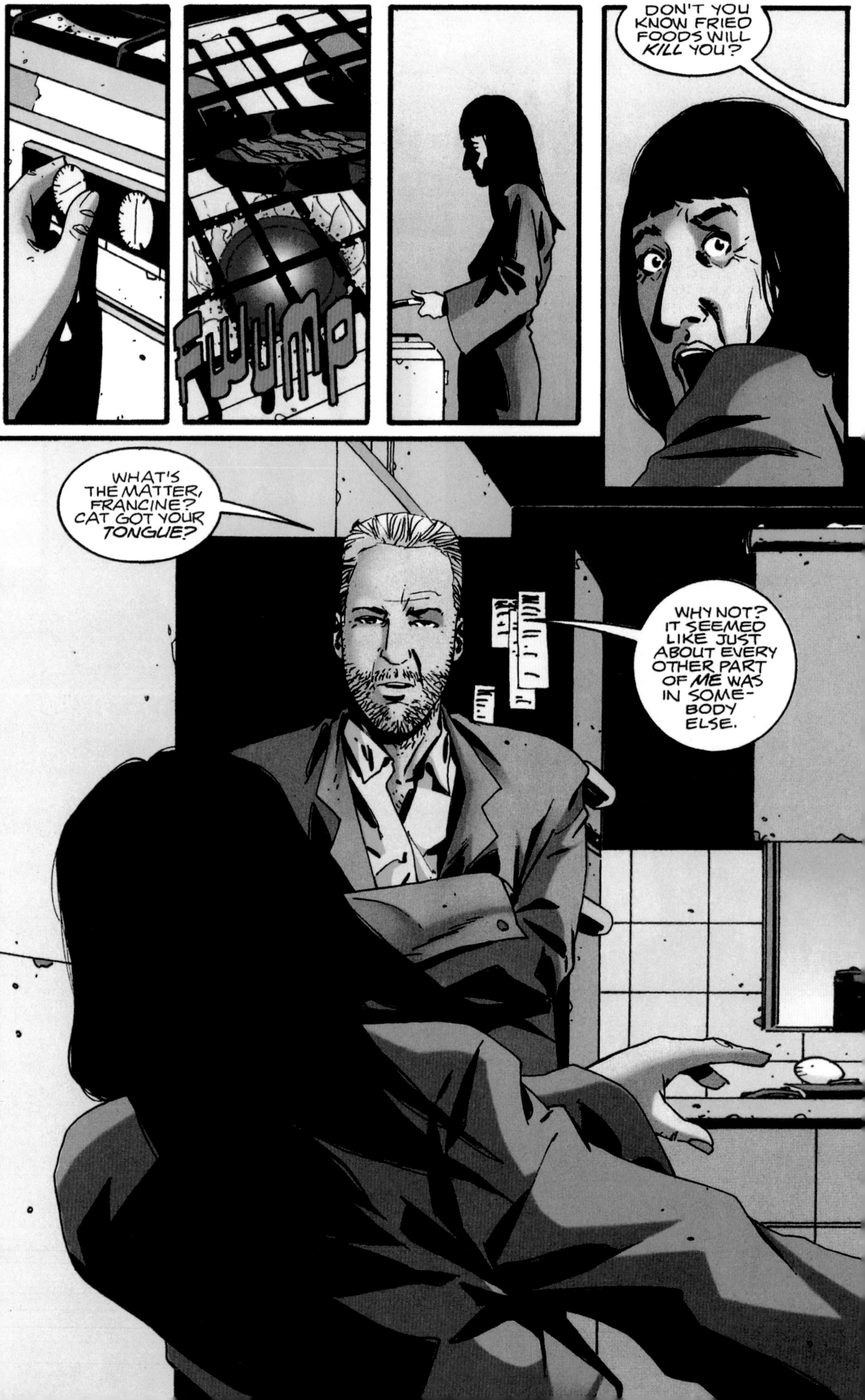
FWUMP
DON'T YOU KNOW FRIED FOODS WILL KILL YOU?
WHAT'S THE MATTER, FRANCINE? CAT GOT YOUR TONGUE?
WHY NOT? IT SEEMED LIKE JUST ABOUT EVERY OTHER PART OF ME WAS IN SOME-BODY ELSE.

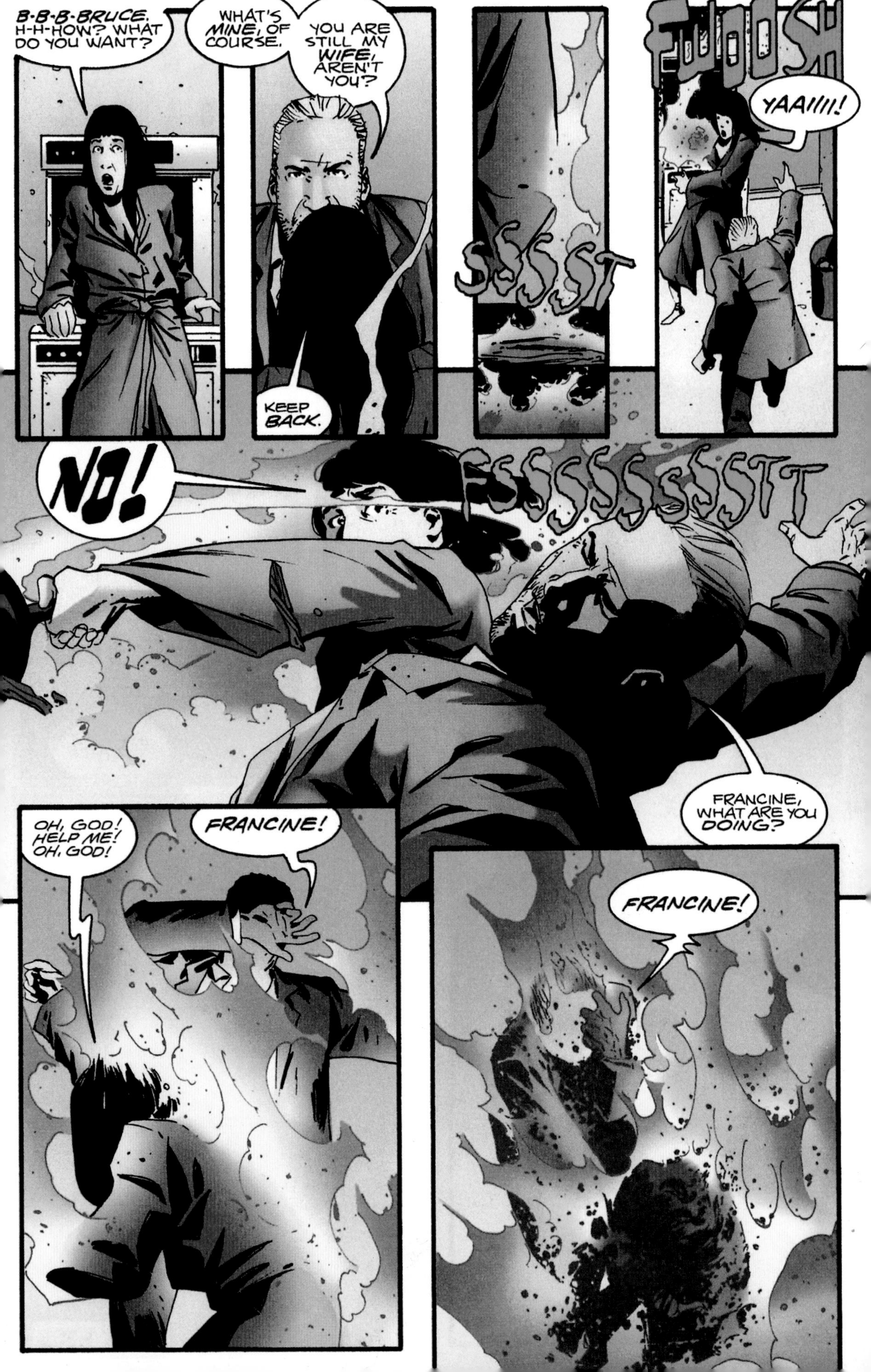
B-B-B-BRUCE. H-H-HOW? WHAT DO YOU WANT?
WHAT'S MINE, OF COURSE.
YOU ARE STILL MY WIFE, AREN'T YOU?
KEEP BACK.
SSSST
FWOOSH
YAAIIII!
NO!
FSSSSSSSSTT
FRANCINE, WHAT ARE YOU DOING?
OH, GOD! HELP ME! OH, GOD!
FRANCINE!
FRANCINE!

IT SMELLS LIKE AN ARBY'S IN HERE.

DID YOU FIND ANYTHING?

DENTAL RECORDS MATCH THOSE OF FRANCINE AND BRUCE MILLER.

DESPITE ITS POOR CONDITION, BRUCE'S BODY DID REVEAL A FEW THINGS TO ME ABOUT HIS DONATED ORGANS.

SUCH AS?

THE DONOR ORGANS WERE ALL BACK IN PLACE, ALTHOUGH NOT ATTACHED TO ANY OF THE SURROUNDING CONNECTIVE TISSUES.

MY GUESS IS THAT FRANCINE MILLER WAS FEELING GUILTY OVER GIVING UP HER HUSBAND'S ORGANS, REPOSSESSED THEM, STUFFED THEM BACK IN PLACE, AND COMMITTED SUICIDE BY IMMOLATION WHEN SHE WAS DONE.

CLEARLY, HER GUILT WASN'T ON BEHALF OF BRUCE'S FAMILY. I DOUBT THEY APPROVE OF CREMATION, EITHER.

NO. PROBABLY NOT.

IT LOOKS LIKE WE STILL GET A GRUESOME SOLUTION TO THIS CASE, WITHOUT RESORTING TO ANY SUPERNATURAL EXPLANATION.

SO MUCH FOR MY VENGEFUL WALKING DEAD SCENARIO.

THERE'S ALWAYS NEXT TIME.

**THE END**

CHAPTER 2

# SILVER LINING

STORY: John Rozum
ART: Gordon Purcell

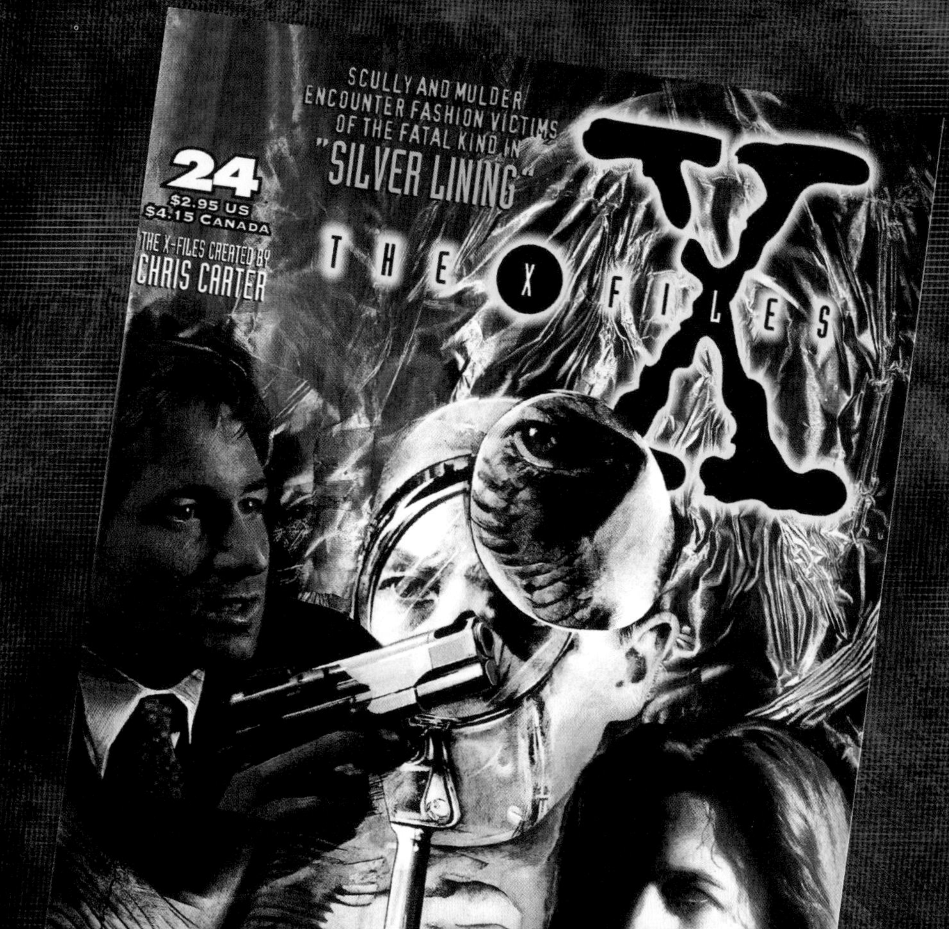
SCULLY AND MULDER ENCOUNTER FASHION VICTIMS OF THE FATAL KIND IN "SILVER LINING"
24
$2.95 US
$4.15 CANADA
THE X-FILES CREATED BY CHRIS CARTER
THE X FILES
JOHN ROZUM
GORDON PURCELL
JOSEF RUBINSTEIN
MIRAN KIM
DIRECT SALES

WHAT DID I TELL YOU? IT'S NOT POLITE TO STARE.

BROOKLYN, NEW YORK
NOVEMBER 18
8:36 A.M.

"IT'S THE SAME EVERY MORNING, EVERY NIGHT, EVERY DAY, EVERYWHERE.

"THEY ALL STARE AT ME. THEY TRY TO DO IT SO I WON'T NOTICE. THIS ONLY MAKES IT WORSE. I NOTICE IT MORE.

"I HATE IT. I CAN READ THE LANGUAGE OF THEIR STARES. EVERY STARE SAYS THE SAME THING.

"EVERY STARE SAYS, 'THAT POOR GUY' OR 'THANK GOD THAT ISN'T ME.'

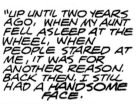

"UP UNTIL TWO YEARS AGO, WHEN MY AUNT FELL ASLEEP AT THE WHEEL, WHEN PEOPLE STARED AT ME, IT WAS FOR ANOTHER REASON. BACK THEN, I STILL HAD A HANDSOME FACE.

"I DIDN'T MIND THOSE STARES.

"THEY WERE MADE BY EYES THAT STILL SAW ME AS A HUMAN BEING.

"EYES BELONGING TO PEOPLE WHO SAW ME AS ONE OF THEIR OWN.

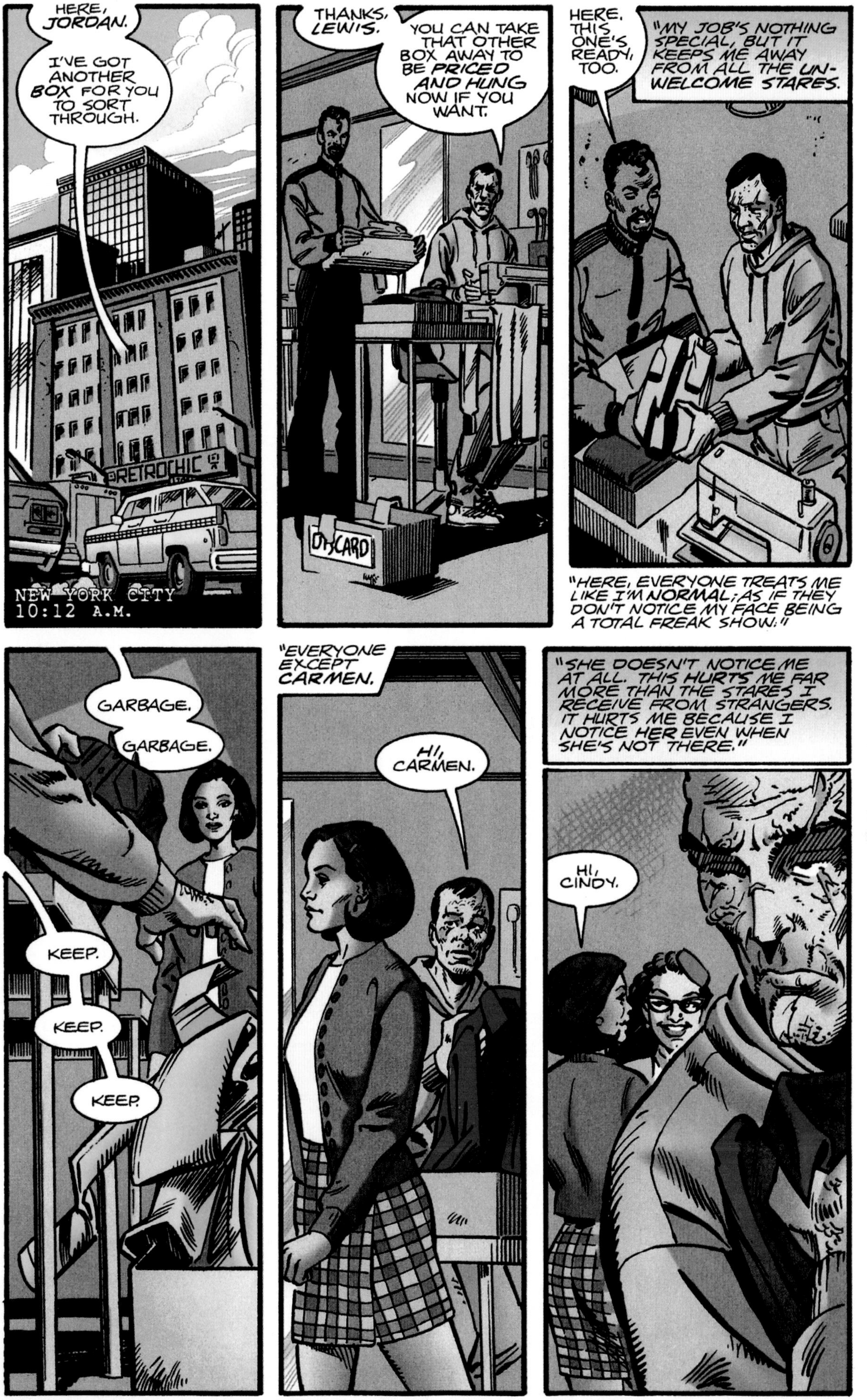
HERE, JORDAN.
I'VE GOT ANOTHER BOX FOR YOU TO SORT THROUGH.
RETROCHIC
NEW YORK CITY 10:12 A.M.
THANKS, LEWIS.
YOU CAN TAKE THAT OTHER BOX AWAY TO BE PRICED AND HUNG NOW IF YOU WANT.
DISCARD
HERE. THIS ONE'S READY, TOO.
"MY JOB'S NOTHING SPECIAL, BUT IT KEEPS ME AWAY FROM ALL THE UNWELCOME STARES.
"HERE, EVERYONE TREATS ME LIKE I'M NORMAL; AS IF THEY DON'T NOTICE MY FACE BEING A TOTAL FREAK SHOW."
GARBAGE.
GARBAGE.
KEEP.
KEEP.
KEEP.
"EVERYONE EXCEPT CARMEN.
HI, CARMEN.
"SHE DOESN'T NOTICE ME AT ALL. THIS HURTS ME FAR MORE THAN THE STARES I RECEIVE FROM STRANGERS. IT HURTS ME BECAUSE I NOTICE HER EVEN WHEN SHE'S NOT THERE."
HI, CINDY.

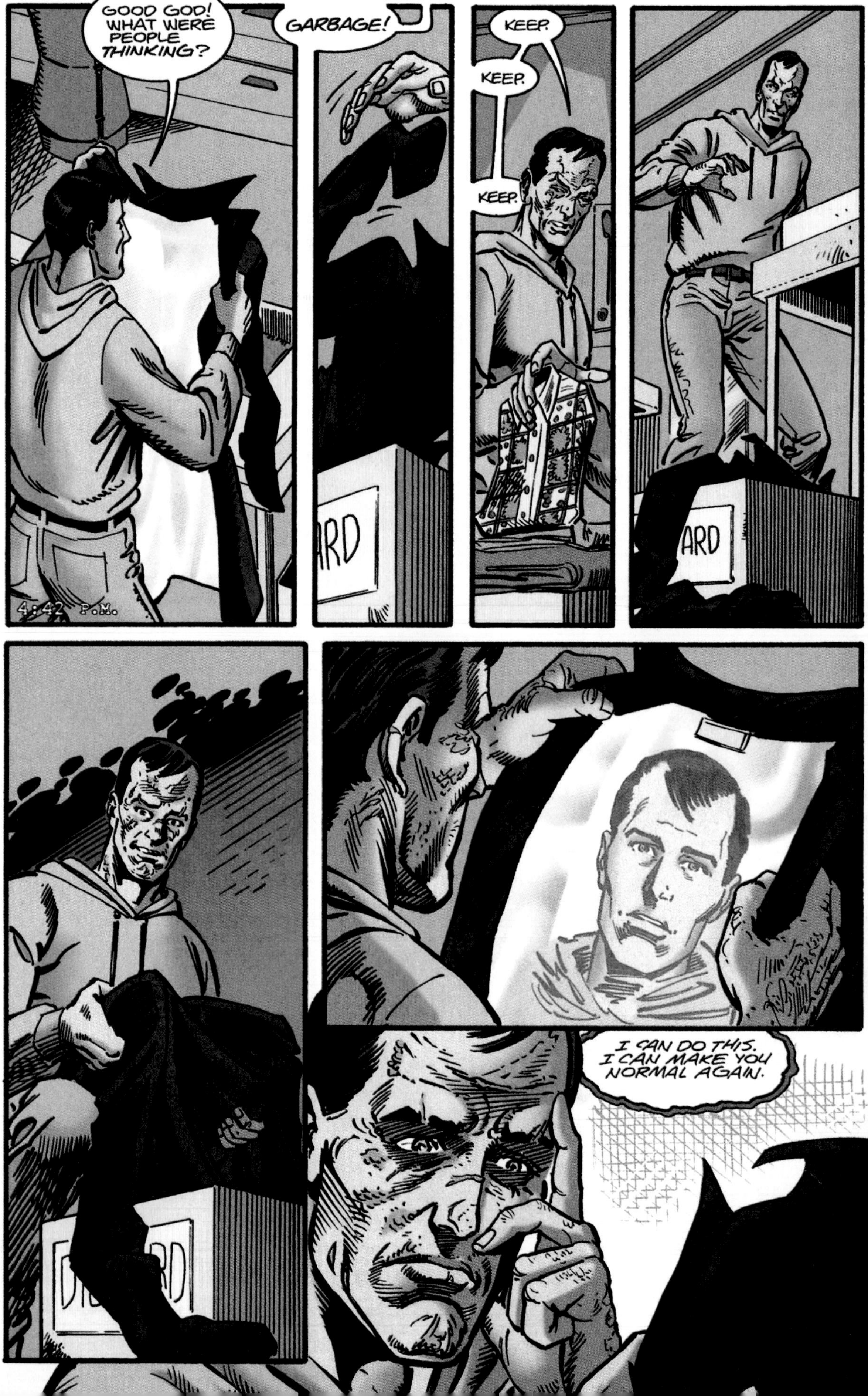
GOOD GOD! WHAT WERE PEOPLE THINKING?
4:42 P.M.
GARBAGE!
KEEP.
KEEP.
KEEP.
ARD
ARD
DI RD
I CAN DO THIS. I CAN MAKE YOU NORMAL AGAIN.

CANDY GROCERY

WE ACCEPT FOOD STAMPS

ONE WAY

BROOKLYN, NY
7:53 P.M.

FOLLOW HER.

SHE'LL BE THE FIRST TO MAKE YOU AS YOU WERE.

AS I SHOWED YOU.

CALL HER TO YOU, I'LL DO THE REST.

EXCUSE ME...

MISS?

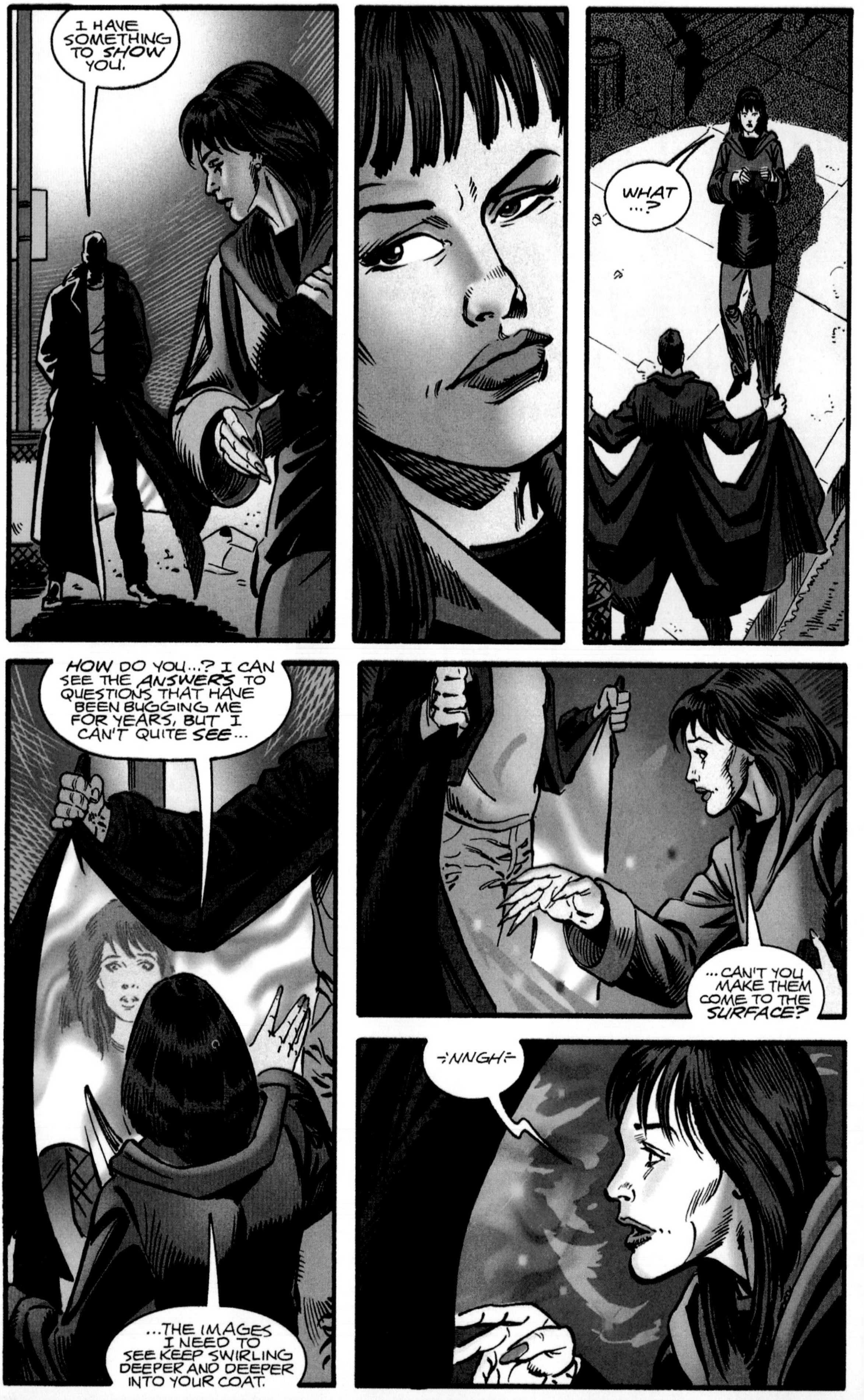
I HAVE SOMETHING TO SHOW YOU.
WHAT ...?
HOW DO YOU...? I CAN SEE THE ANSWERS TO QUESTIONS THAT HAVE BEEN BUGGING ME FOR YEARS, BUT I CAN'T QUITE SEE...
...THE IMAGES I NEED TO SEE KEEP SWIRLING DEEPER AND DEEPER INTO YOUR COAT.
...CAN'T YOU MAKE THEM COME TO THE SURFACE?
-NNGH-

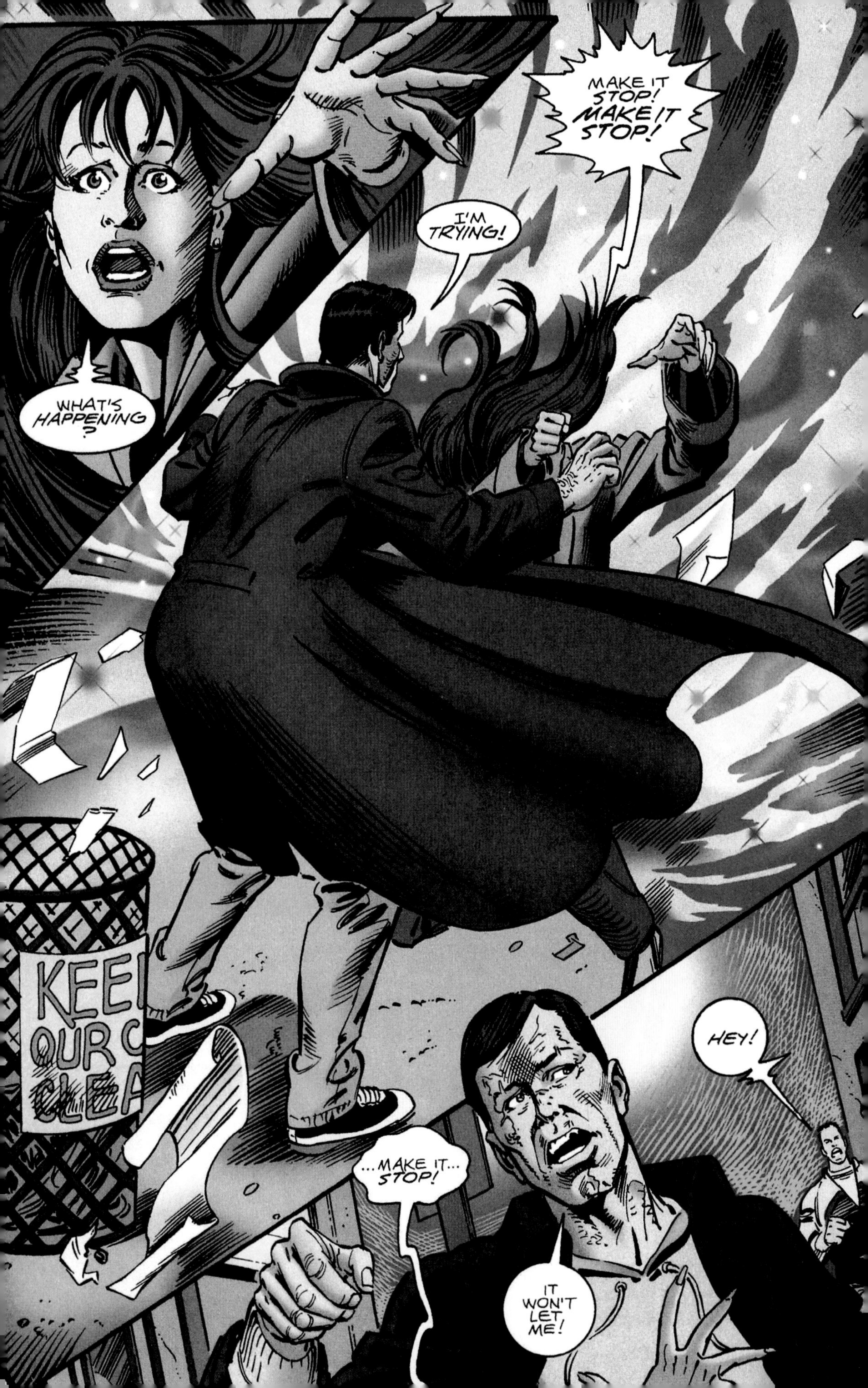
WHAT'S HAPPENING?
MAKE IT STOP! MAKE IT STOP!
I'M TRYING!
KEE
OUR C
CLEA
HEY!
...MAKE IT... STOP!
IT WON'T LET ME!

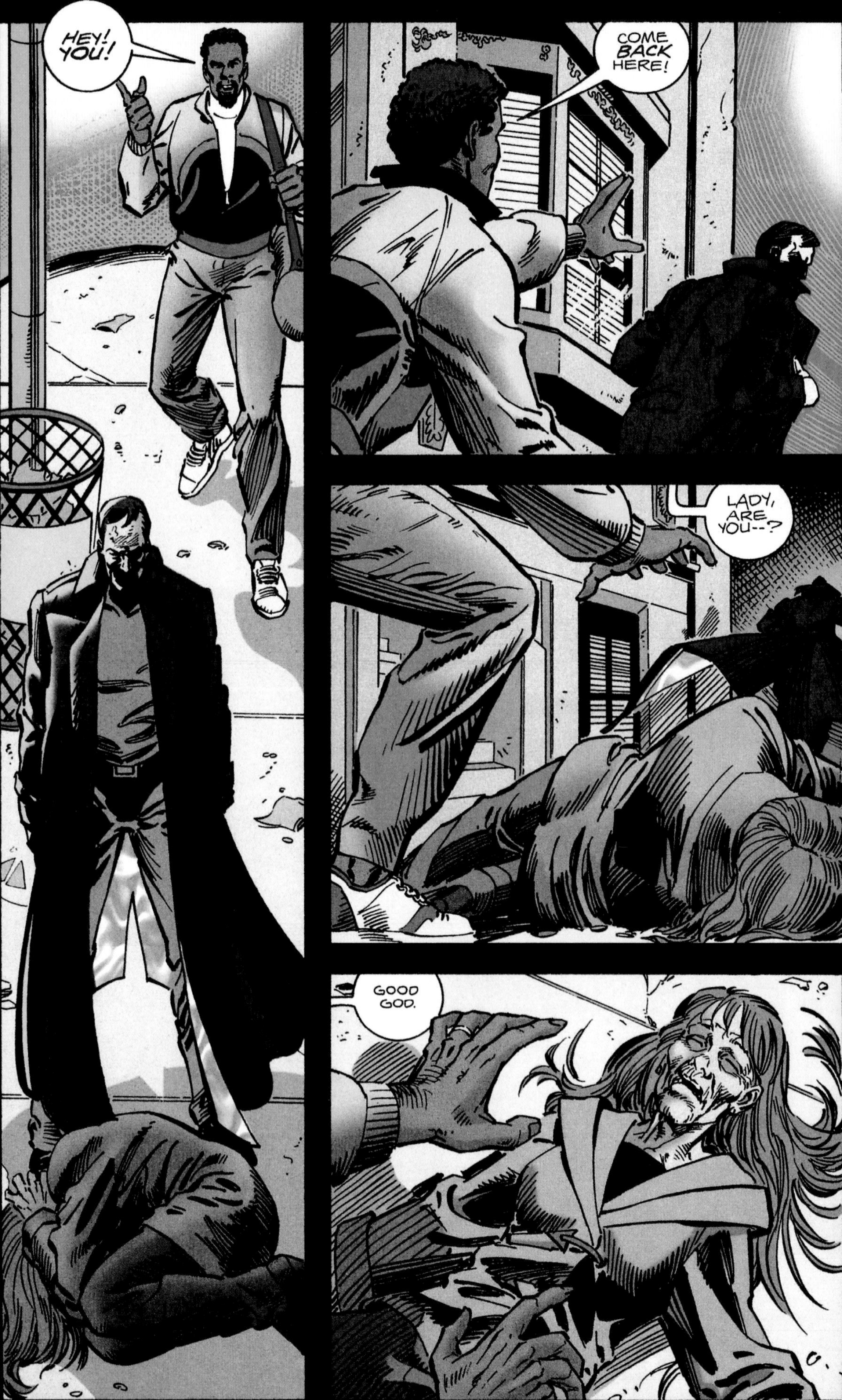
HEY! YOU!
COME BACK HERE!
LADY, ARE YOU--?
GOOD GOD.

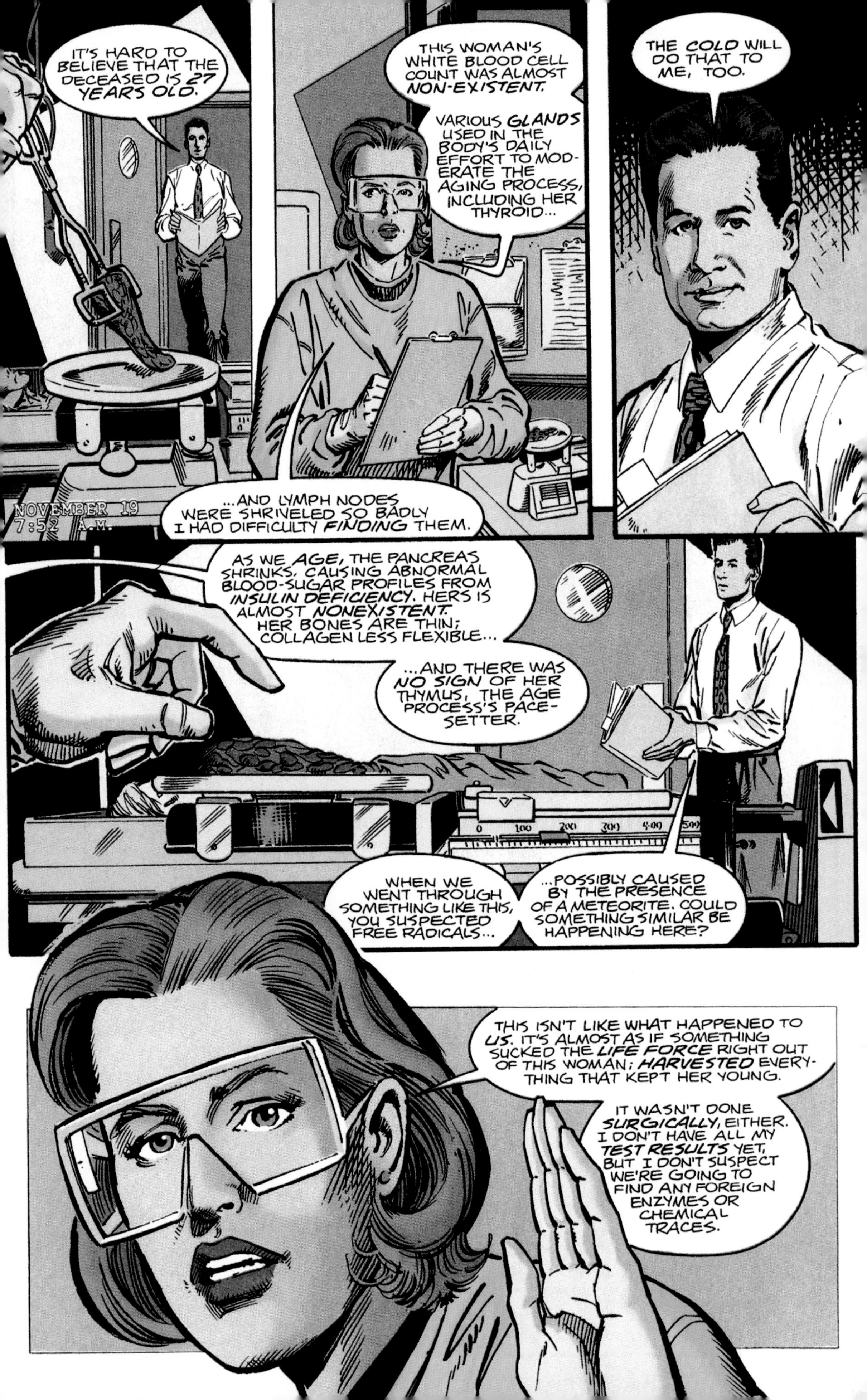
IT'S HARD TO BELIEVE THAT THE DECEASED IS 27 YEARS OLD.
THIS WOMAN'S WHITE BLOOD CELL COUNT WAS ALMOST NON-EXISTENT.
VARIOUS GLANDS USED IN THE BODY'S DAILY EFFORT TO MODERATE THE AGING PROCESS, INCLUDING HER THYROID...
NOVEMBER 19 7:52 A.M.
...AND LYMPH NODES WERE SHRIVELED SO BADLY I HAD DIFFICULTY FINDING THEM.
THE COLD WILL DO THAT TO ME, TOO.
AS WE AGE, THE PANCREAS SHRINKS, CAUSING ABNORMAL BLOOD-SUGAR PROFILES FROM INSULIN DEFICIENCY. HERS IS ALMOST NONEXISTENT. HER BONES ARE THIN; COLLAGEN LESS FLEXIBLE...
...AND THERE WAS NO SIGN OF HER THYMUS, THE AGE PROCESS'S PACE-SETTER.
WHEN WE WENT THROUGH SOMETHING LIKE THIS, YOU SUSPECTED FREE RADICALS...
...POSSIBLY CAUSED BY THE PRESENCE OF A METEORITE. COULD SOMETHING SIMILAR BE HAPPENING HERE?
THIS ISN'T LIKE WHAT HAPPENED TO US. IT'S ALMOST AS IF SOMETHING SUCKED THE LIFE FORCE RIGHT OUT OF THIS WOMAN; HARVESTED EVERYTHING THAT KEPT HER YOUNG.
IT WASN'T DONE SURGICALLY, EITHER. I DON'T HAVE ALL MY TEST RESULTS YET, BUT I DON'T SUSPECT WE'RE GOING TO FIND ANY FOREIGN ENZYMES OR CHEMICAL TRACES.

WHAT ABOUT *RADIATION*?

NORMAL.

DID YOU CHECK HER *SINUS CAVITIES*?

WHAT AM I LOOKING FOR?

YOU'LL KNOW WHEN YOU FIND IT.

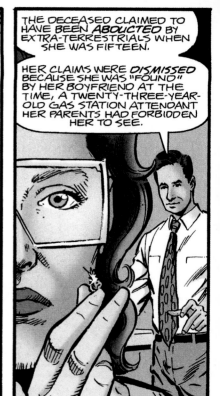

THE DECEASED CLAIMED TO HAVE BEEN *ABDUCTED* BY EXTRA-TERRESTRIALS WHEN SHE WAS FIFTEEN.

HER CLAIMS WERE *DISMISSED* BECAUSE SHE WAS "FOUND" BY HER BOYFRIEND AT THE TIME, A TWENTY-THREE-YEAR-OLD GAS STATION ATTENDANT HER PARENTS HAD FORBIDDEN HER TO SEE.

THAT'S MERELY *COINCIDENCE*, MULDER.

EVEN IF SHE *HAD* BEEN ABDUCTED AND THAT EXPLAINED THE IMPLANT, THE MURDER WAS PROBABLY A RANDOM KILLING. THE WITNESS SAW A *MAN* FLEEING THE SCENE, NOT AN EXTRA-TERRESTRIAL.

HE SAW A MAN IN *BLACK*, SCULLY.

MULDER, YOU'RE GETTING TOO *PARANOID*.

I WOULD HAVE DISMISSED IT AS A COINCIDENCE, AS WELL...

...BUT HOW MANY KILLERS MURDER THEIR *VICTIMS* BY *AGING* THEM TO DEATH?

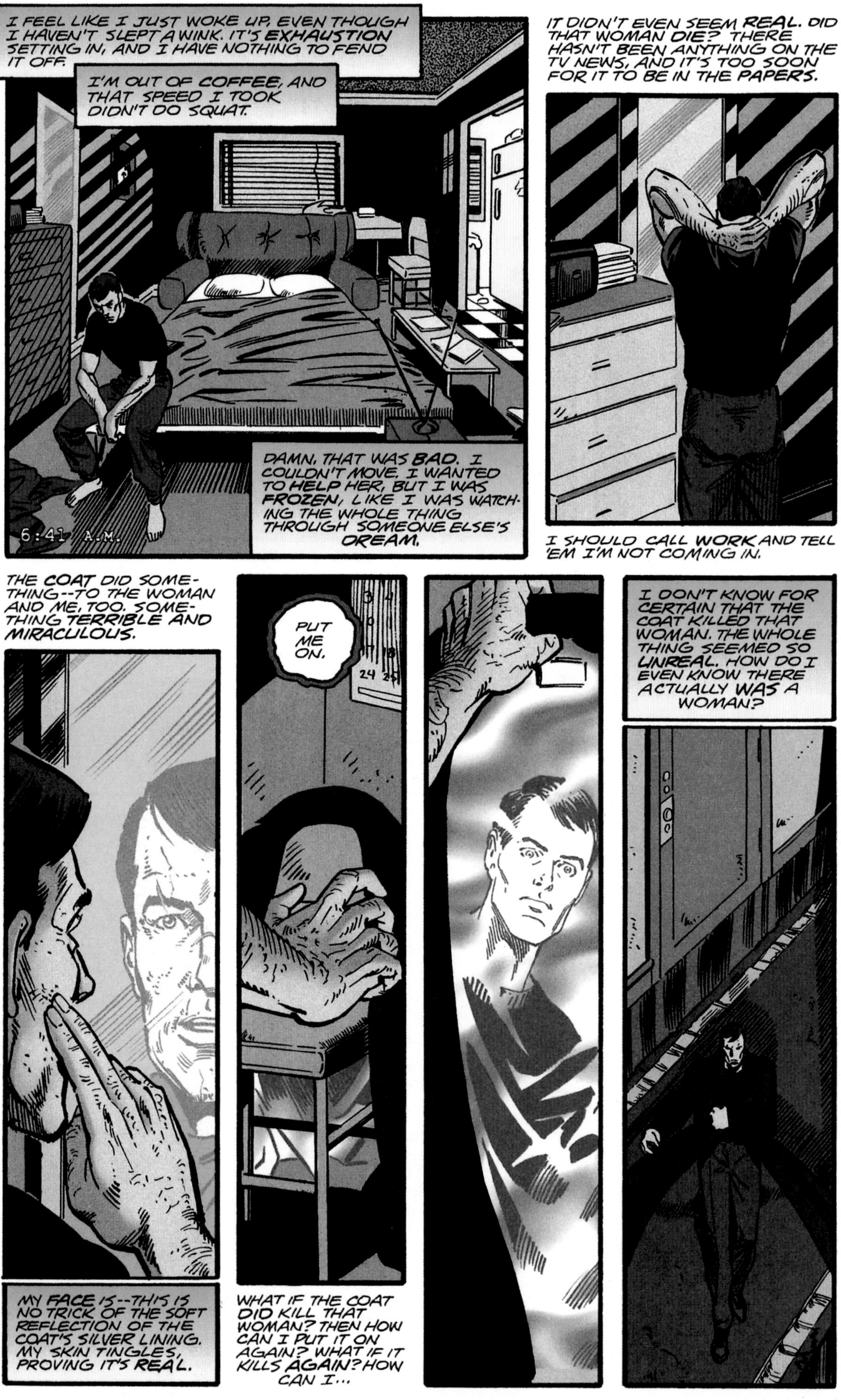
I FEEL LIKE I JUST WOKE UP, EVEN THOUGH I HAVEN'T SLEPT A WINK. IT'S EXHAUSTION SETTING IN, AND I HAVE NOTHING TO FEND IT OFF.
I'M OUT OF COFFEE, AND THAT SPEED I TOOK DIDN'T DO SQUAT.
6:41 A.M.
DAMN, THAT WAS BAD. I COULDN'T MOVE. I WANTED TO HELP HER, BUT I WAS FROZEN, LIKE I WAS WATCHING THE WHOLE THING THROUGH SOMEONE ELSE'S DREAM.
IT DIDN'T EVEN SEEM REAL. DID THAT WOMAN DIE? THERE HASN'T BEEN ANYTHING ON THE TV NEWS, AND IT'S TOO SOON FOR IT TO BE IN THE PAPERS.
I SHOULD CALL WORK AND TELL 'EM I'M NOT COMING IN.
THE COAT DID SOMETHING--TO THE WOMAN AND ME, TOO. SOMETHING TERRIBLE AND MIRACULOUS.
MY FACE IS--THIS IS NO TRICK OF THE SOFT REFLECTION OF THE COAT'S SILVER LINING. MY SKIN TINGLES, PROVING IT'S REAL.
PUT ME ON.
WHAT IF THE COAT DID KILL THAT WOMAN? THEN HOW CAN I PUT IT ON AGAIN? WHAT IF IT KILLS AGAIN? HOW CAN I...
I DON'T KNOW FOR CERTAIN THAT THE COAT KILLED THAT WOMAN. THE WHOLE THING SEEMED SO UNREAL. HOW DO I EVEN KNOW THERE ACTUALLY WAS A WOMAN?

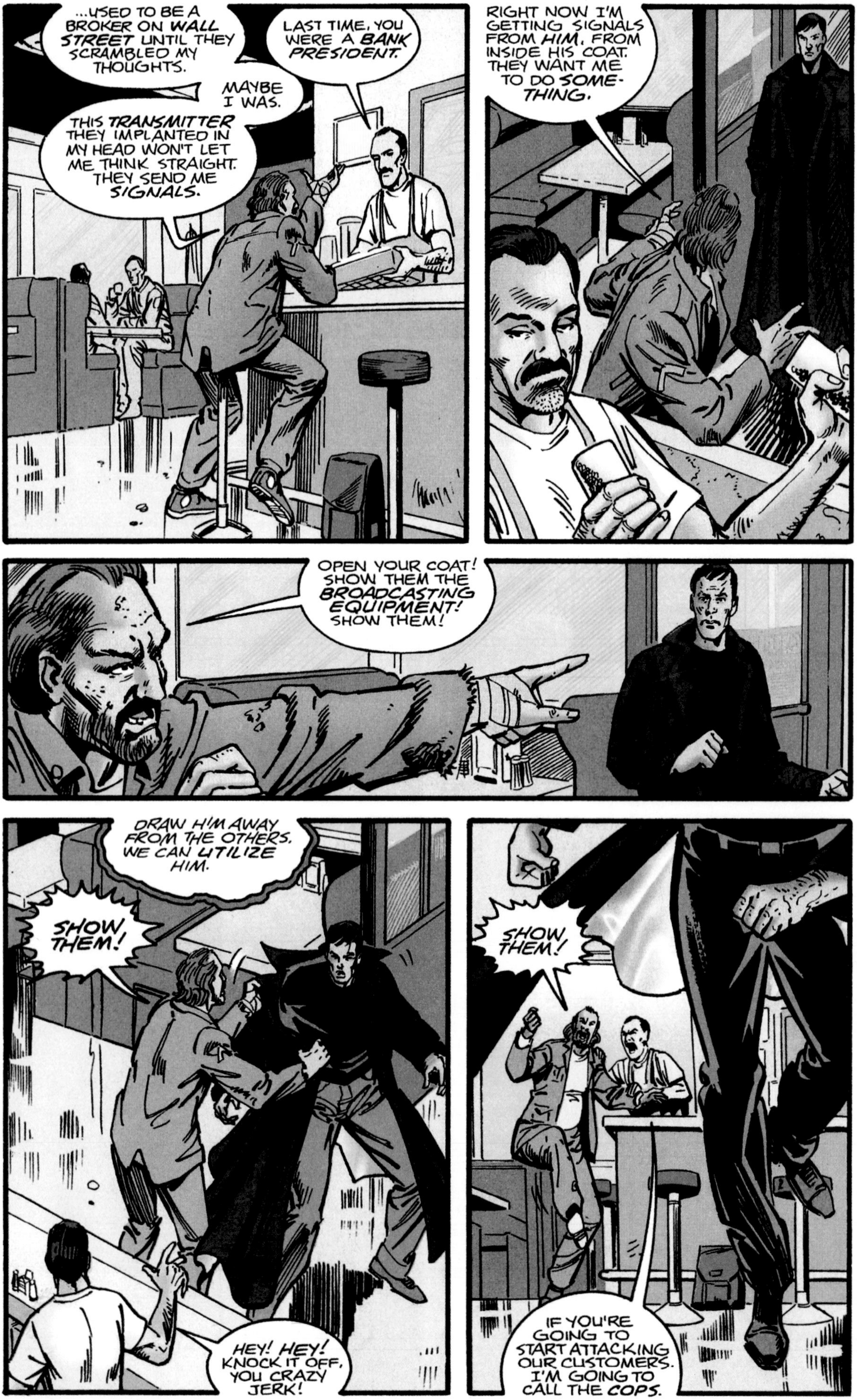
...USED TO BE A BROKER ON WALL STREET UNTIL THEY SCRAMBLED MY THOUGHTS.
LAST TIME, YOU WERE A BANK PRESIDENT.
MAYBE I WAS.
THIS TRANSMITTER THEY IMPLANTED IN MY HEAD WON'T LET ME THINK STRAIGHT. THEY SEND ME SIGNALS.
RIGHT NOW I'M GETTING SIGNALS FROM HIM. FROM INSIDE HIS COAT. THEY WANT ME TO DO SOME-THING.
OPEN YOUR COAT! SHOW THEM THE BROADCASTING EQUIPMENT! SHOW THEM!
DRAW HIM AWAY FROM THE OTHERS. WE CAN UTILIZE HIM.
SHOW THEM!
HEY! HEY! KNOCK IT OFF, YOU CRAZY JERK!
SHOW THEM!
IF YOU'RE GOING TO START ATTACKING OUR CUSTOMERS. I'M GOING TO CALL THE COPS.

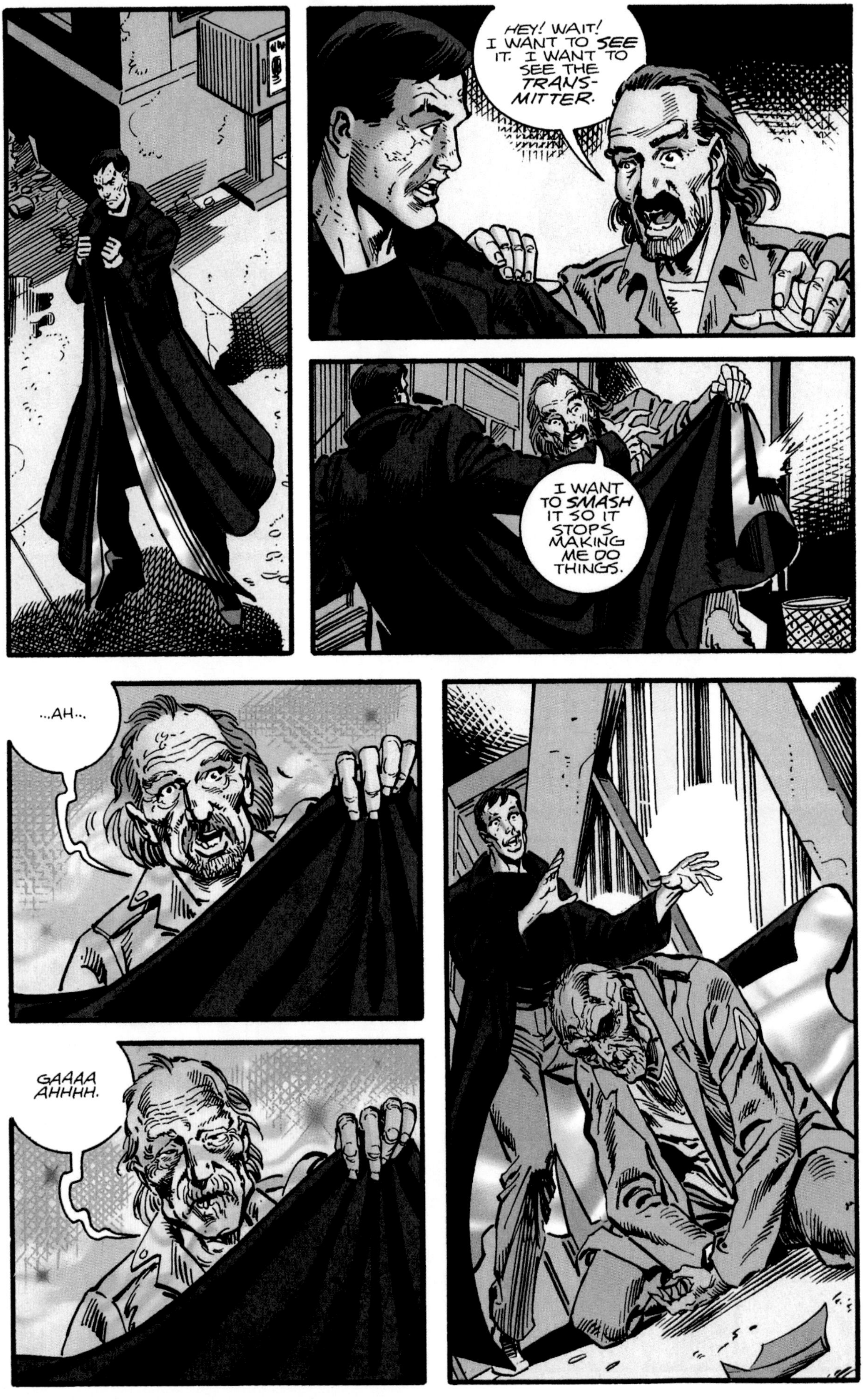
HEY! WAIT! I WANT TO SEE IT. I WANT TO SEE THE TRANS-MITTER.
I WANT TO SMASH IT SO IT STOPS MAKING ME DO THINGS.
...AH...
GAAAA AHHHH.

9:33 A.M.

THE WITNESSES ALL TOLD THE *SAME STORY.* METHUSELAH THERE IS KNOWN FOR RANTING ABOUT HOW ALIENS WERE *BROADCAST-ING* TO HIM THROUGH A DEVICE PLANTED IN HIS HEAD.

IT GETS *BETTER.*

THE VICTIM ACCOSTED A YOUNG MAN WHO ENTERED THE DINER, CLAIMING THAT HE HAD THE BROADCASTING DE-VICE HIDDEN IN HIS *COAT.*

HE CHASED THE YOUNG MAN OUTSIDE AND WAS FOUND LIKE THIS MOMENTS LATER WHEN THE DISH-WASHER CAME OUT TO CHECK ON THEM.

WE HAVE A *DESCRIPTION* OF THE MAN IN QUESTION.

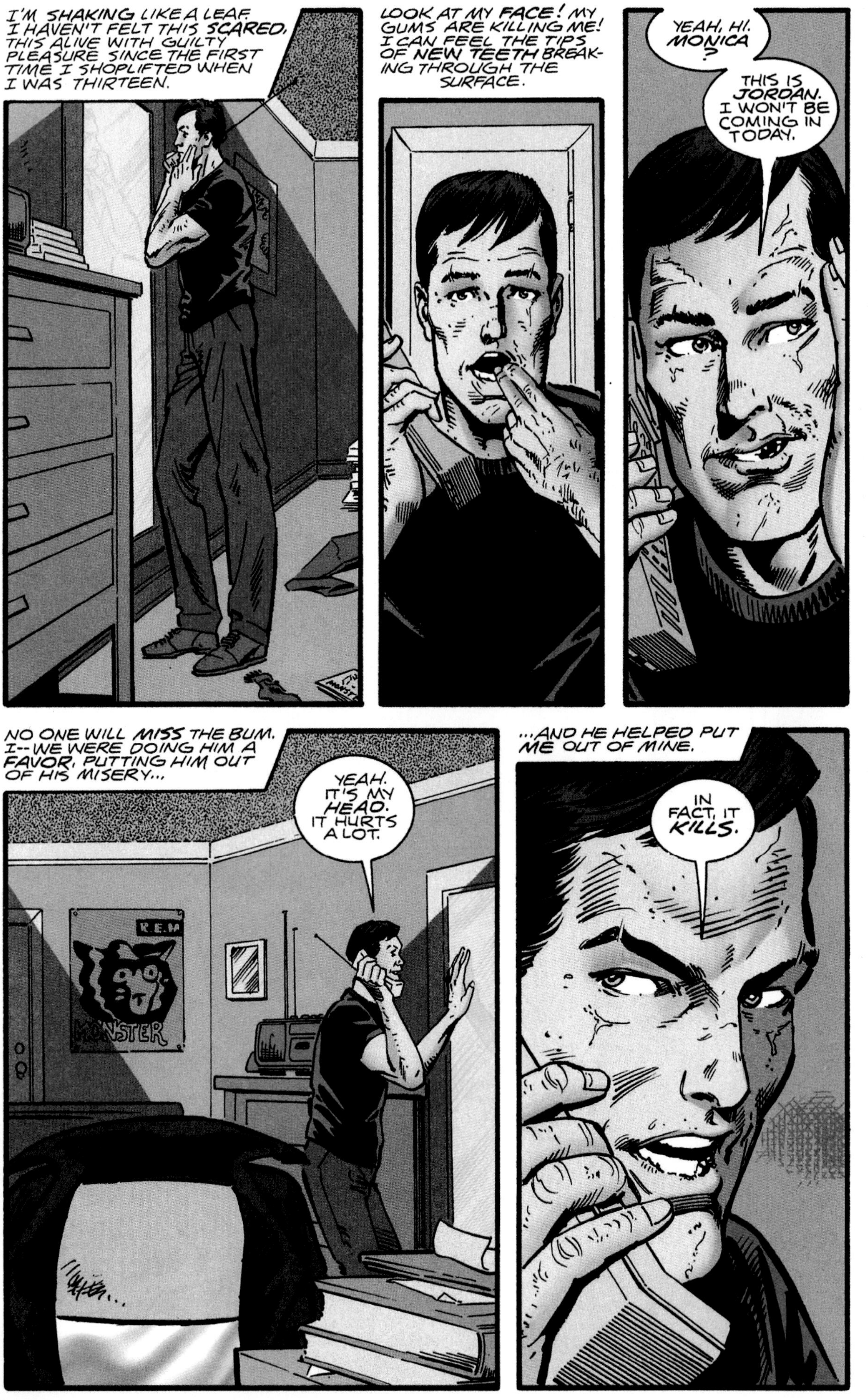
I'M SHAKING LIKE A LEAF. I HAVEN'T FELT THIS SCARED, THIS ALIVE WITH GUILTY PLEASURE SINCE THE FIRST TIME I SHOPLIFTED WHEN I WAS THIRTEEN.
LOOK AT MY FACE! MY GUMS ARE KILLING ME! I CAN FEEL THE TIPS OF NEW TEETH BREAKING THROUGH THE SURFACE.
YEAH, HI. MONICA?
THIS IS JORDAN. I WON'T BE COMING IN TODAY.
NO ONE WILL MISS THE BUM. I--WE WERE DOING HIM A FAVOR, PUTTING HIM OUT OF HIS MISERY...
YEAH. IT'S MY HEAD. IT HURTS A LOT.
R.E.M
MONSTER
...AND HE HELPED PUT ME OUT OF MINE.
IN FACT, IT KILLS.

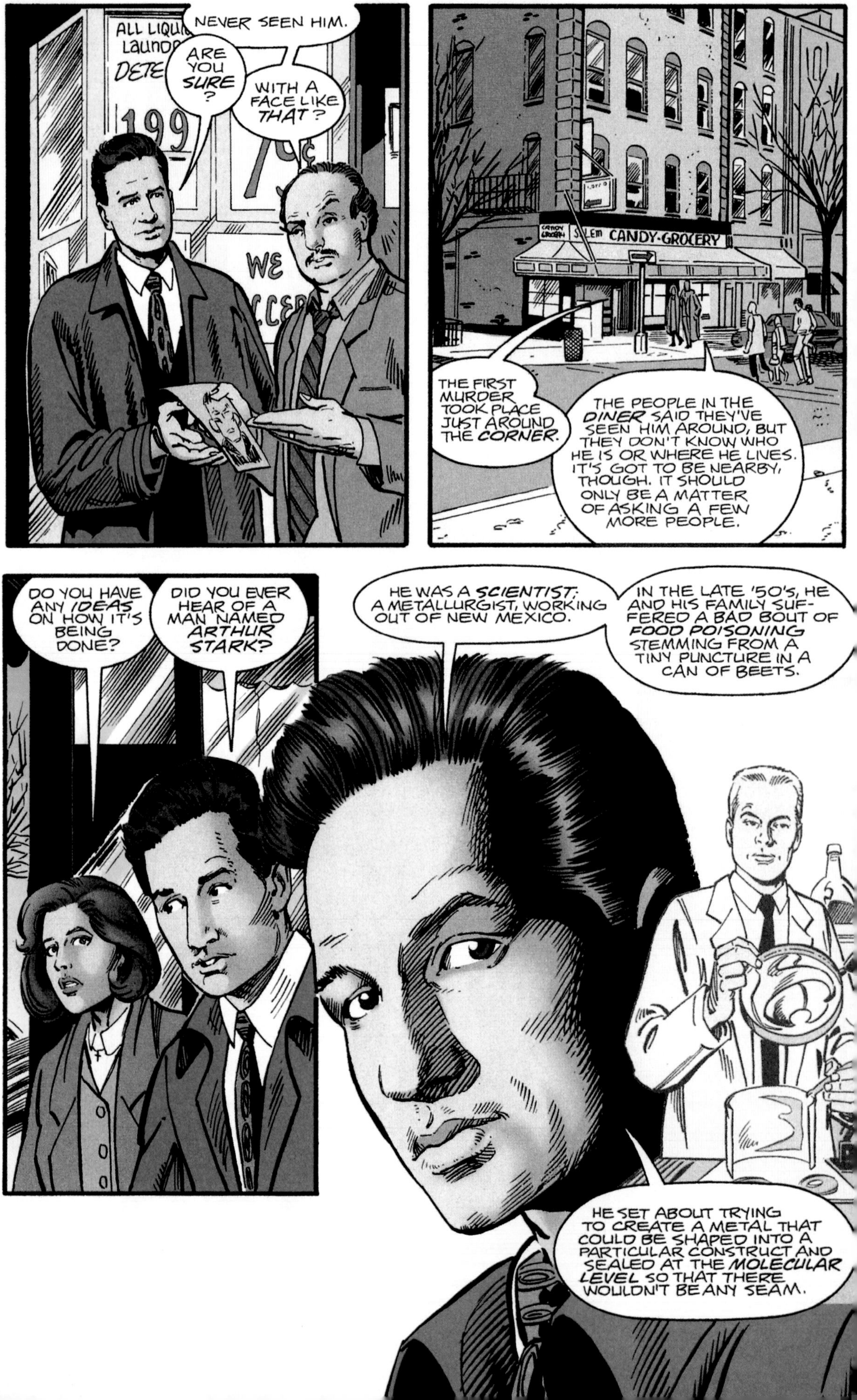
ALL LIQUI
LAUNDR
DETE
199
79¢
WE
CCEP
NEVER SEEN HIM.
ARE YOU SURE?
WITH A FACE LIKE THAT?
CANDY GROCERY
SALEM CANDY-GROCERY
THE FIRST MURDER TOOK PLACE JUST AROUND THE CORNER.
THE PEOPLE IN THE DINER SAID THEY'VE SEEN HIM AROUND, BUT THEY DON'T KNOW WHO HE IS OR WHERE HE LIVES. IT'S GOT TO BE NEARBY, THOUGH. IT SHOULD ONLY BE A MATTER OF ASKING A FEW MORE PEOPLE.
DO YOU HAVE ANY IDEAS ON HOW IT'S BEING DONE?
DID YOU EVER HEAR OF A MAN NAMED ARTHUR STARK?
HE WAS A SCIENTIST: A METALLURGIST, WORKING OUT OF NEW MEXICO.
IN THE LATE '50'S, HE AND HIS FAMILY SUFFERED A BAD BOUT OF FOOD POISONING STEMMING FROM A TINY PUNCTURE IN A CAN OF BEETS.
HE SET ABOUT TRYING TO CREATE A METAL THAT COULD BE SHAPED INTO A PARTICULAR CONSTRUCT AND SEALED AT THE MOLECULAR LEVEL SO THAT THERE WOULDN'T BE ANY SEAM.

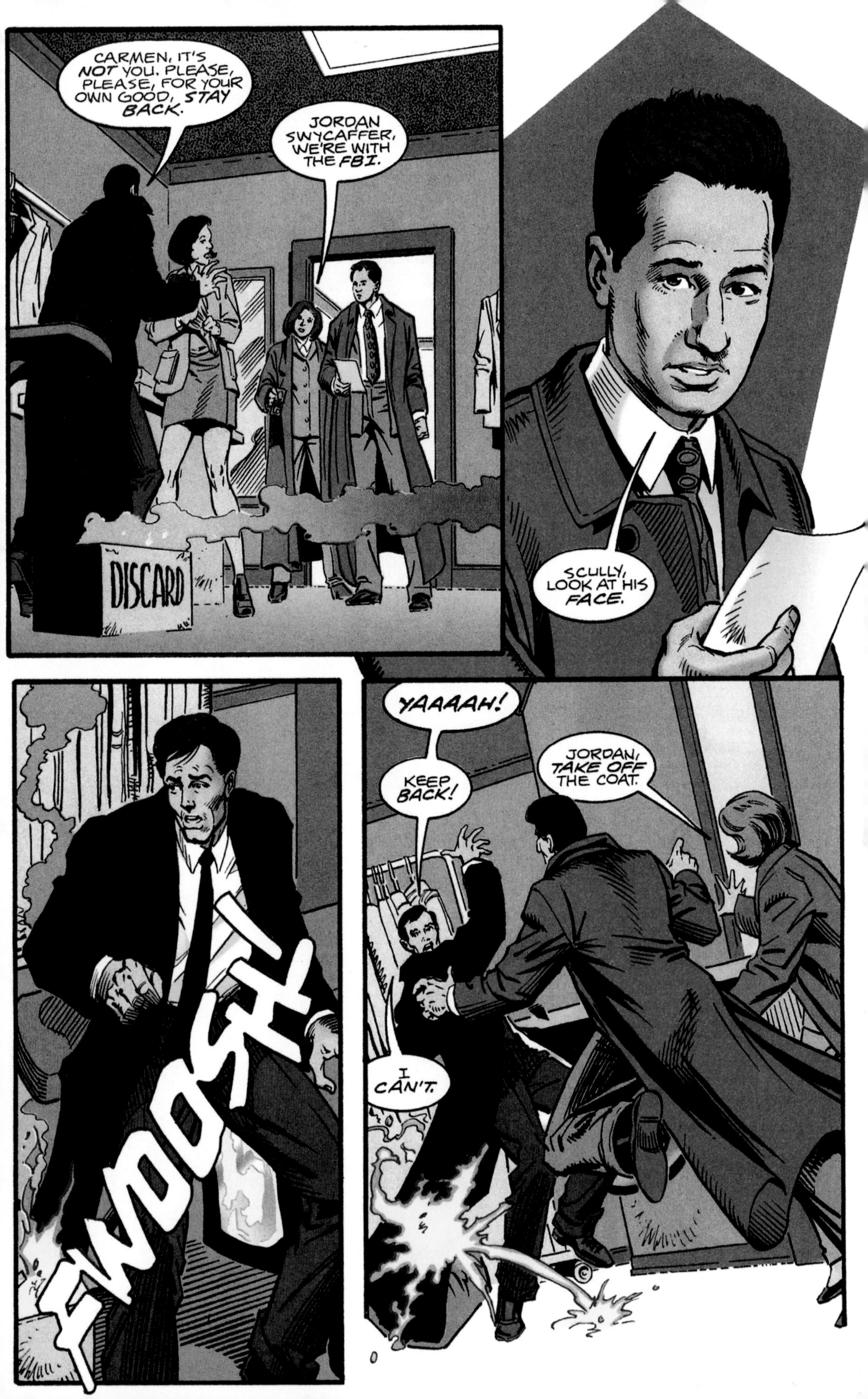
CARMEN, IT'S NOT YOU. PLEASE, PLEASE, FOR YOUR OWN GOOD, STAY BACK.
JORDAN SWYCAFFER, WE'RE WITH THE FBI.
DISCARD
SCULLY, LOOK AT HIS FACE.
FWOOSH!
YAAAAH!
KEEP BACK!
JORDAN, TAKE OFF THE COAT.
I CAN'T.

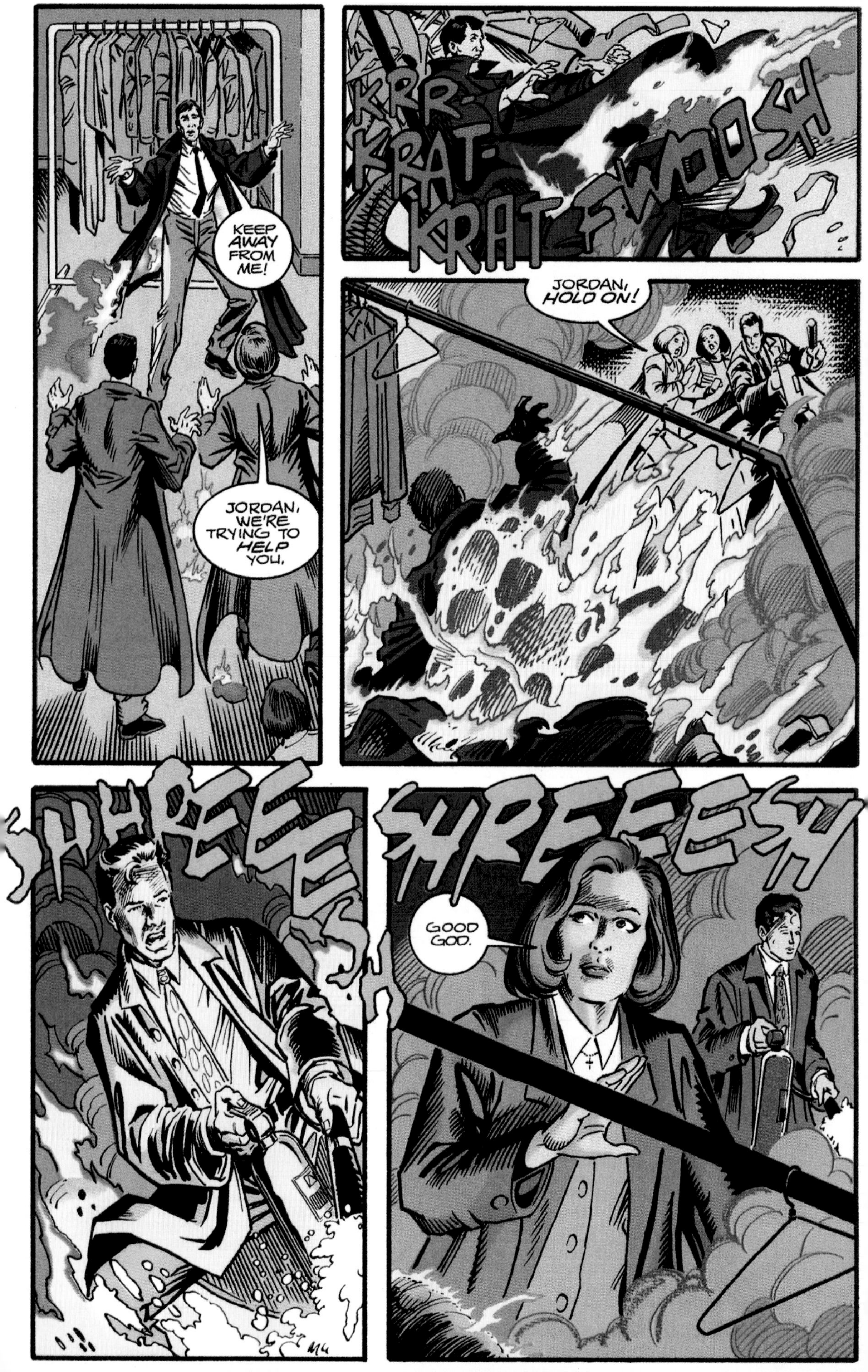
KEEP AWAY FROM ME!
JORDAN, WE'RE TRYING TO HELP YOU.
KRR-KRAT-KRAT
FWOOSH
JORDAN, HOLD ON!
SHREEESH
SHREEESH
GOOD GOD.

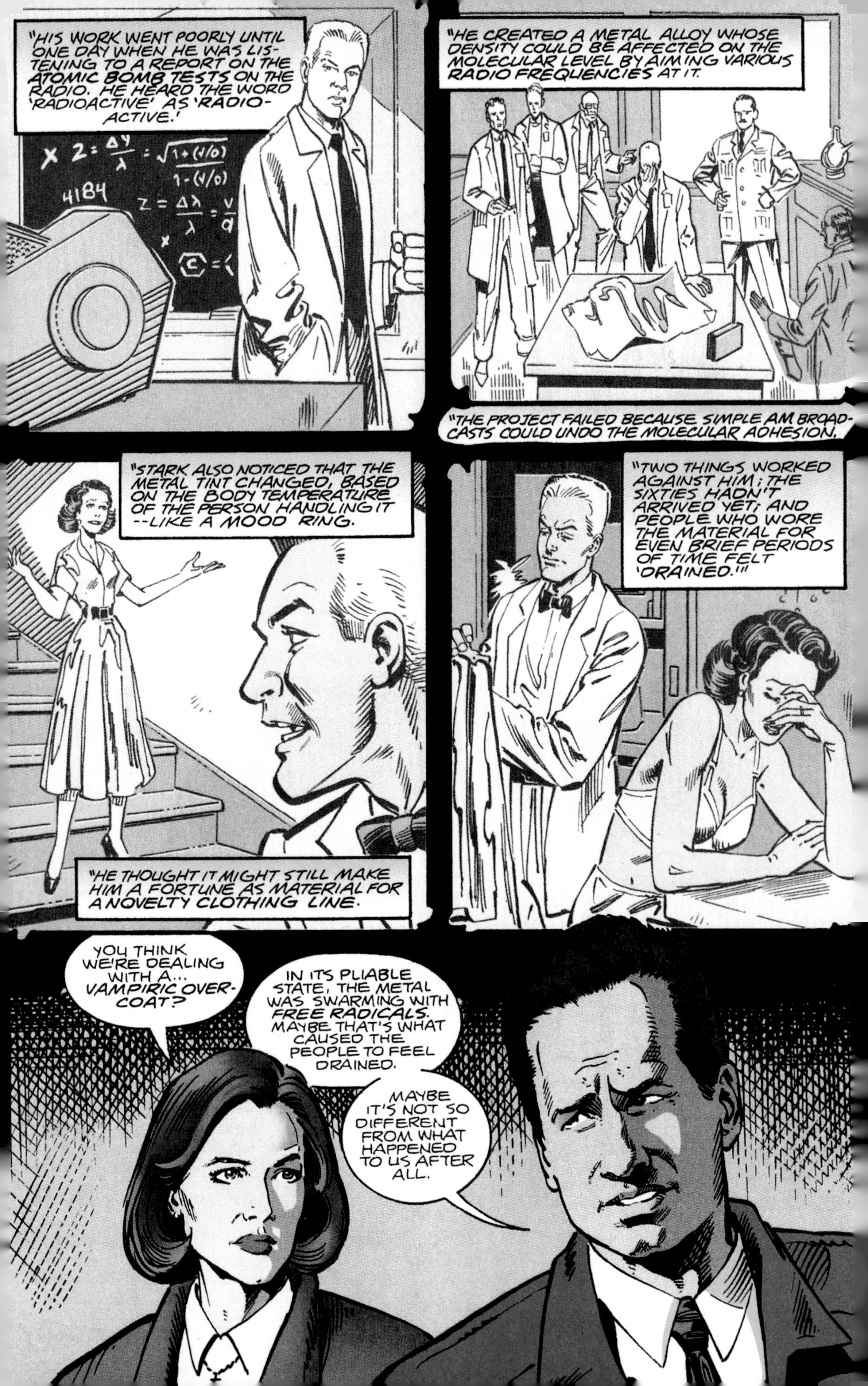
"HIS WORK WENT POORLY UNTIL ONE DAY WHEN HE WAS LISTENING TO A REPORT ON THE ATOMIC BOMB TESTS ON THE RADIO. HE HEARD THE WORD 'RADIOACTIVE' AS 'RADIO-ACTIVE.'
"HE CREATED A METAL ALLOY WHOSE DENSITY COULD BE AFFECTED ON THE MOLECULAR LEVEL BY AIMING VARIOUS RADIO FREQUENCIES AT IT.
"THE PROJECT FAILED BECAUSE SIMPLE AM BROADCASTS COULD UNDO THE MOLECULAR ADHESION.
"STARK ALSO NOTICED THAT THE METAL TINT CHANGED, BASED ON THE BODY TEMPERATURE OF THE PERSON HANDLING IT --LIKE A MOOD RING.
"HE THOUGHT IT MIGHT STILL MAKE HIM A FORTUNE AS MATERIAL FOR A NOVELTY CLOTHING LINE.
"TWO THINGS WORKED AGAINST HIM; THE SIXTIES HADN'T ARRIVED YET; AND PEOPLE WHO WORE THE MATERIAL FOR EVEN BRIEF PERIODS OF TIME FELT 'DRAINED.'"
YOU THINK WE'RE DEALING WITH A... VAMPIRIC OVER-COAT?
IN ITS PLIABLE STATE, THE METAL WAS SWARMING WITH FREE RADICALS. MAYBE THAT'S WHAT CAUSED THE PEOPLE TO FEEL DRAINED.
MAYBE IT'S NOT SO DIFFERENT FROM WHAT HAPPENED TO US AFTER ALL.

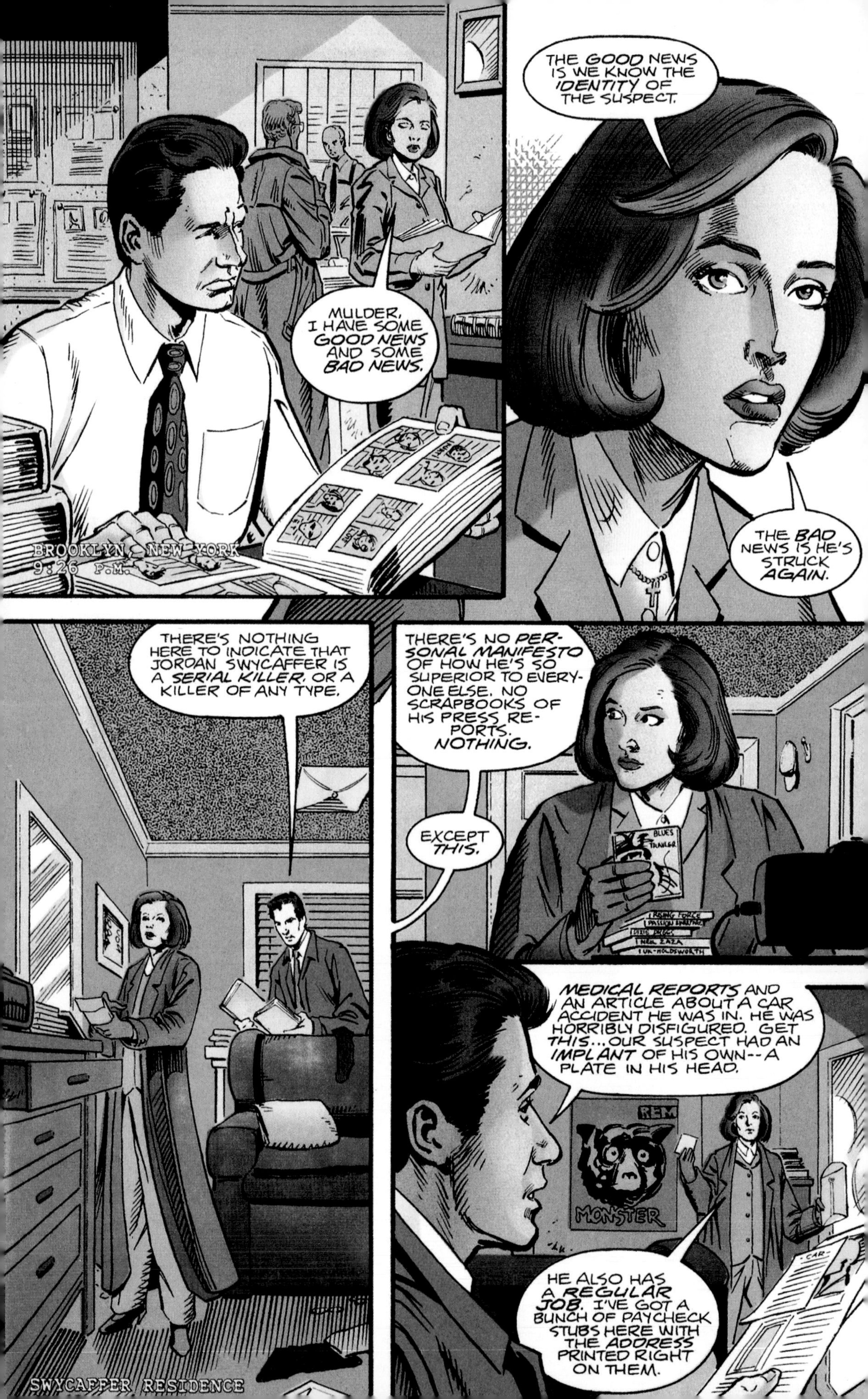
BROOKLYN, NEW YORK 9:26 P.M.
MULDER, I HAVE SOME GOOD NEWS AND SOME BAD NEWS.
THE GOOD NEWS IS WE KNOW THE IDENTITY OF THE SUSPECT.
THE BAD NEWS IS HE'S STRUCK AGAIN.
SWYCAFFER RESIDENCE
THERE'S NOTHING HERE TO INDICATE THAT JORDAN SWYCAFFER IS A SERIAL KILLER, OR A KILLER OF ANY TYPE.
THERE'S NO PERSONAL MANIFESTO OF HOW HE'S SO SUPERIOR TO EVERYONE ELSE. NO SCRAPBOOKS OF HIS PRESS REPORTS. NOTHING.
EXCEPT THIS.
BLUES TRAVELER
MEDICAL REPORTS AND AN ARTICLE ABOUT A CAR ACCIDENT HE WAS IN. HE WAS HORRIBLY DISFIGURED. GET THIS... OUR SUSPECT HAD AN IMPLANT OF HIS OWN--A PLATE IN HIS HEAD.
R.E.M.
MONSTER
HE ALSO HAS A REGULAR JOB. I'VE GOT A BUNCH OF PAYCHECK STUBS HERE WITH THE ADDRESS PRINTED RIGHT ON THEM.

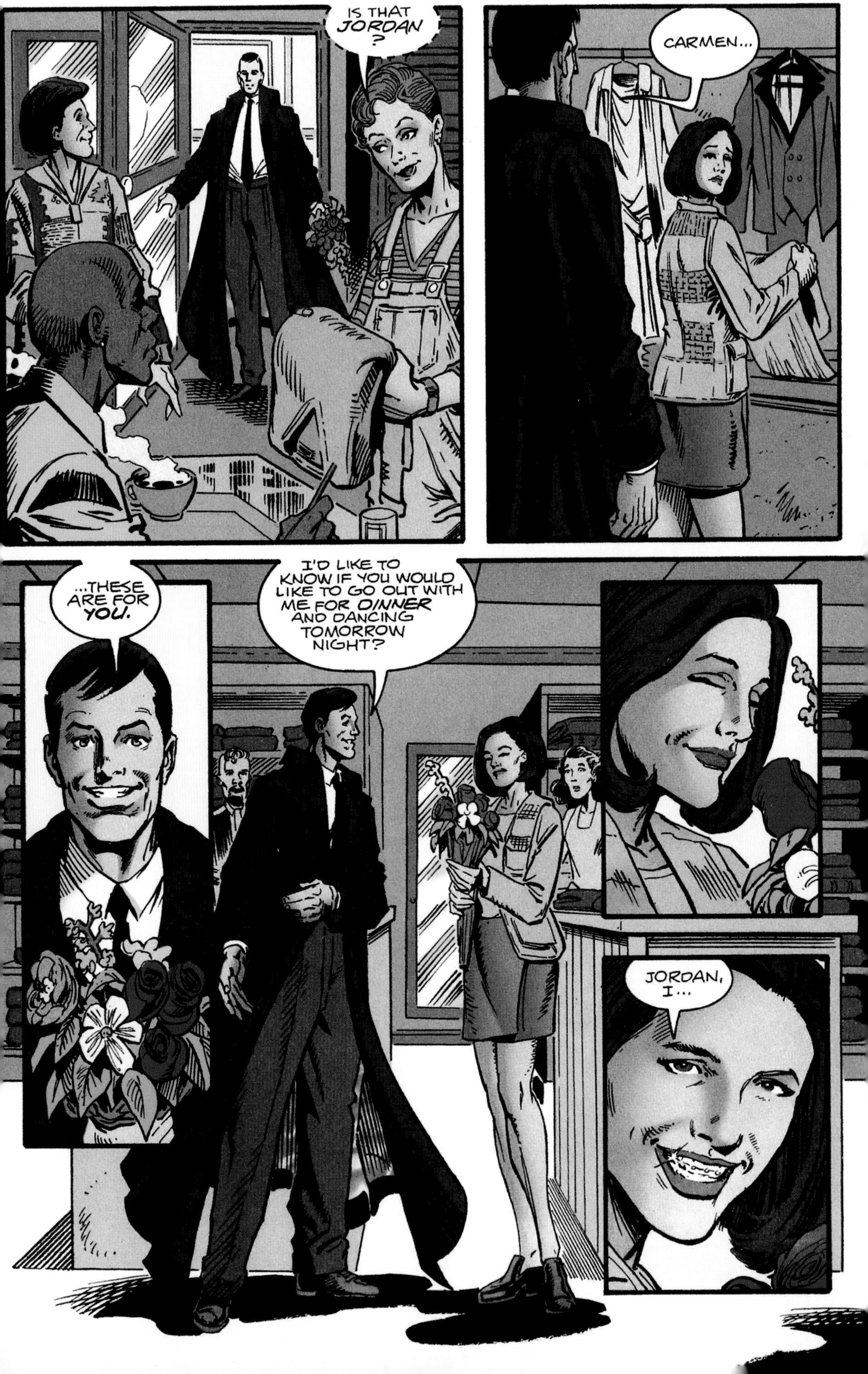
IS THAT JORDAN ?
CARMEN...
...THESE ARE FOR YOU.
I'D LIKE TO KNOW IF YOU WOULD LIKE TO GO OUT WITH ME FOR DINNER AND DANCING TOMORROW NIGHT?
JORDAN, I...

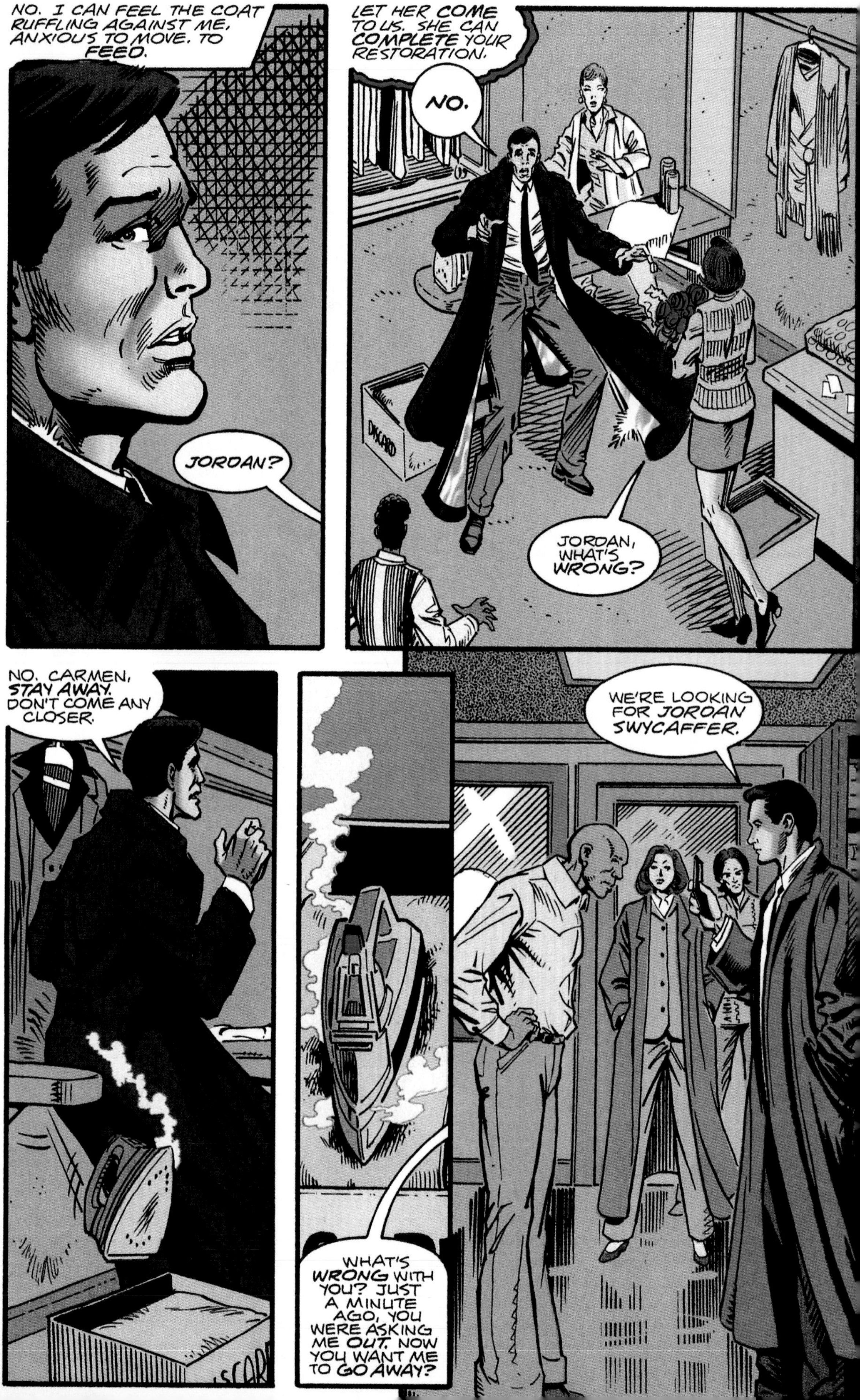

NO. I CAN FEEL THE COAT RUFFLING AGAINST ME, ANXIOUS TO MOVE. TO FEED.
JORDAN?
LET HER COME TO US. SHE CAN COMPLETE YOUR RESTORATION.
NO.
DISCARD
JORDAN, WHAT'S WRONG?
NO. CARMEN, STAY AWAY. DON'T COME ANY CLOSER.
WHAT'S WRONG WITH YOU? JUST A MINUTE AGO, YOU WERE ASKING ME OUT. NOW YOU WANT ME TO GO AWAY?
WE'RE LOOKING FOR JORDAN SWYCAFFER.

# BE PREPARED PART 1 (of 2)

STORY: John Rozum
ART: Gordon Purcell

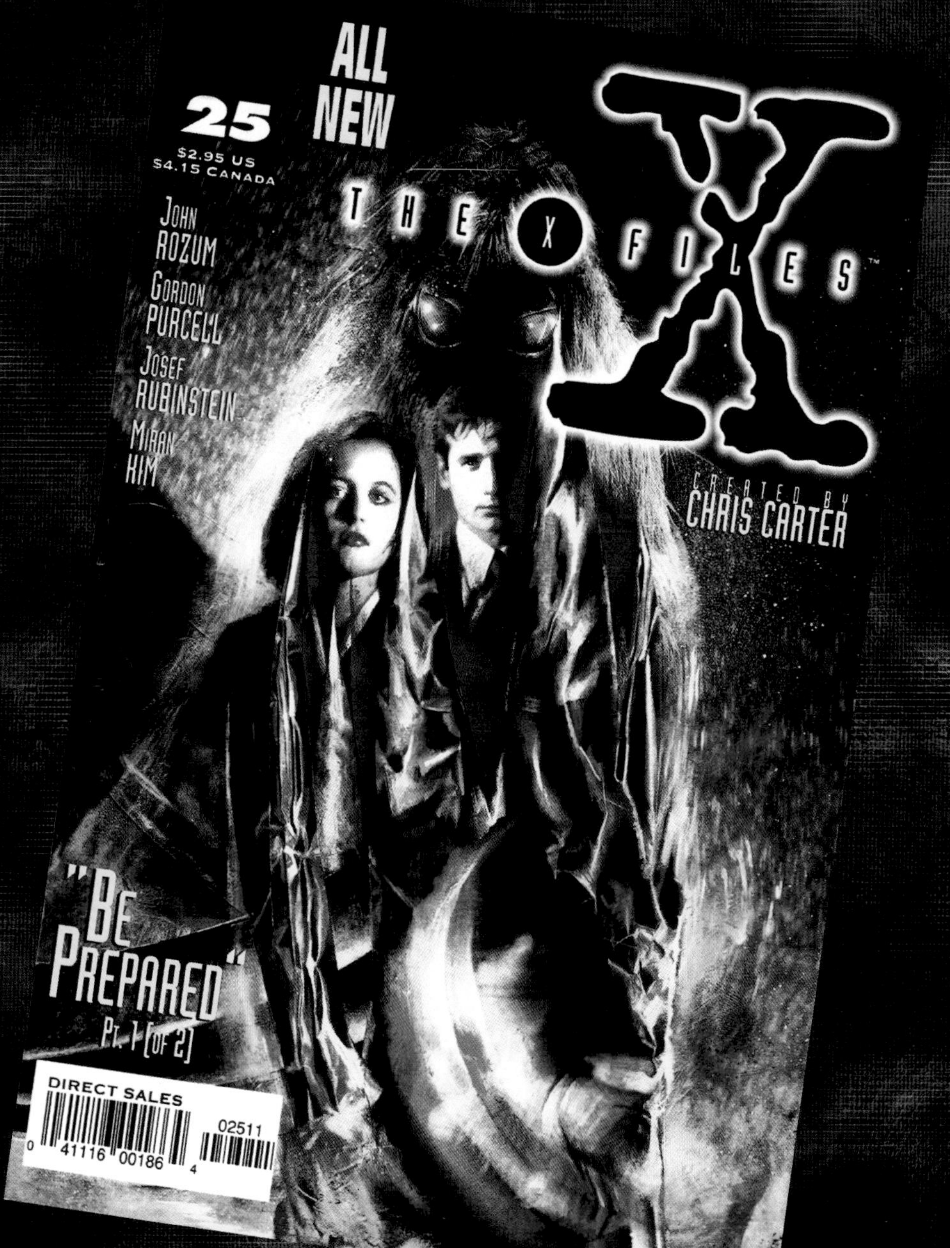

ALL NEW
25
$2.95 US
$4.15 CANADA
THE X FILES
JOHN ROZUM
GORDON PURCELL
JOSEF RUBINSTEIN
MIRAN KIM
CREATED BY CHRIS CARTER
"BE PREPARED"
PT. 1 (OF 2)
DIRECT SALES

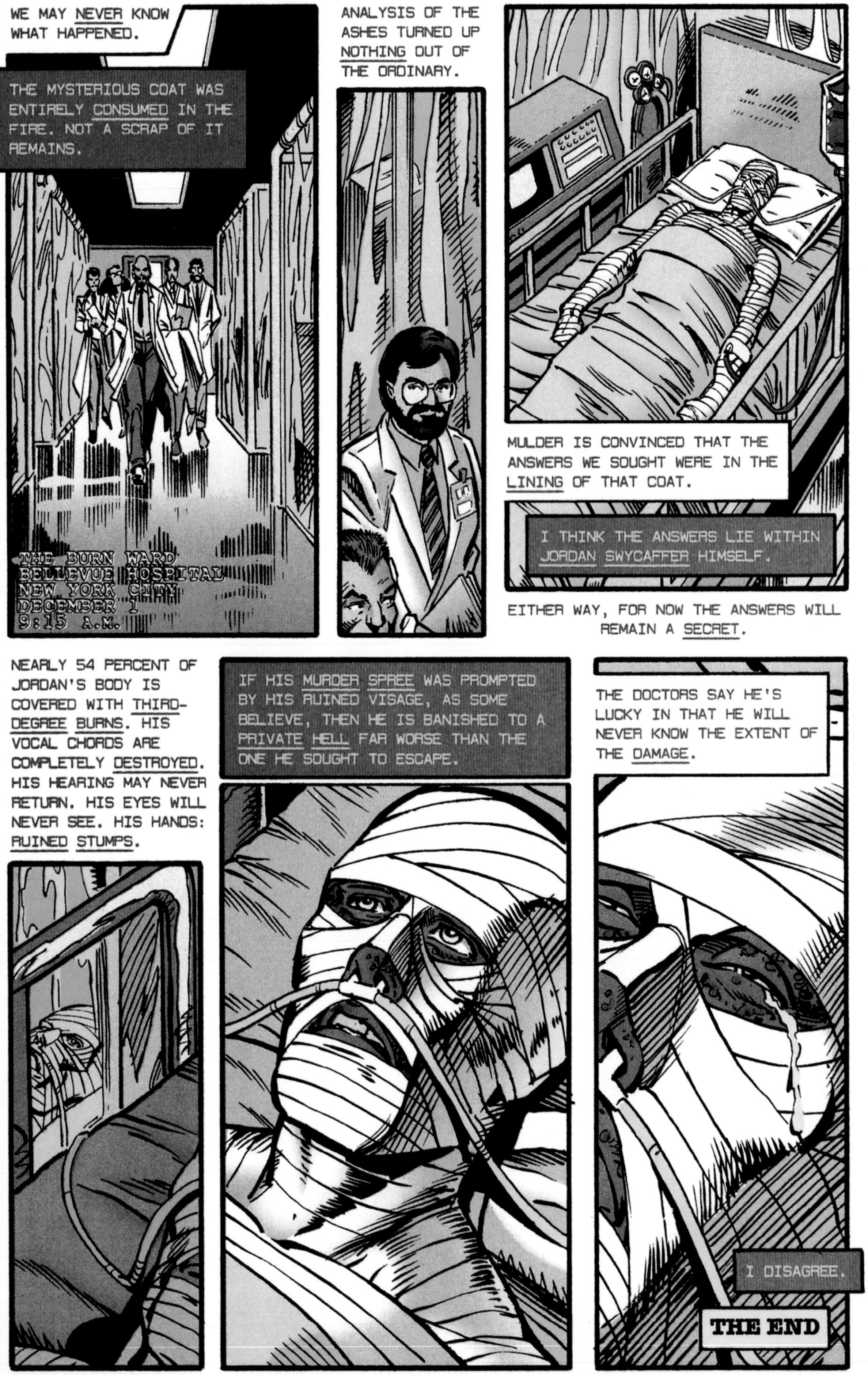
WE MAY NEVER KNOW WHAT HAPPENED.
THE MYSTERIOUS COAT WAS ENTIRELY CONSUMED IN THE FIRE. NOT A SCRAP OF IT REMAINS.
THE BURN WARD
BELLEVUE HOSPITAL
NEW YORK CITY
DECEMBER 1
9:15 A.M.
ANALYSIS OF THE ASHES TURNED UP NOTHING OUT OF THE ORDINARY.
MULDER IS CONVINCED THAT THE ANSWERS WE SOUGHT WERE IN THE LINING OF THAT COAT.
I THINK THE ANSWERS LIE WITHIN JORDAN SWYCAFFER HIMSELF.
EITHER WAY, FOR NOW THE ANSWERS WILL REMAIN A SECRET.
NEARLY 54 PERCENT OF JORDAN'S BODY IS COVERED WITH THIRD-DEGREE BURNS. HIS VOCAL CHORDS ARE COMPLETELY DESTROYED. HIS HEARING MAY NEVER RETURN. HIS EYES WILL NEVER SEE. HIS HANDS: RUINED STUMPS.
IF HIS MURDER SPREE WAS PROMPTED BY HIS RUINED VISAGE, AS SOME BELIEVE, THEN HE IS BANISHED TO A PRIVATE HELL FAR WORSE THAN THE ONE HE SOUGHT TO ESCAPE.
THE DOCTORS SAY HE'S LUCKY IN THAT HE WILL NEVER KNOW THE EXTENT OF THE DAMAGE.
I DISAGREE.
THE END

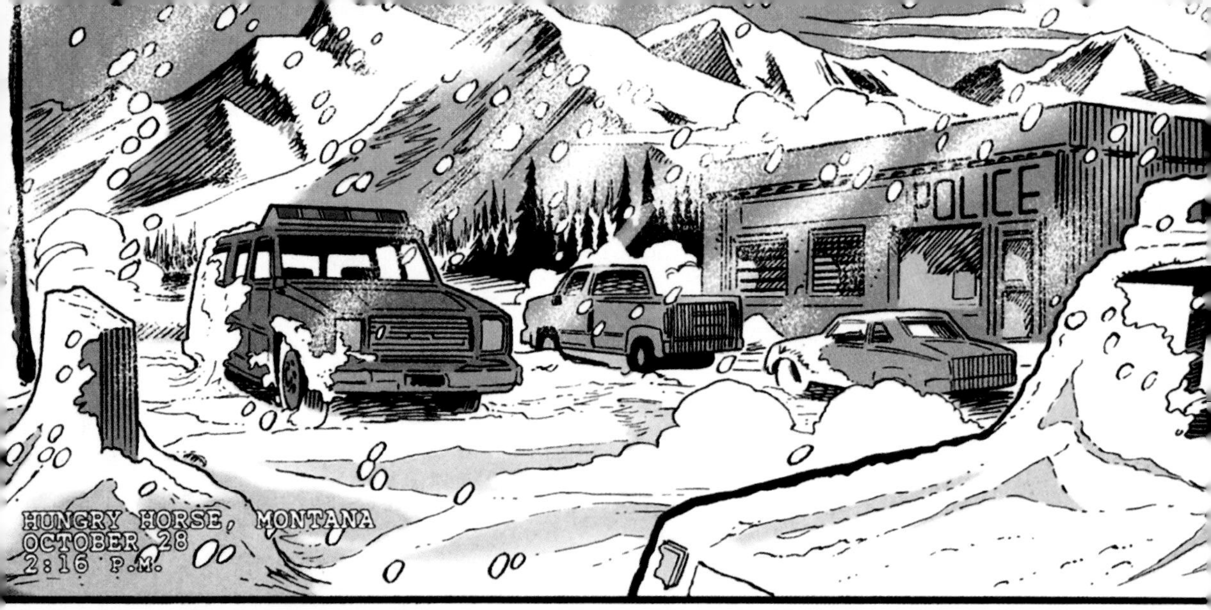
POLICE
HUNGRY HORSE, MONTANA
OCTOBER 28
2:16 P.M.

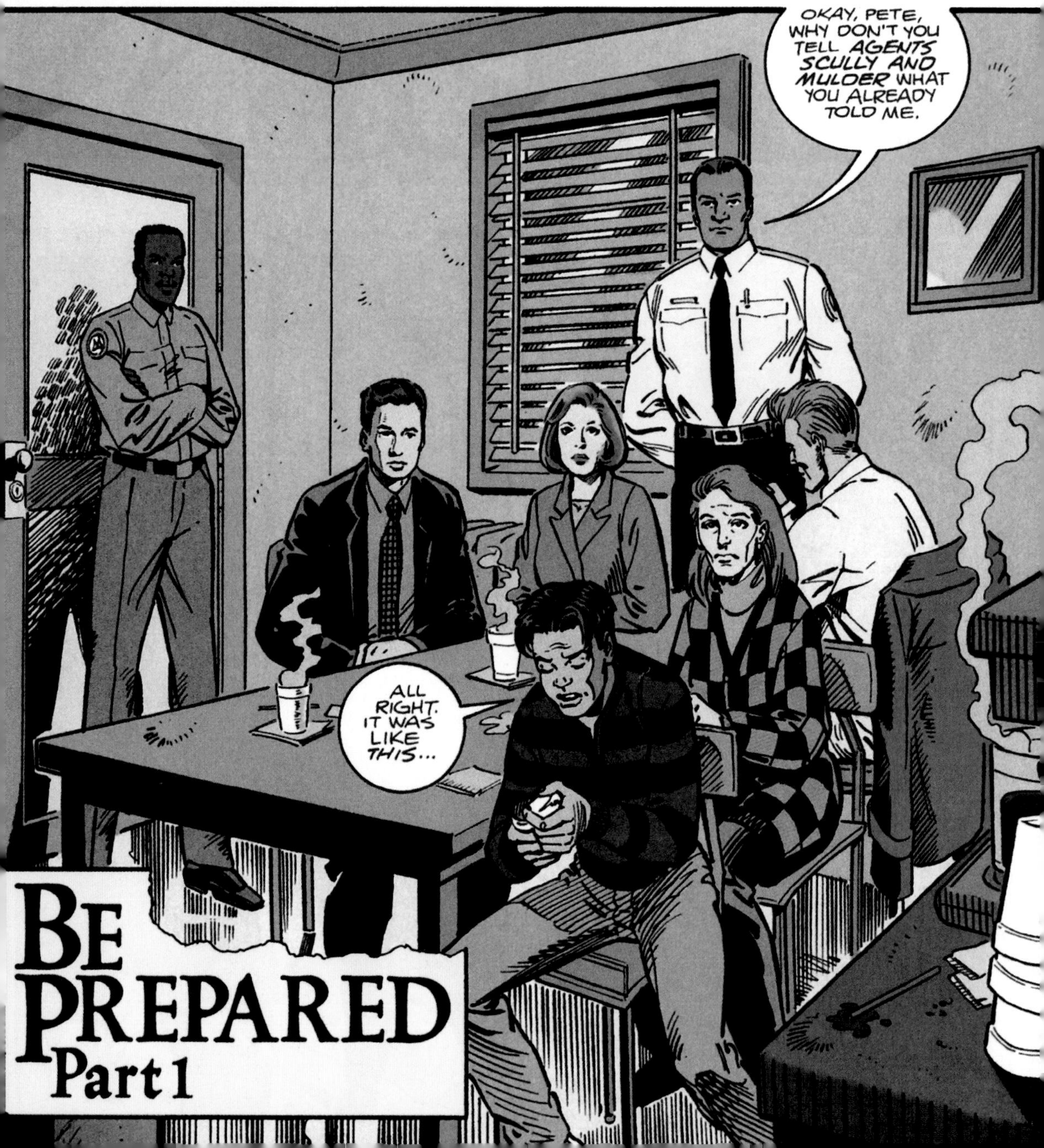
OKAY, PETE, WHY DON'T YOU TELL AGENTS SCULLY AND MULDER WHAT YOU ALREADY TOLD ME.
ALL RIGHT. IT WAS LIKE THIS...
BE PREPARED
Part 1

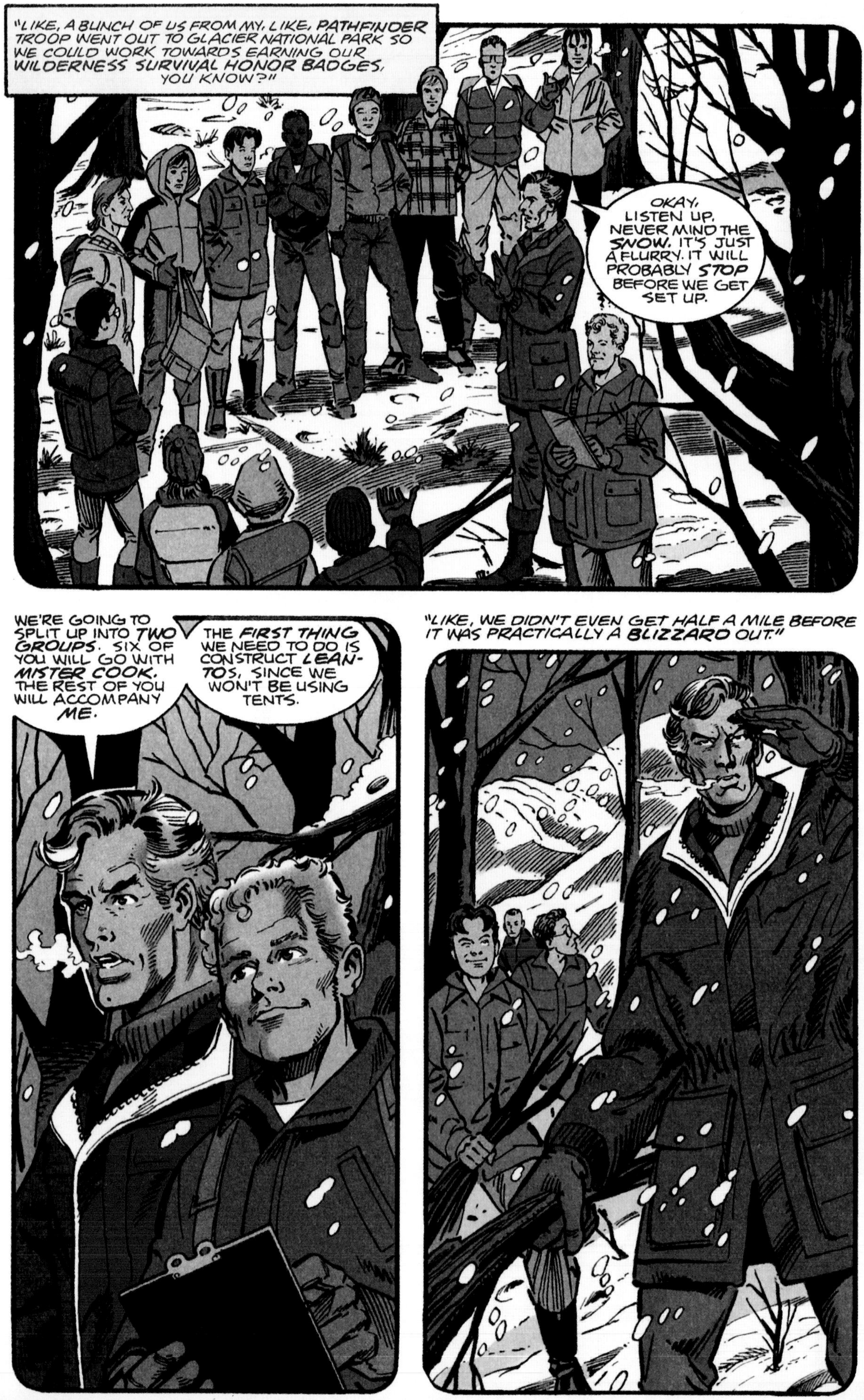
"LIKE, A BUNCH OF US FROM MY, LIKE, PATHFINDER TROOP WENT OUT TO GLACIER NATIONAL PARK SO WE COULD WORK TOWARDS EARNING OUR WILDERNESS SURVIVAL HONOR BADGES, YOU KNOW?"
OKAY, LISTEN UP. NEVER MIND THE SNOW. IT'S JUST A FLURRY. IT WILL PROBABLY STOP BEFORE WE GET SET UP.
WE'RE GOING TO SPLIT UP INTO TWO GROUPS. SIX OF YOU WILL GO WITH MISTER COOK. THE REST OF YOU WILL ACCOMPANY ME.
THE FIRST THING WE NEED TO DO IS CONSTRUCT LEAN-TOS, SINCE WE WON'T BE USING TENTS.
"LIKE, WE DIDN'T EVEN GET HALF A MILE BEFORE IT WAS PRACTICALLY A BLIZZARD OUT."

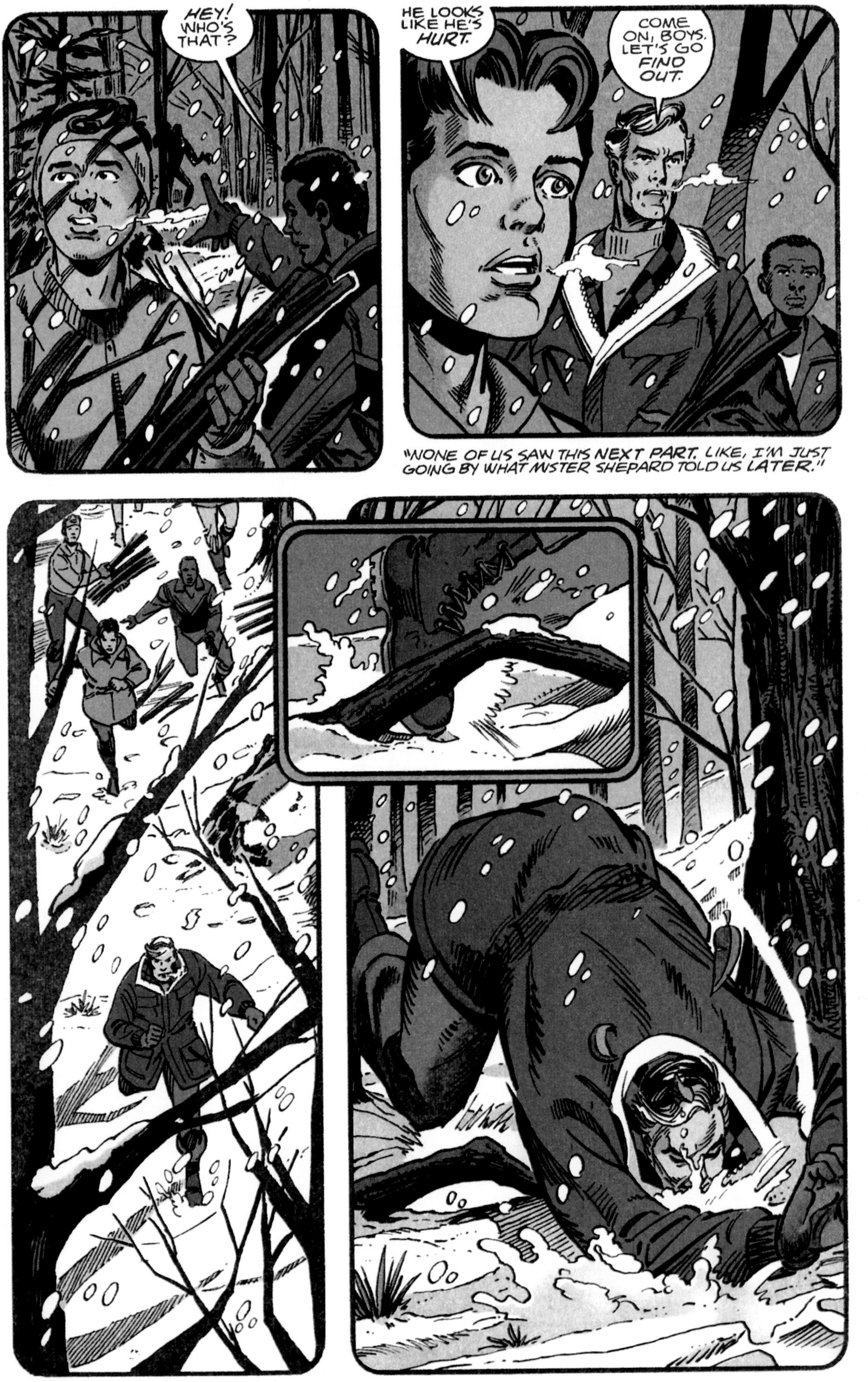
HEY! WHO'S THAT?
HE LOOKS LIKE HE'S HURT.
COME ON, BOYS. LET'S GO FIND OUT.
"NONE OF US SAW THIS NEXT PART. LIKE, I'M JUST GOING BY WHAT MISTER SHEPARD TOLD US LATER."

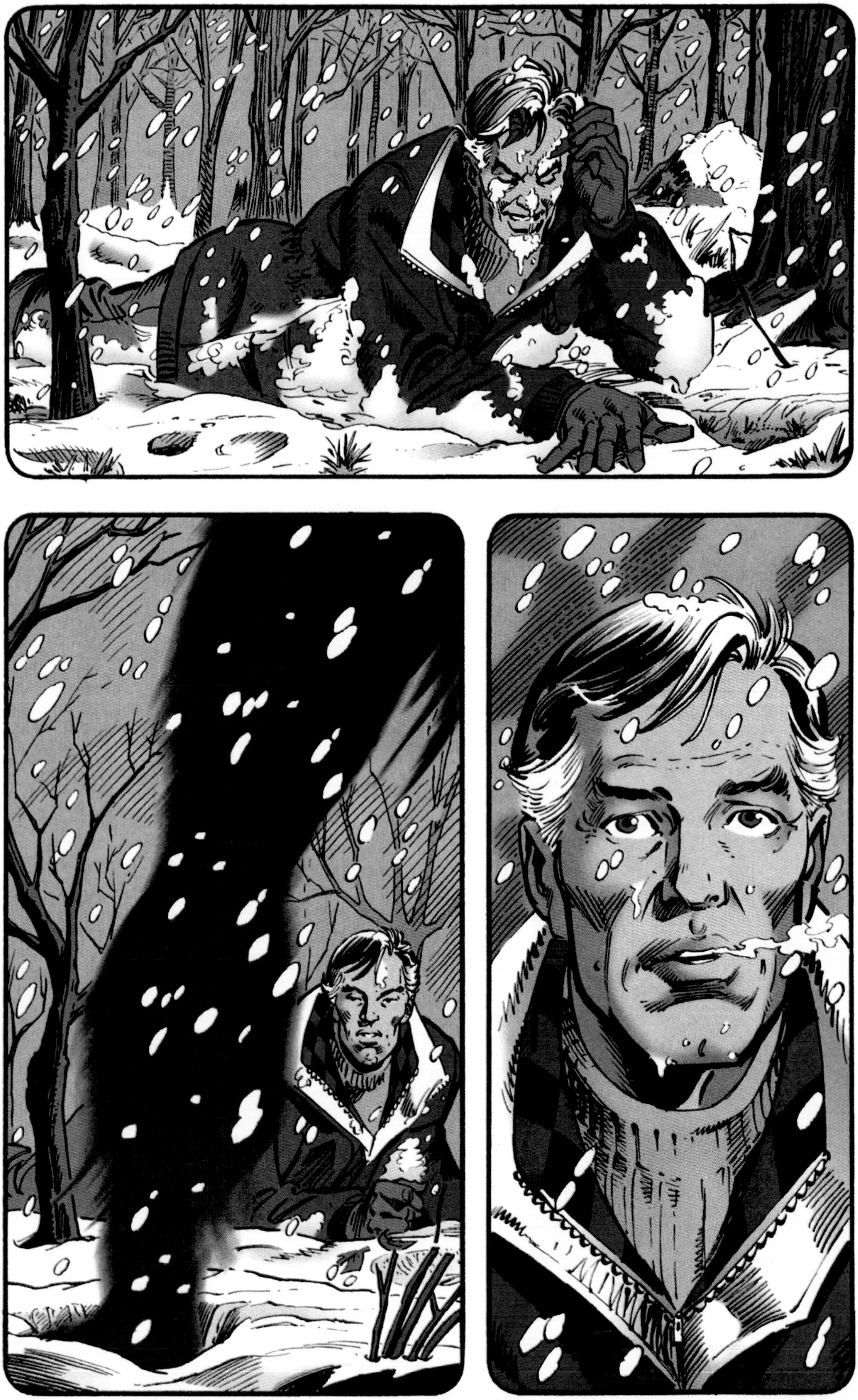

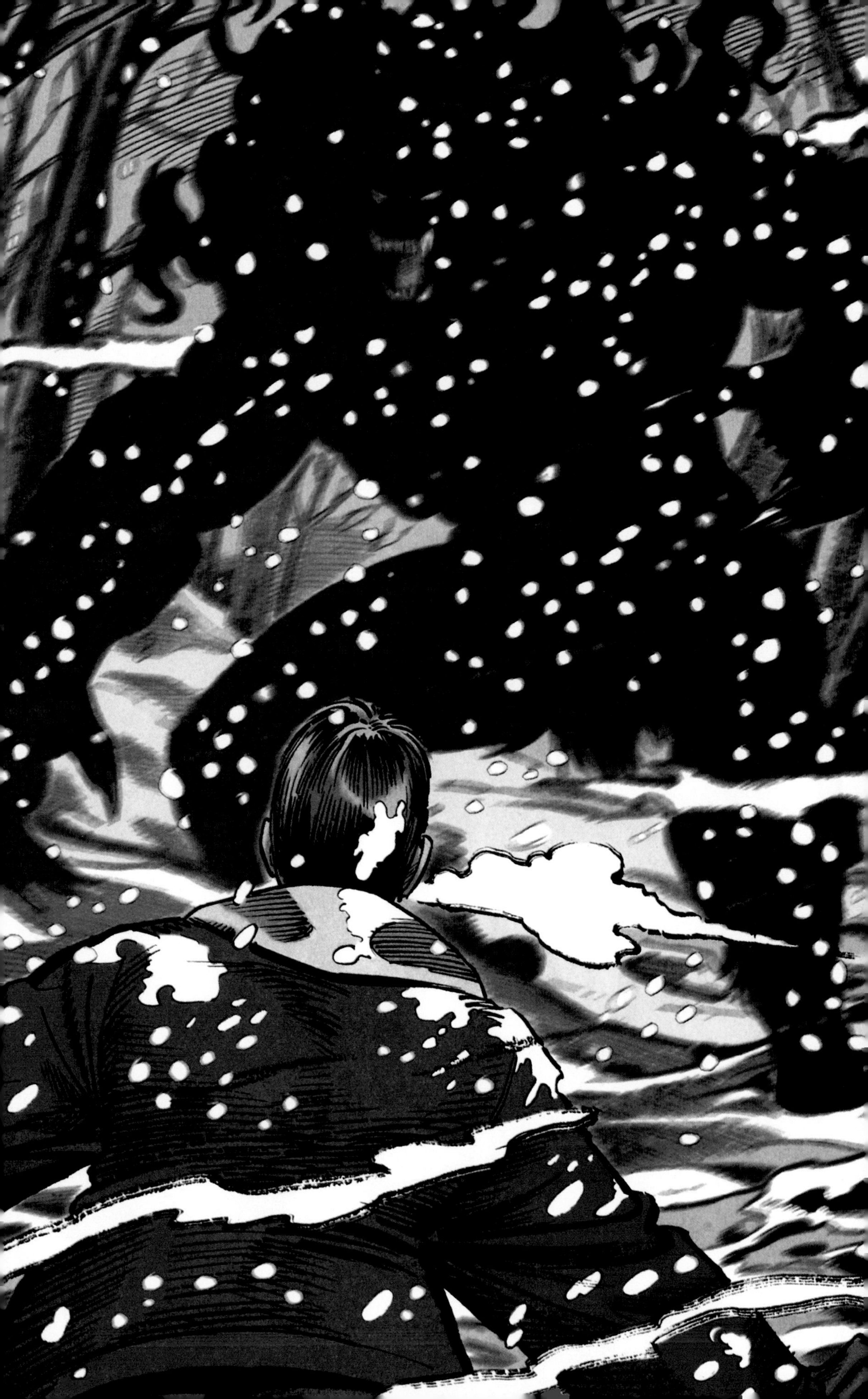

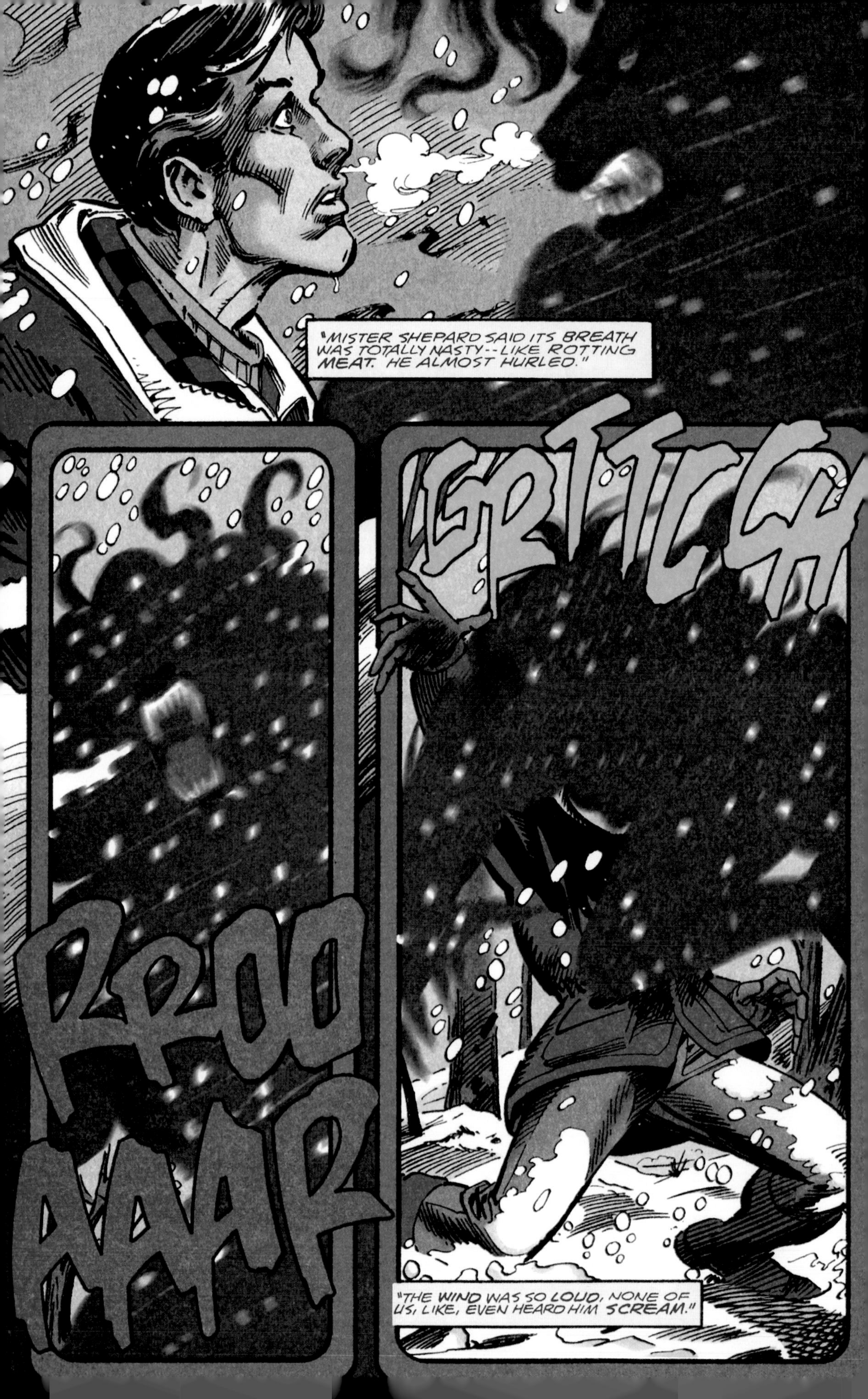
"MISTER SHEPARD SAID ITS BREATH WAS TOTALLY NASTY--LIKE ROTTING MEAT. HE ALMOST HURLED."
RROOAAAR
GRTTCCH
"THE WIND WAS SO LOUD, NONE OF US, LIKE, EVEN HEARD HIM SCREAM."

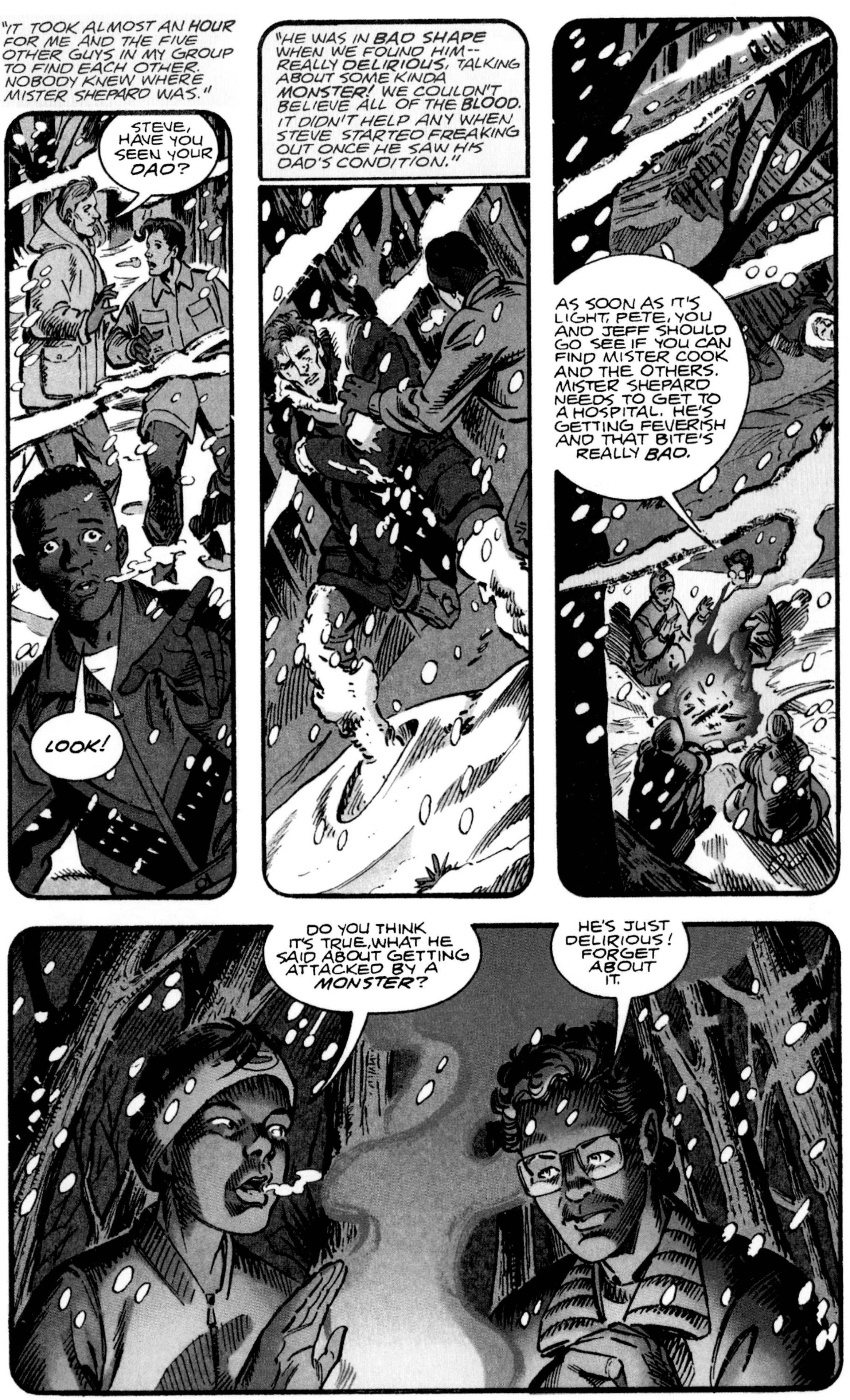
"IT TOOK ALMOST AN HOUR FOR ME AND THE FIVE OTHER GUYS IN MY GROUP TO FIND EACH OTHER. NOBODY KNEW WHERE MISTER SHEPARD WAS."
STEVE, HAVE YOU SEEN YOUR DAD?
LOOK!
"HE WAS IN BAD SHAPE WHEN WE FOUND HIM-- REALLY DELIRIOUS, TALKING ABOUT SOME KINDA MONSTER! WE COULDN'T BELIEVE ALL OF THE BLOOD. IT DIDN'T HELP ANY WHEN STEVE STARTED FREAKING OUT ONCE HE SAW HIS DAD'S CONDITION."
AS SOON AS IT'S LIGHT, PETE, YOU AND JEFF SHOULD GO SEE IF YOU CAN FIND MISTER COOK AND THE OTHERS. MISTER SHEPARD NEEDS TO GET TO A HOSPITAL. HE'S GETTING FEVERISH AND THAT BITE'S REALLY BAD.
DO YOU THINK IT'S TRUE, WHAT HE SAID ABOUT GETTING ATTACKED BY A MONSTER?
HE'S JUST DELIRIOUS! FORGET ABOUT IT.

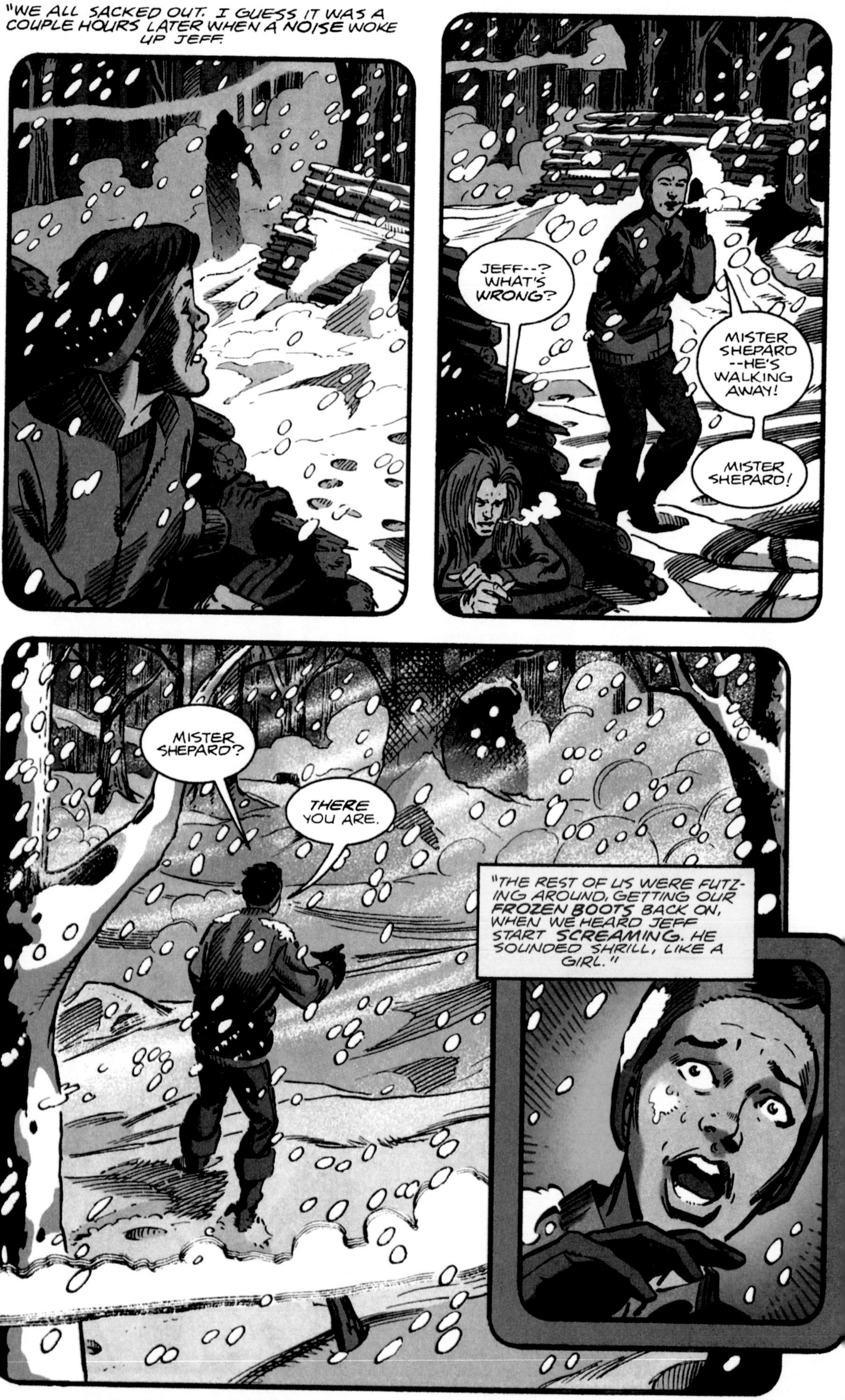
"WE ALL SACKED OUT. I GUESS IT WAS A COUPLE HOURS LATER WHEN A NOISE WOKE UP JEFF.
JEFF--? WHAT'S WRONG?
MISTER SHEPARD --HE'S WALKING AWAY!
MISTER SHEPARD!
MISTER SHEPARD?
THERE YOU ARE.
"THE REST OF US WERE FUTZ-ING AROUND, GETTING OUR FROZEN BOOTS BACK ON, WHEN WE HEARD JEFF START SCREAMING. HE SOUNDED SHRILL, LIKE A GIRL."

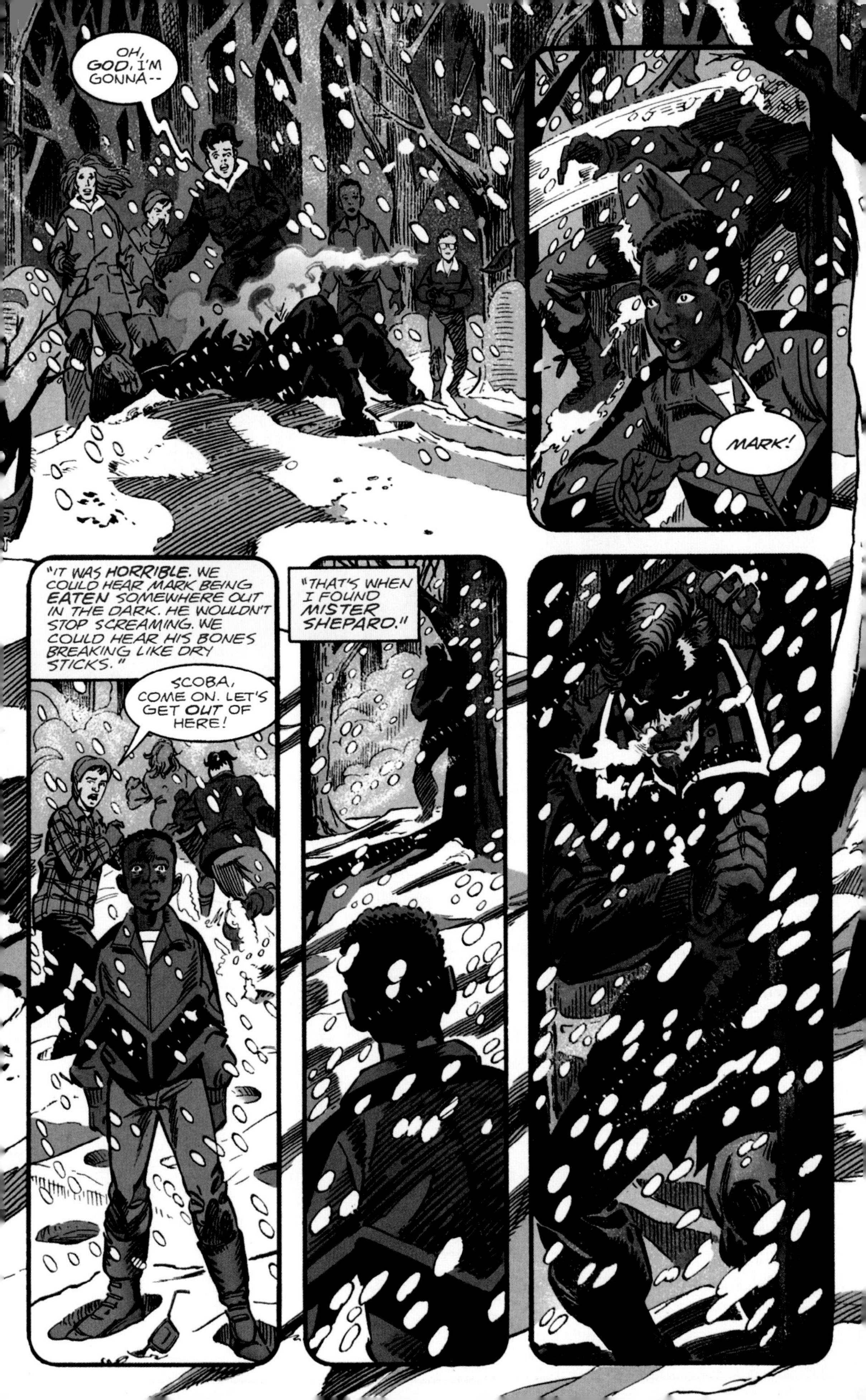
OH, GOD, I'M GONNA--
MARK!
"IT WAS HORRIBLE. WE COULD HEAR MARK BEING EATEN SOMEWHERE OUT IN THE DARK. HE WOULDN'T STOP SCREAMING. WE COULD HEAR HIS BONES BREAKING LIKE DRY STICKS."
SCOBA, COME ON. LET'S GET OUT OF HERE!
"THAT'S WHEN I FOUND MISTER SHEPARD."

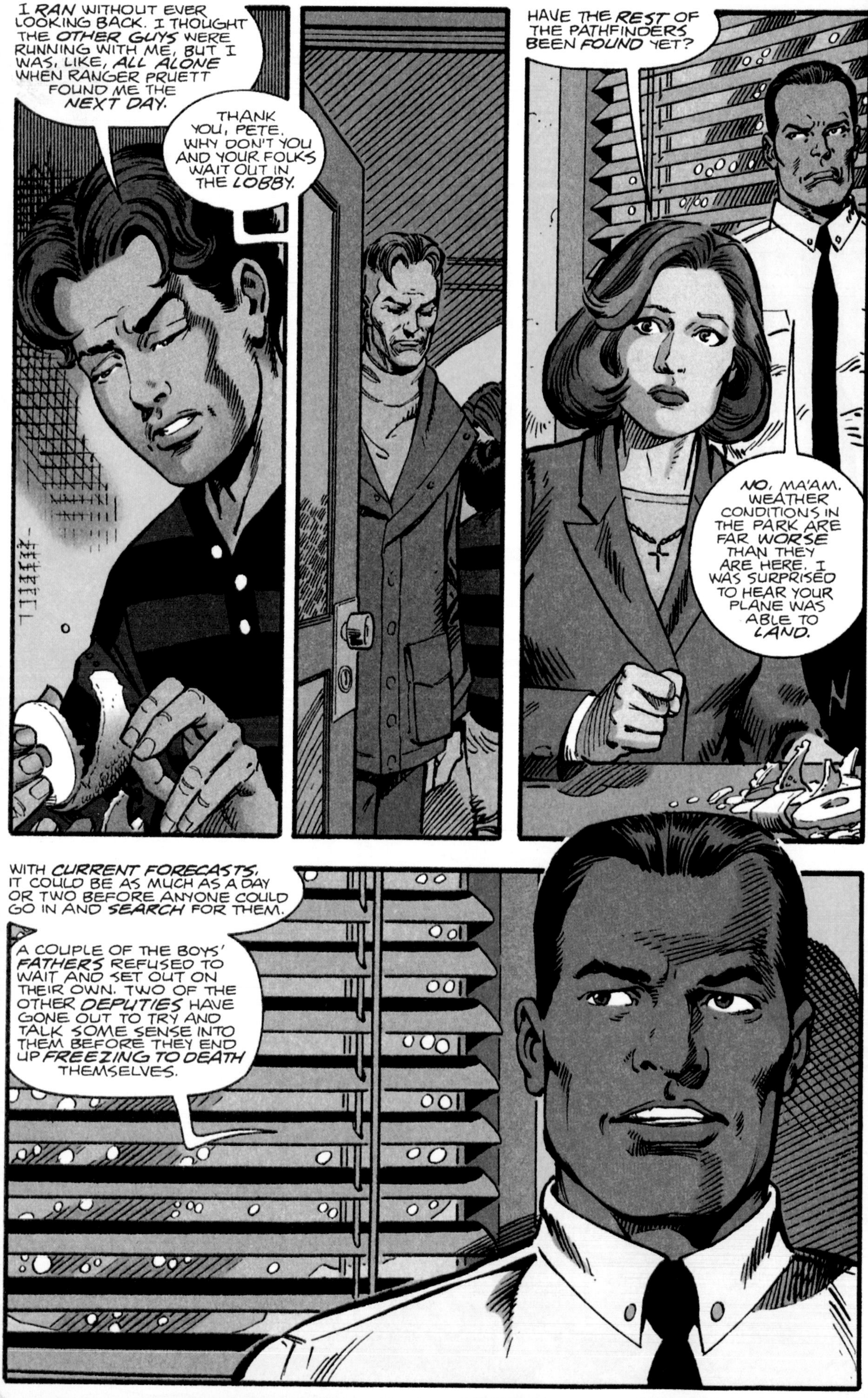

I RAN WITHOUT EVER LOOKING BACK. I THOUGHT THE OTHER GUYS WERE RUNNING WITH ME, BUT I WAS, LIKE, ALL ALONE WHEN RANGER PRUETT FOUND ME THE NEXT DAY.
THANK YOU, PETE. WHY DON'T YOU AND YOUR FOLKS WAIT OUT IN THE LOBBY.
HAVE THE REST OF THE PATHFINDERS BEEN FOUND YET?
NO, MA'AM. WEATHER CONDITIONS IN THE PARK ARE FAR WORSE THAN THEY ARE HERE. I WAS SURPRISED TO HEAR YOUR PLANE WAS ABLE TO LAND.
WITH CURRENT FORECASTS, IT COULD BE AS MUCH AS A DAY OR TWO BEFORE ANYONE COULD GO IN AND SEARCH FOR THEM.
A COUPLE OF THE BOYS' FATHERS REFUSED TO WAIT AND SET OUT ON THEIR OWN. TWO OF THE OTHER DEPUTIES HAVE GONE OUT TO TRY AND TALK SOME SENSE INTO THEM BEFORE THEY END UP FREEZING TO DEATH THEMSELVES.

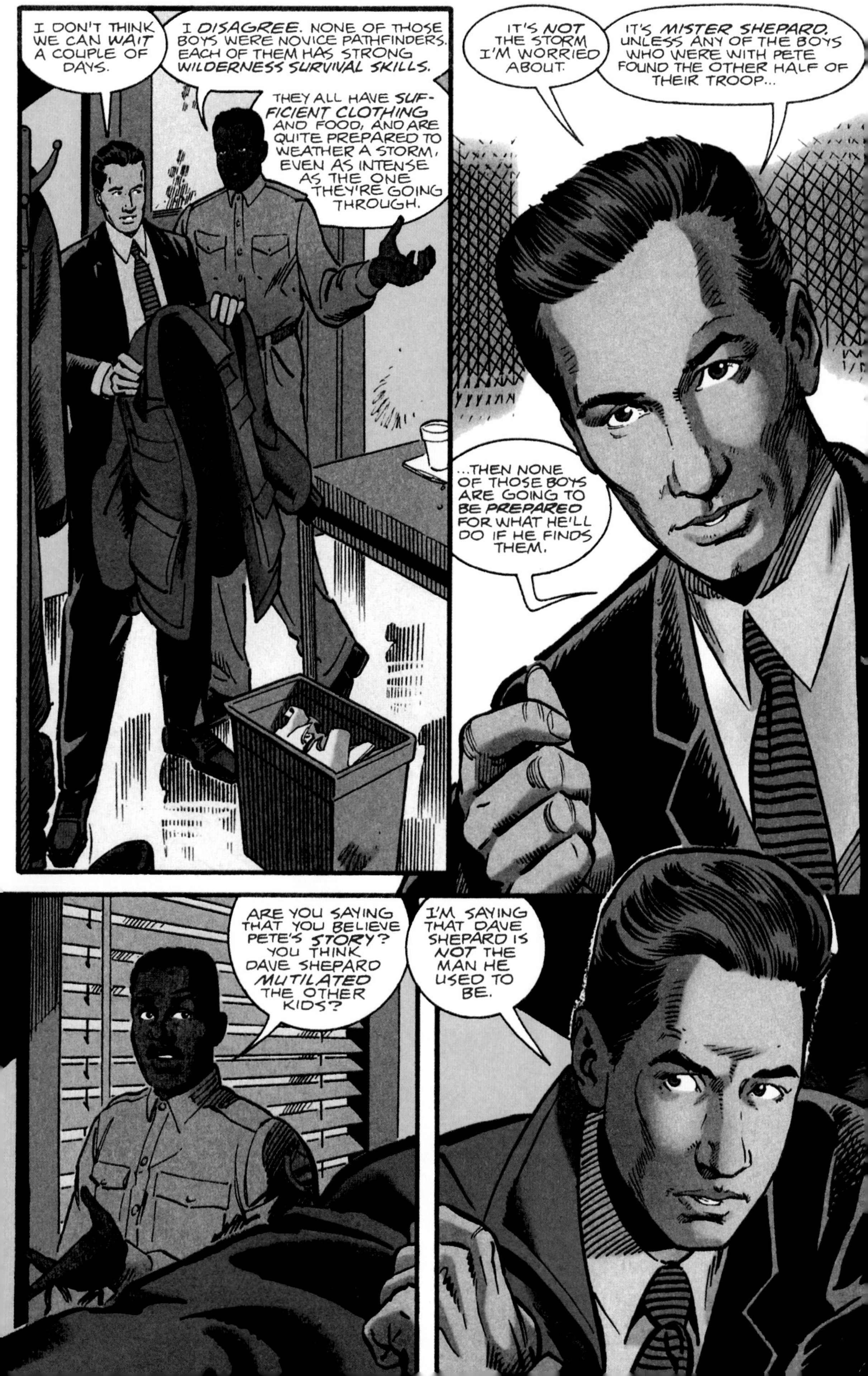

I DON'T THINK WE CAN WAIT A COUPLE OF DAYS.
I DISAGREE. NONE OF THOSE BOYS WERE NOVICE PATHFINDERS. EACH OF THEM HAS STRONG WILDERNESS SURVIVAL SKILLS.
THEY ALL HAVE SUFFICIENT CLOTHING AND FOOD, AND ARE QUITE PREPARED TO WEATHER A STORM, EVEN AS INTENSE AS THE ONE THEY'RE GOING THROUGH.
IT'S NOT THE STORM I'M WORRIED ABOUT.
IT'S MISTER SHEPARD. UNLESS ANY OF THE BOYS WHO WERE WITH PETE FOUND THE OTHER HALF OF THEIR TROOP...
...THEN NONE OF THOSE BOYS ARE GOING TO BE PREPARED FOR WHAT HE'LL DO IF HE FINDS THEM.
ARE YOU SAYING THAT YOU BELIEVE PETE'S STORY? YOU THINK DAVE SHEPARD MUTILATED THE OTHER KIDS?
I'M SAYING THAT DAVE SHEPARD IS NOT THE MAN HE USED TO BE.

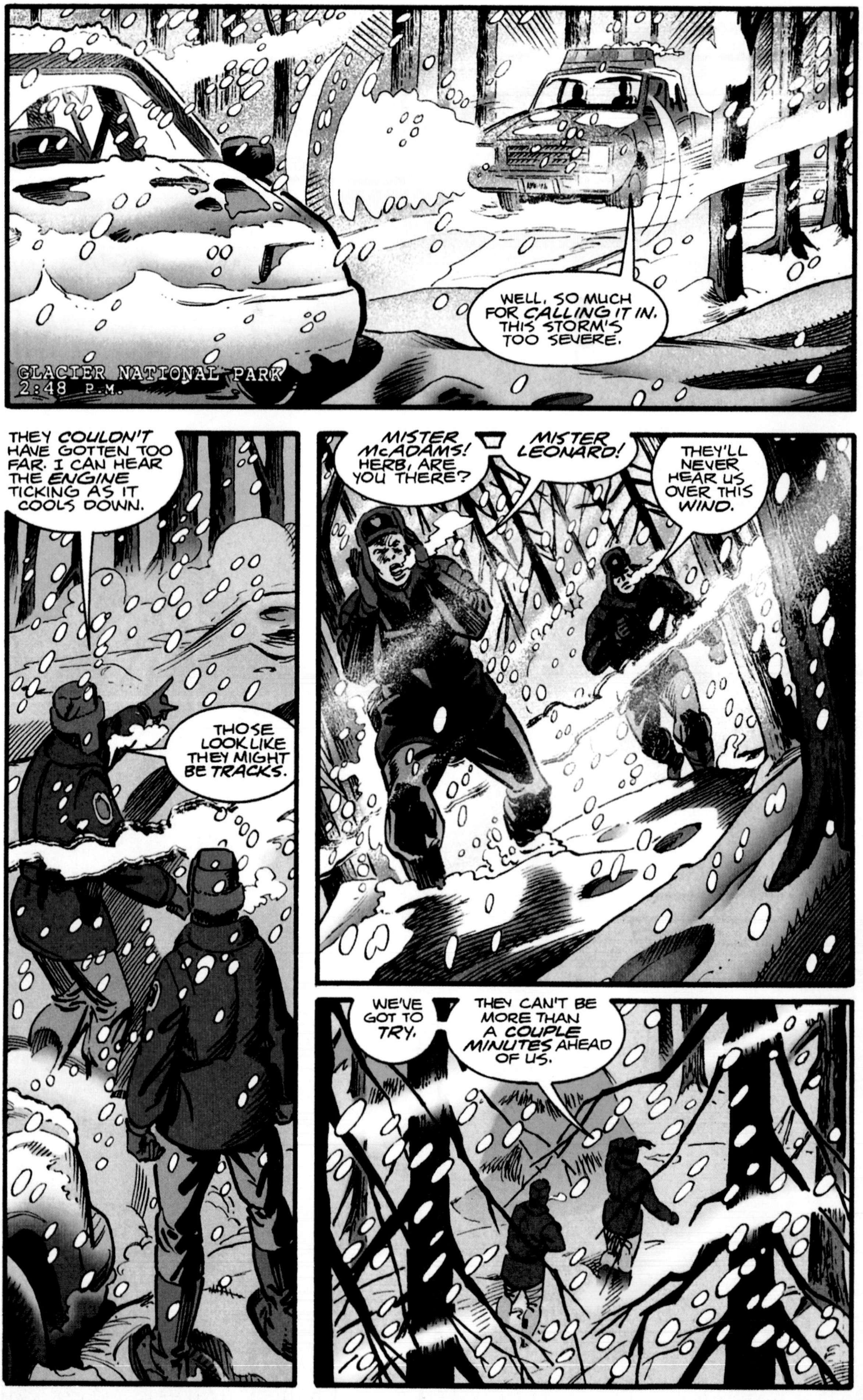
GLACIER NATIONAL PARK
2:48 P.M.
WELL, SO MUCH FOR CALLING IT IN. THIS STORM'S TOO SEVERE.
THEY COULDN'T HAVE GOTTEN TOO FAR. I CAN HEAR THE ENGINE TICKING AS IT COOLS DOWN.
THOSE LOOK LIKE THEY MIGHT BE TRACKS.
MISTER McADAMS! HERB, ARE YOU THERE?
MISTER LEONARD!
THEY'LL NEVER HEAR US OVER THIS WIND.
WE'VE GOT TO TRY.
THEY CAN'T BE MORE THAN A COUPLE MINUTES AHEAD OF US.

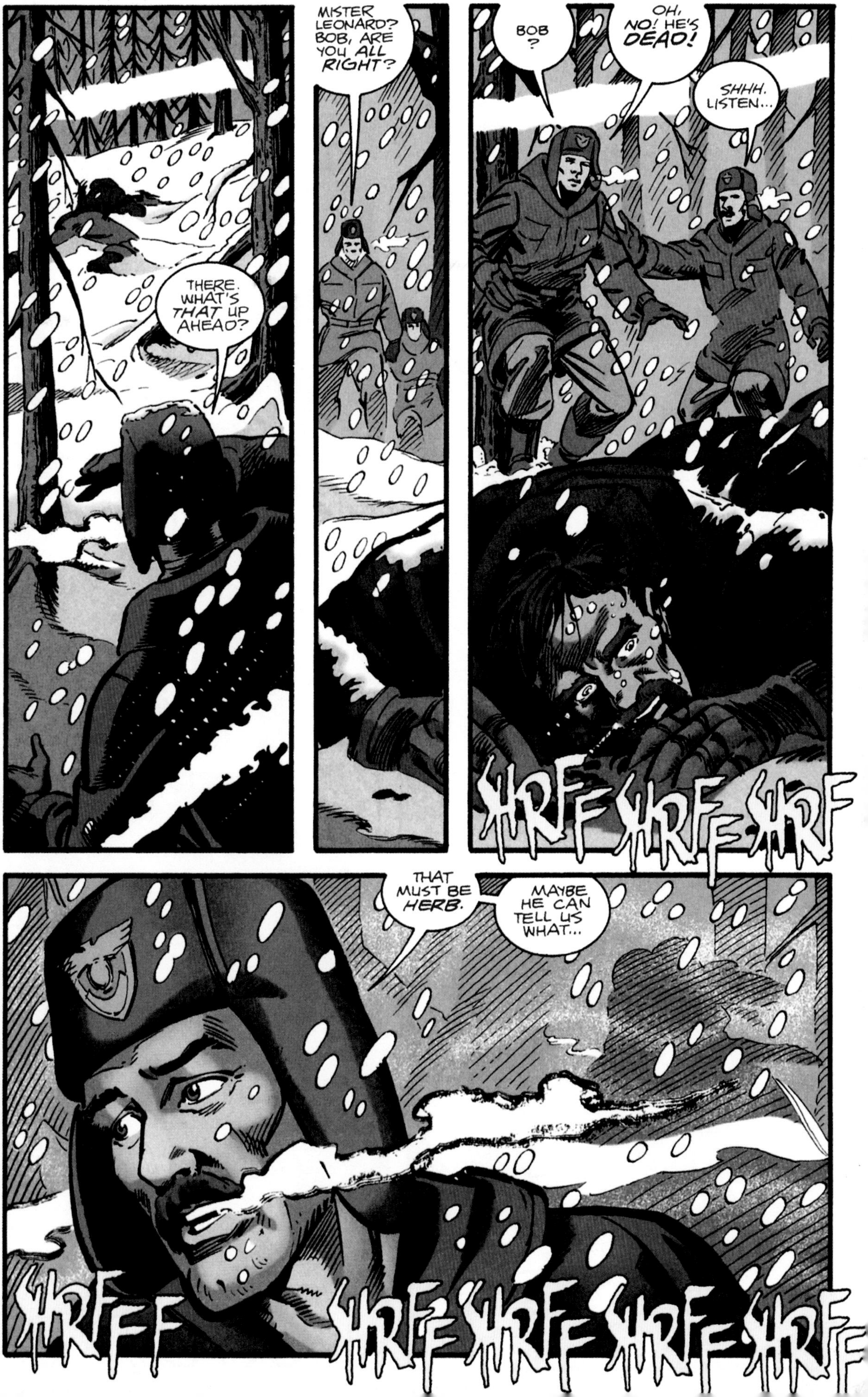

THERE. WHAT'S *THAT* UP AHEAD?
MISTER LEONARD? BOB, ARE YOU *ALL RIGHT*?
BOB?
OH, *NO!* HE'S *DEAD!*
SHHH. LISTEN...
SHRFF SHRFF SHRF
THAT MUST BE *HERB*.
MAYBE HE CAN TELL US WHAT...
SHRFF SHRFF SHRFF SHRFF SHRFF

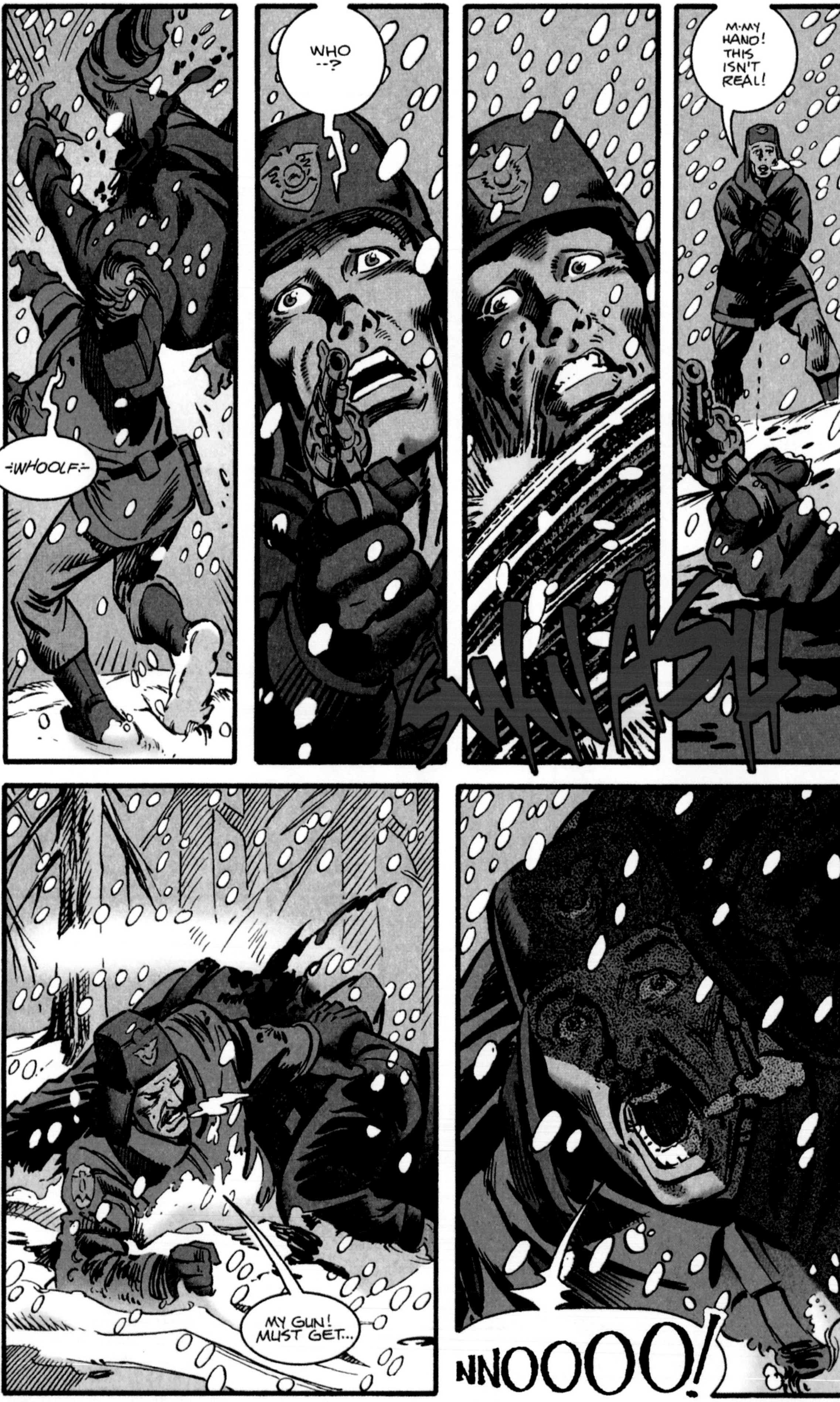
-WHOOLF-
WHO --?
M-MY HAND! THIS ISN'T REAL!
SHWASH
MY GUN! MUST GET...
NNOOOO!

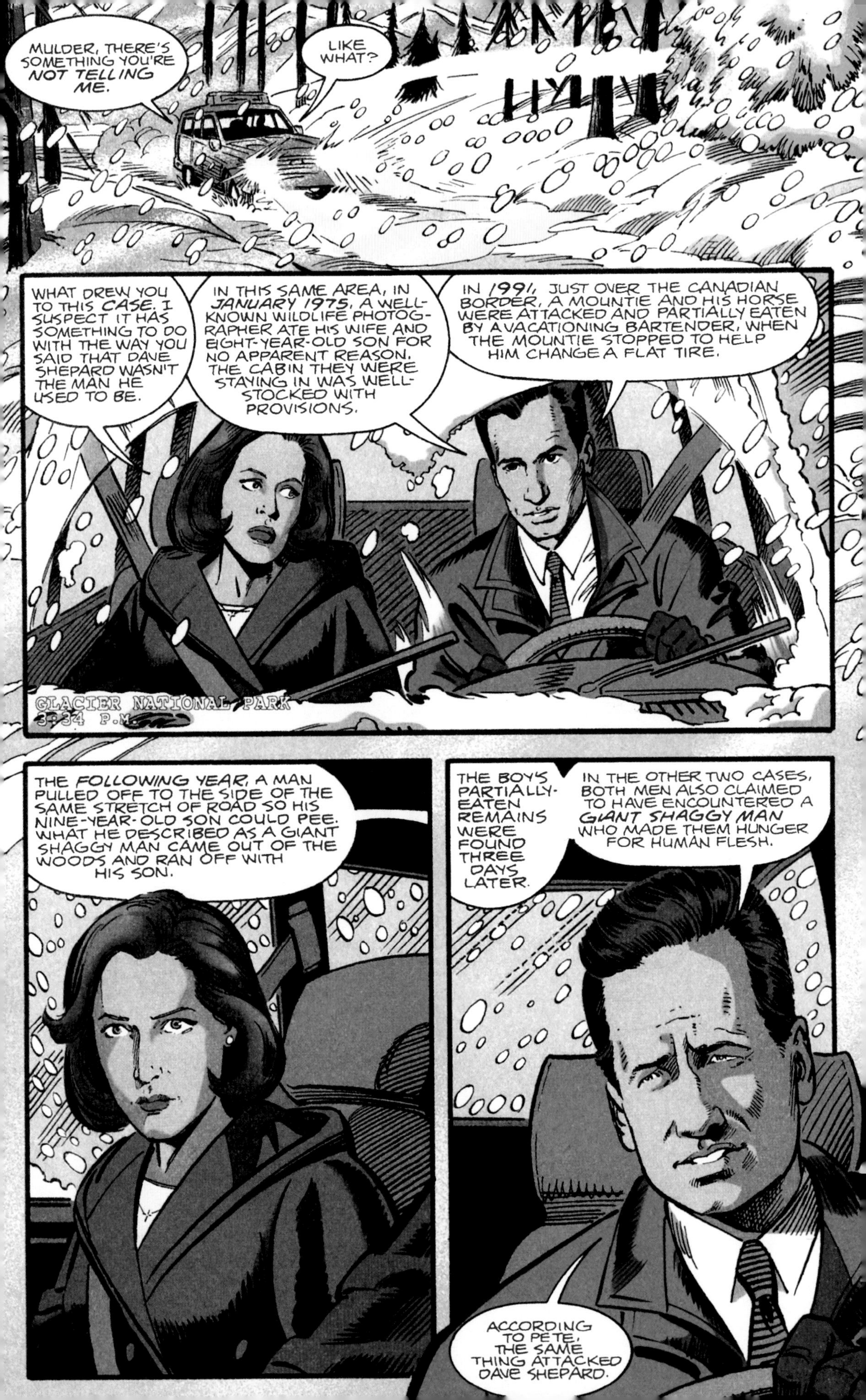
MULDER, THERE'S SOMETHING YOU'RE *NOT TELLING ME.*
LIKE WHAT?
WHAT DREW YOU TO THIS *CASE.* I SUSPECT IT HAS SOMETHING TO DO WITH THE WAY YOU SAID THAT DAVE SHEPARD WASN'T THE MAN HE USED TO BE.
IN THIS SAME AREA, IN *JANUARY 1975,* A WELL-KNOWN WILDLIFE PHOTOGRAPHER ATE HIS WIFE AND EIGHT-YEAR-OLD SON FOR NO APPARENT REASON. THE CABIN THEY WERE STAYING IN WAS WELL-STOCKED WITH PROVISIONS.
IN *1991,* JUST OVER THE CANADIAN BORDER, A MOUNTIE AND HIS HORSE WERE ATTACKED AND PARTIALLY EATEN BY A VACATIONING BARTENDER, WHEN THE MOUNTIE STOPPED TO HELP HIM CHANGE A FLAT TIRE.
GLACIER NATIONAL PARK
3:34 P.M.
THE *FOLLOWING YEAR,* A MAN PULLED OFF TO THE SIDE OF THE SAME STRETCH OF ROAD SO HIS NINE-YEAR-OLD SON COULD PEE. WHAT HE DESCRIBED AS A GIANT SHAGGY MAN CAME OUT OF THE WOODS AND RAN OFF WITH HIS SON.
THE BOY'S PARTIALLY-EATEN REMAINS WERE FOUND THREE DAYS LATER.
IN THE OTHER TWO CASES, BOTH MEN ALSO CLAIMED TO HAVE ENCOUNTERED A *GIANT SHAGGY MAN* WHO MADE THEM HUNGER FOR HUMAN FLESH.
ACCORDING TO PETE, THE SAME THING ATTACKED DAVE SHEPARD.

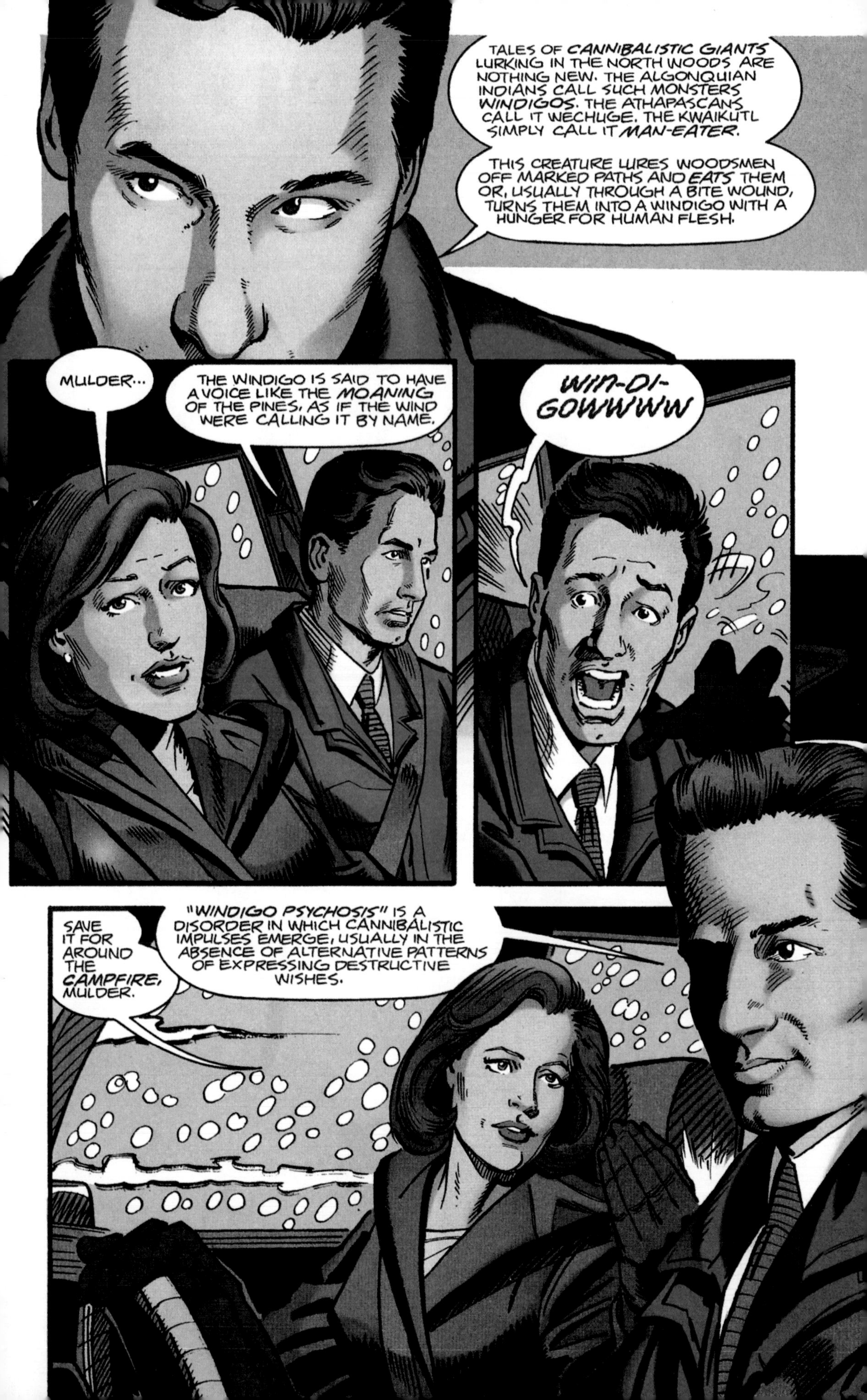
TALES OF CANNIBALISTIC GIANTS LURKING IN THE NORTH WOODS ARE NOTHING NEW. THE ALGONQUIAN INDIANS CALL SUCH MONSTERS WINDIGOS. THE ATHAPASCANS CALL IT WECHUGE. THE KWAIKUTL SIMPLY CALL IT MAN-EATER.
THIS CREATURE LURES WOODSMEN OFF MARKED PATHS AND EATS THEM OR, USUALLY THROUGH A BITE WOUND, TURNS THEM INTO A WINDIGO WITH A HUNGER FOR HUMAN FLESH.
MULDER...
THE WINDIGO IS SAID TO HAVE A VOICE LIKE THE MOANING OF THE PINES, AS IF THE WIND WERE CALLING IT BY NAME.
WIN-DI-GOWWWW
SAVE IT FOR AROUND THE CAMPFIRE, MULDER.
"WINDIGO PSYCHOSIS" IS A DISORDER IN WHICH CANNIBALISTIC IMPULSES EMERGE, USUALLY IN THE ABSENCE OF ALTERNATIVE PATTERNS OF EXPRESSING DESTRUCTIVE WISHES.

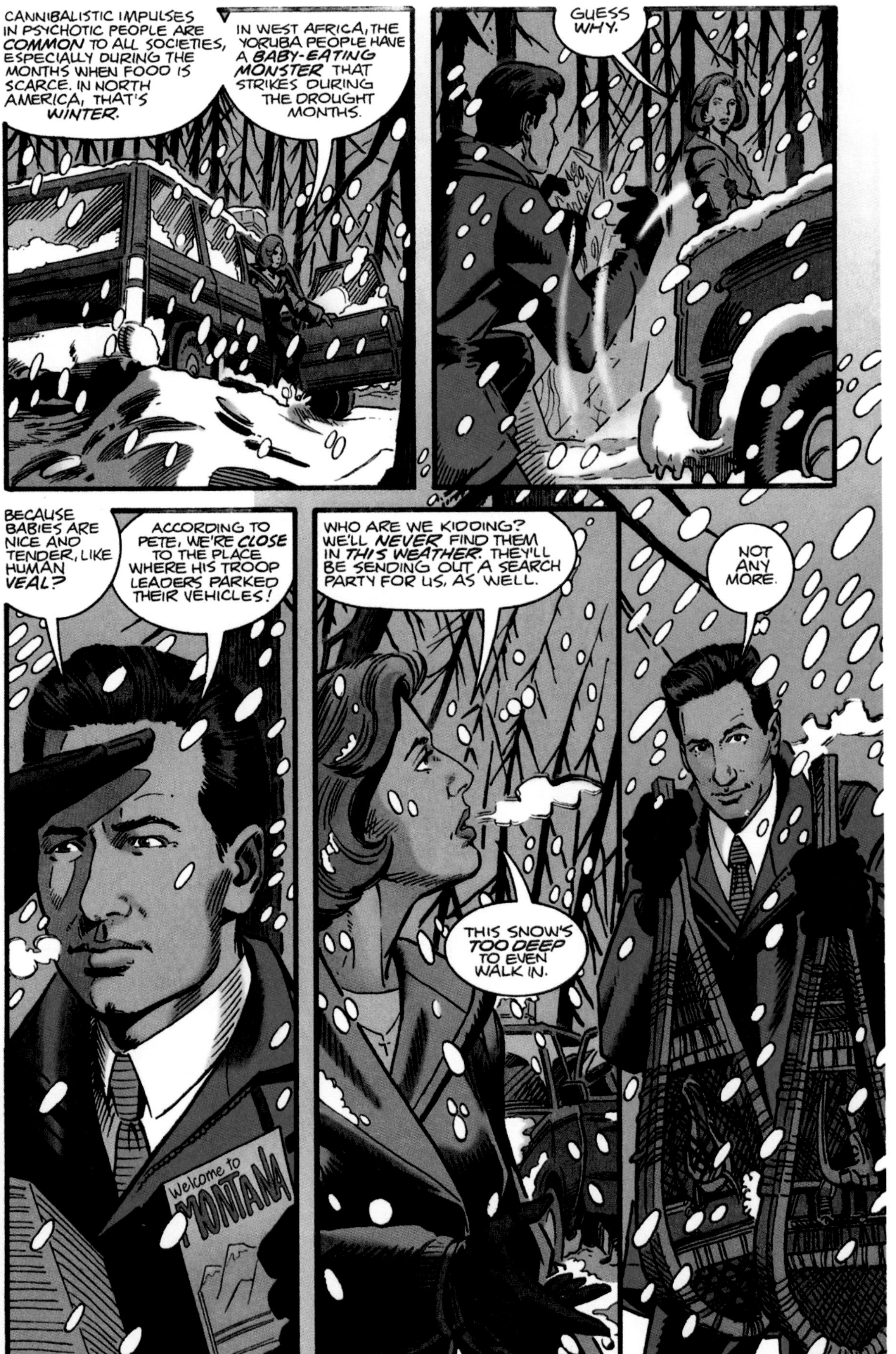
CANNIBALISTIC IMPULSES IN PSYCHOTIC PEOPLE ARE COMMON TO ALL SOCIETIES, ESPECIALLY DURING THE MONTHS WHEN FOOD IS SCARCE. IN NORTH AMERICA, THAT'S WINTER.
IN WEST AFRICA, THE YORUBA PEOPLE HAVE A BABY-EATING MONSTER THAT STRIKES DURING THE DROUGHT MONTHS.
GUESS WHY.
BECAUSE BABIES ARE NICE AND TENDER, LIKE HUMAN VEAL?
ACCORDING TO PETE, WE'RE CLOSE TO THE PLACE WHERE HIS TROOP LEADERS PARKED THEIR VEHICLES!
Welcome to MONTANA
WHO ARE WE KIDDING? WE'LL NEVER FIND THEM IN THIS WEATHER. THEY'LL BE SENDING OUT A SEARCH PARTY FOR US, AS WELL.
THIS SNOW'S TOO DEEP TO EVEN WALK IN.
NOT ANY MORE.

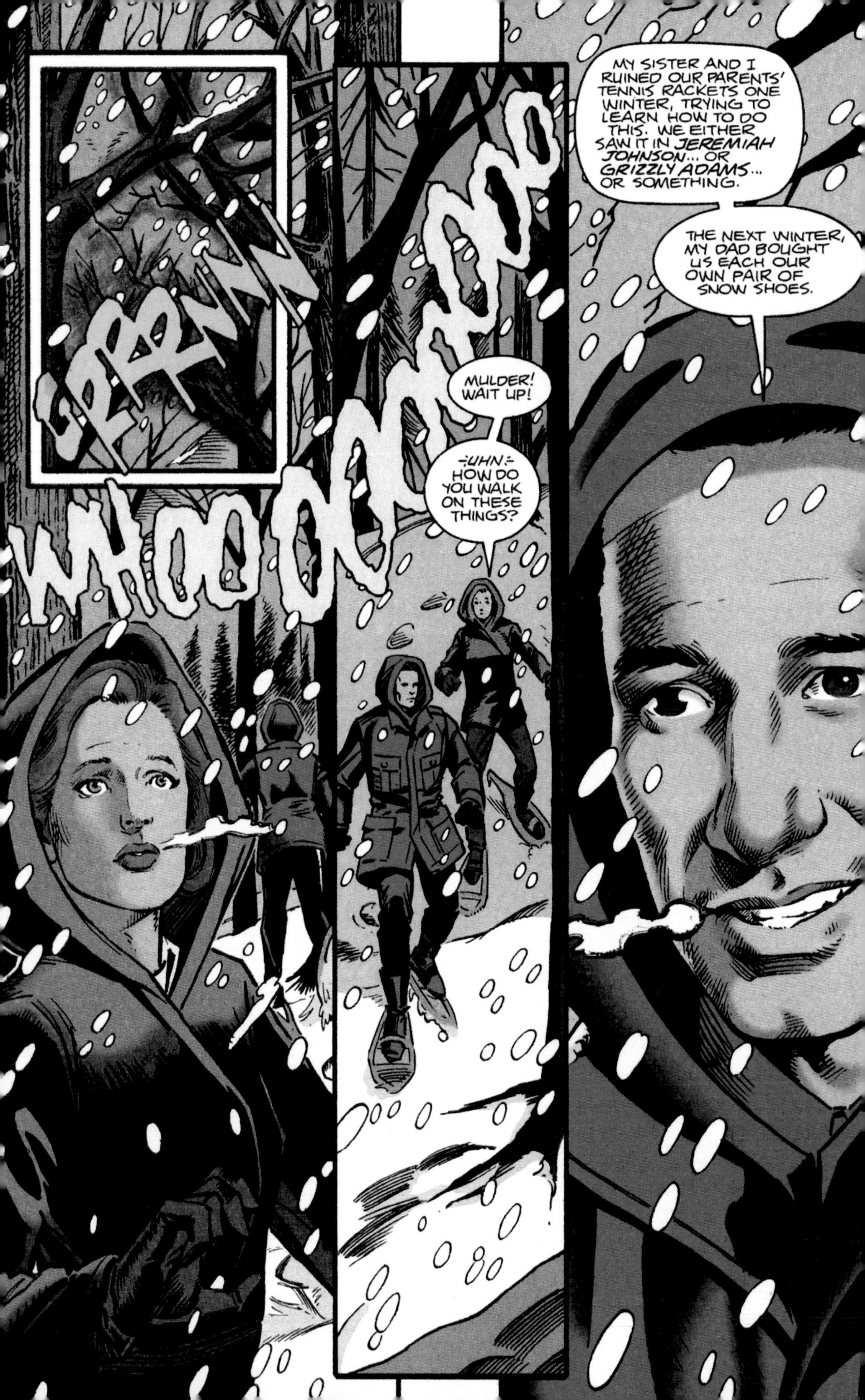

SPRRANNG
WHOOOOOOOOOSHHHH
MULDER! WAIT UP!
-UHN- HOW DO YOU WALK ON THESE THINGS?
MY SISTER AND I RUINED OUR PARENTS' TENNIS RACKETS ONE WINTER, TRYING TO LEARN HOW TO DO THIS. WE EITHER SAW IT IN *JEREMIAH JOHNSON*... OR *GRIZZLY ADAMS*... OR SOMETHING.
THE NEXT WINTER, MY DAD BOUGHT US EACH OUR OWN PAIR OF SNOW SHOES.

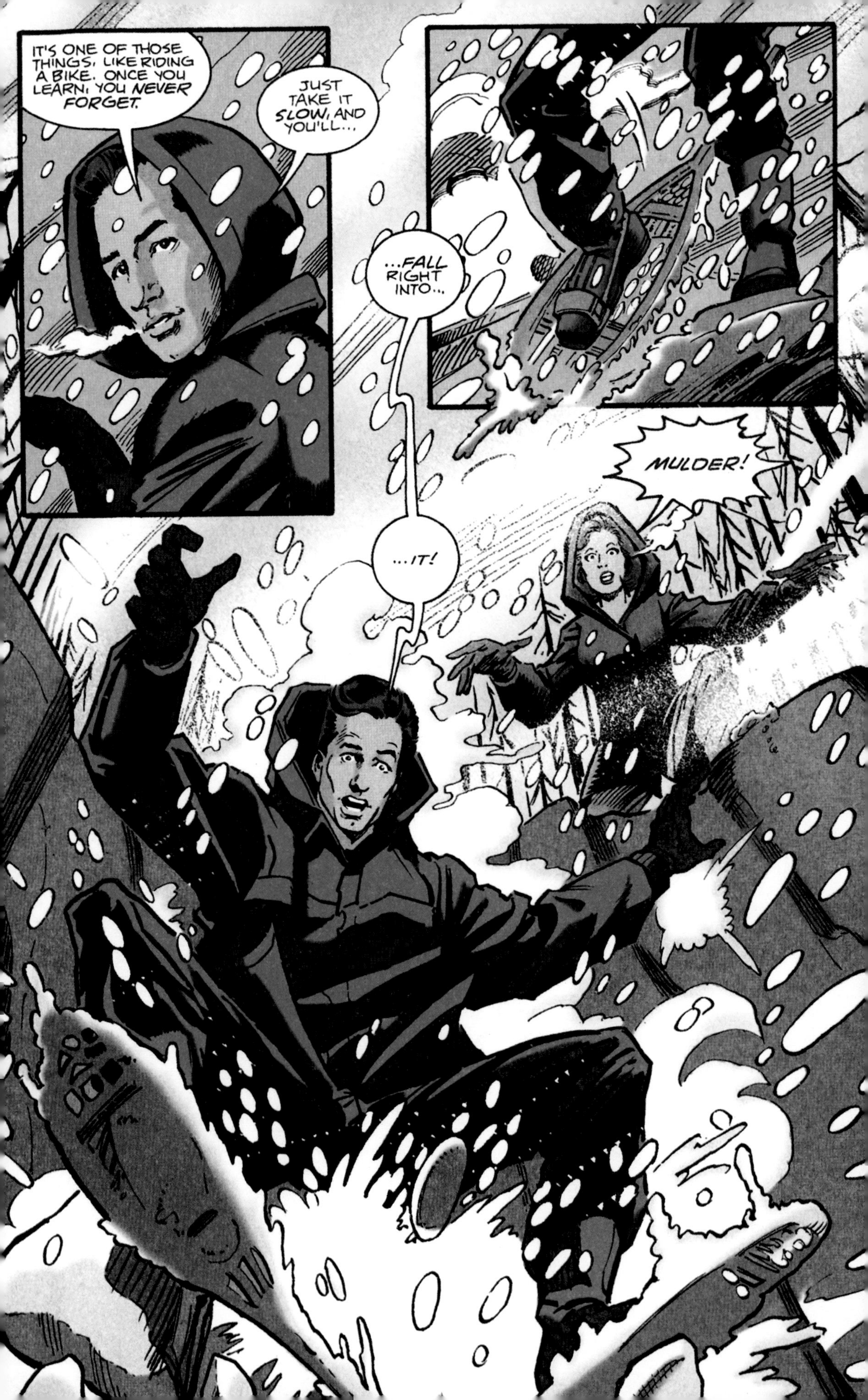
IT'S ONE OF THOSE THINGS, LIKE RIDING A BIKE. ONCE YOU LEARN, YOU NEVER FORGET.
JUST TAKE IT SLOW, AND YOU'LL...
...FALL RIGHT INTO...
...IT!
MULDER!

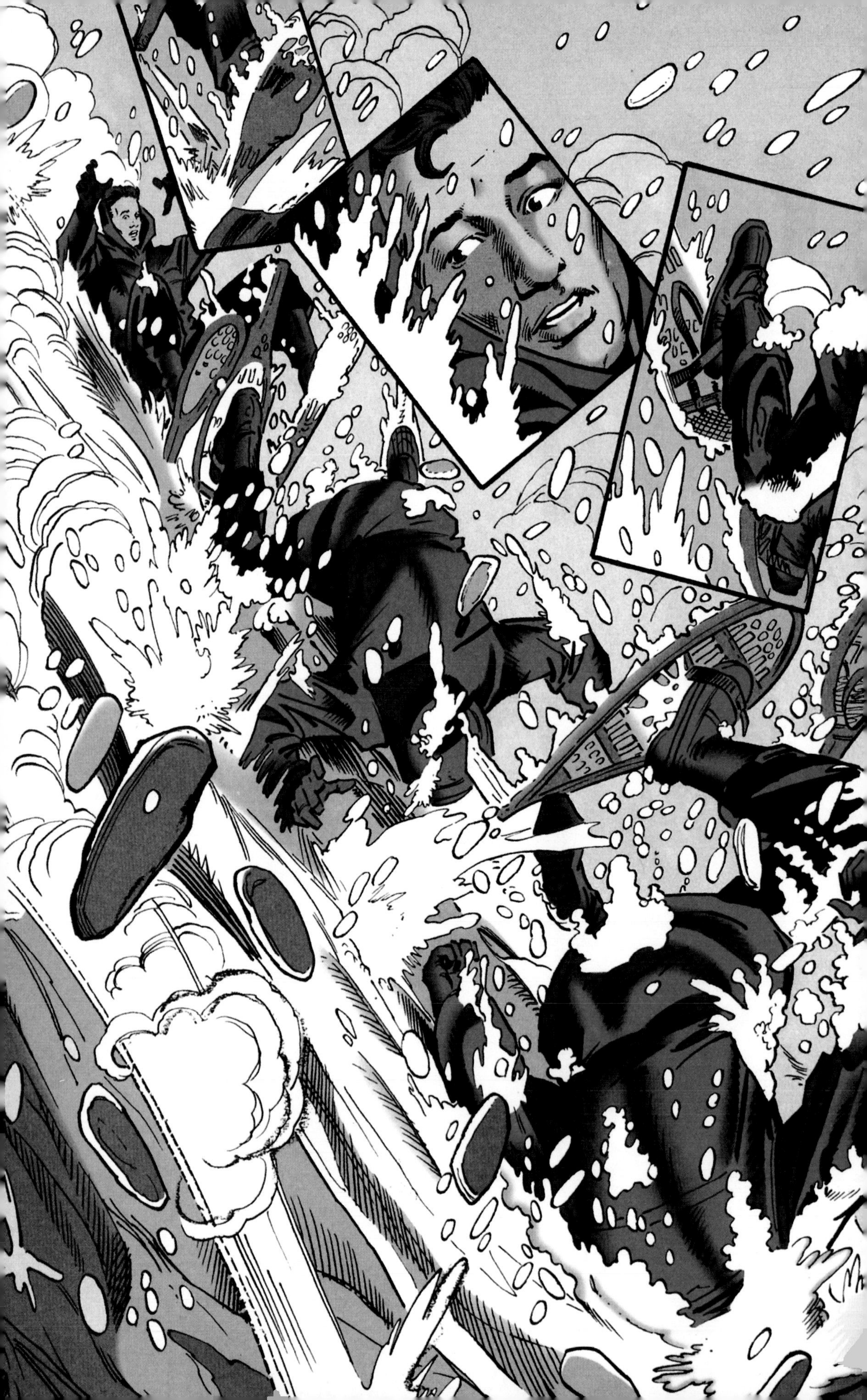

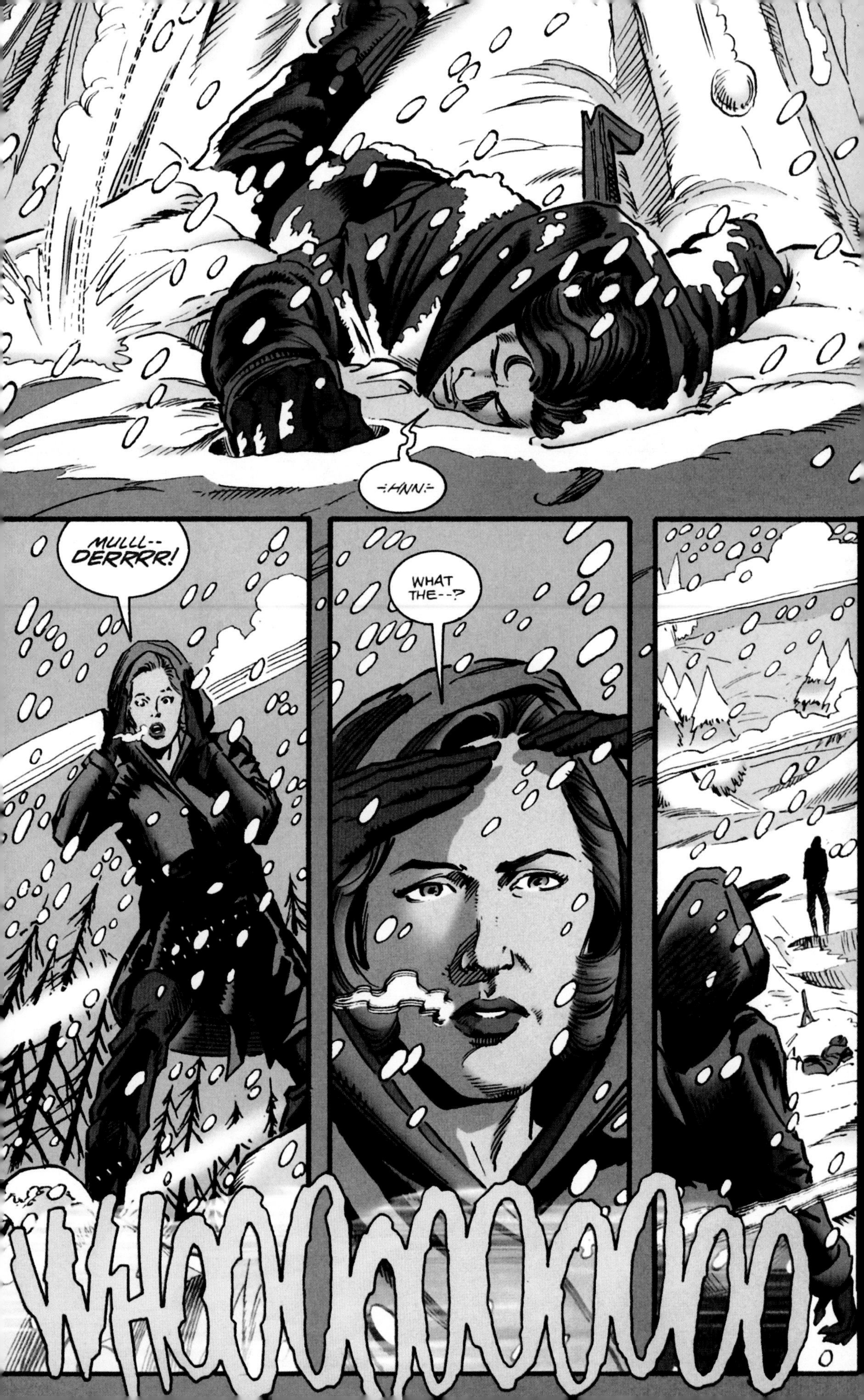
-HNN-
MULLL--DERRRR!
WHAT THE--?
WHOOOOOOOOOOOO

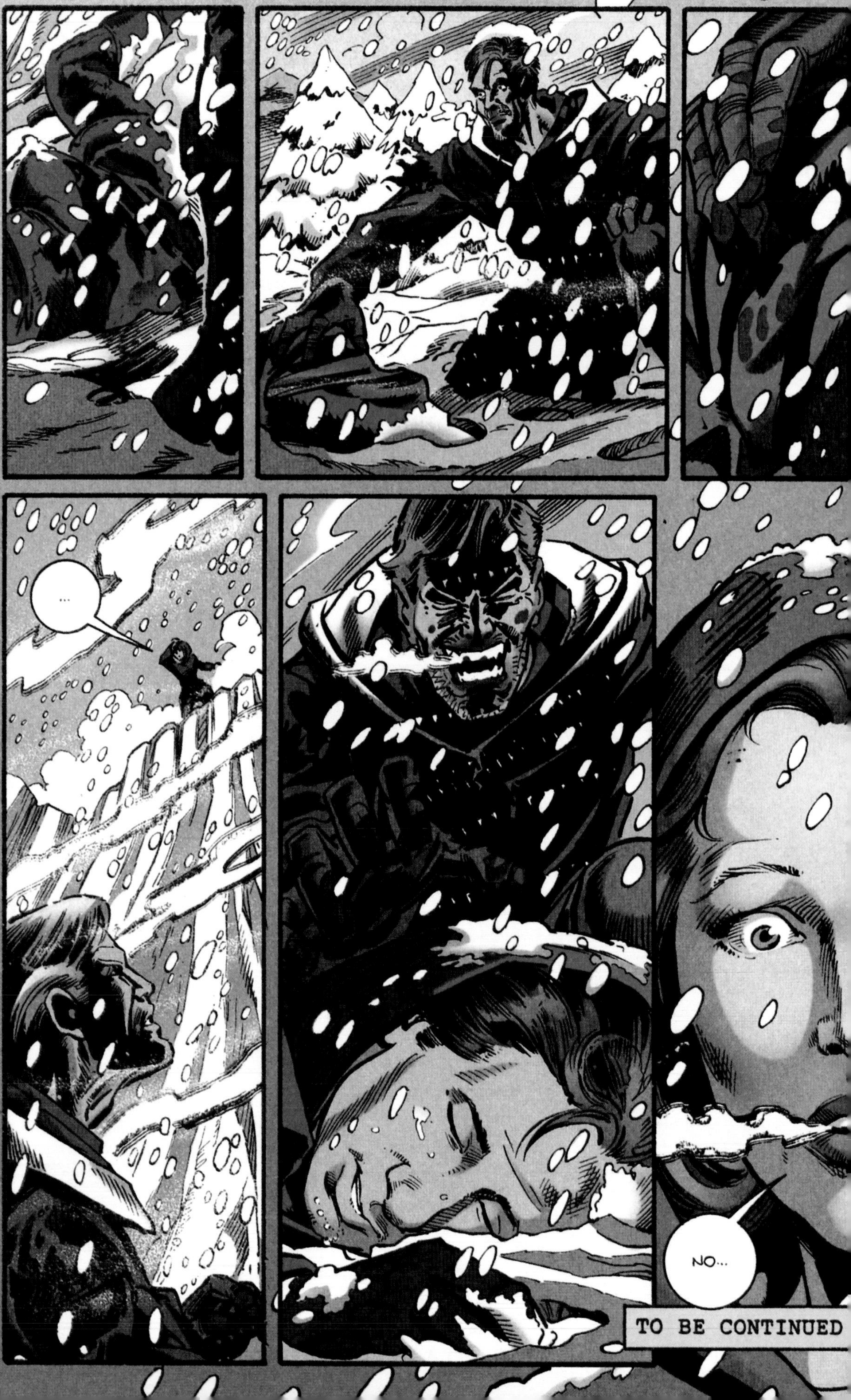
...
NO...
TO BE CONTINUED

CHAPTER 4

# BE PREPARED PART 2 (of 2)

STORY: John Rozum
ART: Gordon Purcell

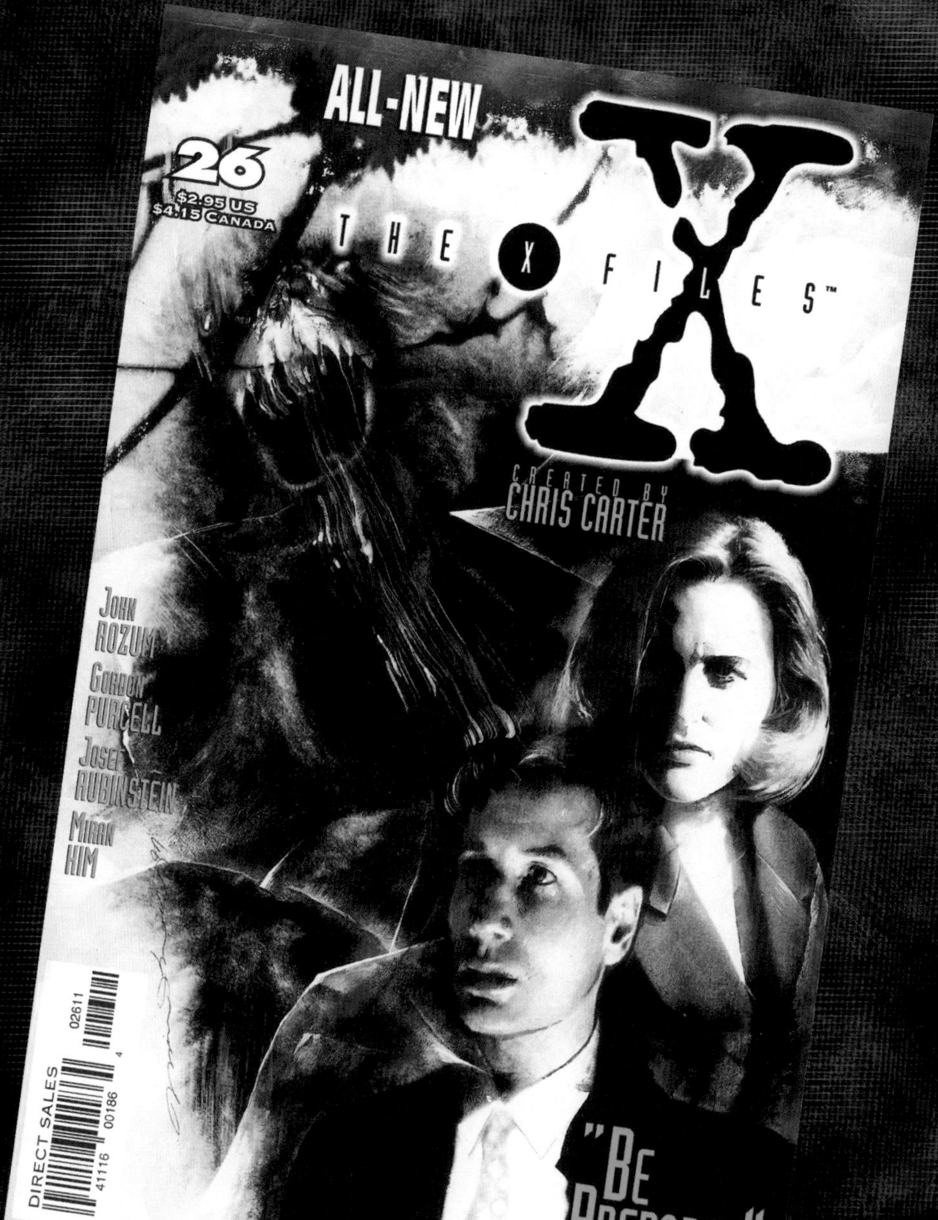
ALL-NEW
26
$2.95 US
$4.15 CANADA
THE X FILES™
CREATED BY
CHRIS CARTER
JOHN ROZUM
GORDON PURCELL
JOSEF RUBINSTEIN
MIRAN KIM
DIRECT SALES
"BE PREPARED"
PT. 2 (OF 2)

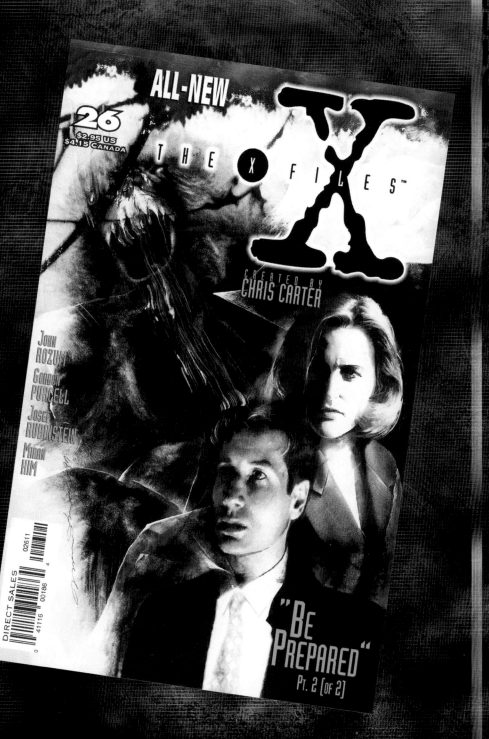

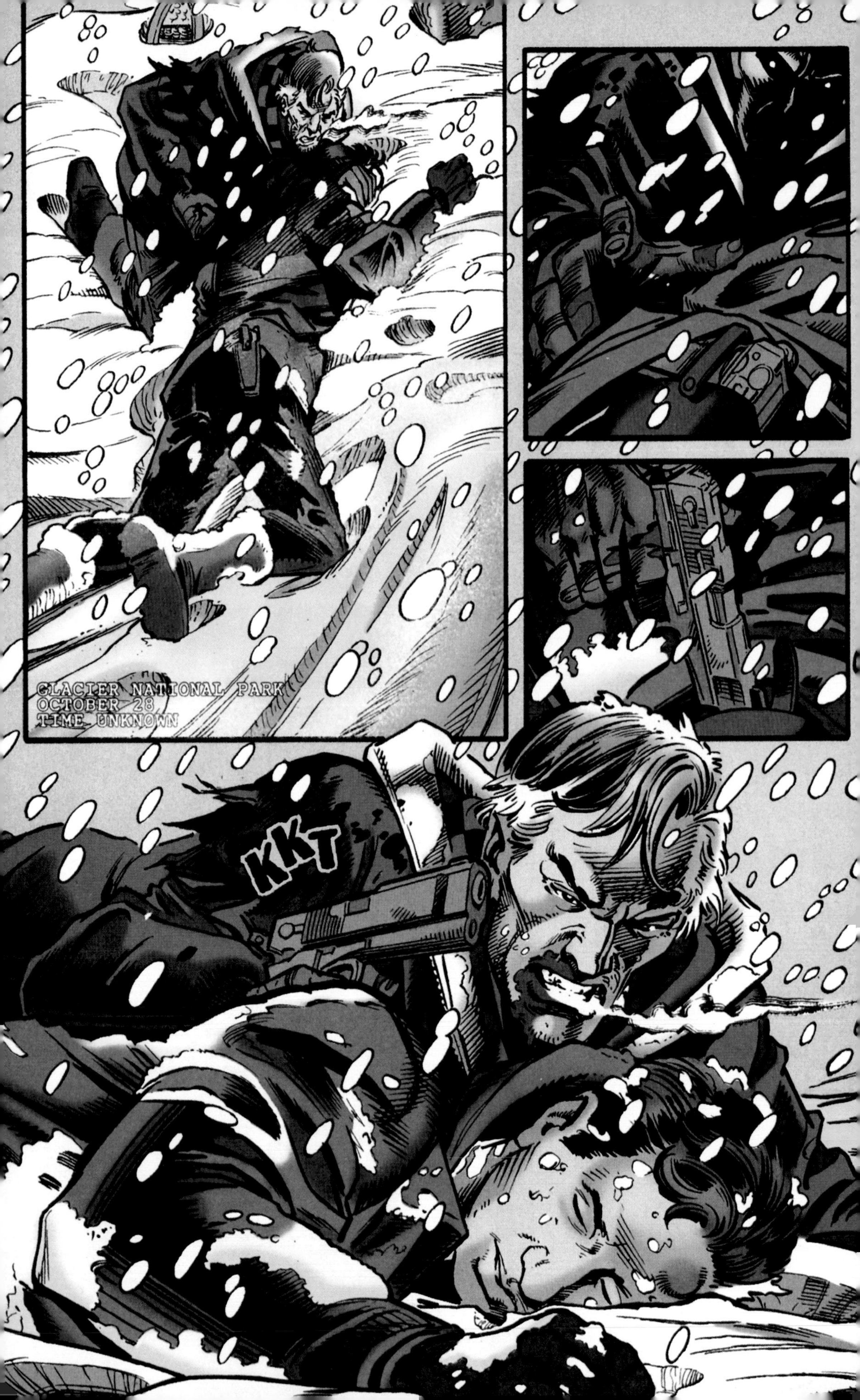
GLACIER NATIONAL PARK
OCTOBER 28
TIME UNKNOWN
KKT

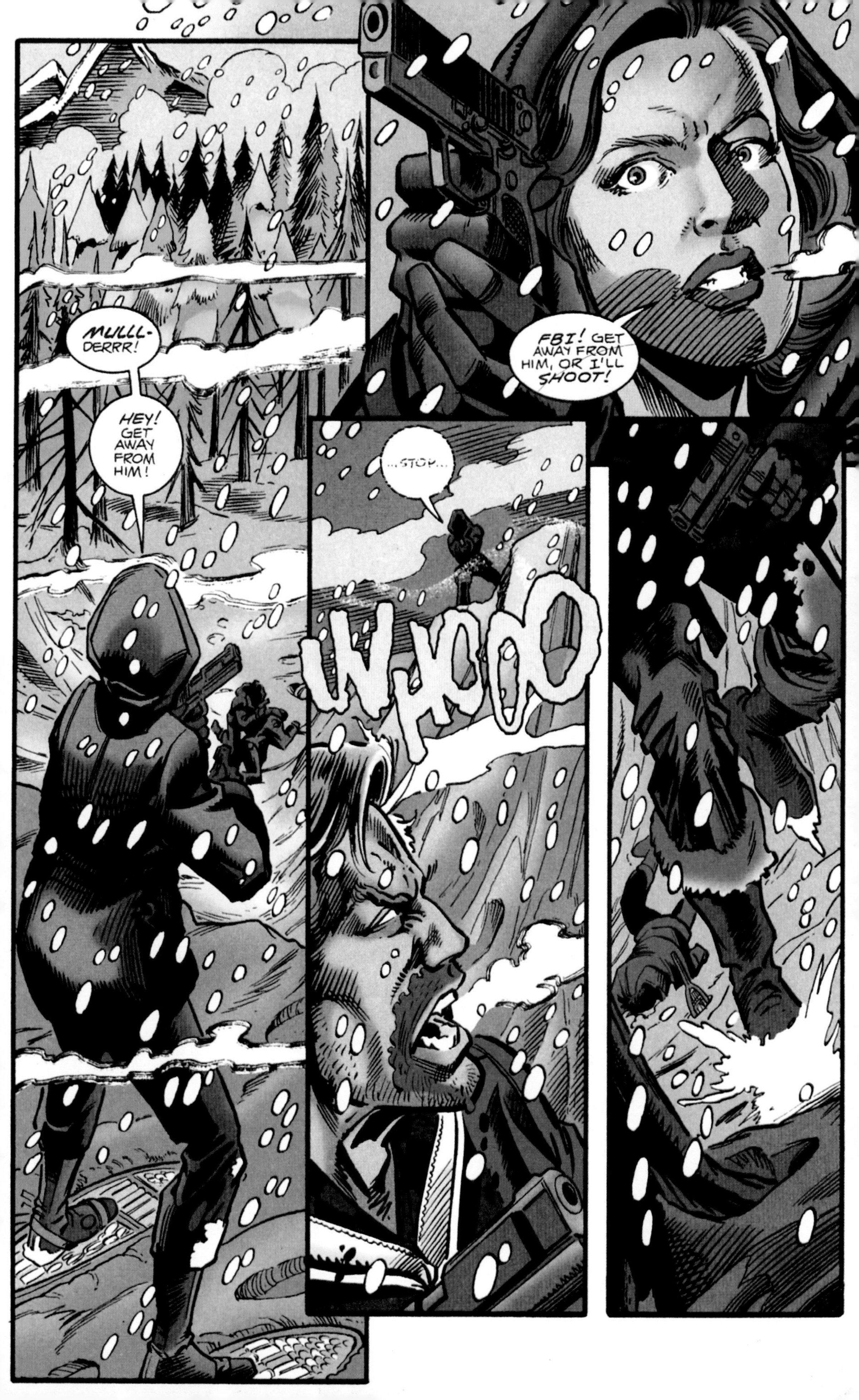
MULLL-DERRR!
HEY! GET AWAY FROM HIM!
FBI! GET AWAY FROM HIM, OR I'LL SHOOT!
...STOP...

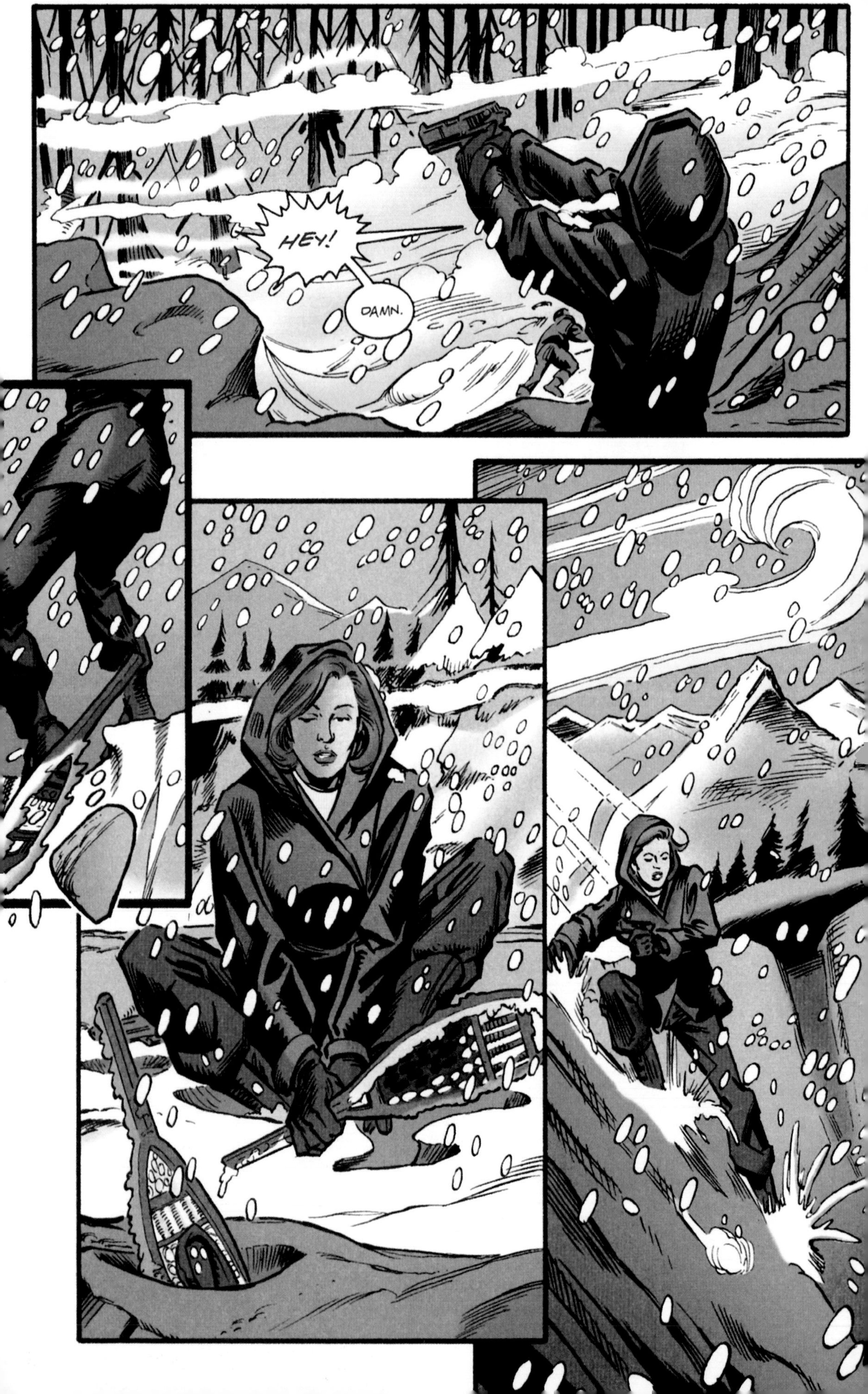
HEY!
DAMN.

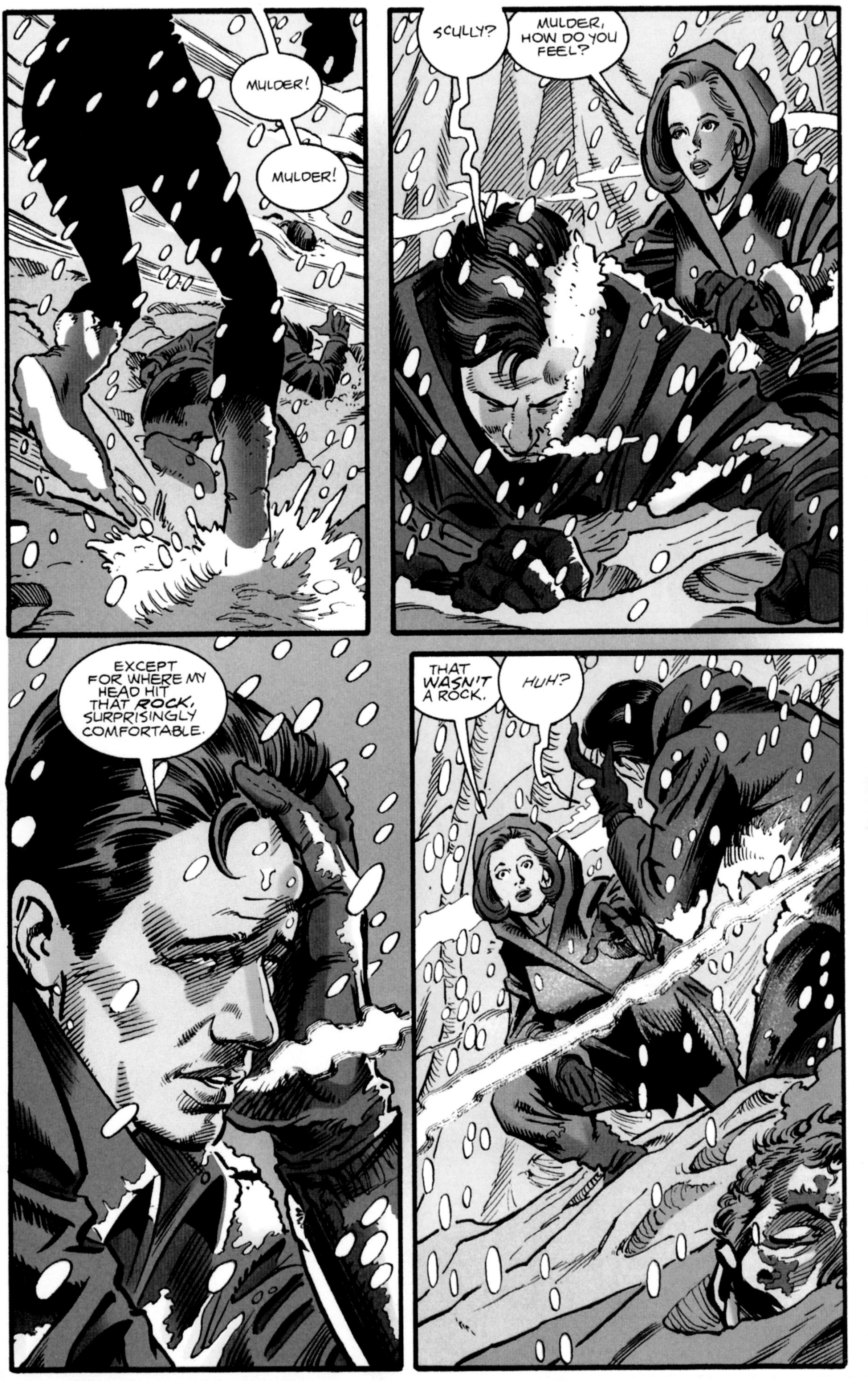
MULDER!
MULDER!
SCULLY?
MULDER, HOW DO YOU FEEL?
EXCEPT FOR WHERE MY HEAD HIT THAT ROCK, SURPRISINGLY COMFORTABLE.
THAT WASN'T A ROCK.
HUH?

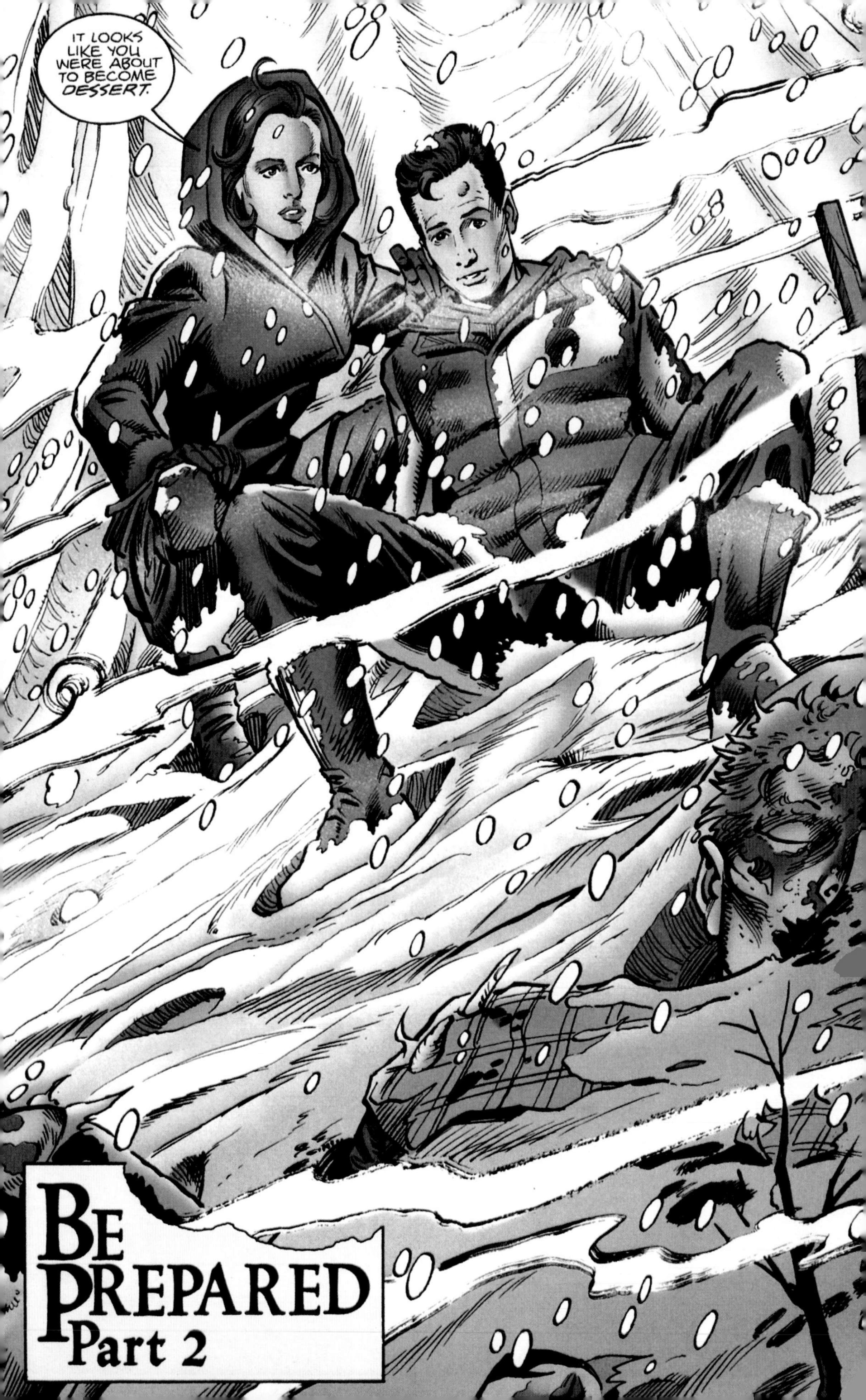
IT LOOKS LIKE YOU WERE ABOUT TO BECOME DESSERT.
BE PREPARED
Part 2

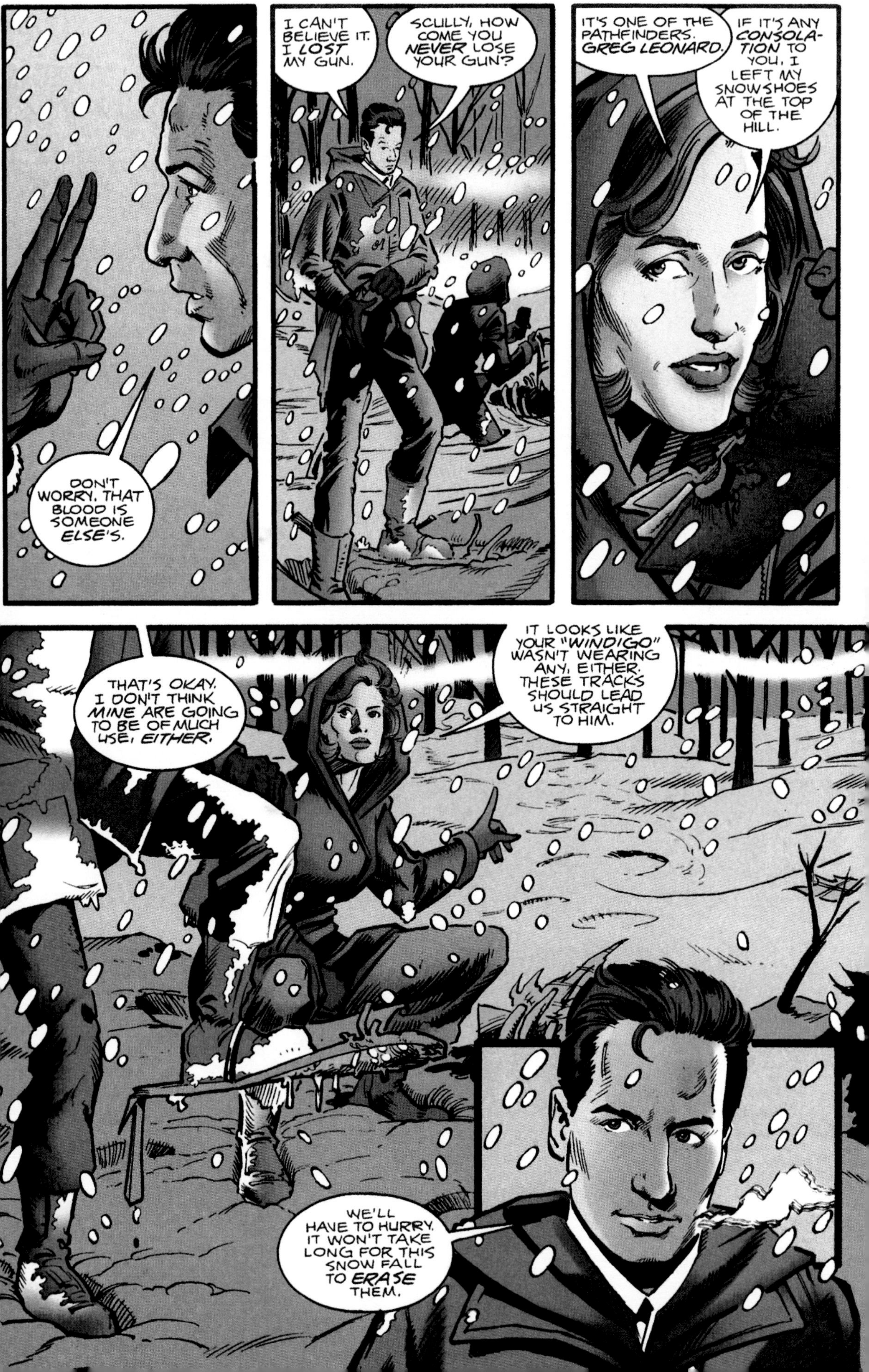
DON'T WORRY. THAT BLOOD IS SOMEONE ELSE'S.
I CAN'T BELIEVE IT. I LOST MY GUN.
SCULLY, HOW COME YOU NEVER LOSE YOUR GUN?
IT'S ONE OF THE PATHFINDERS. GREG LEONARD.
IF IT'S ANY CONSOLATION TO YOU, I LEFT MY SNOWSHOES AT THE TOP OF THE HILL.
THAT'S OKAY. I DON'T THINK MINE ARE GOING TO BE OF MUCH USE, EITHER.
IT LOOKS LIKE YOUR "WINDIGO" WASN'T WEARING ANY, EITHER. THESE TRACKS SHOULD LEAD US STRAIGHT TO HIM.
WE'LL HAVE TO HURRY. IT WON'T TAKE LONG FOR THIS SNOW FALL TO ERASE THEM.

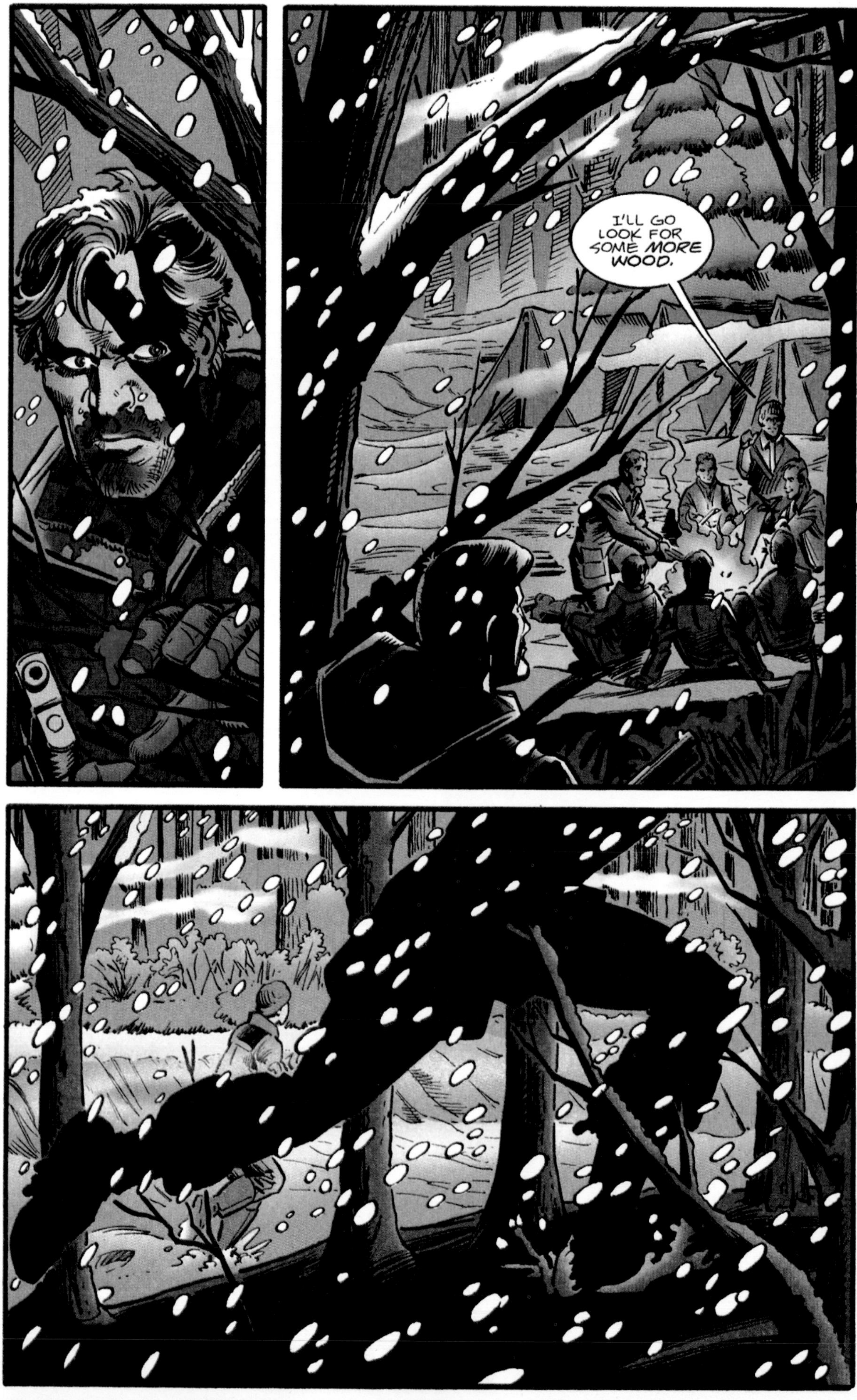
I'LL GO LOOK FOR SOME MORE WOOD.

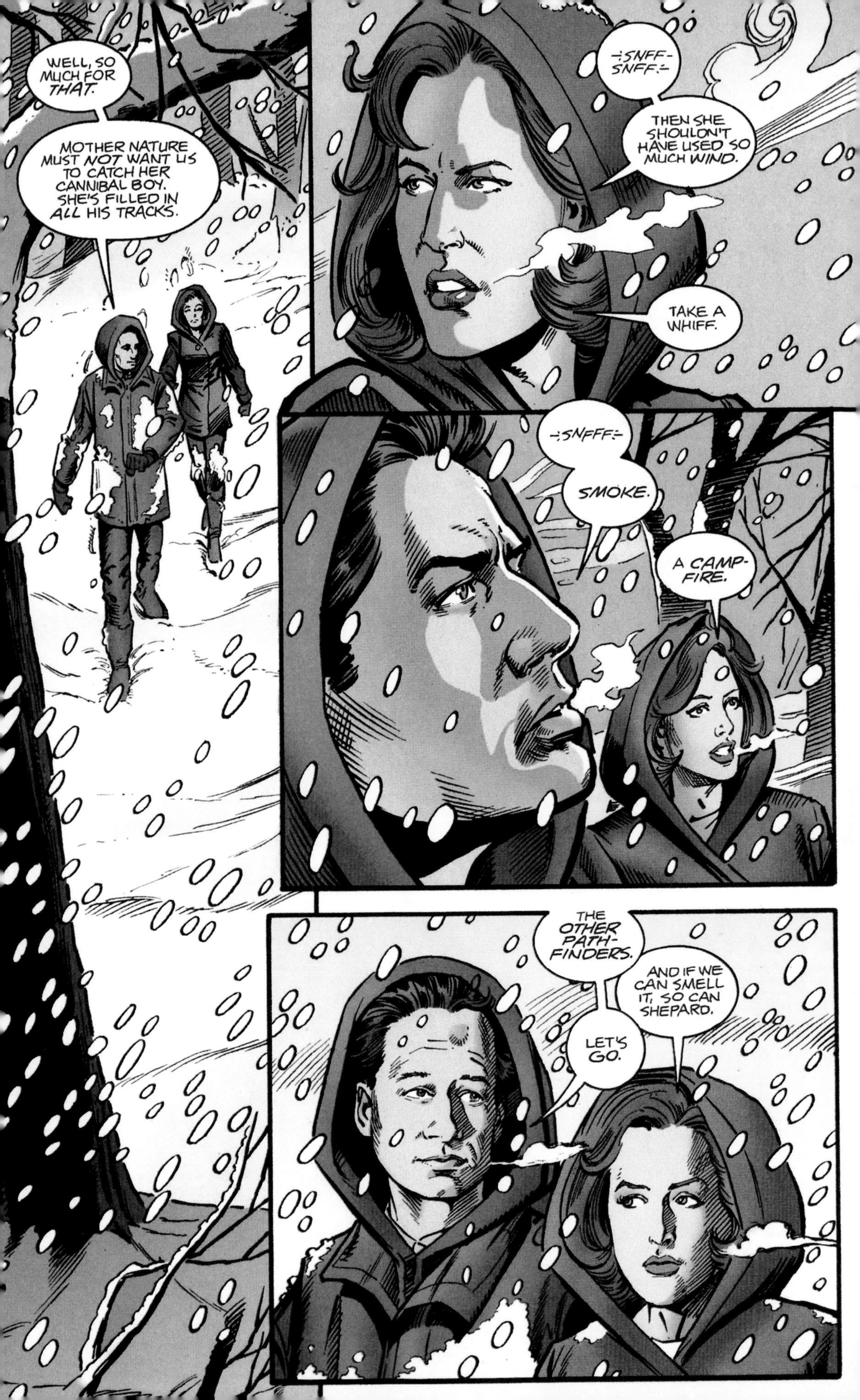
WELL, SO MUCH FOR THAT.
MOTHER NATURE MUST NOT WANT US TO CATCH HER CANNIBAL BOY. SHE'S FILLED IN ALL HIS TRACKS.
-:SNFF-SNFF:-
THEN SHE SHOULDN'T HAVE USED SO MUCH WIND.
TAKE A WHIFF.
-:SNFFF:-
SMOKE.
A CAMP-FIRE.
THE OTHER PATH-FINDERS.
AND IF WE CAN SMELL IT, SO CAN SHEPARD.
LET'S GO.

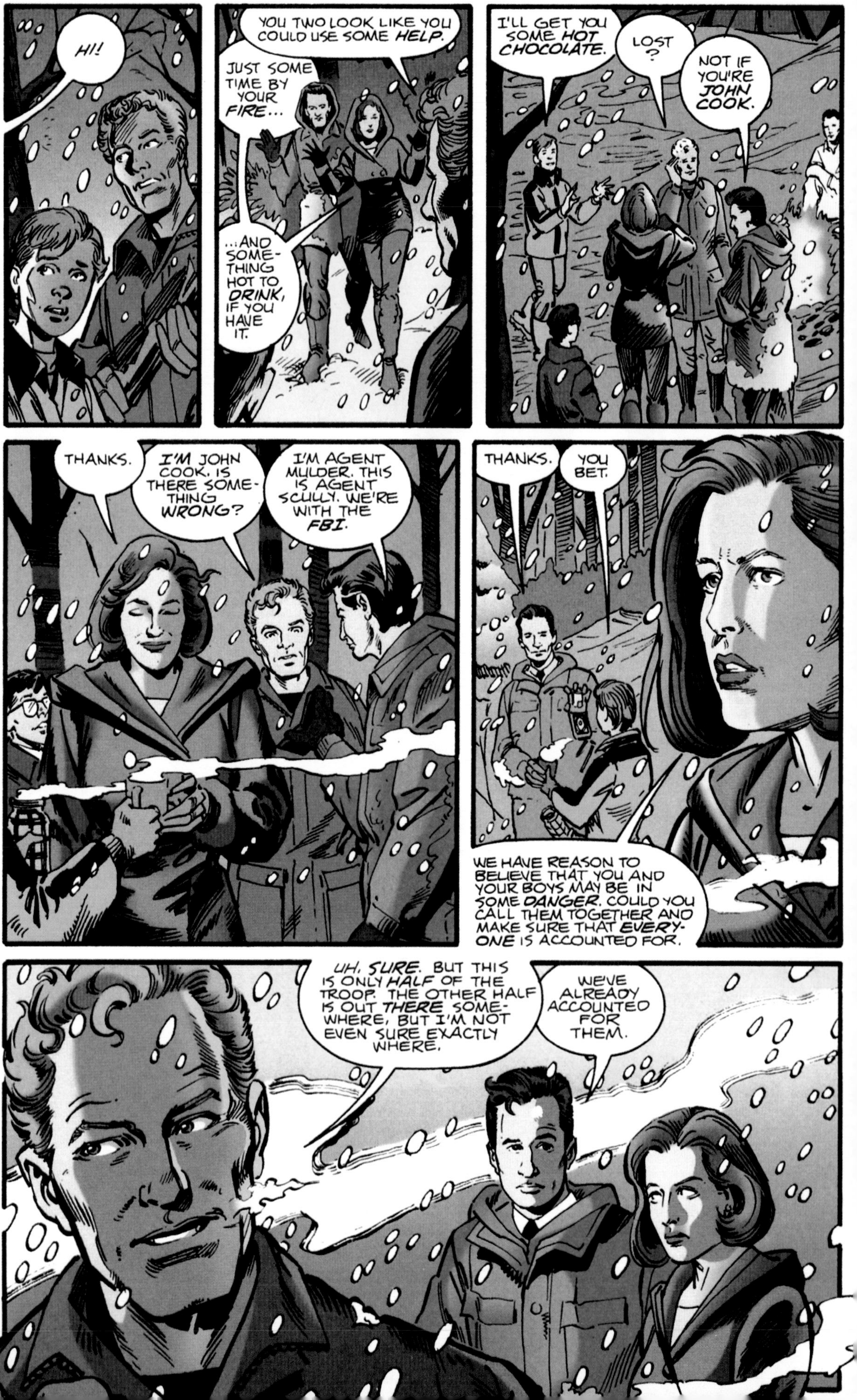
HI!
YOU TWO LOOK LIKE YOU COULD USE SOME HELP.
JUST SOME TIME BY YOUR FIRE...
...AND SOMETHING HOT TO DRINK, IF YOU HAVE IT.
I'LL GET YOU SOME HOT CHOCOLATE.
LOST?
NOT IF YOU'RE JOHN COOK.
THANKS.
I'M JOHN COOK. IS THERE SOMETHING WRONG?
I'M AGENT MULDER. THIS IS AGENT SCULLY. WE'RE WITH THE FBI.
THANKS.
YOU BET.
WE HAVE REASON TO BELIEVE THAT YOU AND YOUR BOYS MAY BE IN SOME DANGER. COULD YOU CALL THEM TOGETHER AND MAKE SURE THAT EVERYONE IS ACCOUNTED FOR.
UH, SURE. BUT THIS IS ONLY HALF OF THE TROOP. THE OTHER HALF IS OUT THERE SOMEWHERE, BUT I'M NOT EVEN SURE EXACTLY WHERE.
WE'VE ALREADY ACCOUNTED FOR THEM.

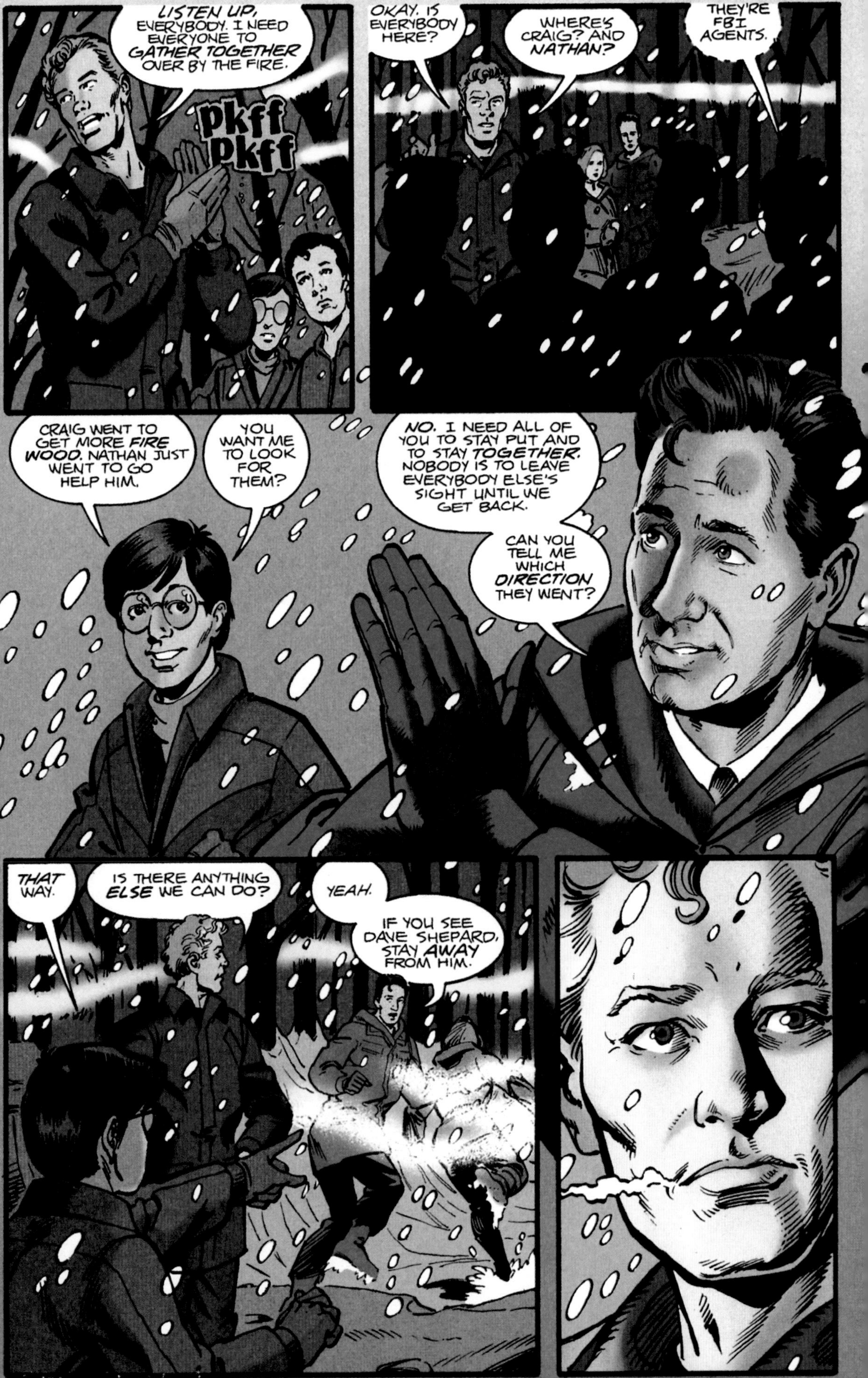
LISTEN UP, EVERYBODY. I NEED EVERYONE TO GATHER TOGETHER OVER BY THE FIRE.
pkff pkff
OKAY. IS EVERYBODY HERE?
WHERE'S CRAIG? AND NATHAN?
THEY'RE FBI AGENTS.
CRAIG WENT TO GET MORE FIRE WOOD. NATHAN JUST WENT TO GO HELP HIM.
YOU WANT ME TO LOOK FOR THEM?
NO. I NEED ALL OF YOU TO STAY PUT AND TO STAY TOGETHER. NOBODY IS TO LEAVE EVERYBODY ELSE'S SIGHT UNTIL WE GET BACK.
CAN YOU TELL ME WHICH DIRECTION THEY WENT?
THAT WAY.
IS THERE ANYTHING ELSE WE CAN DO?
YEAH.
IF YOU SEE DAVE SHEPARD, STAY AWAY FROM HIM.

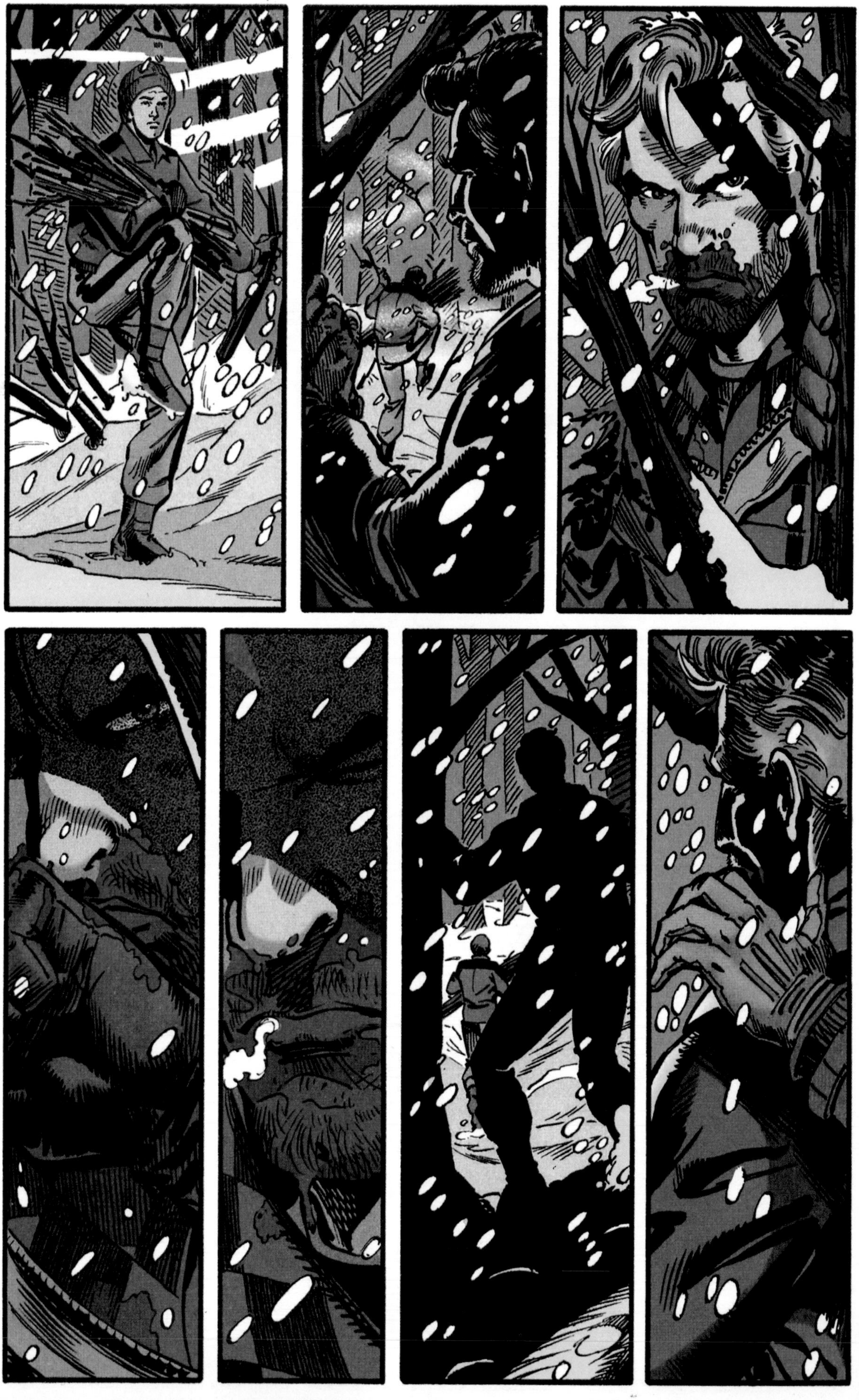

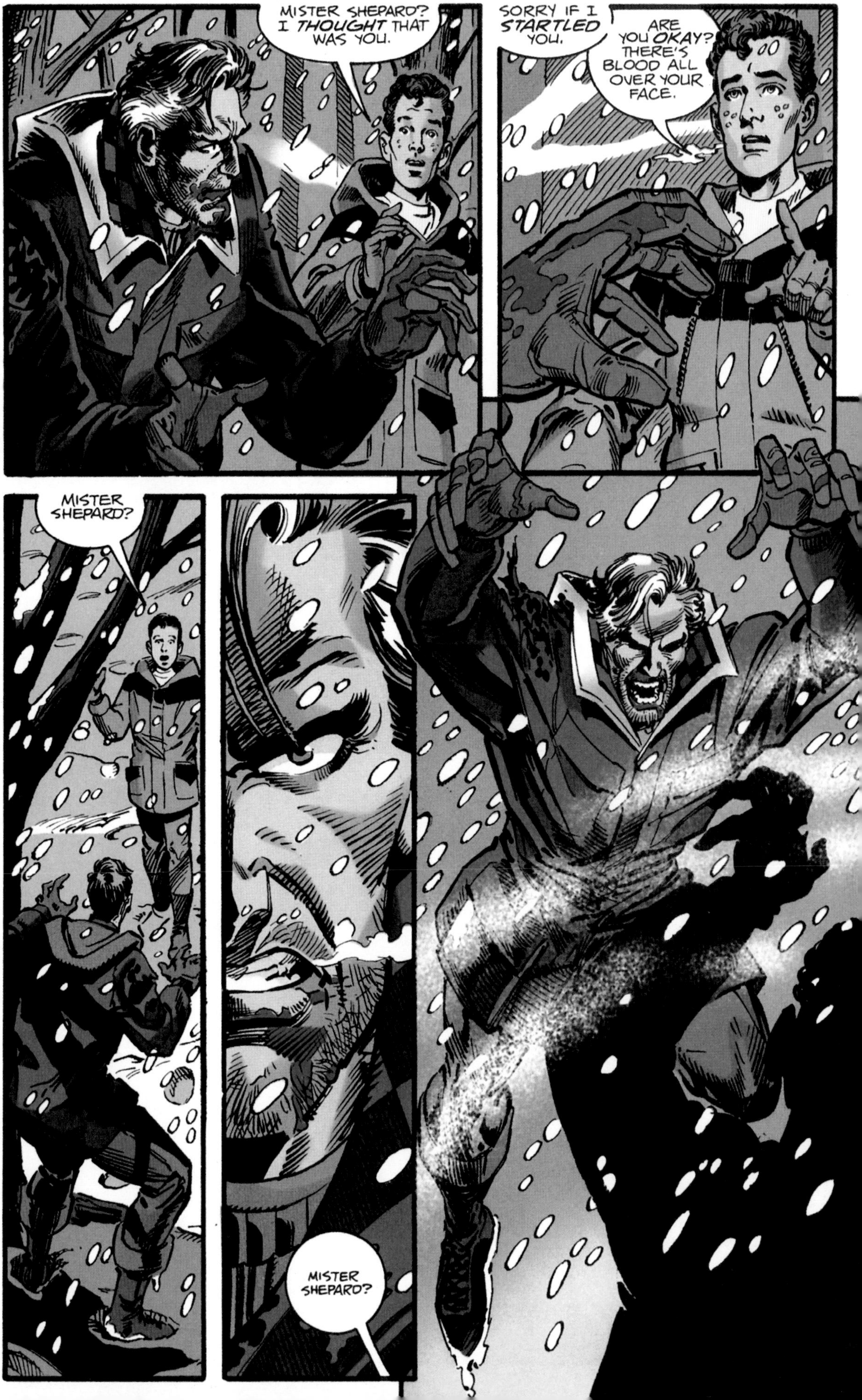

MISTER SHEPARD? I *THOUGHT* THAT WAS YOU.
SORRY IF I *STARTLED* YOU.
ARE YOU *OKAY*? THERE'S BLOOD ALL OVER YOUR FACE.
MISTER SHEPARD?
MISTER SHEPARD?

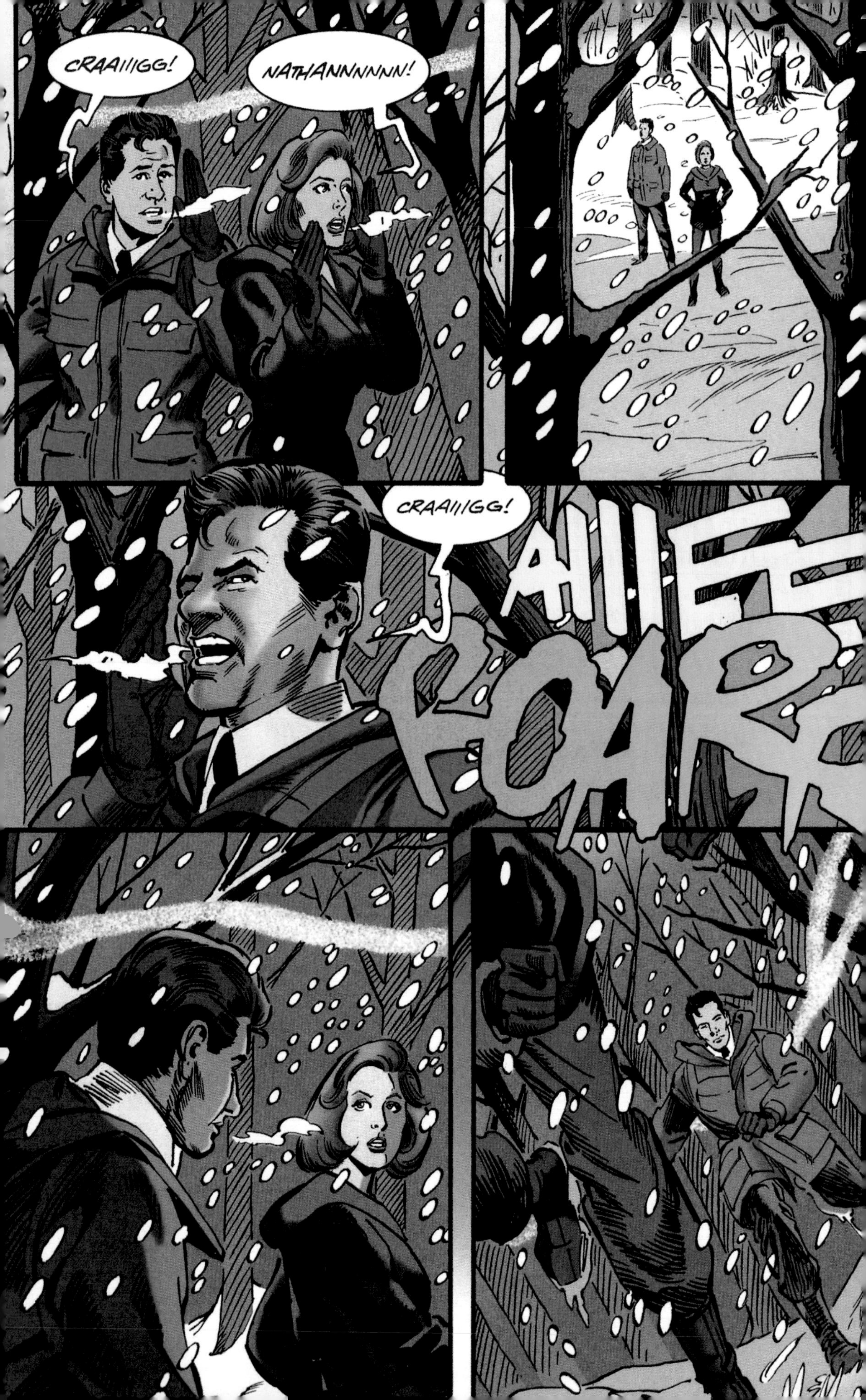
CRAAIIIGG!
NATHANNNNNN!
CRAAIIIGG!
AIIIEE
ROAR

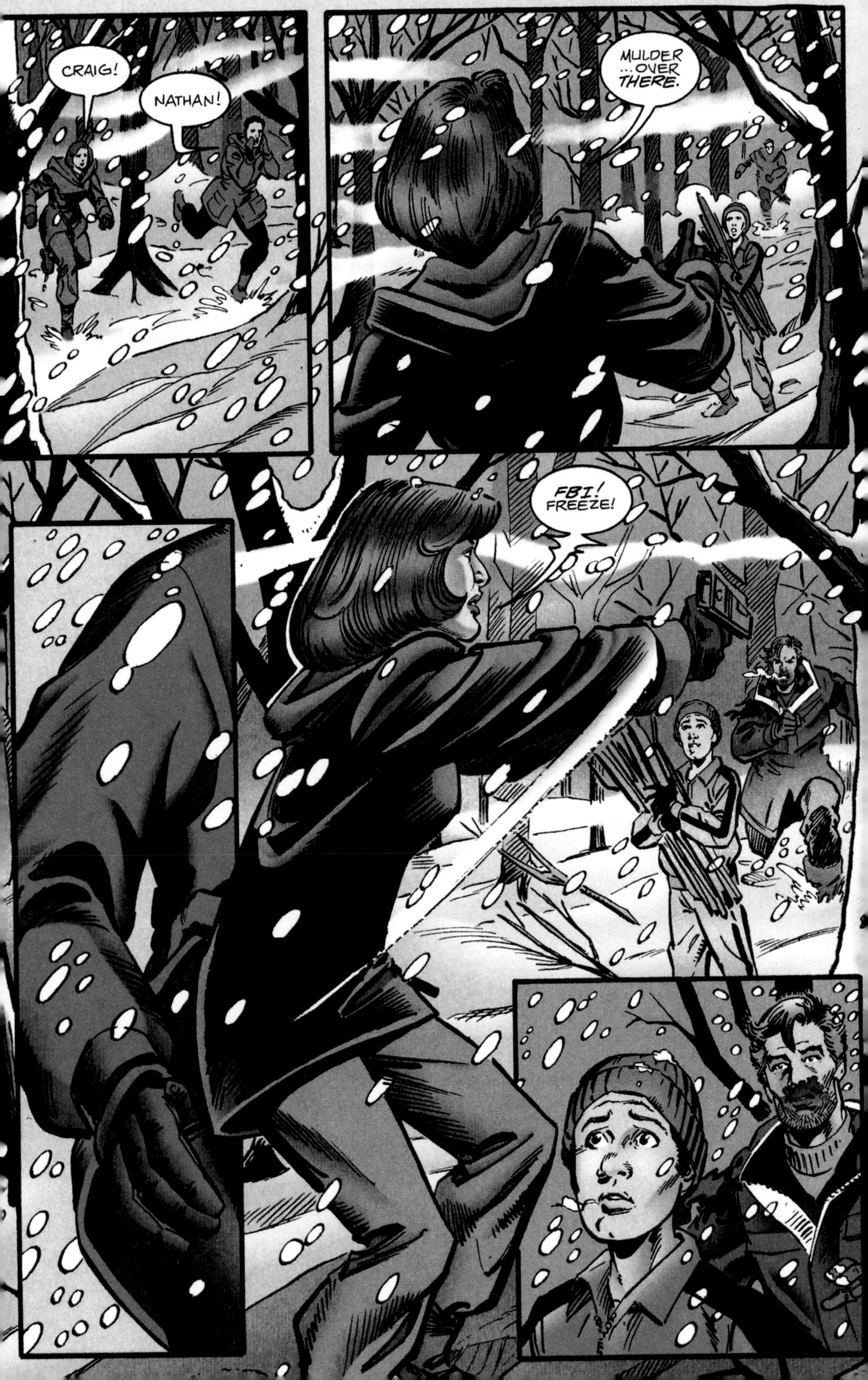
CRAIG!
NATHAN!
MULDER ...OVER THERE.
FBI! FREEZE!

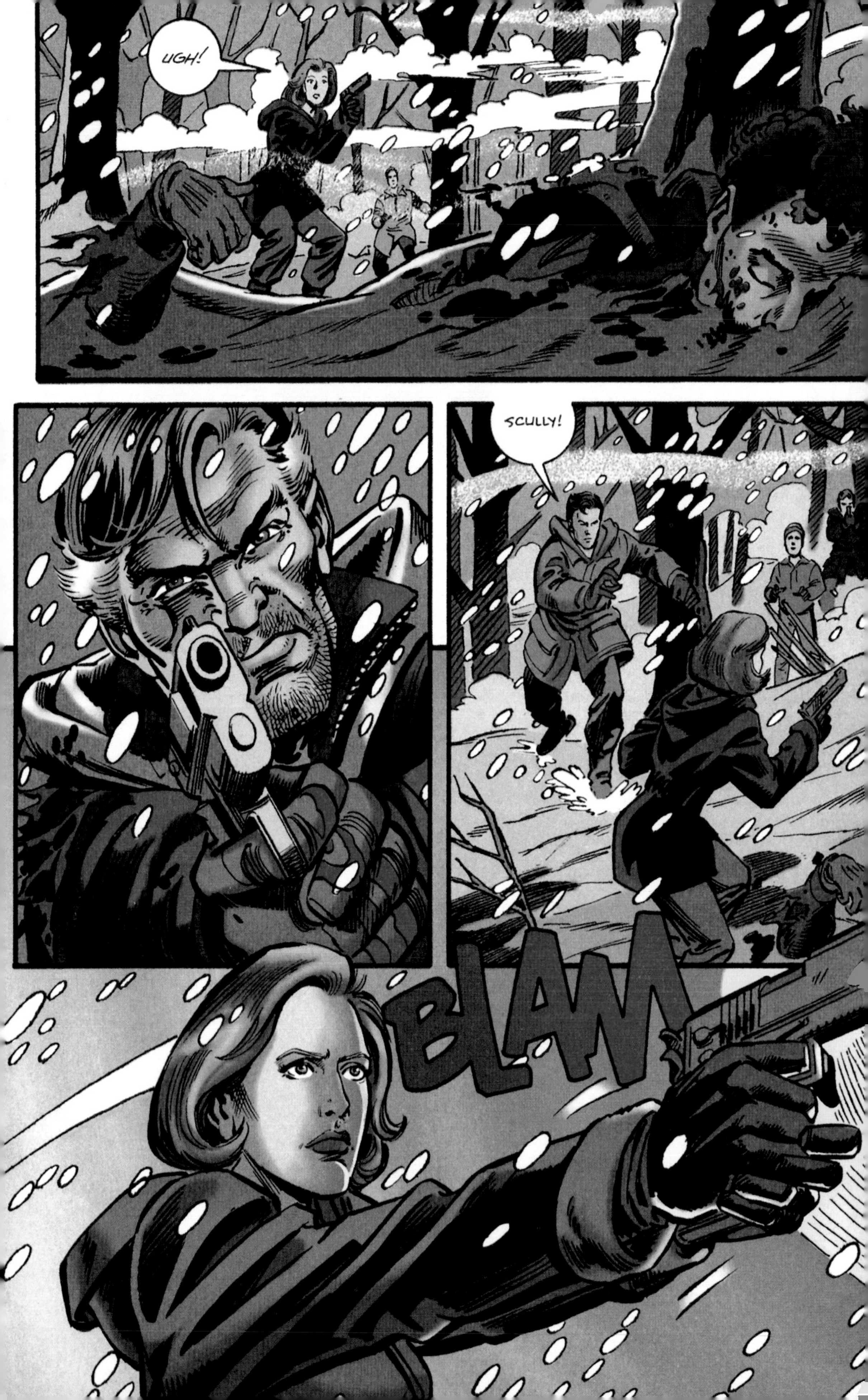
UGH!
SCULLY!
BLAM

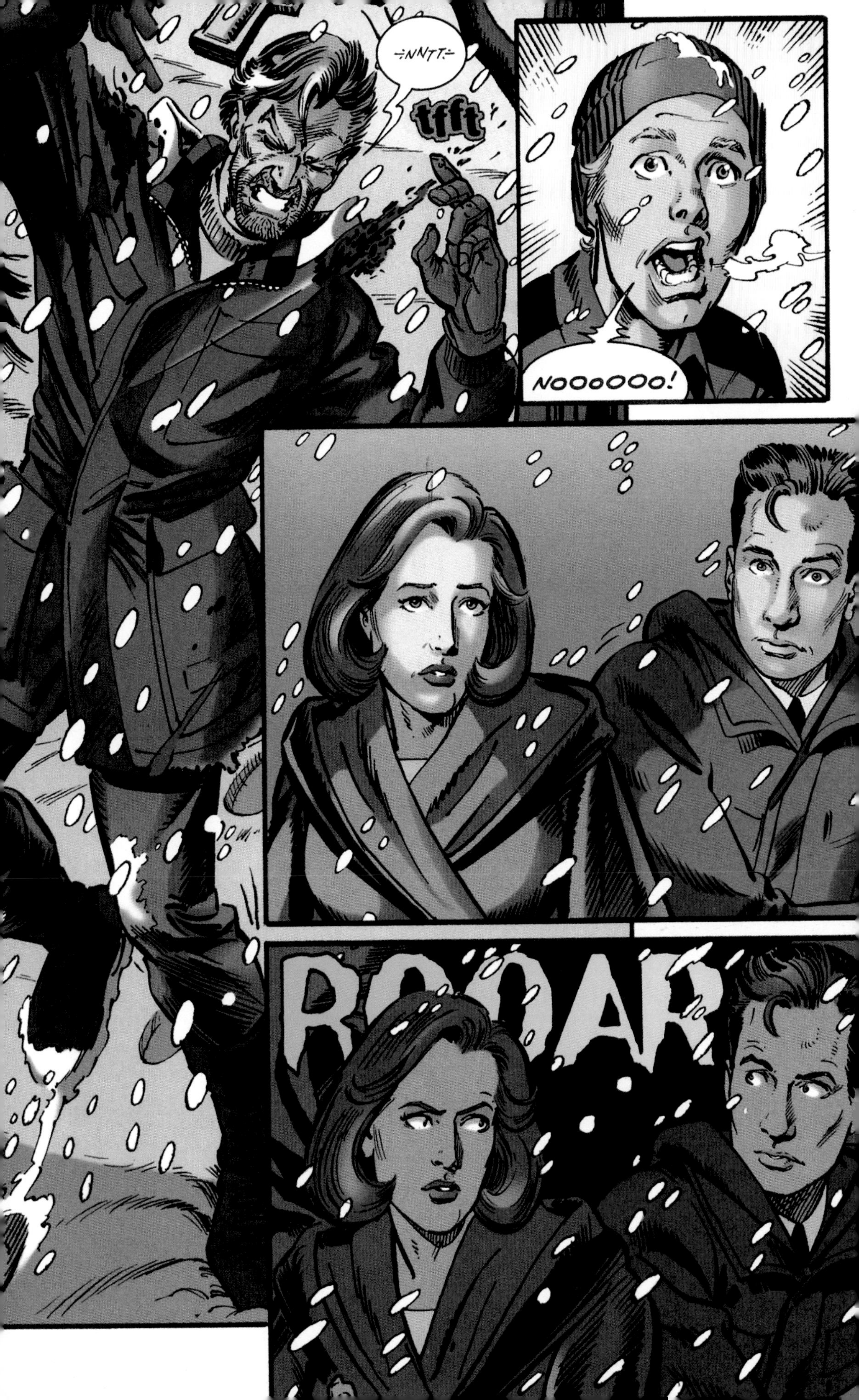
NNTT
tfft
NOOOOOO!
ROOAR

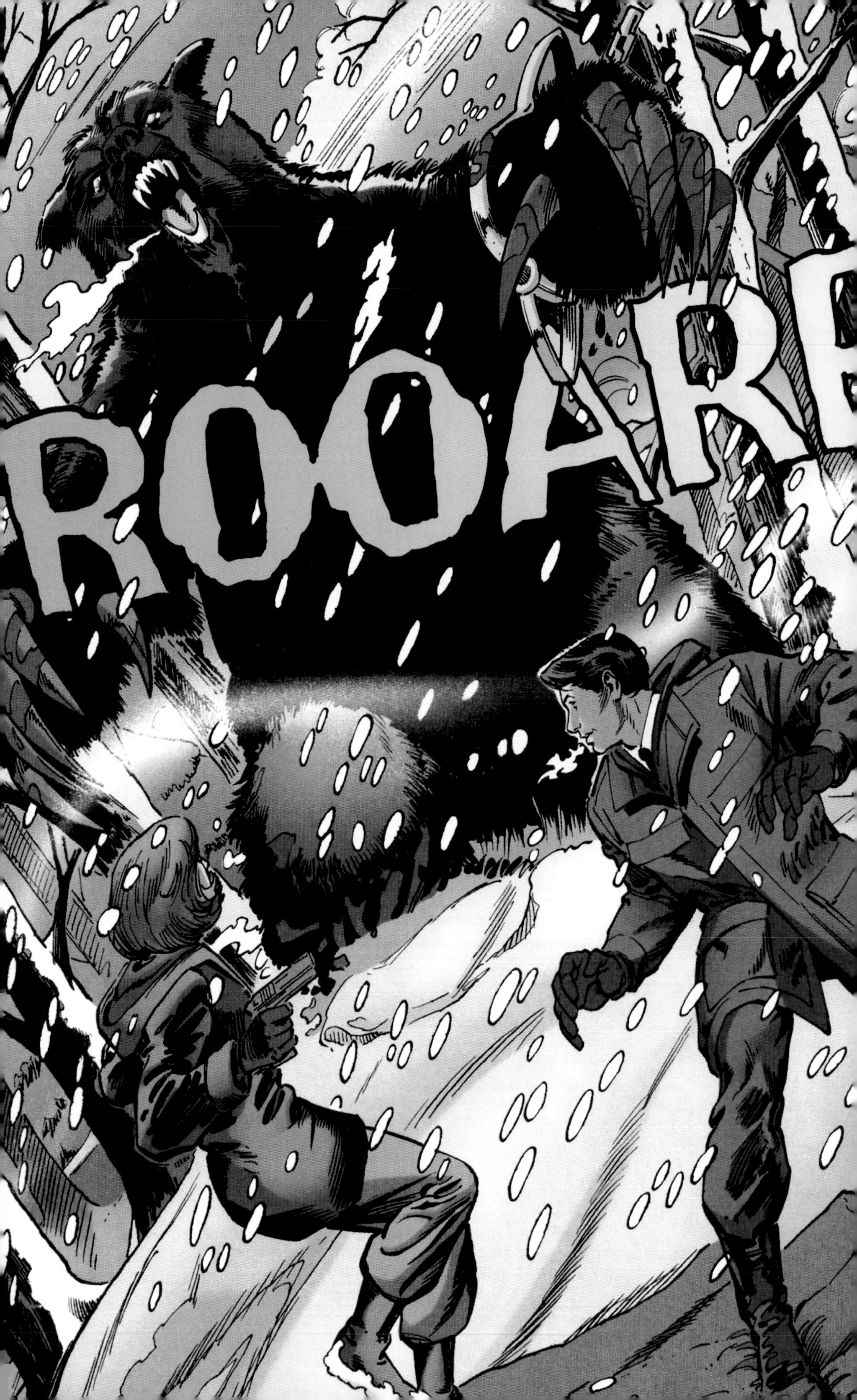
ROOAR

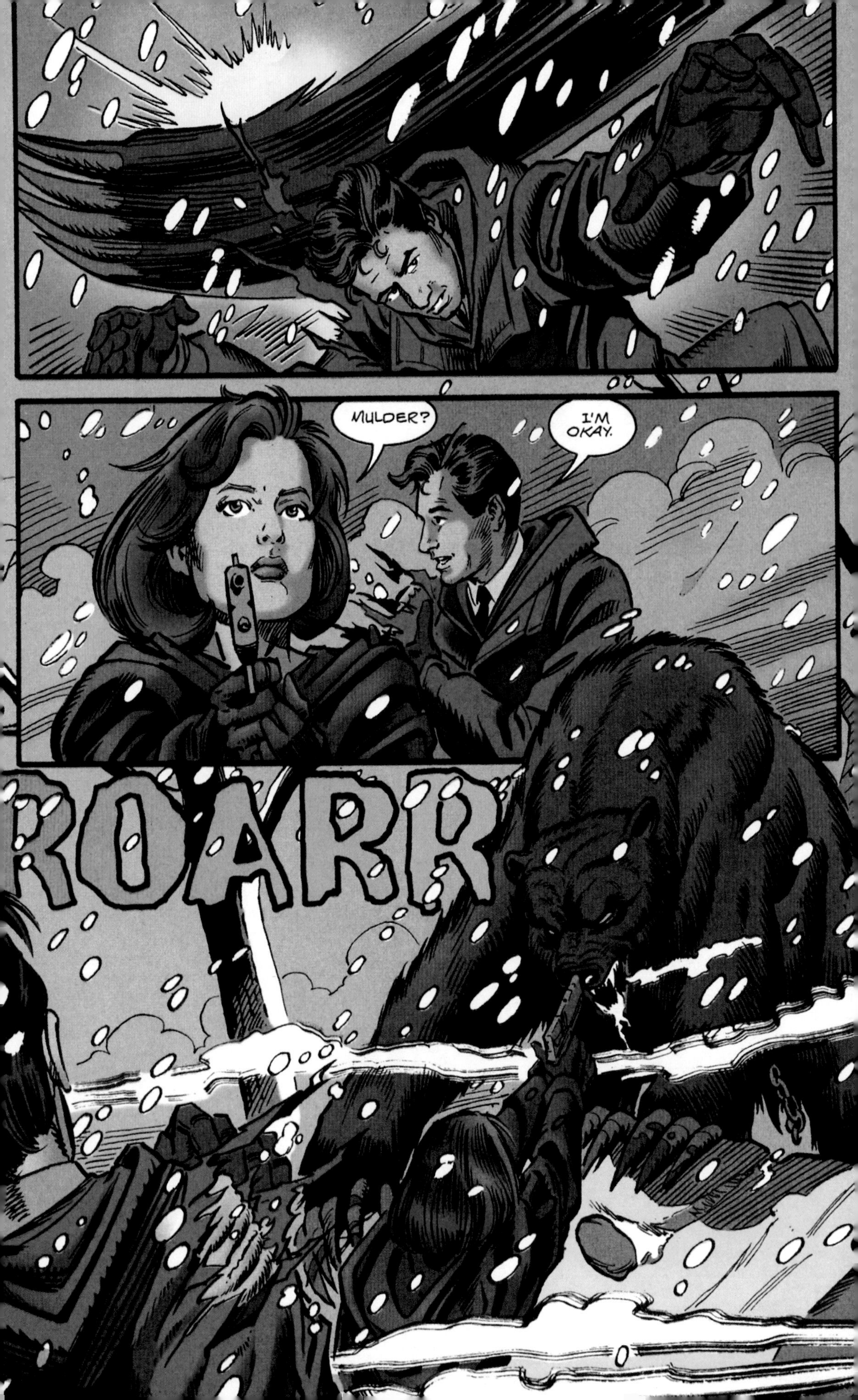
MULDER?
I'M OKAY.
ROARR

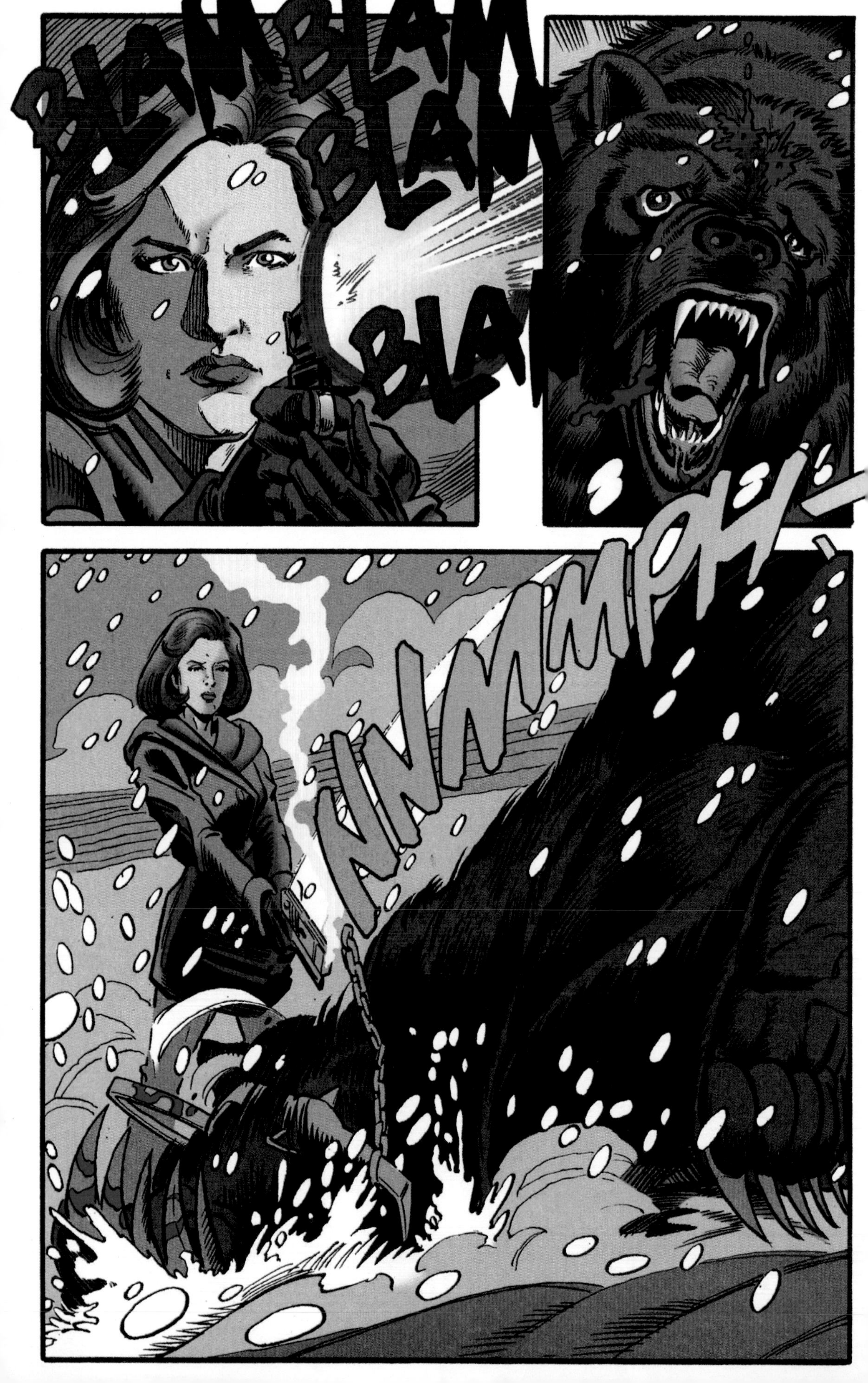
BLAMBLAMBLAM
BLAM
BLAM

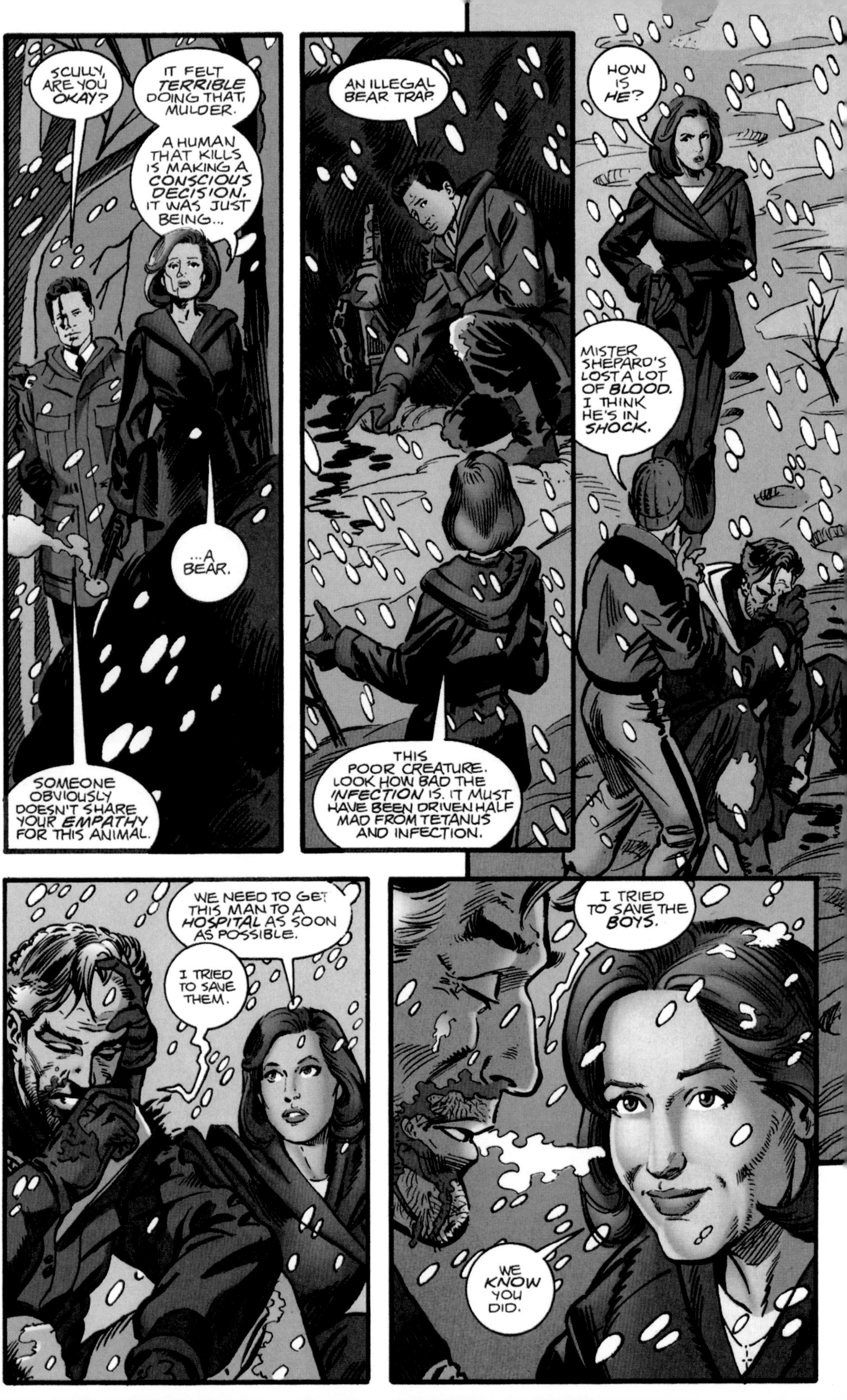
SCULLY, ARE YOU OKAY?
IT FELT TERRIBLE DOING THAT, MULDER.
A HUMAN THAT KILLS IS MAKING A CONSCIOUS DECISION. IT WAS JUST BEING...
...A BEAR.
SOMEONE OBVIOUSLY DOESN'T SHARE YOUR EMPATHY FOR THIS ANIMAL.
AN ILLEGAL BEAR TRAP.
THIS POOR CREATURE. LOOK HOW BAD THE INFECTION IS. IT MUST HAVE BEEN DRIVEN HALF MAD FROM TETANUS AND INFECTION.
HOW IS HE?
MISTER SHEPARD'S LOST A LOT OF BLOOD. I THINK HE'S IN SHOCK.
WE NEED TO GET THIS MAN TO A HOSPITAL AS SOON AS POSSIBLE.
I TRIED TO SAVE THEM.
I TRIED TO SAVE THE BOYS.
WE KNOW YOU DID.

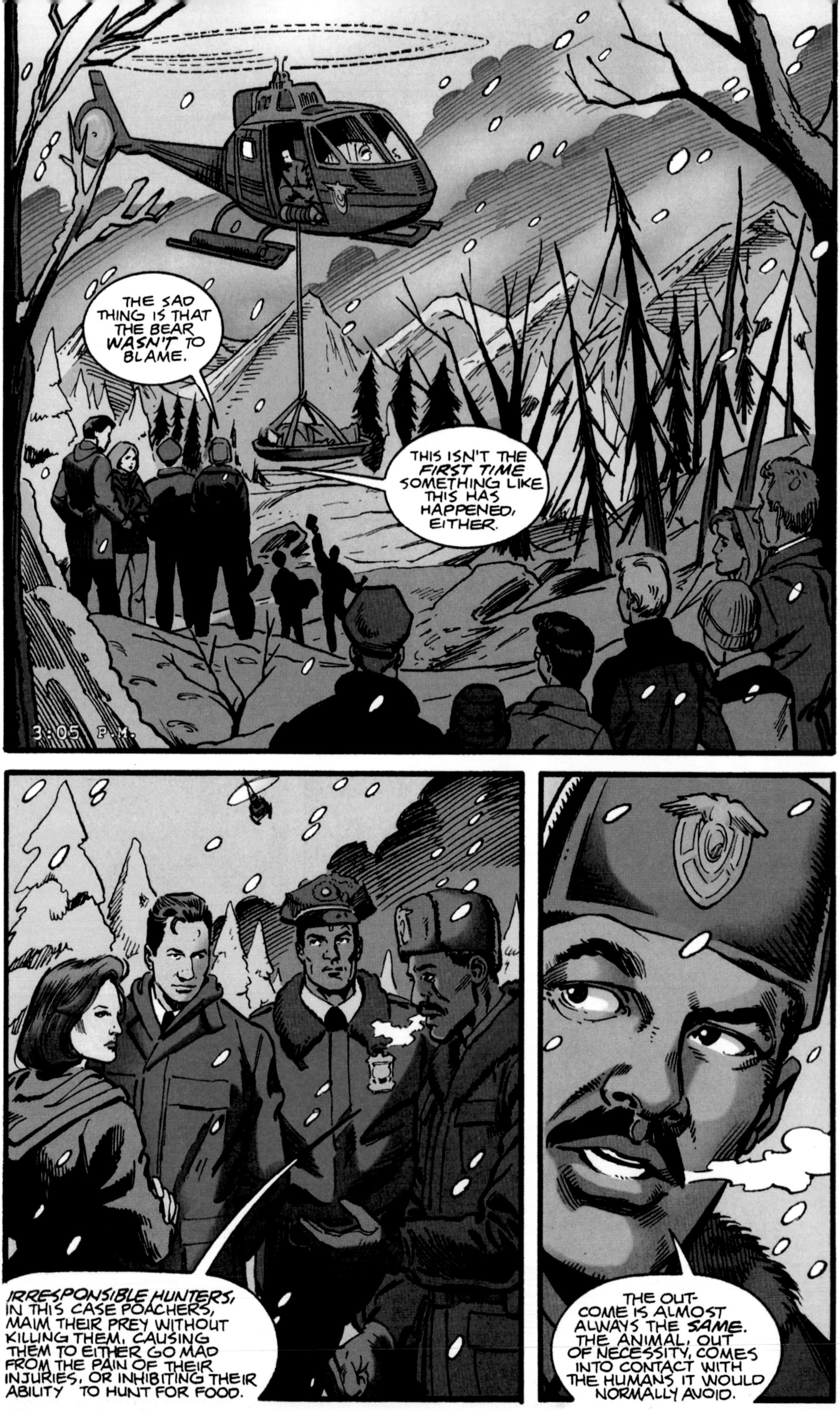
THE SAD THING IS THAT THE BEAR WASN'T TO BLAME.
THIS ISN'T THE FIRST TIME SOMETHING LIKE THIS HAS HAPPENED, EITHER.
3:05 P.M.
IRRESPONSIBLE HUNTERS, IN THIS CASE POACHERS, MAIM THEIR PREY WITHOUT KILLING THEM, CAUSING THEM TO EITHER GO MAD FROM THE PAIN OF THEIR INJURIES, OR INHIBITING THEIR ABILITY TO HUNT FOR FOOD.
THE OUT-COME IS ALMOST ALWAYS THE SAME. THE ANIMAL, OUT OF NECESSITY, COMES INTO CONTACT WITH THE HUMANS IT WOULD NORMALLY AVOID.

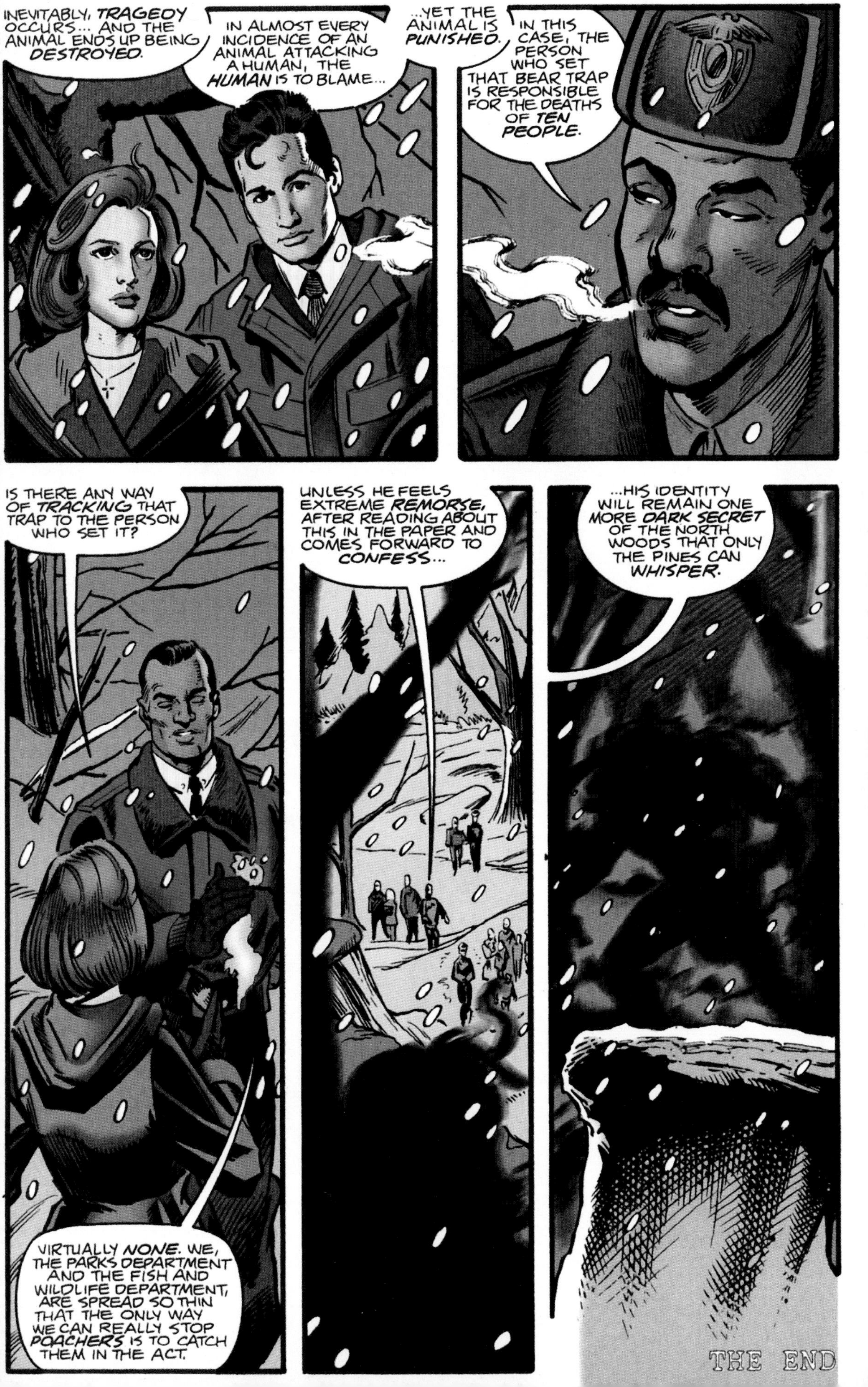
INEVITABLY, TRAGEDY OCCURS... AND THE ANIMAL ENDS UP BEING DESTROYED.
IN ALMOST EVERY INCIDENCE OF AN ANIMAL ATTACKING A HUMAN, THE HUMAN IS TO BLAME...
...YET THE ANIMAL IS PUNISHED.
IN THIS CASE, THE PERSON WHO SET THAT BEAR TRAP IS RESPONSIBLE FOR THE DEATHS OF TEN PEOPLE.
IS THERE ANY WAY OF TRACKING THAT TRAP TO THE PERSON WHO SET IT?
VIRTUALLY NONE. WE, THE PARKS DEPARTMENT AND THE FISH AND WILDLIFE DEPARTMENT, ARE SPREAD SO THIN THAT THE ONLY WAY WE CAN REALLY STOP POACHERS IS TO CATCH THEM IN THE ACT.
UNLESS HE FEELS EXTREME REMORSE, AFTER READING ABOUT THIS IN THE PAPER AND COMES FORWARD TO CONFESS...
...HIS IDENTITY WILL REMAIN ONE MORE DARK SECRET OF THE NORTH WOODS THAT ONLY THE PINES CAN WHISPER.
THE END

CHAPTER 5

# FIRE

STORY: Roy Thomas
ART: John Van Fleet

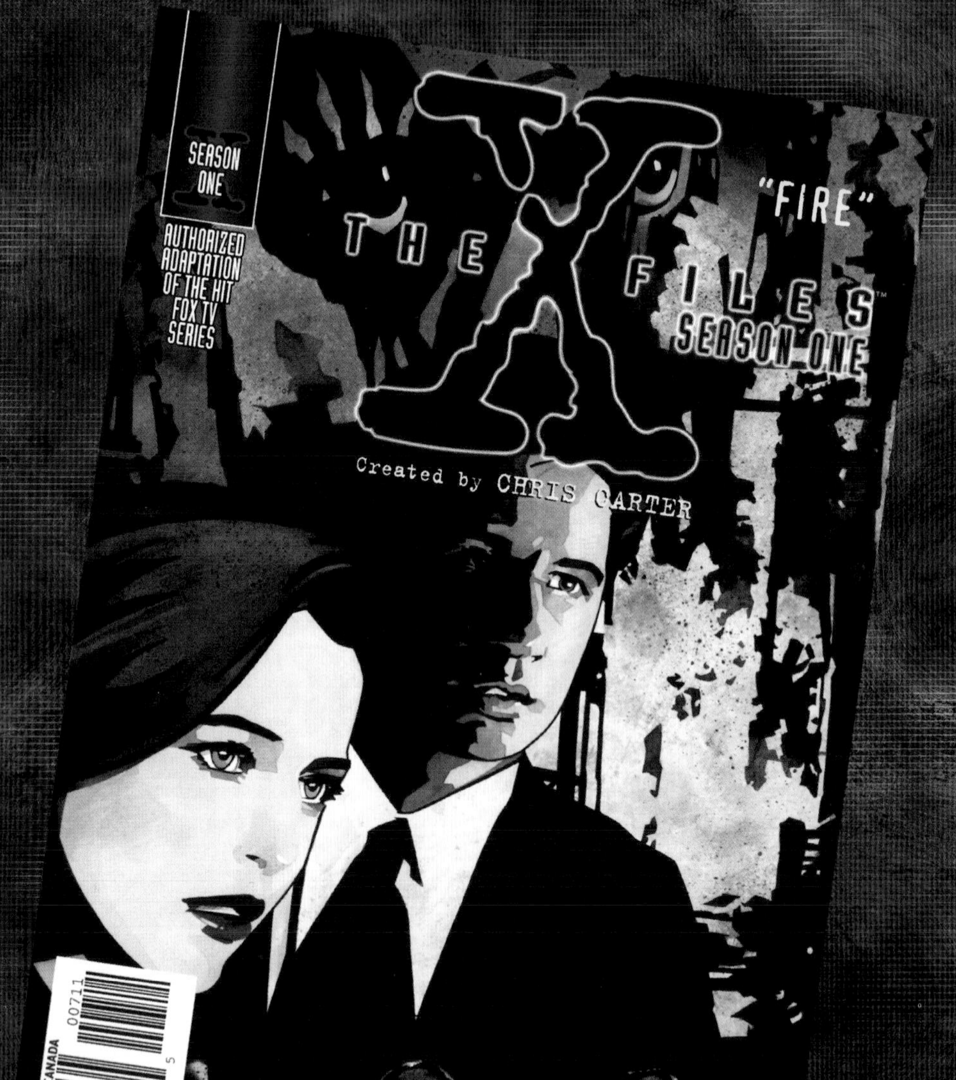
SEASON ONE
AUTHORIZED ADAPTATION OF THE HIT FOX TV SERIES
"FIRE"
THE X FILES™
SEASON ONE
Created by CHRIS CARTER
$4.95 U.S. / $6.95 CANADA
SCREENPLAY BY CHRIS CARTER
ADAPTED BY ROY THOMAS AND JOHN VAN FLEET

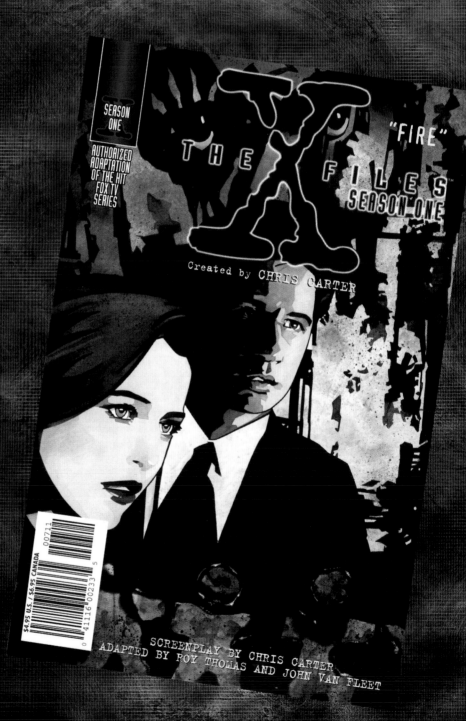

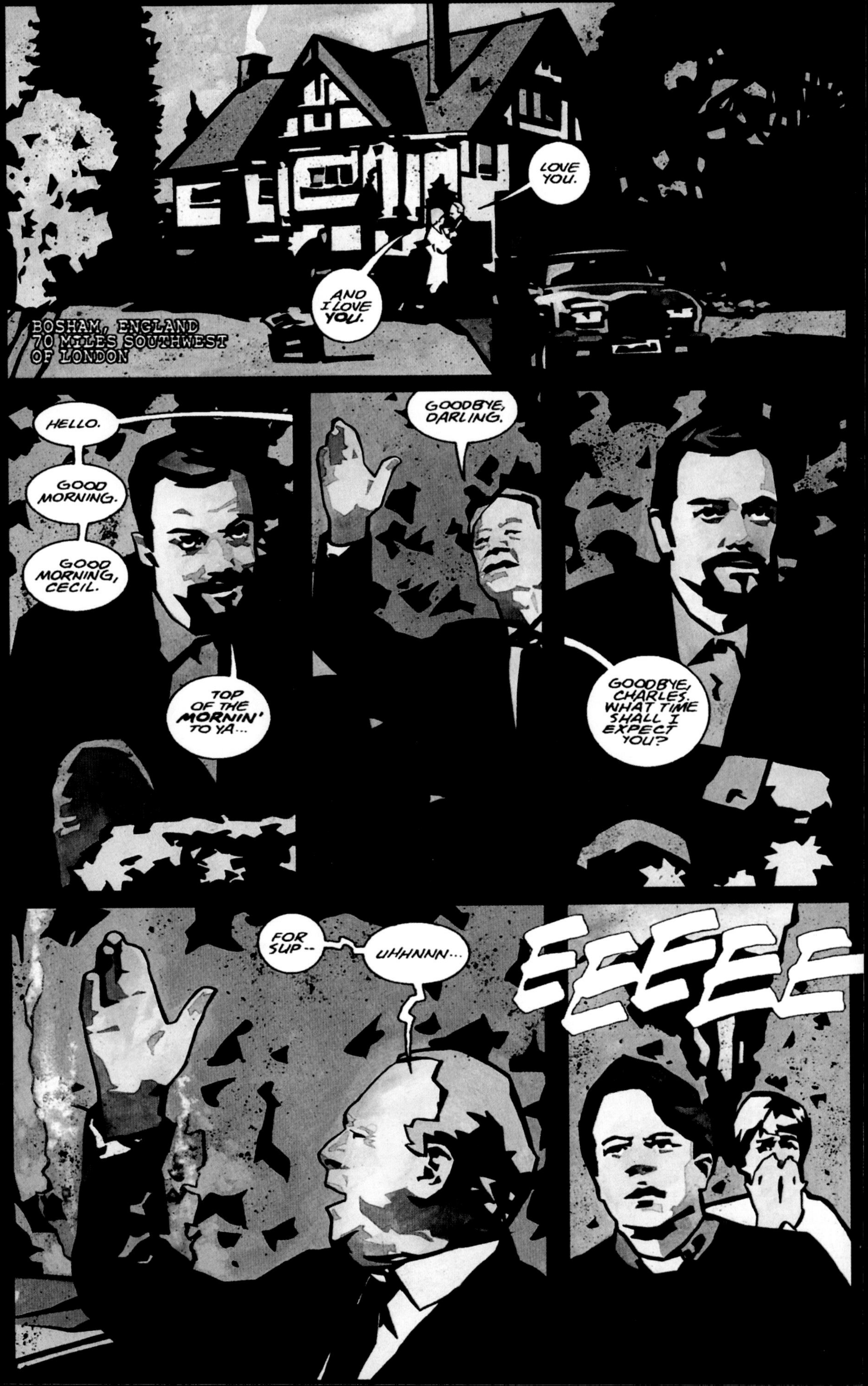

BOSHAM, ENGLAND
70 MILES SOUTHWEST
OF LONDON
LOVE YOU.
AND I LOVE YOU.
HELLO.
GOOD MORNING.
GOOD MORNING, CECIL.
TOP OF THE MORNIN' TO YA...
GOODBYE, DARLING.
GOODBYE, CHARLES. WHAT TIME SHALL I EXPECT YOU?
FOR SUP--
UHHNNN...
EEEEE

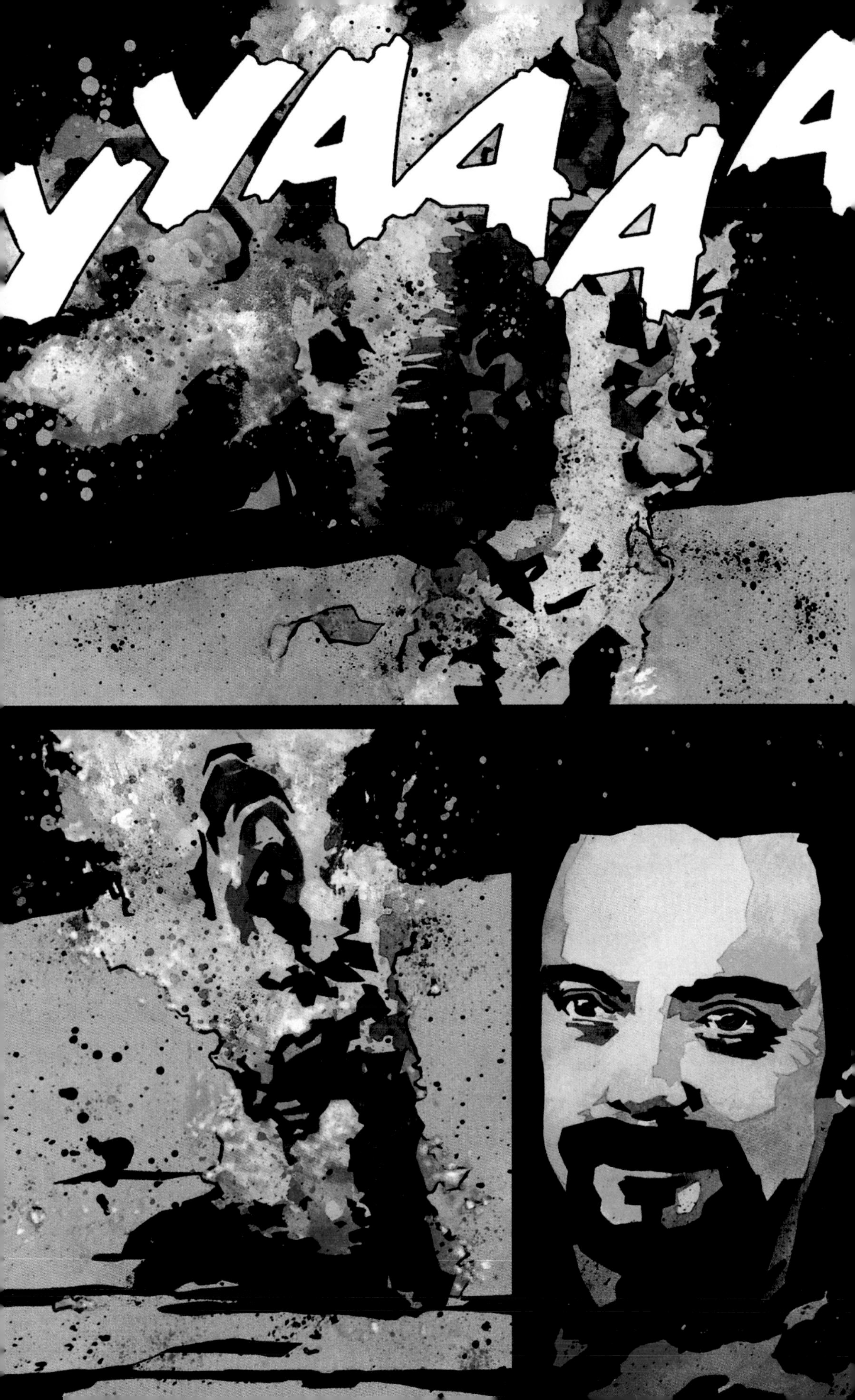
YAAAAA

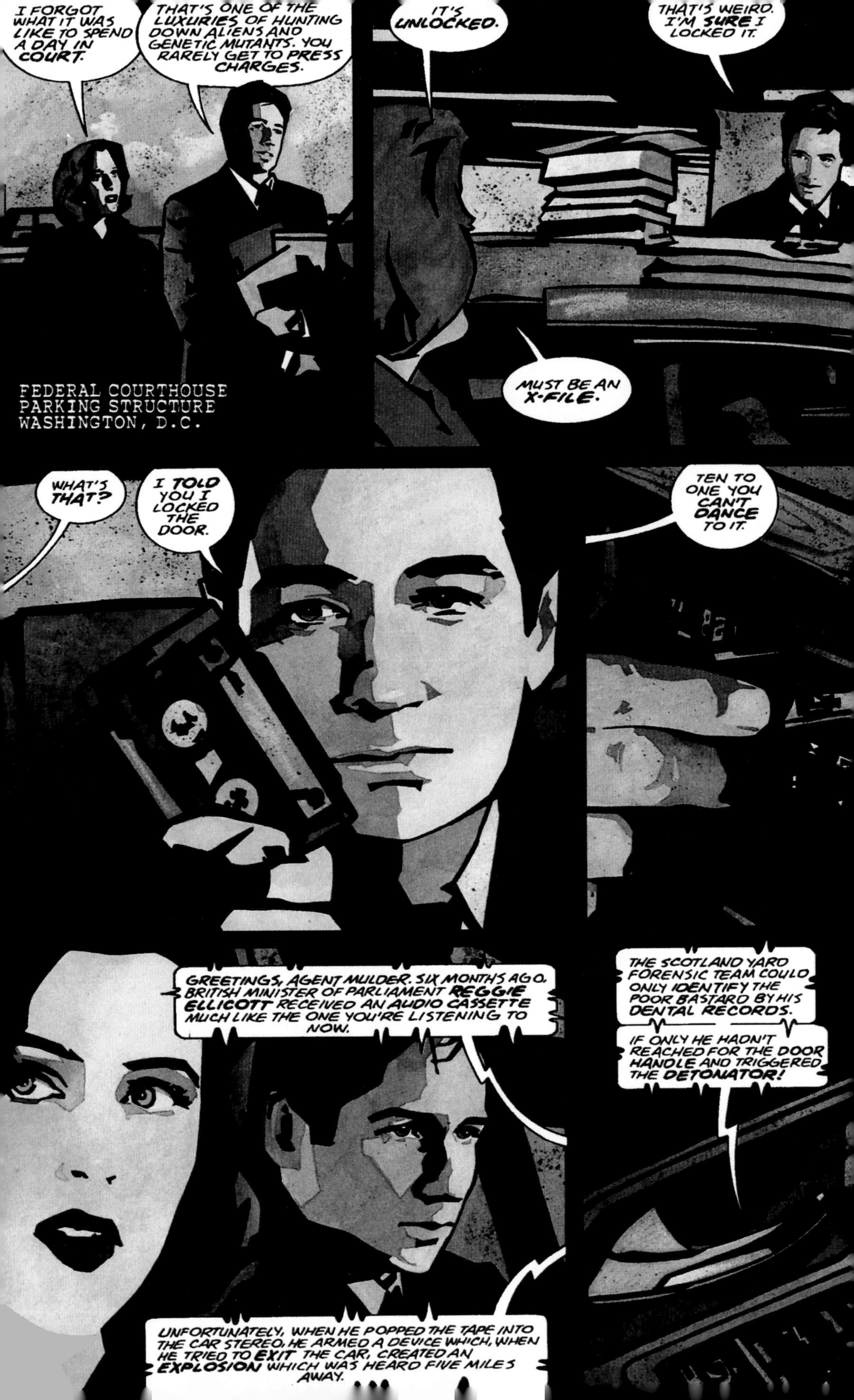
I FORGOT WHAT IT WAS LIKE TO SPEND A DAY IN COURT.
THAT'S ONE OF THE LUXURIES OF HUNTING DOWN ALIENS AND GENETIC MUTANTS. YOU RARELY GET TO PRESS CHARGES.
FEDERAL COURTHOUSE
PARKING STRUCTURE
WASHINGTON, D.C.
IT'S UNLOCKED.
THAT'S WEIRD. I'M SURE I LOCKED IT.
MUST BE AN X-FILE.
WHAT'S THAT?
I TOLD YOU I LOCKED THE DOOR.
TEN TO ONE YOU CAN'T DANCE TO IT.
GREETINGS, AGENT MULDER. SIX MONTHS AGO, BRITISH MINISTER OF PARLIAMENT REGGIE ELLICOTT RECEIVED AN AUDIO CASSETTE MUCH LIKE THE ONE YOU'RE LISTENING TO NOW.
UNFORTUNATELY, WHEN HE POPPED THE TAPE INTO THE CAR STEREO, HE ARMED A DEVICE WHICH, WHEN HE TRIED TO EXIT THE CAR, CREATED AN EXPLOSION WHICH WAS HEARD FIVE MILES AWAY...
THE SCOTLAND YARD FORENSIC TEAM COULD ONLY IDENTIFY THE POOR BASTARD BY HIS DENTAL RECORDS.
IF ONLY HE HADN'T REACHED FOR THE DOOR HANDLE AND TRIGGERED THE DETONATOR!

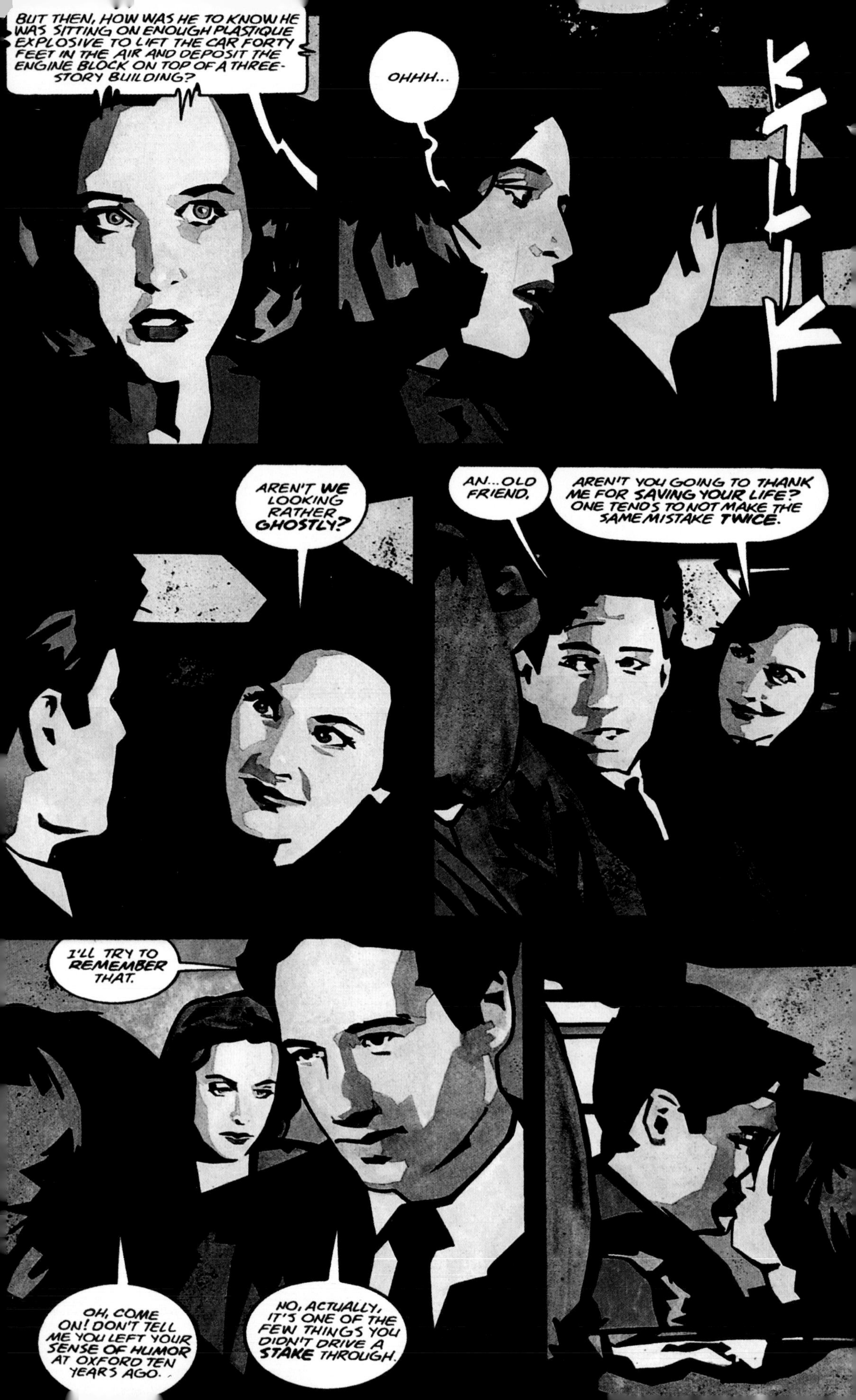
BUT THEN, HOW WAS HE TO KNOW HE WAS SITTING ON ENOUGH PLASTIQUE EXPLOSIVE TO LIFT THE CAR FORTY FEET IN THE AIR AND DEPOSIT THE ENGINE BLOCK ON TOP OF A THREE-STORY BUILDING?
OHHH...
AREN'T WE LOOKING RATHER GHOSTLY?
AN...OLD FRIEND.
AREN'T YOU GOING TO THANK ME FOR SAVING YOUR LIFE? ONE TENDS TO NOT MAKE THE SAME MISTAKE TWICE.
I'LL TRY TO REMEMBER THAT.
OH, COME ON! DON'T TELL ME YOU LEFT YOUR SENSE OF HUMOR AT OXFORD TEN YEARS AGO.
NO, ACTUALLY, IT'S ONE OF THE FEW THINGS YOU DIDN'T DRIVE A STAKE THROUGH.

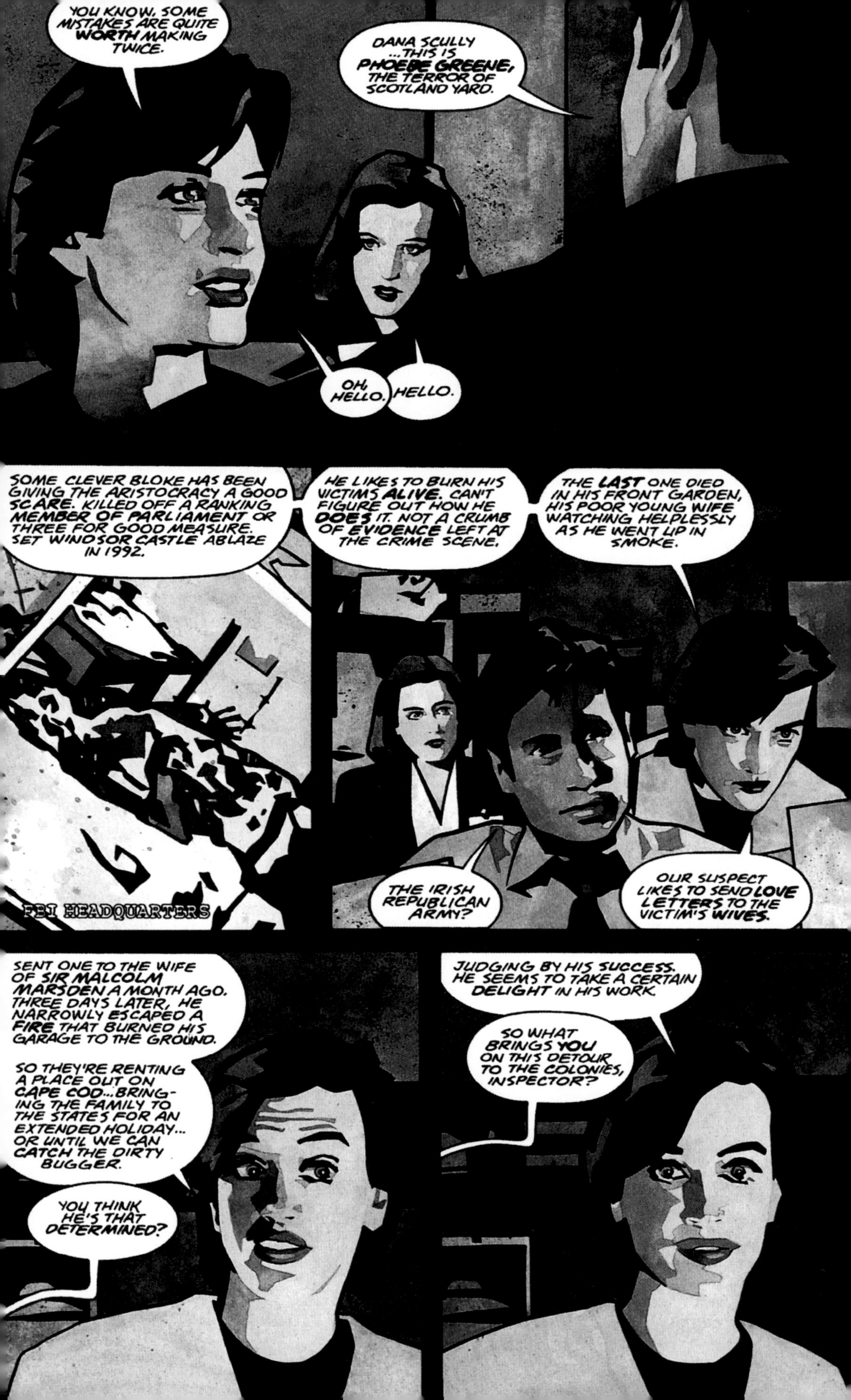
YOU KNOW, SOME MISTAKES ARE QUITE WORTH MAKING TWICE.
DANA SCULLY ...THIS IS PHOEBE GREENE, THE TERROR OF SCOTLAND YARD.
OH, HELLO.
HELLO.
SOME CLEVER BLOKE HAS BEEN GIVING THE ARISTOCRACY A GOOD SCARE. KILLED OFF A RANKING MEMBER OF PARLIAMENT OR THREE FOR GOOD MEASURE. SET WINDSOR CASTLE ABLAZE IN 1992.
FBI HEADQUARTERS
HE LIKES TO BURN HIS VICTIMS ALIVE. CAN'T FIGURE OUT HOW HE DOES IT. NOT A CRUMB OF EVIDENCE LEFT AT THE CRIME SCENE.
THE LAST ONE DIED IN HIS FRONT GARDEN, HIS POOR YOUNG WIFE WATCHING HELPLESSLY AS HE WENT UP IN SMOKE.
THE IRISH REPUBLICAN ARMY?
OUR SUSPECT LIKES TO SEND LOVE LETTERS TO THE VICTIM'S WIVES.
SENT ONE TO THE WIFE OF SIR MALCOLM MARSDEN A MONTH AGO. THREE DAYS LATER, HE NARROWLY ESCAPED A FIRE THAT BURNED HIS GARAGE TO THE GROUND.
SO THEY'RE RENTING A PLACE OUT ON CAPE COD...BRINGING THE FAMILY TO THE STATES FOR AN EXTENDED HOLIDAY... OR UNTIL WE CAN CATCH THE DIRTY BUGGER.
YOU THINK HE'S THAT DETERMINED?
JUDGING BY HIS SUCCESS. HE SEEMS TO TAKE A CERTAIN DELIGHT IN HIS WORK.
SO WHAT BRINGS YOU ON THIS DETOUR TO THE COLONIES, INSPECTOR?

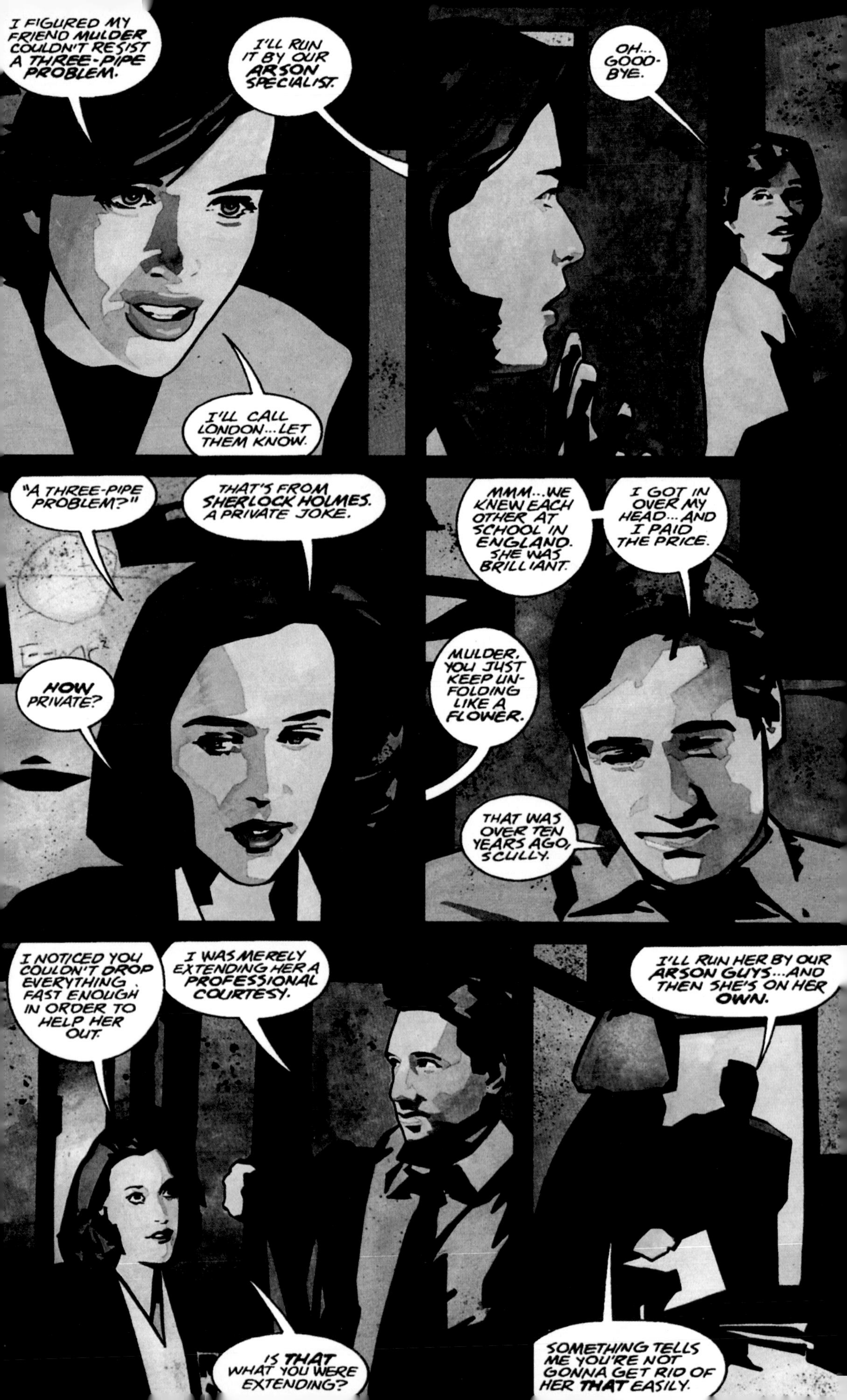
I FIGURED MY FRIEND MULDER COULDN'T RESIST A THREE-PIPE PROBLEM.
I'LL RUN IT BY OUR ARSON SPECIALIST.
I'LL CALL LONDON... LET THEM KNOW.
OH... GOOD-BYE.
"A THREE-PIPE PROBLEM?"
THAT'S FROM SHERLOCK HOLMES. A PRIVATE JOKE.
HOW PRIVATE?
MMM... WE KNEW EACH OTHER AT SCHOOL IN ENGLAND. SHE WAS BRILLIANT.
I GOT IN OVER MY HEAD... AND I PAID THE PRICE.
MULDER, YOU JUST KEEP UN-FOLDING LIKE A FLOWER.
THAT WAS OVER TEN YEARS AGO, SCULLY.
I NOTICED YOU COULDN'T DROP EVERYTHING FAST ENOUGH IN ORDER TO HELP HER OUT.
I WAS MERELY EXTENDING HER A PROFESSIONAL COURTESY.
IS THAT WHAT YOU WERE EXTENDING?
I'LL RUN HER BY OUR ARSON GUYS... AND THEN SHE'S ON HER OWN.
SOMETHING TELLS ME YOU'RE NOT GONNA GET RID OF HER THAT EASILY.

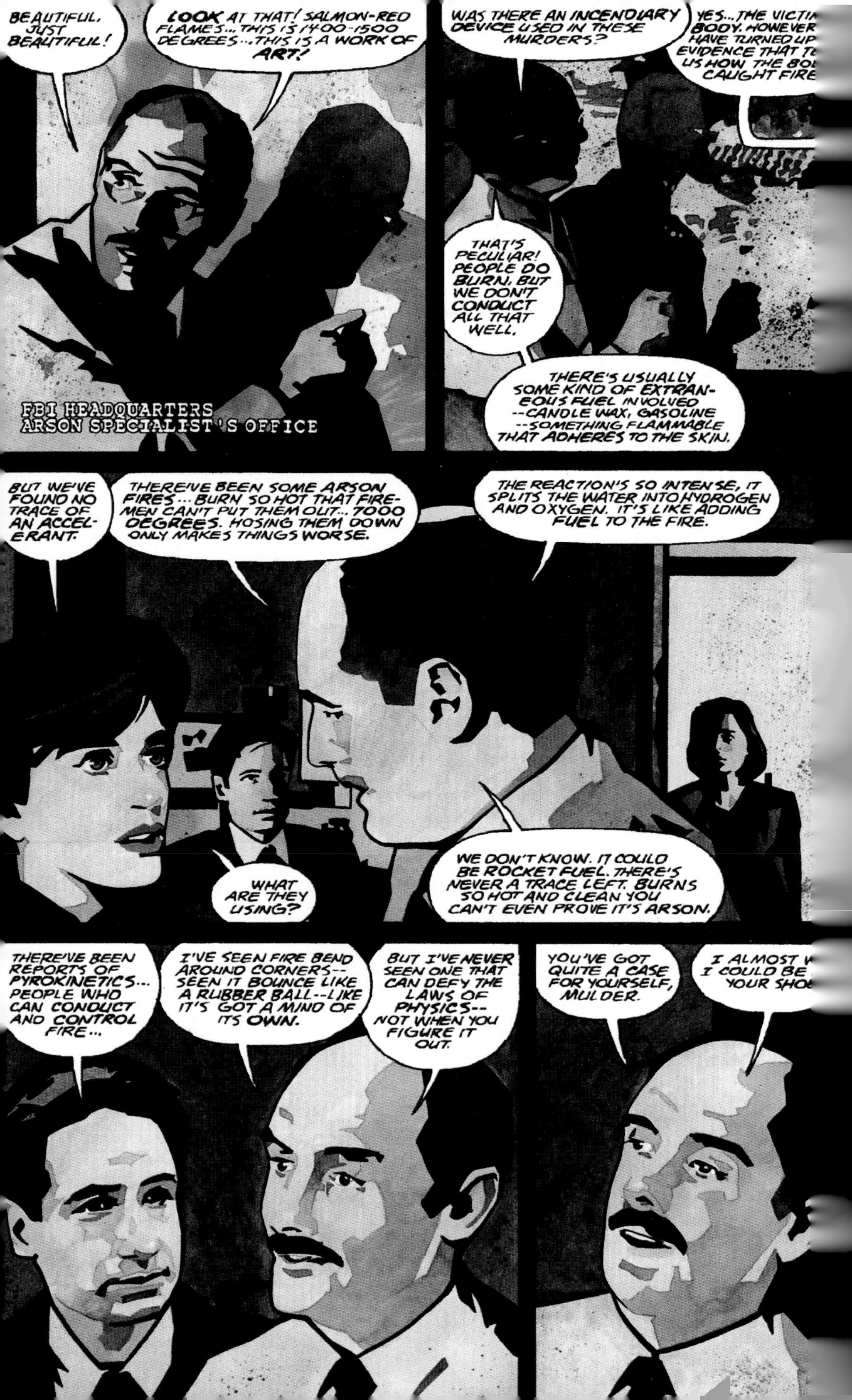

BEAUTIFUL. JUST BEAUTIFUL!
LOOK AT THAT! SALMON-RED FLAMES... THIS IS 1400-1500 DEGREES... THIS IS A WORK OF ART!
FBI HEADQUARTERS ARSON SPECIALIST'S OFFICE
WAS THERE AN INCENDIARY DEVICE USED IN THESE MURDERS?
YES...THE VICTI BODY. HOWEVER HAVE TURNED UP EVIDENCE THAT T US HOW THE BO CAUGHT FIRE
THAT'S PECULIAR! PEOPLE DO BURN, BUT WE DON'T CONDUCT ALL THAT WELL.
THERE'S USUALLY SOME KIND OF EXTRANEOUS FUEL INVOLVED --CANDLE WAX, GASOLINE --SOMETHING FLAMMABLE THAT ADHERES TO THE SKIN.
BUT WE'VE FOUND NO TRACE OF AN ACCELERANT.
THERE'VE BEEN SOME ARSON FIRES... BURN SO HOT THAT FIREMEN CAN'T PUT THEM OUT... 7000 DEGREES. HOSING THEM DOWN ONLY MAKES THINGS WORSE.
THE REACTION'S SO INTENSE, IT SPLITS THE WATER INTO HYDROGEN AND OXYGEN. IT'S LIKE ADDING FUEL TO THE FIRE.
WHAT ARE THEY USING?
WE DON'T KNOW. IT COULD BE ROCKET FUEL. THERE'S NEVER A TRACE LEFT. BURNS SO HOT AND CLEAN YOU CAN'T EVEN PROVE IT'S ARSON.
THERE'VE BEEN REPORTS OF PYROKINETICS... PEOPLE WHO CAN CONDUCT AND CONTROL FIRE...
I'VE SEEN FIRE BEND AROUND CORNERS--SEEN IT BOUNCE LIKE A RUBBER BALL--LIKE IT'S GOT A MIND OF ITS OWN.
BUT I'VE NEVER SEEN ONE THAT CAN DEFY THE LAWS OF PHYSICS--NOT WHEN YOU FIGURE IT OUT.
YOU'VE GOT QUITE A CASE FOR YOURSELF, MULDER.
I ALMOST I COULD BE YOUR SHO

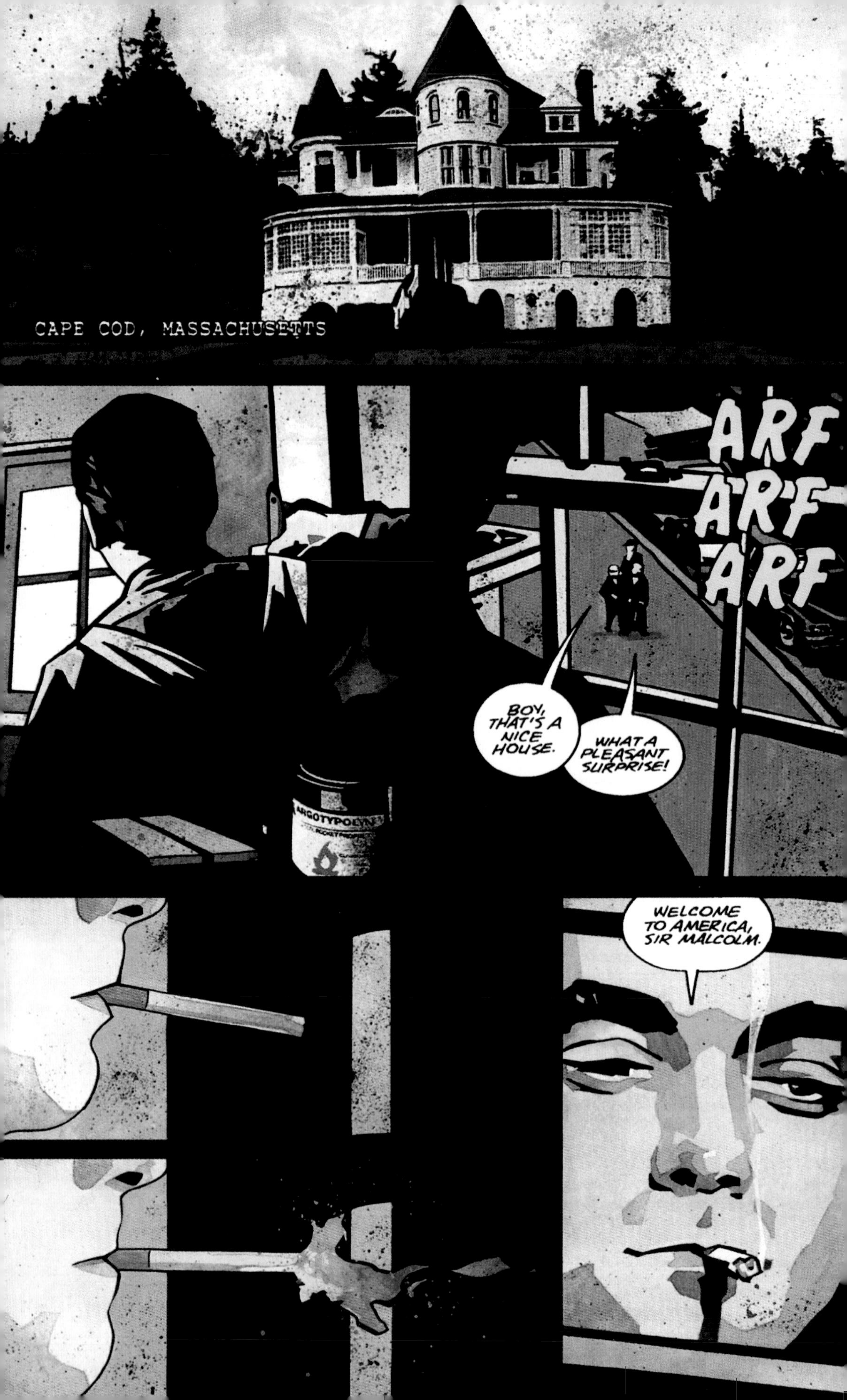
CAPE COD, MASSACHUSETTS
ARF ARF ARF
BOY, THAT'S A NICE HOUSE.
WHAT A PLEASANT SURPRISE!
WELCOME TO AMERICA, SIR MALCOLM.

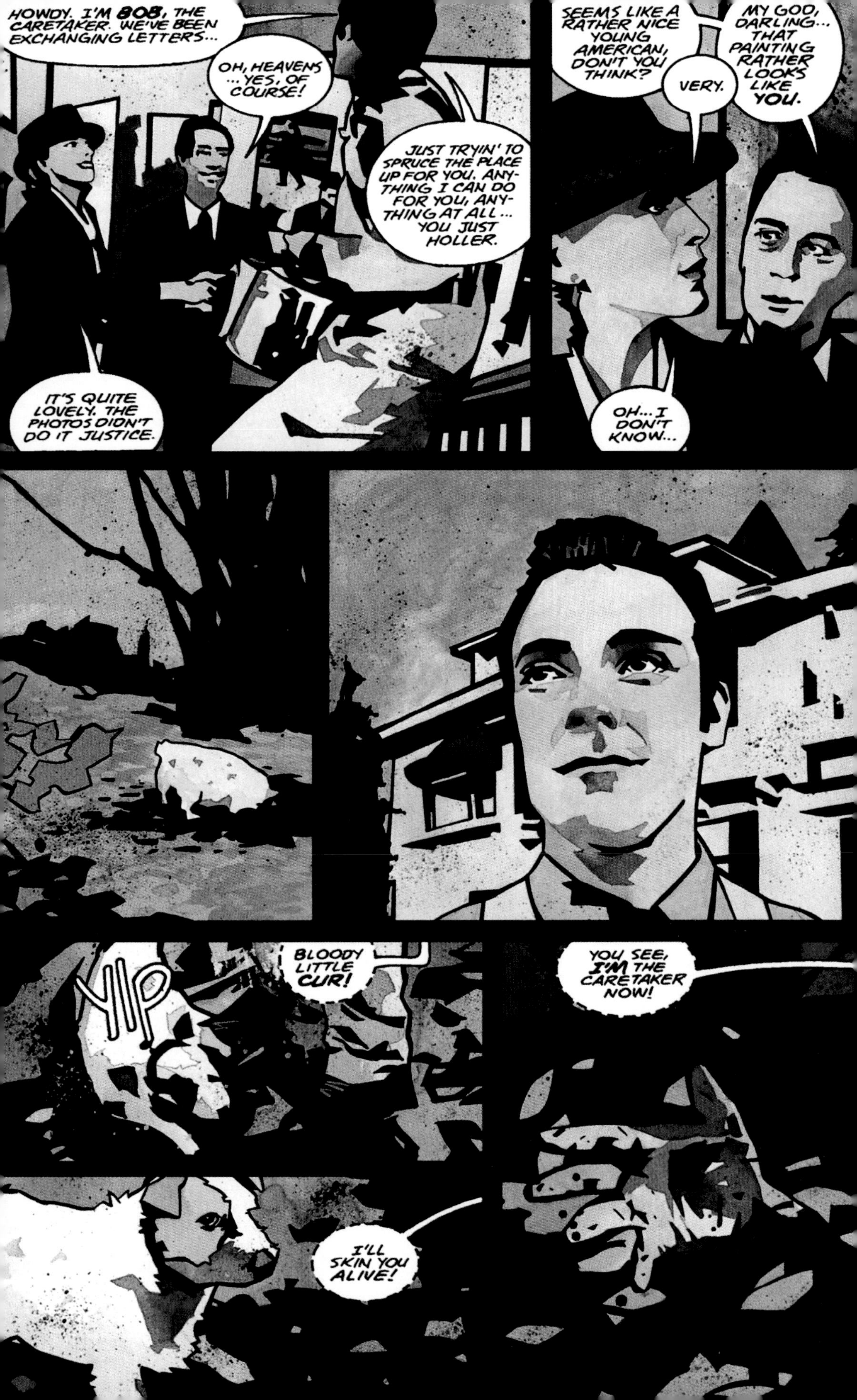
HOWDY. I'M BOB, THE CARETAKER. WE'VE BEEN EXCHANGING LETTERS...
OH, HEAVENS ...YES, OF COURSE!
JUST TRYIN' TO SPRUCE THE PLACE UP FOR YOU. ANYTHING I CAN DO FOR YOU, ANYTHING AT ALL... YOU JUST HOLLER.
IT'S QUITE LOVELY. THE PHOTOS DIDN'T DO IT JUSTICE.
SEEMS LIKE A RATHER NICE YOUNG AMERICAN, DON'T YOU THINK?
VERY.
MY GOD, DARLING... THAT PAINTING RATHER LOOKS LIKE YOU.
OH... I DON'T KNOW...
YIP
BLOODY LITTLE CUR!
YOU SEE, I'M THE CARETAKER NOW!
I'LL SKIN YOU ALIVE!

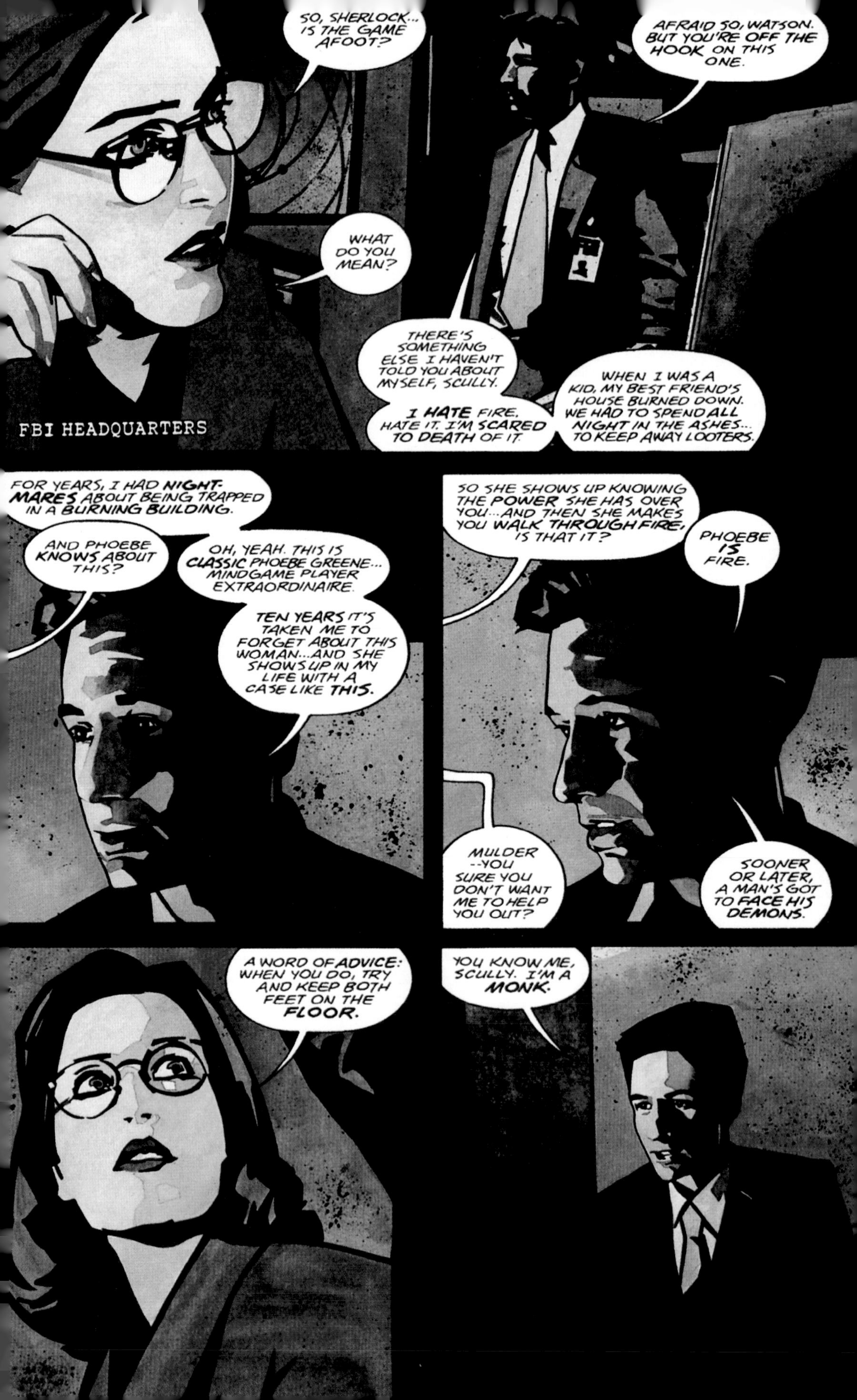
SO, SHERLOCK... IS THE GAME AFOOT?
AFRAID SO, WATSON. BUT YOU'RE OFF THE HOOK ON THIS ONE.
WHAT DO YOU MEAN?
THERE'S SOMETHING ELSE I HAVEN'T TOLD YOU ABOUT MYSELF, SCULLY.
I HATE FIRE. HATE IT. I'M SCARED TO DEATH OF IT.
WHEN I WAS A KID, MY BEST FRIEND'S HOUSE BURNED DOWN. WE HAD TO SPEND ALL NIGHT IN THE ASHES... TO KEEP AWAY LOOTERS.
FBI HEADQUARTERS
FOR YEARS, I HAD NIGHT-MARES ABOUT BEING TRAPPED IN A BURNING BUILDING.
AND PHOEBE KNOWS ABOUT THIS?
OH, YEAH. THIS IS CLASSIC PHOEBE GREENE... MINDGAME PLAYER EXTRAORDINAIRE.
TEN YEARS IT'S TAKEN ME TO FORGET ABOUT THIS WOMAN...AND SHE SHOWS UP IN MY LIFE WITH A CASE LIKE THIS.
SO SHE SHOWS UP KNOWING THE POWER SHE HAS OVER YOU...AND THEN SHE MAKES YOU WALK THROUGH FIRE, IS THAT IT?
PHOEBE IS FIRE.
MULDER --YOU SURE YOU DON'T WANT ME TO HELP YOU OUT?
SOONER OR LATER, A MAN'S GOT TO FACE HIS DEMONS.
A WORD OF ADVICE: WHEN YOU DO, TRY AND KEEP BOTH FEET ON THE FLOOR.
YOU KNOW ME, SCULLY. I'M A MONK.

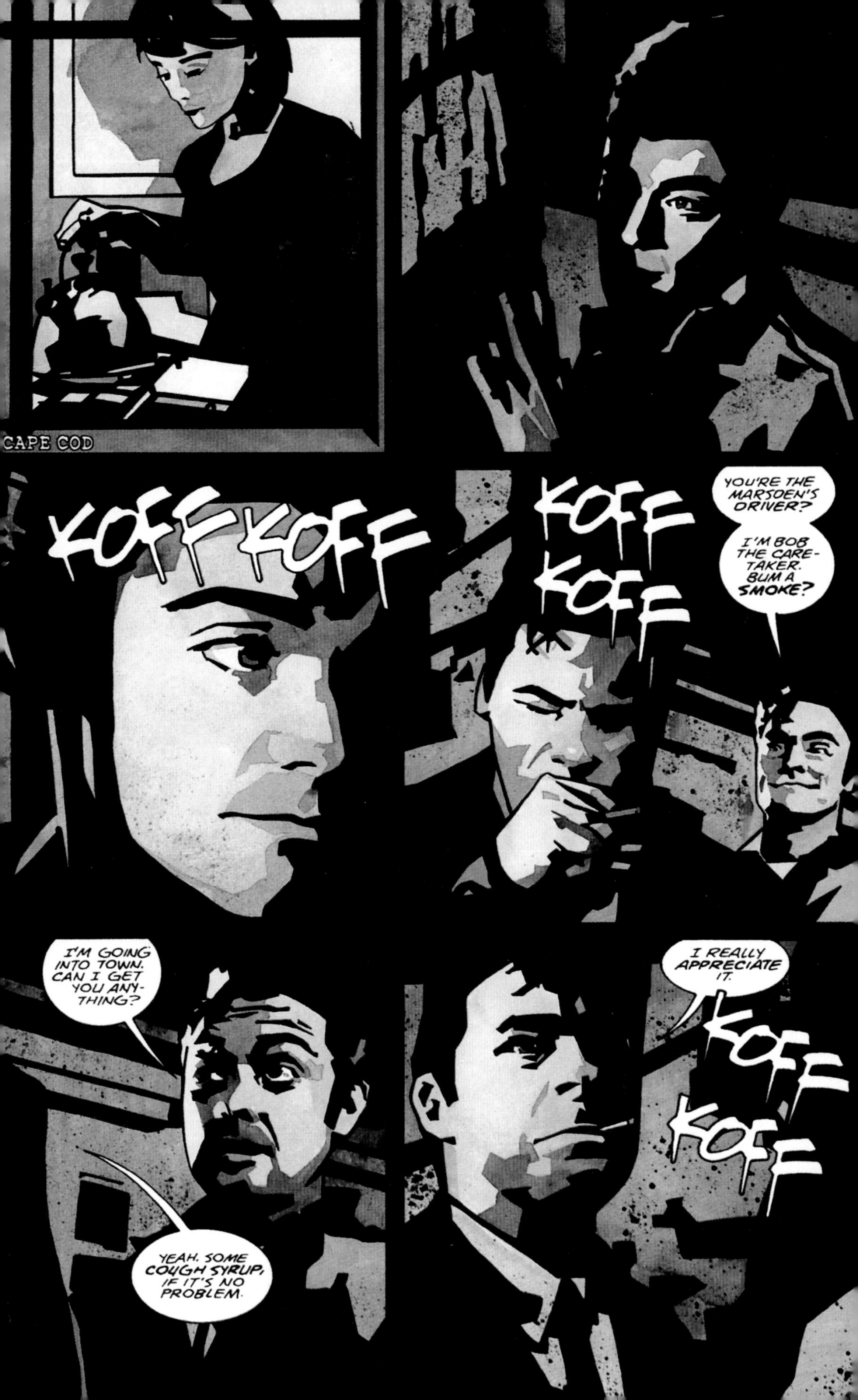
CAPE COD
KOFF KOFF
KOFF KOFF
YOU'RE THE MARSOEN'S DRIVER?
I'M BOB THE CARE-TAKER. BUM A SMOKE?
I'M GOING INTO TOWN. CAN I GET YOU ANY-THING?
YEAH. SOME COUGH SYRUP, IF IT'S NO PROBLEM.
I REALLY APPRECIATE IT.
KOFF KOFF

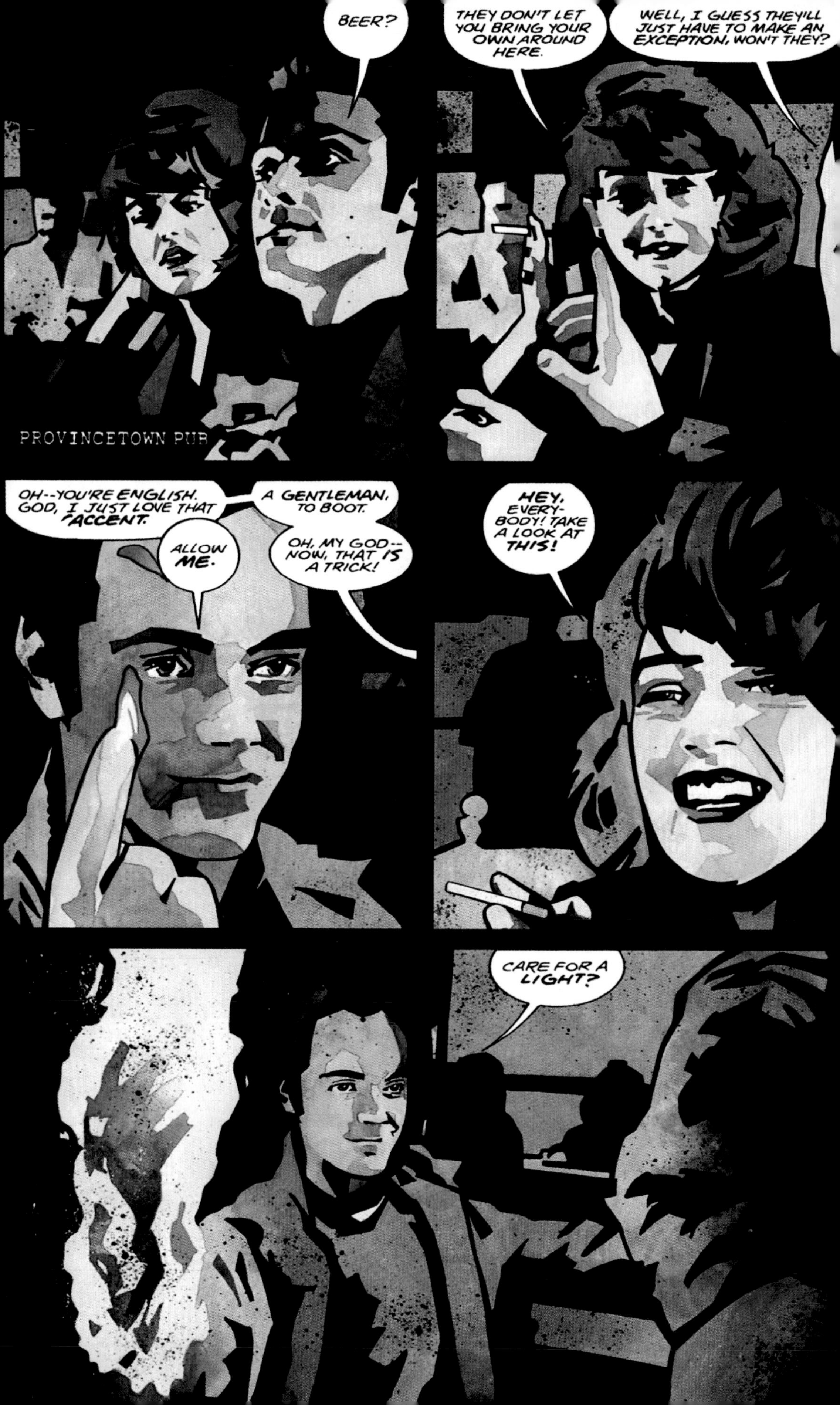
BEER?
PROVINCETOWN PUB
THEY DON'T LET YOU BRING YOUR OWN AROUND HERE.
WELL, I GUESS THEY'LL JUST HAVE TO MAKE AN EXCEPTION, WON'T THEY?
OH--YOU'RE ENGLISH. GOD, I JUST LOVE THAT ACCENT.
A GENTLEMAN, TO BOOT.
ALLOW ME.
OH, MY GOD-- NOW, THAT IS A TRICK!
HEY, EVERYBODY! TAKE A LOOK AT THIS!
CARE FOR A LIGHT?

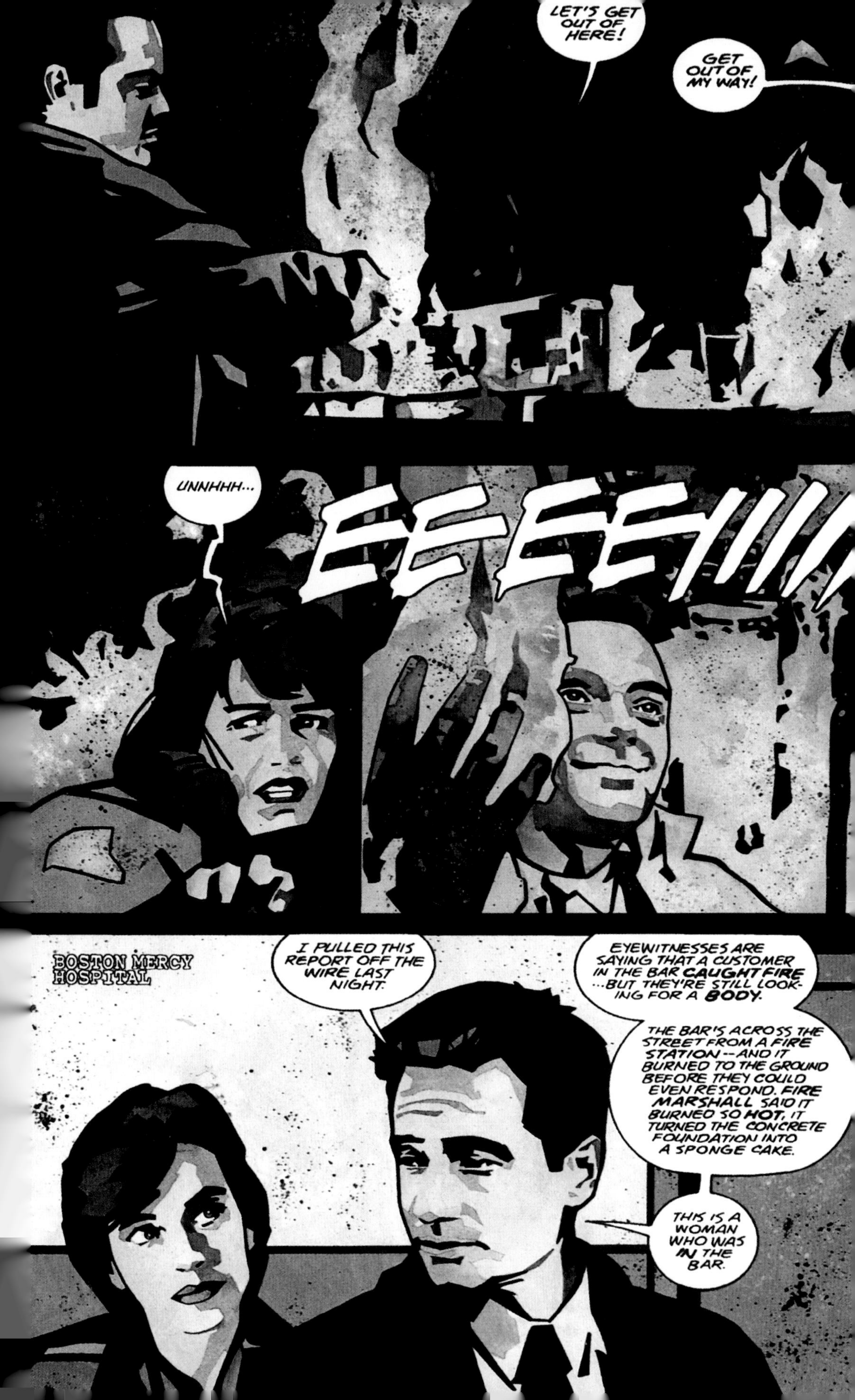
LET'S GET OUT OF HERE!
GET OUT OF MY WAY!
UNNHHH...
EEEEEIIIII
BOSTON MERCY HOSPITAL
I PULLED THIS REPORT OFF THE WIRE LAST NIGHT.
EYEWITNESSES ARE SAYING THAT A CUSTOMER IN THE BAR CAUGHT FIRE ...BUT THEY'RE STILL LOOKING FOR A BODY.
THE BAR'S ACROSS THE STREET FROM A FIRE STATION -- AND IT BURNED TO THE GROUND BEFORE THEY COULD EVEN RESPOND. FIRE MARSHALL SAID IT BURNED SO HOT, IT TURNED THE CONCRETE FOUNDATION INTO A SPONGE CAKE.
THIS IS A WOMAN WHO WAS IN THE BAR.

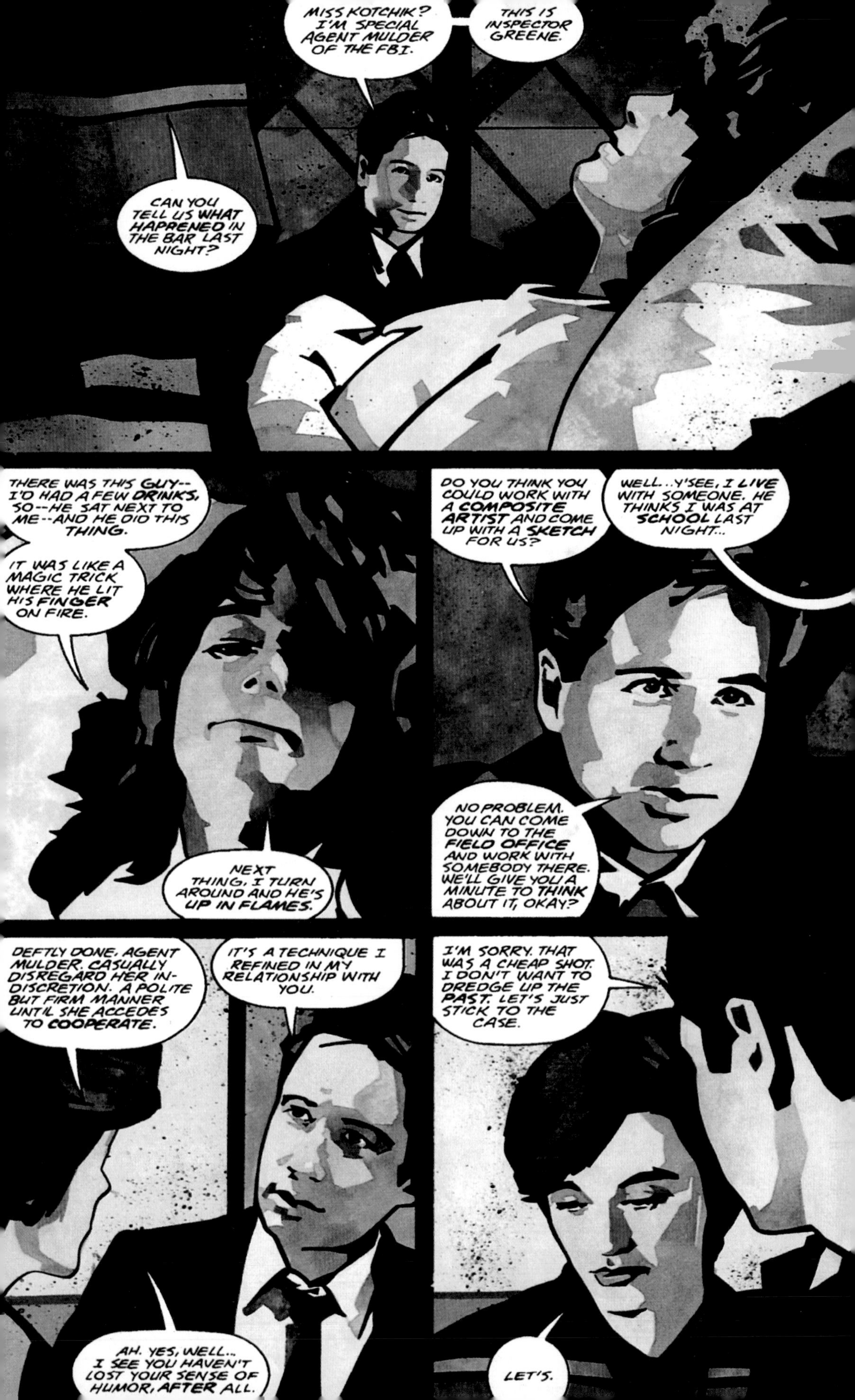
MISS KOTCHIK? I'M SPECIAL AGENT MULDER OF THE FBI.
THIS IS INSPECTOR GREENE.
CAN YOU TELL US WHAT HAPPENED IN THE BAR LAST NIGHT?
THERE WAS THIS GUY-- I'D HAD A FEW DRINKS, SO--HE SAT NEXT TO ME--AND HE DID THIS THING.
IT WAS LIKE A MAGIC TRICK WHERE HE LIT HIS FINGER ON FIRE.
NEXT THING, I TURN AROUND AND HE'S UP IN FLAMES.
DO YOU THINK YOU COULD WORK WITH A COMPOSITE ARTIST AND COME UP WITH A SKETCH FOR US?
WELL...Y'SEE, I LIVE WITH SOMEONE. HE THINKS I WAS AT SCHOOL LAST NIGHT...
NO PROBLEM. YOU CAN COME DOWN TO THE FIELD OFFICE AND WORK WITH SOMEBODY THERE. WE'LL GIVE YOU A MINUTE TO THINK ABOUT IT, OKAY?
DEFTLY DONE, AGENT MULDER. CASUALLY DISREGARD HER INDISCRETION. A POLITE BUT FIRM MANNER UNTIL SHE ACCEDES TO COOPERATE.
IT'S A TECHNIQUE I REFINED IN MY RELATIONSHIP WITH YOU.
AH. YES, WELL... I SEE YOU HAVEN'T LOST YOUR SENSE OF HUMOR, AFTER ALL.
I'M SORRY. THAT WAS A CHEAP SHOT. I DON'T WANT TO DREDGE UP THE PAST. LET'S JUST STICK TO THE CASE.
LET'S.

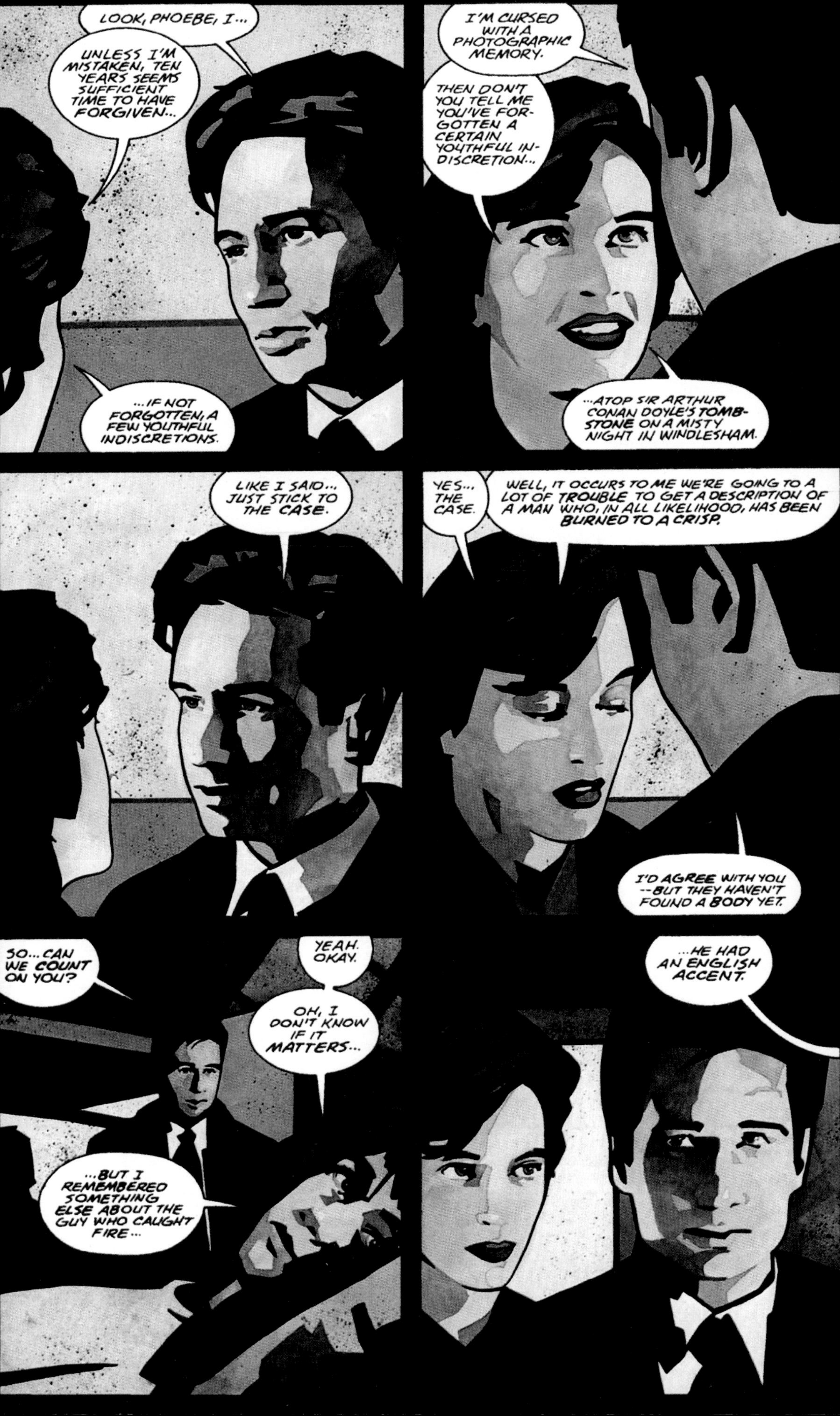
LOOK, PHOEBE, I...
UNLESS I'M MISTAKEN, TEN YEARS SEEMS SUFFICIENT TIME TO HAVE FORGIVEN...
...IF NOT FORGOTTEN, A FEW YOUTHFUL INDISCRETIONS.
I'M CURSED WITH A PHOTOGRAPHIC MEMORY.
THEN DON'T YOU TELL ME YOU'VE FORGOTTEN A CERTAIN YOUTHFUL INDISCRETION...
...ATOP SIR ARTHUR CONAN DOYLE'S TOMBSTONE ON A MISTY NIGHT IN WINDLESHAM.
LIKE I SAID... JUST STICK TO THE CASE.
YES... THE CASE.
WELL, IT OCCURS TO ME WE'RE GOING TO A LOT OF TROUBLE TO GET A DESCRIPTION OF A MAN WHO, IN ALL LIKELIHOOD, HAS BEEN BURNED TO A CRISP.
I'D AGREE WITH YOU --BUT THEY HAVEN'T FOUND A BODY YET.
SO... CAN WE COUNT ON YOU?
YEAH. OKAY.
OH, I DON'T KNOW IF IT MATTERS...
...BUT I REMEMBERED SOMETHING ELSE ABOUT THE GUY WHO CAUGHT FIRE...
...HE HAD AN ENGLISH ACCENT.

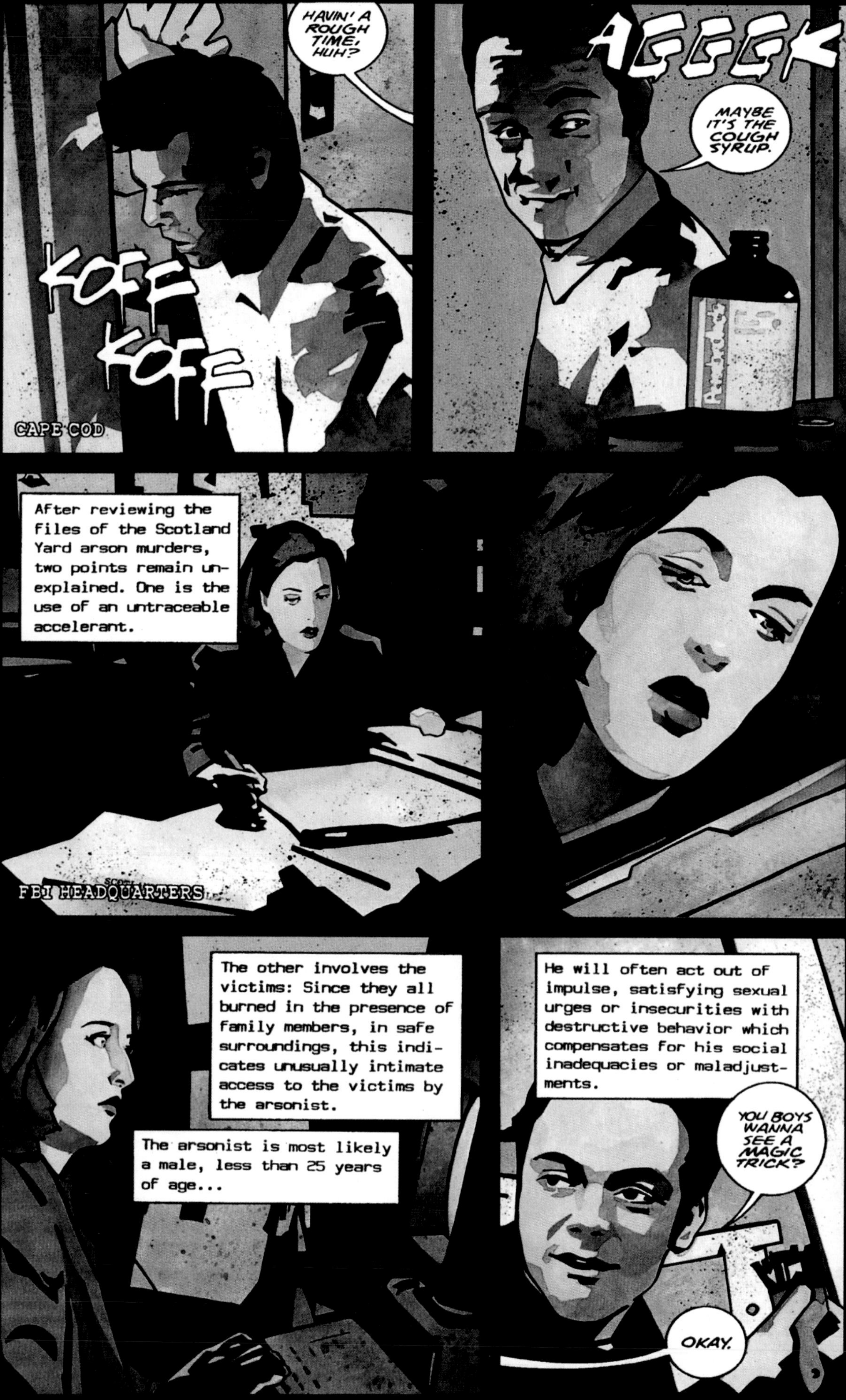
HAVIN' A ROUGH TIME, HUH?
KOFF KOFF
CAPE COD
AGGGK
MAYBE IT'S THE COUGH SYRUP.
After reviewing the files of the Scotland Yard arson murders, two points remain unexplained. One is the use of an untraceable accelerant.
FBI HEADQUARTERS
The other involves the victims: Since they all burned in the presence of family members, in safe surroundings, this indicates unusually intimate access to the victims by the arsonist.
The arsonist is most likely a male, less than 25 years of age...
He will often act out of impulse, satisfying sexual urges or insecurities with destructive behavior which compensates for his social inadequacies or maladjustments.
YOU BOYS WANNA SEE A MAGIC TRICK?
OKAY.

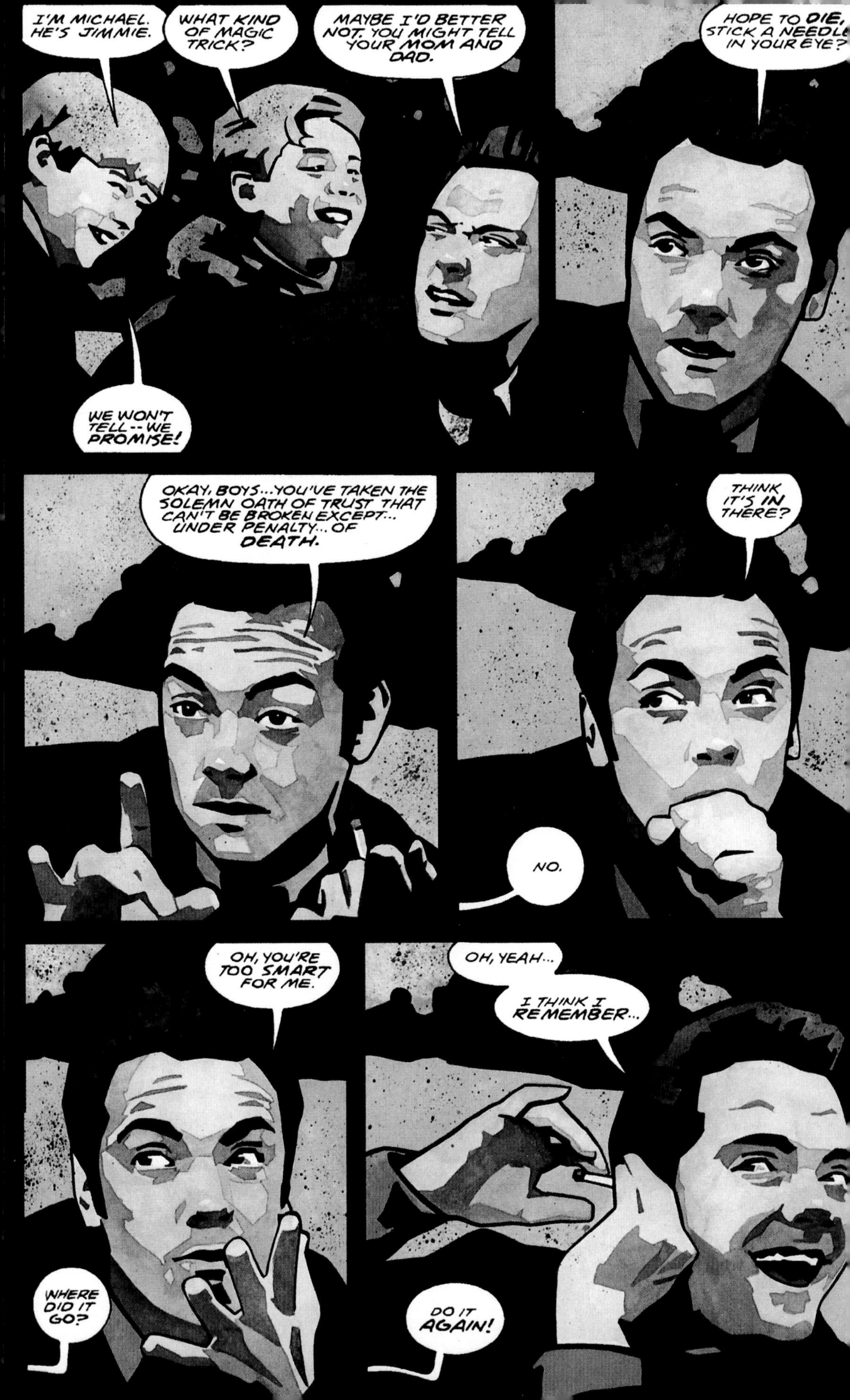
I'M MICHAEL. HE'S JIMMIE.
WHAT KIND OF MAGIC TRICK?
MAYBE I'D BETTER NOT. YOU MIGHT TELL YOUR MOM AND DAD.
WE WON'T TELL -- WE PROMISE!
HOPE TO DIE, STICK A NEEDLE IN YOUR EYE?
OKAY, BOYS... YOU'VE TAKEN THE SOLEMN OATH OF TRUST THAT CAN'T BE BROKEN EXCEPT... UNDER PENALTY... OF DEATH.
THINK IT'S IN THERE?
NO.
OH, YOU'RE TOO SMART FOR ME.
WHERE DID IT GO?
OH, YEAH...
I THINK I REMEMBER...
DO IT AGAIN!

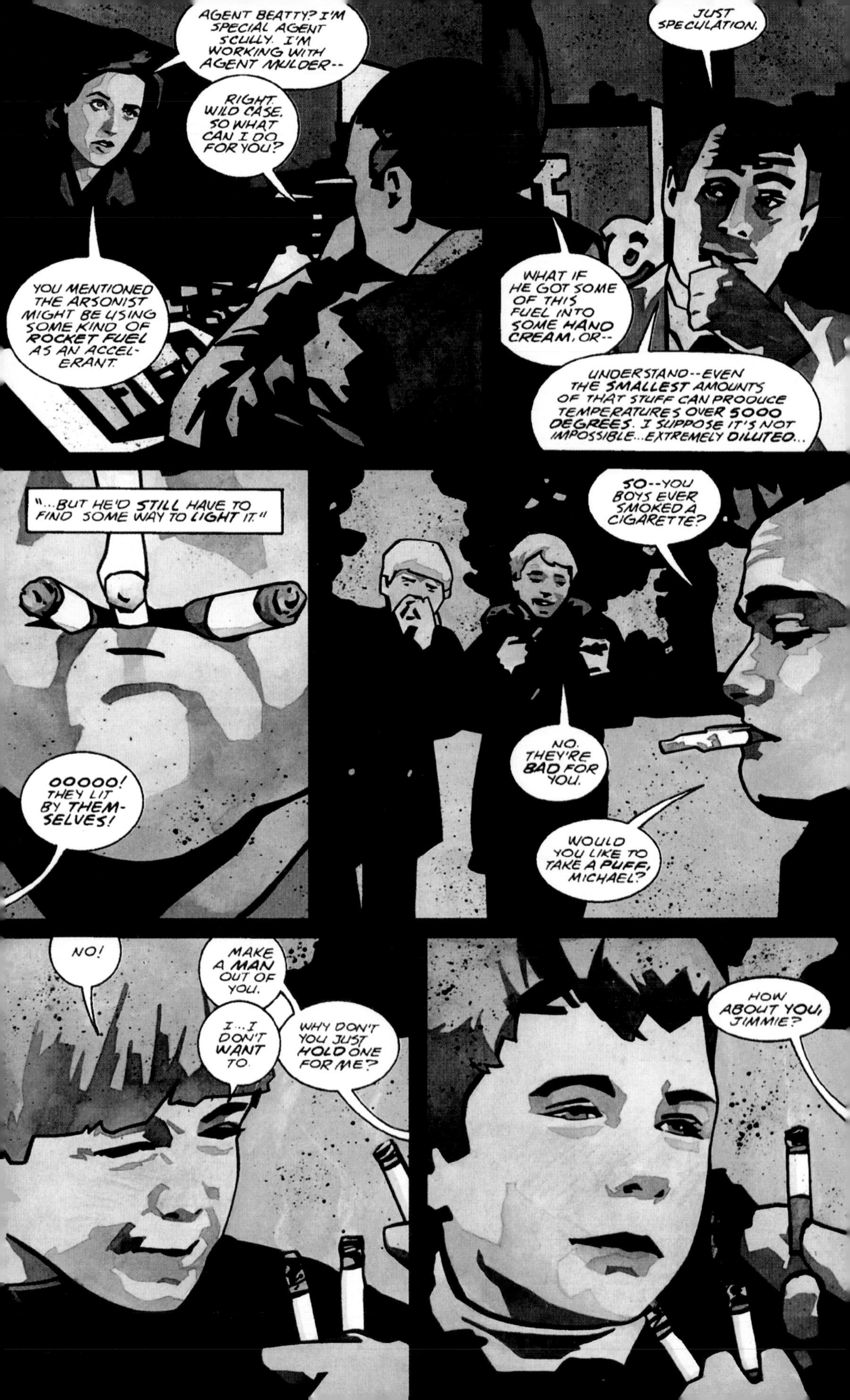
AGENT BEATTY? I'M SPECIAL AGENT SCULLY. I'M WORKING WITH AGENT MULDER--
RIGHT. WILD CASE. SO WHAT CAN I DO FOR YOU?
YOU MENTIONED THE ARSONIST MIGHT BE USING SOME KIND OF ROCKET FUEL AS AN ACCEL-ERANT.
JUST SPECULATION.
WHAT IF HE GOT SOME OF THIS FUEL INTO SOME HAND CREAM, OR--
UNDERSTAND--EVEN THE SMALLEST AMOUNTS OF THAT STUFF CAN PRODUCE TEMPERATURES OVER 5000 DEGREES. I SUPPOSE IT'S NOT IMPOSSIBLE...EXTREMELY DILUTED...
"...BUT HE'D STILL HAVE TO FIND SOME WAY TO LIGHT IT."
OOOOO! THEY LIT BY THEM-SELVES!
SO--YOU BOYS EVER SMOKED A CIGARETTE?
NO. THEY'RE BAD FOR YOU.
WOULD YOU LIKE TO TAKE A PUFF, MICHAEL?
NO!
MAKE A MAN OUT OF YOU.
I...I DON'T WANT TO.
WHY DON'T YOU JUST HOLD ONE FOR ME?
HOW ABOUT YOU, JIMMIE?

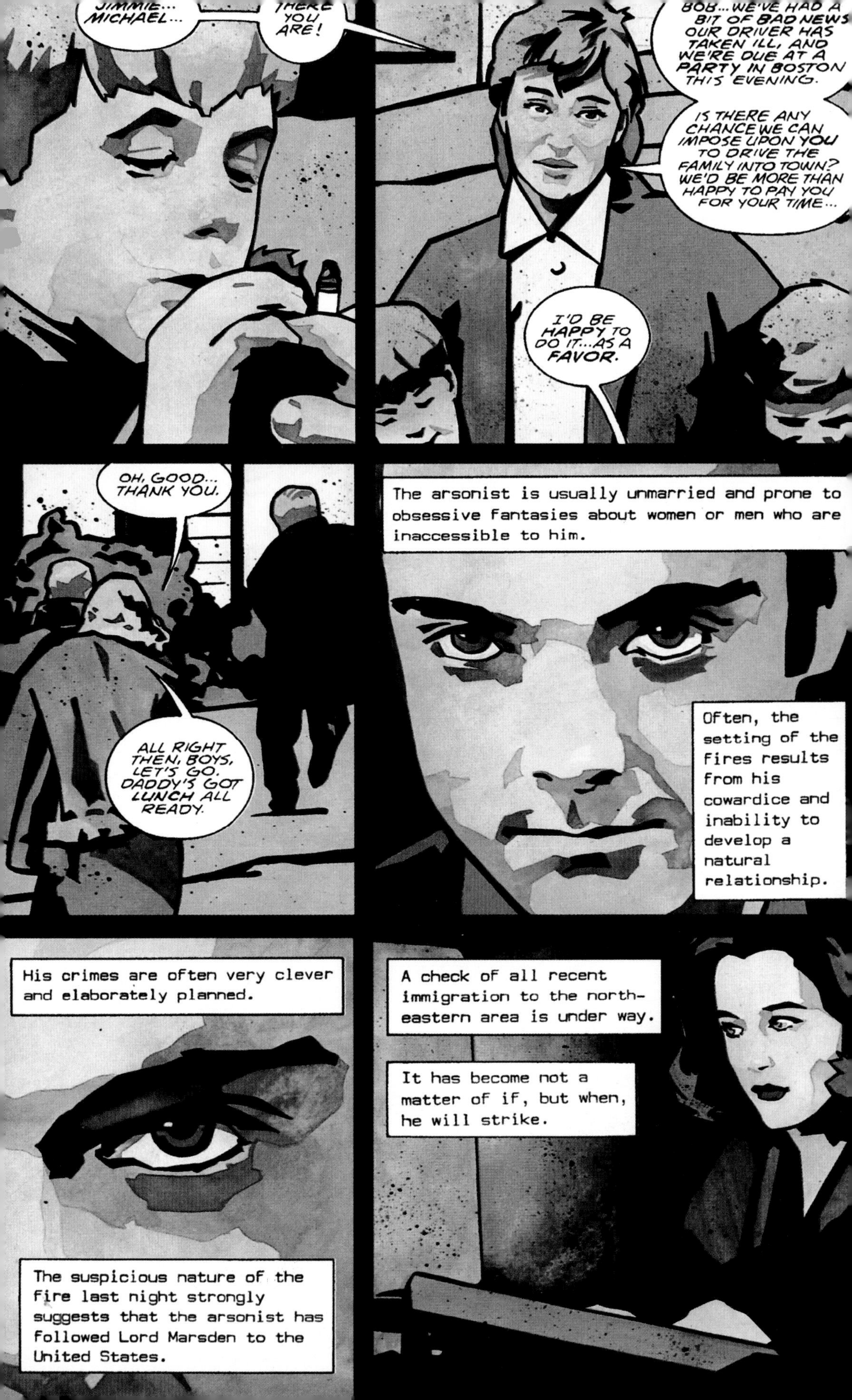
JIMMIE... MICHAEL...
THERE YOU ARE!
BOB... WE'VE HAD A BIT OF BAD NEWS. OUR DRIVER HAS TAKEN ILL, AND WE'RE DUE AT A PARTY IN BOSTON THIS EVENING.
IS THERE ANY CHANCE WE CAN IMPOSE UPON YOU TO DRIVE THE FAMILY INTO TOWN? WE'D BE MORE THAN HAPPY TO PAY YOU FOR YOUR TIME...
I'D BE HAPPY TO DO IT... AS A FAVOR.
OH, GOOD... THANK YOU.
ALL RIGHT THEN, BOYS, LET'S GO. DADDY'S GOT LUNCH ALL READY.
The arsonist is usually unmarried and prone to obsessive fantasies about women or men who are inaccessible to him.
Often, the setting of the fires results from his cowardice and inability to develop a natural relationship.
His crimes are often very clever and elaborately planned.
The suspicious nature of the fire last night strongly suggests that the arsonist has followed Lord Marsden to the United States.
A check of all recent immigration to the north-eastern area is under way.
It has become not a matter of if, but when, he will strike.

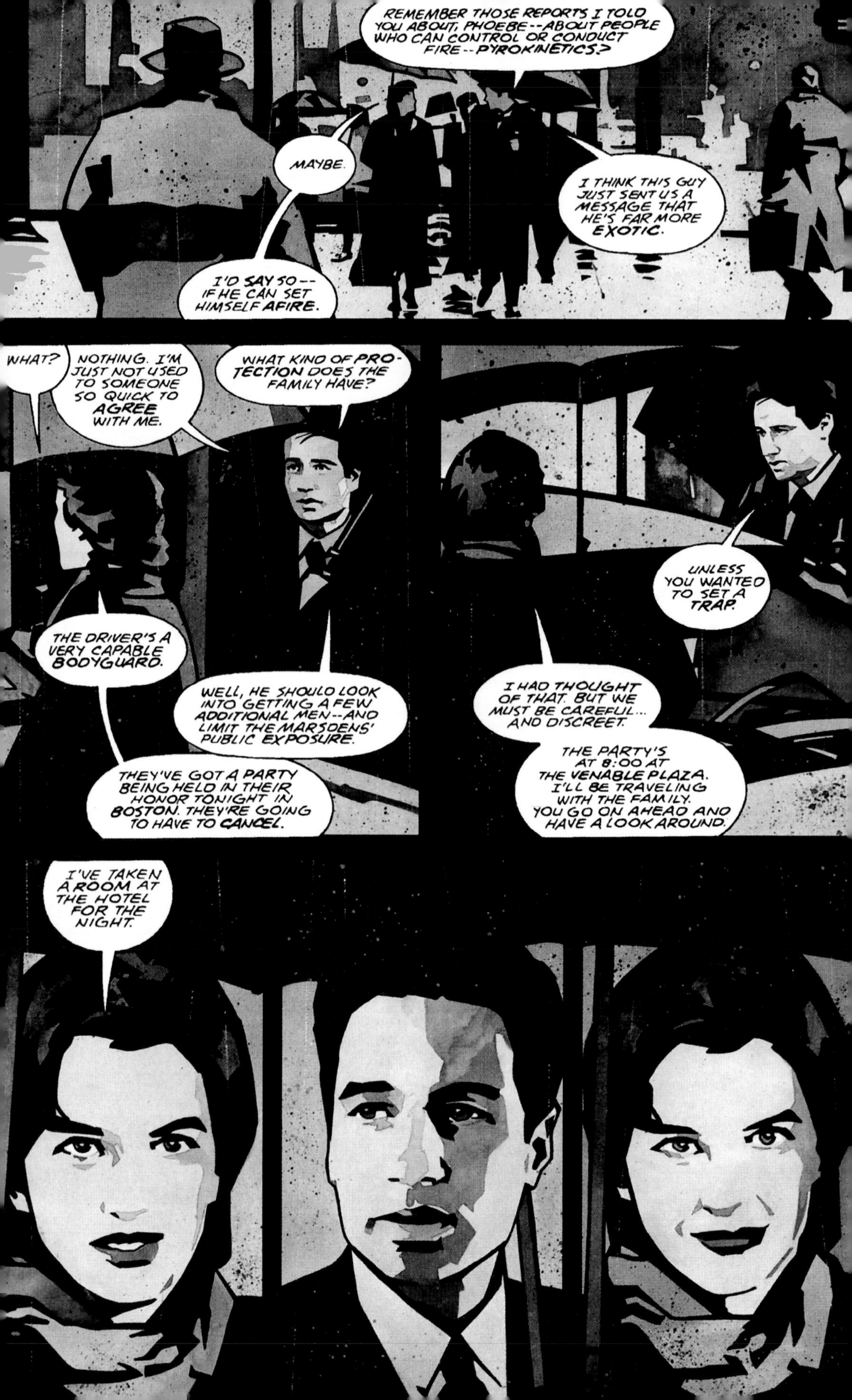
REMEMBER THOSE REPORTS I TOLD YOU ABOUT, PHOEBE--ABOUT PEOPLE WHO CAN CONTROL OR CONDUCT FIRE--PYROKINETICS?
MAYBE.
I THINK THIS GUY JUST SENT US A MESSAGE THAT HE'S FAR MORE EXOTIC.
I'D SAY SO-- IF HE CAN SET HIMSELF AFIRE.
WHAT?
NOTHING. I'M JUST NOT USED TO SOMEONE SO QUICK TO AGREE WITH ME.
WHAT KIND OF PROTECTION DOES THE FAMILY HAVE?
THE DRIVER'S A VERY CAPABLE BODYGUARD.
WELL, HE SHOULD LOOK INTO GETTING A FEW ADDITIONAL MEN--AND LIMIT THE MARSDENS' PUBLIC EXPOSURE.
THEY'VE GOT A PARTY BEING HELD IN THEIR HONOR TONIGHT IN BOSTON. THEY'RE GOING TO HAVE TO CANCEL.
UNLESS YOU WANTED TO SET A TRAP.
I HAD THOUGHT OF THAT. BUT WE MUST BE CAREFUL... AND DISCREET.
THE PARTY'S AT 8:00 AT THE VENABLE PLAZA. I'LL BE TRAVELING WITH THE FAMILY. YOU GO ON AHEAD AND HAVE A LOOK AROUND.
I'VE TAKEN A ROOM AT THE HOTEL FOR THE NIGHT.

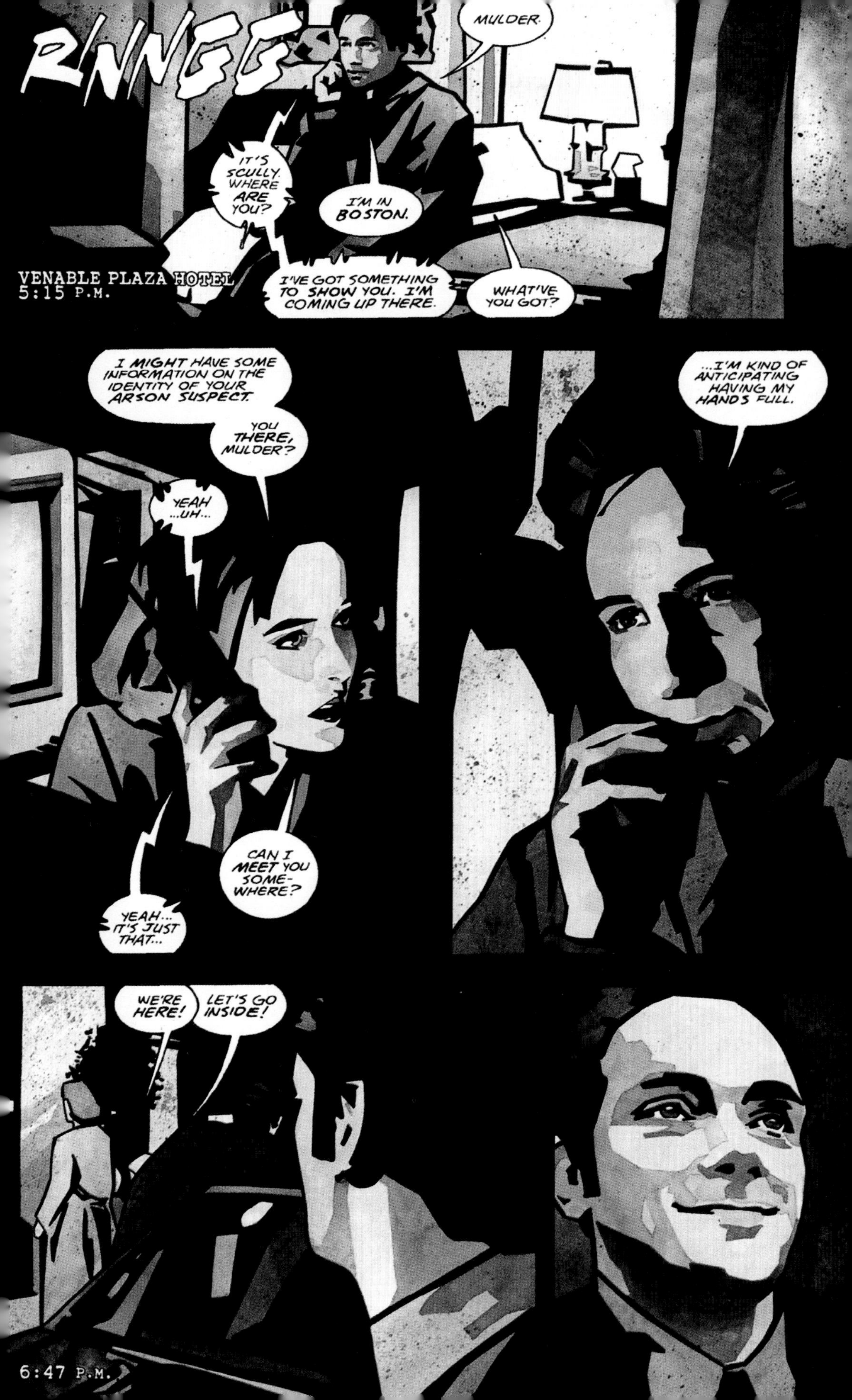
RINNGG
MULDER.
IT'S SCULLY. WHERE ARE YOU?
I'M IN BOSTON.
VENABLE PLAZA HOTEL
5:15 P.M.
I'VE GOT SOMETHING TO SHOW YOU. I'M COMING UP THERE.
WHAT'VE YOU GOT?
I MIGHT HAVE SOME INFORMATION ON THE IDENTITY OF YOUR ARSON SUSPECT.
YOU THERE, MULDER?
YEAH ...UH...
CAN I MEET YOU SOME-WHERE?
YEAH... IT'S JUST THAT...
...I'M KIND OF ANTICIPATING HAVING MY HANDS FULL.
WE'RE HERE!
LET'S GO INSIDE!
6:47 P.M.

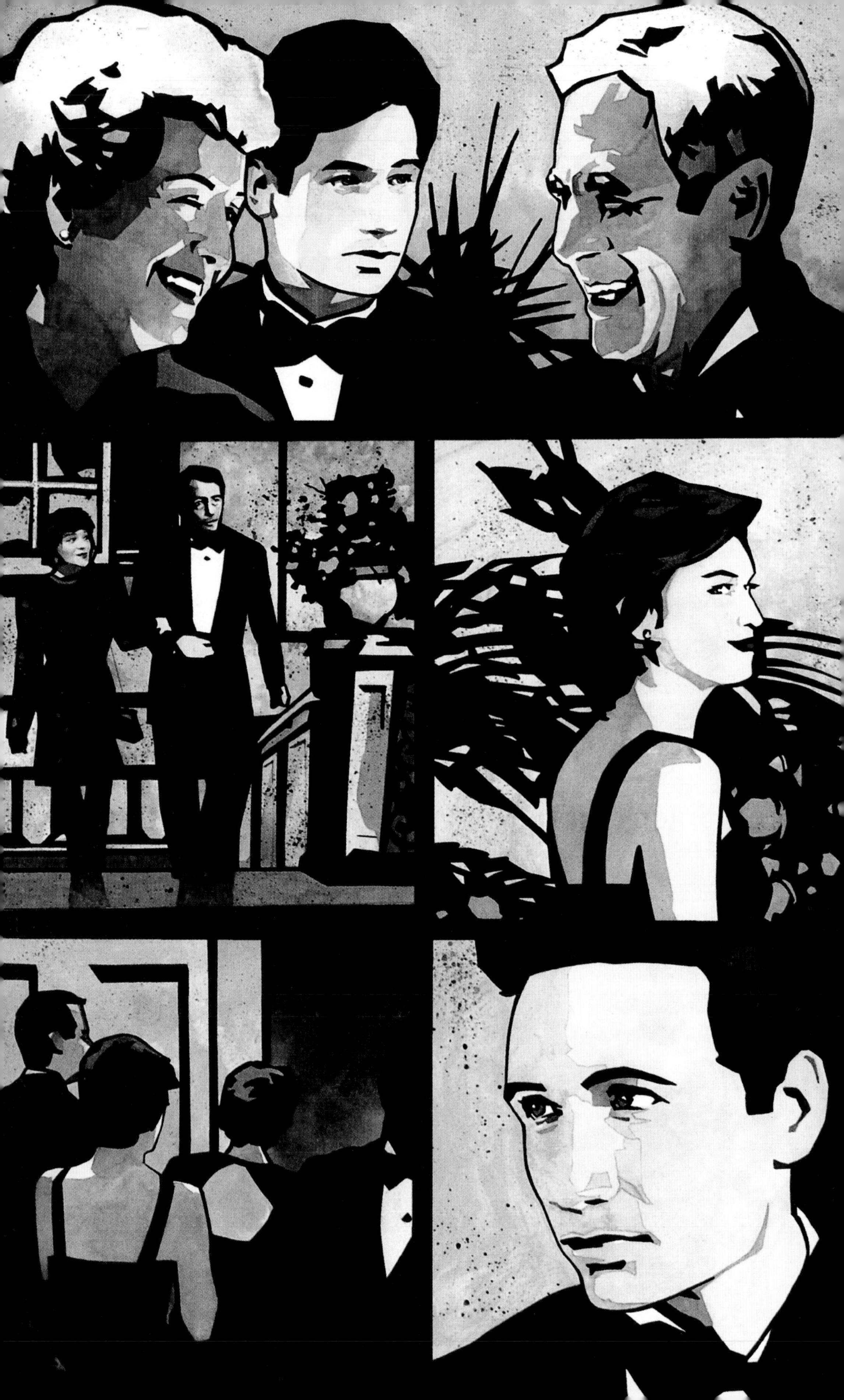

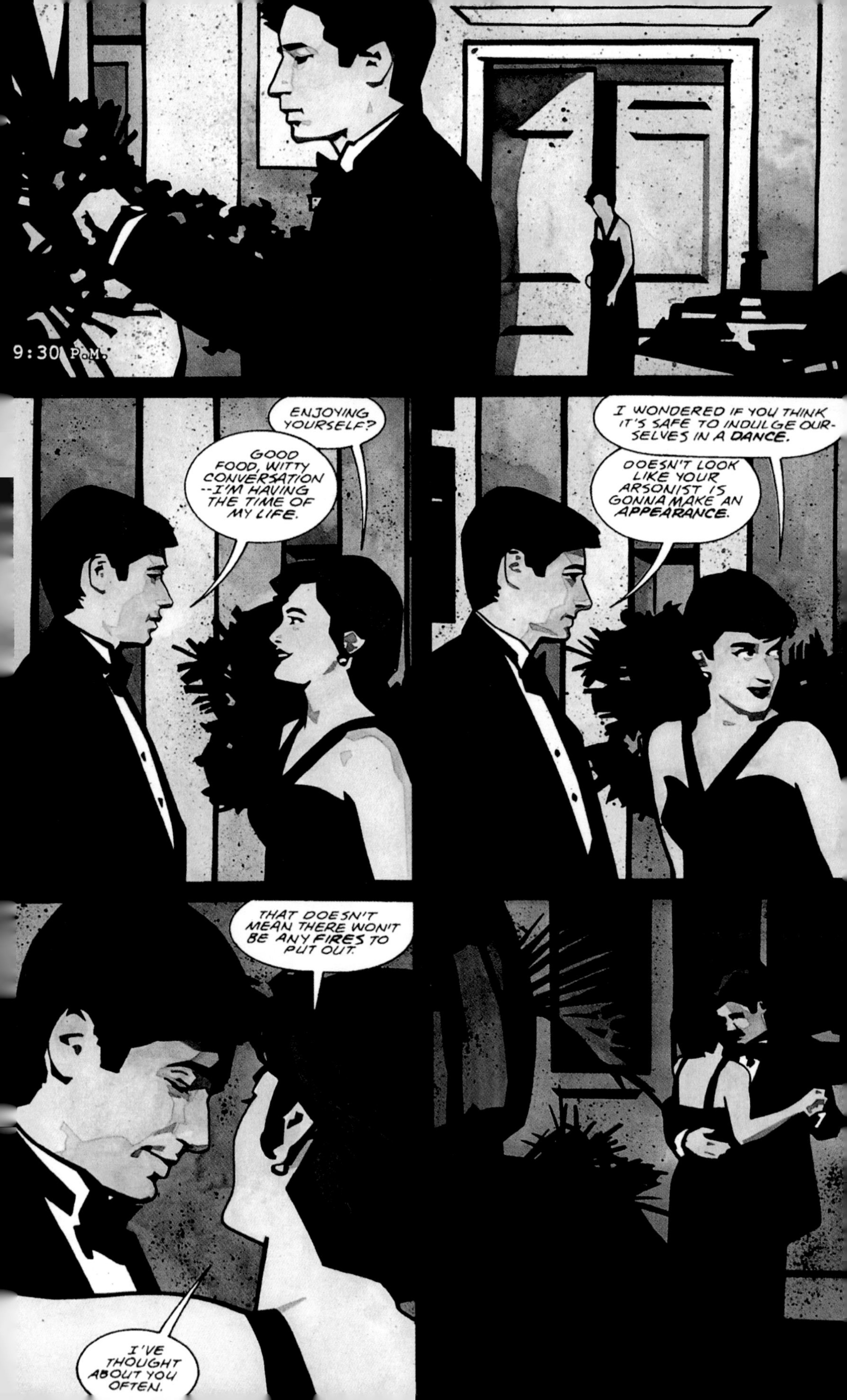
9:30 P.M.
ENJOYING YOURSELF?
GOOD FOOD, WITTY CONVERSATION --I'M HAVING THE TIME OF MY LIFE.
I WONDERED IF YOU THINK IT'S SAFE TO INDULGE OURSELVES IN A DANCE.
DOESN'T LOOK LIKE YOUR ARSONIST IS GONNA MAKE AN APPEARANCE.
THAT DOESN'T MEAN THERE WON'T BE ANY FIRES TO PUT OUT.
I'VE THOUGHT ABOUT YOU OFTEN.

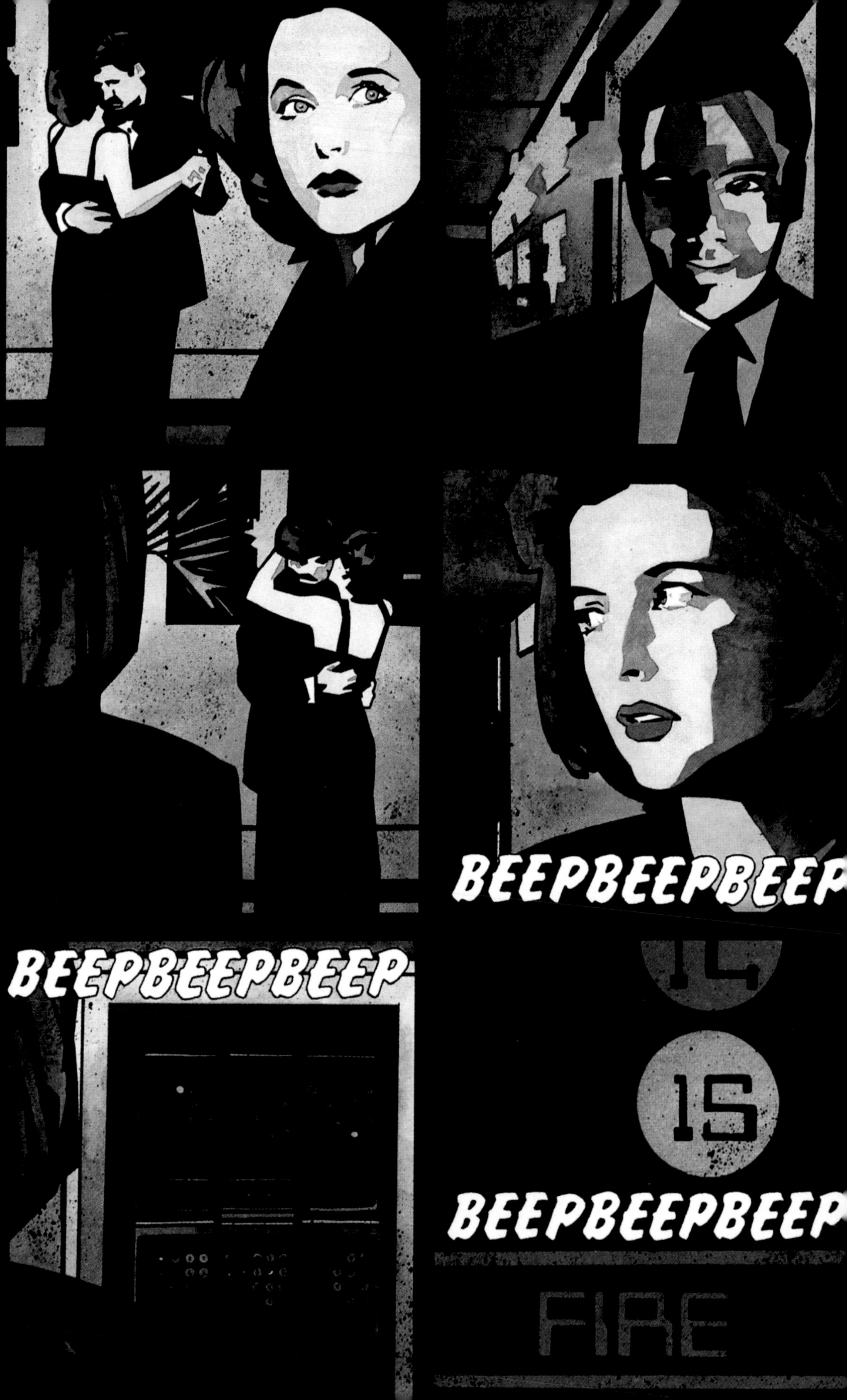
BEEPBEEPBEEP
BEEPBEEPBEEP
15
BEEPBEEPBEEP
FIRE

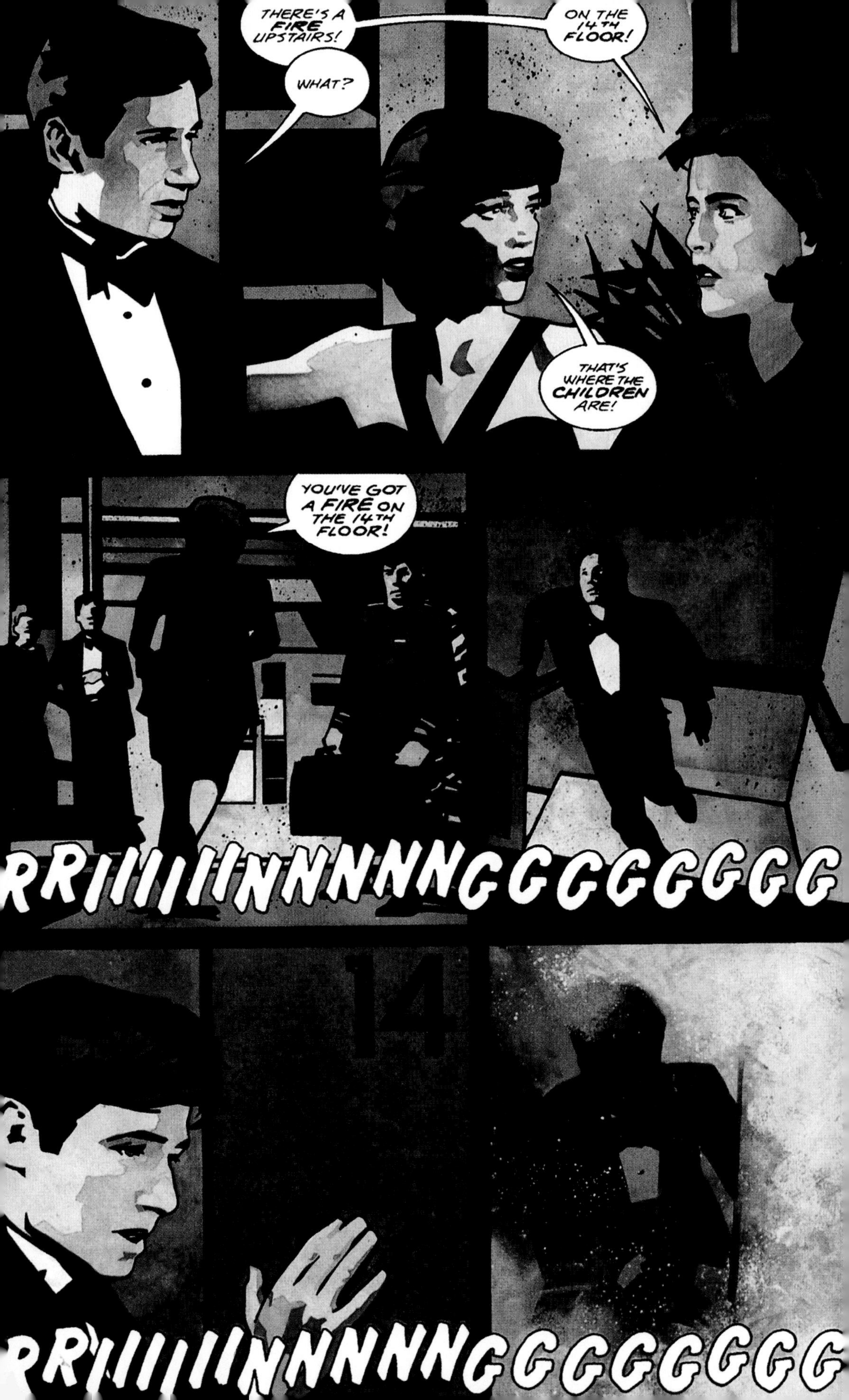
THERE'S A FIRE UPSTAIRS!
WHAT?
ON THE 14TH FLOOR!
THAT'S WHERE THE CHILDREN ARE!
YOU'VE GOT A FIRE ON THE 14TH FLOOR!
RRIIIIIINNNNNGGGGGGGG
14
RRIIIIIINNNNNGGGGGGGG

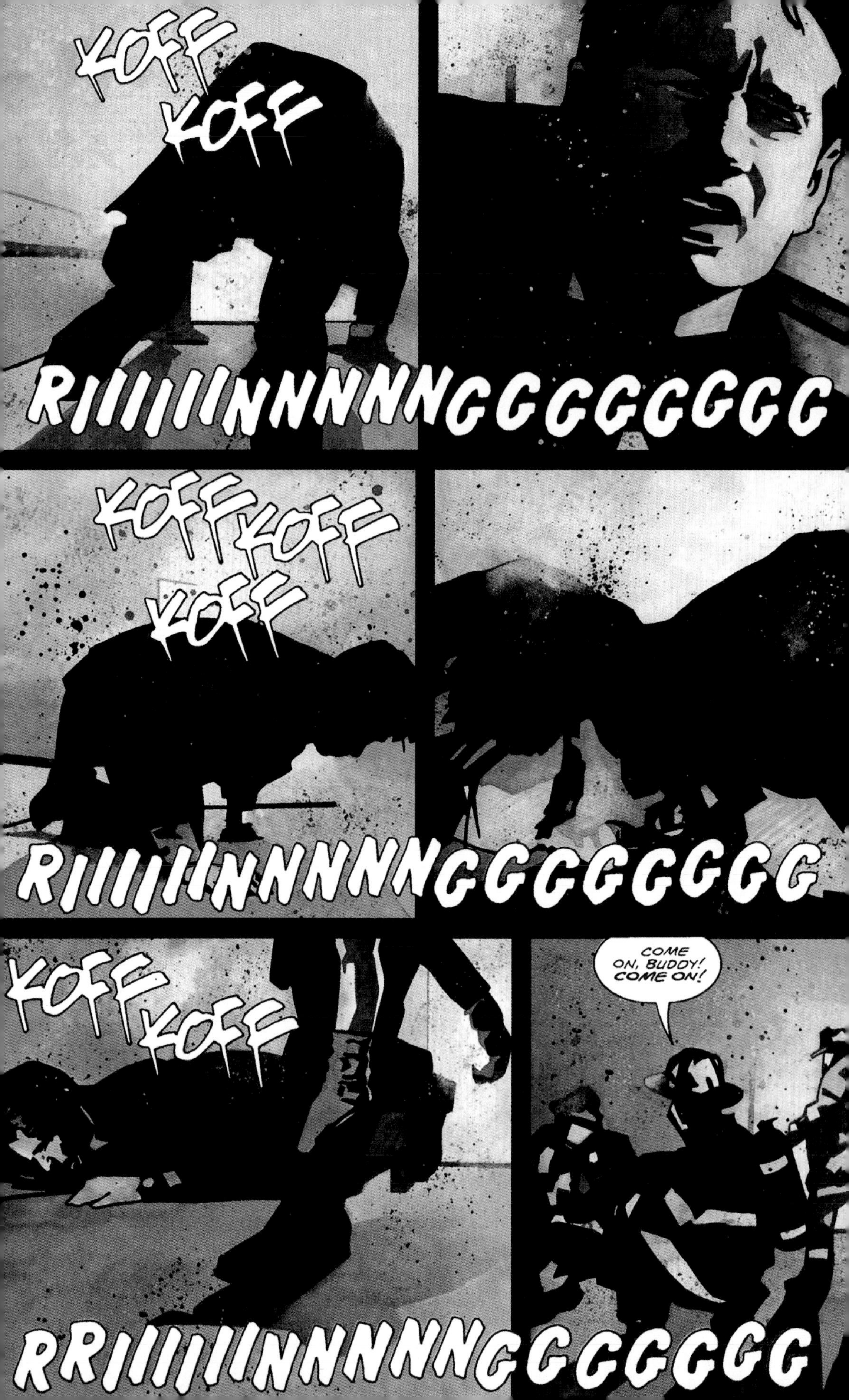
KOFF
KOFF
RIIIIIINNNNNGGGGGGGG
KOFF
KOFF
KOFF
RIIIIIINNNNNGGGGGGGG
KOFF
KOFF
COME ON, BUDDY! COME ON!
RRIIIIIINNNNNGGGGGGG

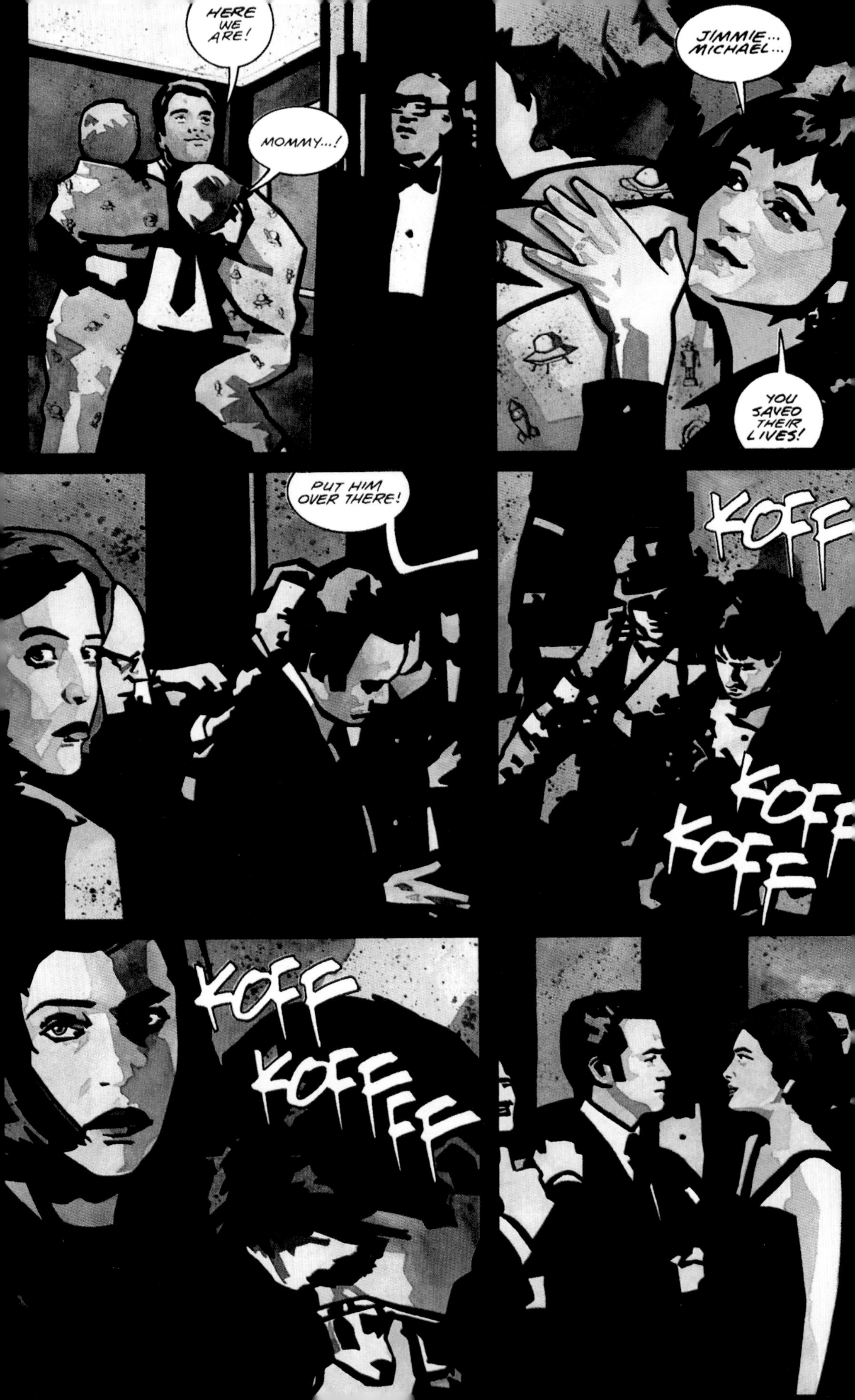
HERE WE ARE!
MOMMY...!
JIMMIE... MICHAEL...
YOU SAVED THEIR LIVES!
PUT HIM OVER THERE!
KOFF
KOFF
KOFF
KOFF
KOFFFF

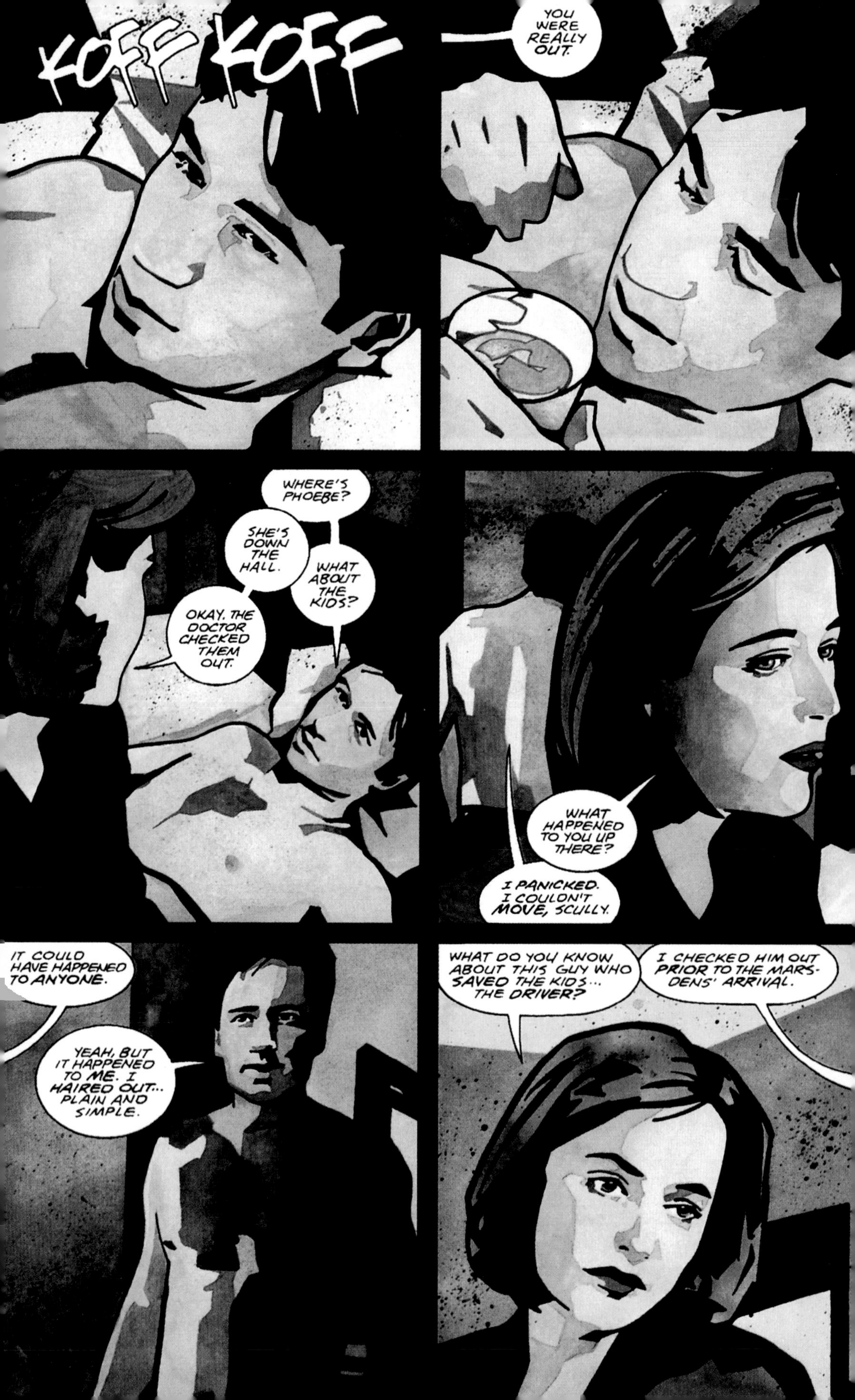
KOFF KOFF
YOU WERE REALLY OUT.
WHERE'S PHOEBE?
SHE'S DOWN THE HALL.
WHAT ABOUT THE KIDS?
OKAY. THE DOCTOR CHECKED THEM OUT.
WHAT HAPPENED TO YOU UP THERE?
I PANICKED. I COULDN'T MOVE, SCULLY.
IT COULD HAVE HAPPENED TO ANYONE.
YEAH, BUT IT HAPPENED TO ME. I HAIRED OUT... PLAIN AND SIMPLE.
WHAT DO YOU KNOW ABOUT THIS GUY WHO SAVED THE KIDS... THE DRIVER?
I CHECKED HIM OUT PRIOR TO THE MARS-DENS' ARRIVAL.

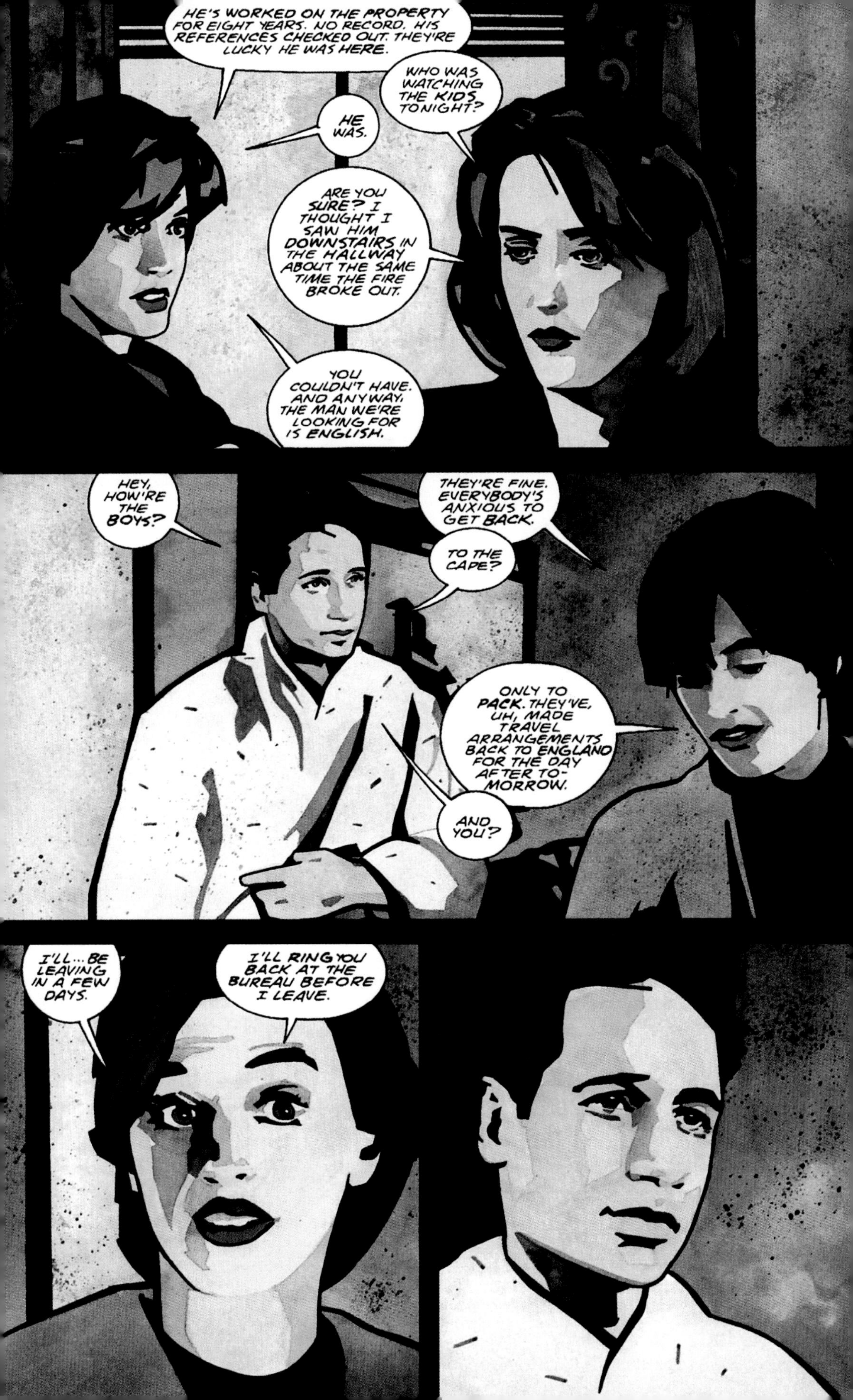
HE'S WORKED ON THE PROPERTY FOR EIGHT YEARS. NO RECORD. HIS REFERENCES CHECKED OUT. THEY'RE LUCKY HE WAS HERE.
WHO WAS WATCHING THE KIDS TONIGHT?
HE WAS.
ARE YOU SURE? I THOUGHT I SAW HIM DOWNSTAIRS IN THE HALLWAY ABOUT THE SAME TIME THE FIRE BROKE OUT.
YOU COULDN'T HAVE. AND ANYWAY, THE MAN WE'RE LOOKING FOR IS ENGLISH.
HEY, HOW'RE THE BOYS?
THEY'RE FINE. EVERYBODY'S ANXIOUS TO GET BACK.
TO THE CAPE?
ONLY TO PACK. THEY'VE, UH, MADE TRAVEL ARRANGEMENTS BACK TO ENGLAND FOR THE DAY AFTER TO-MORROW.
AND YOU?
I'LL... BE LEAVING IN A FEW DAYS.
I'LL RING YOU BACK AT THE BUREAU BEFORE I LEAVE.

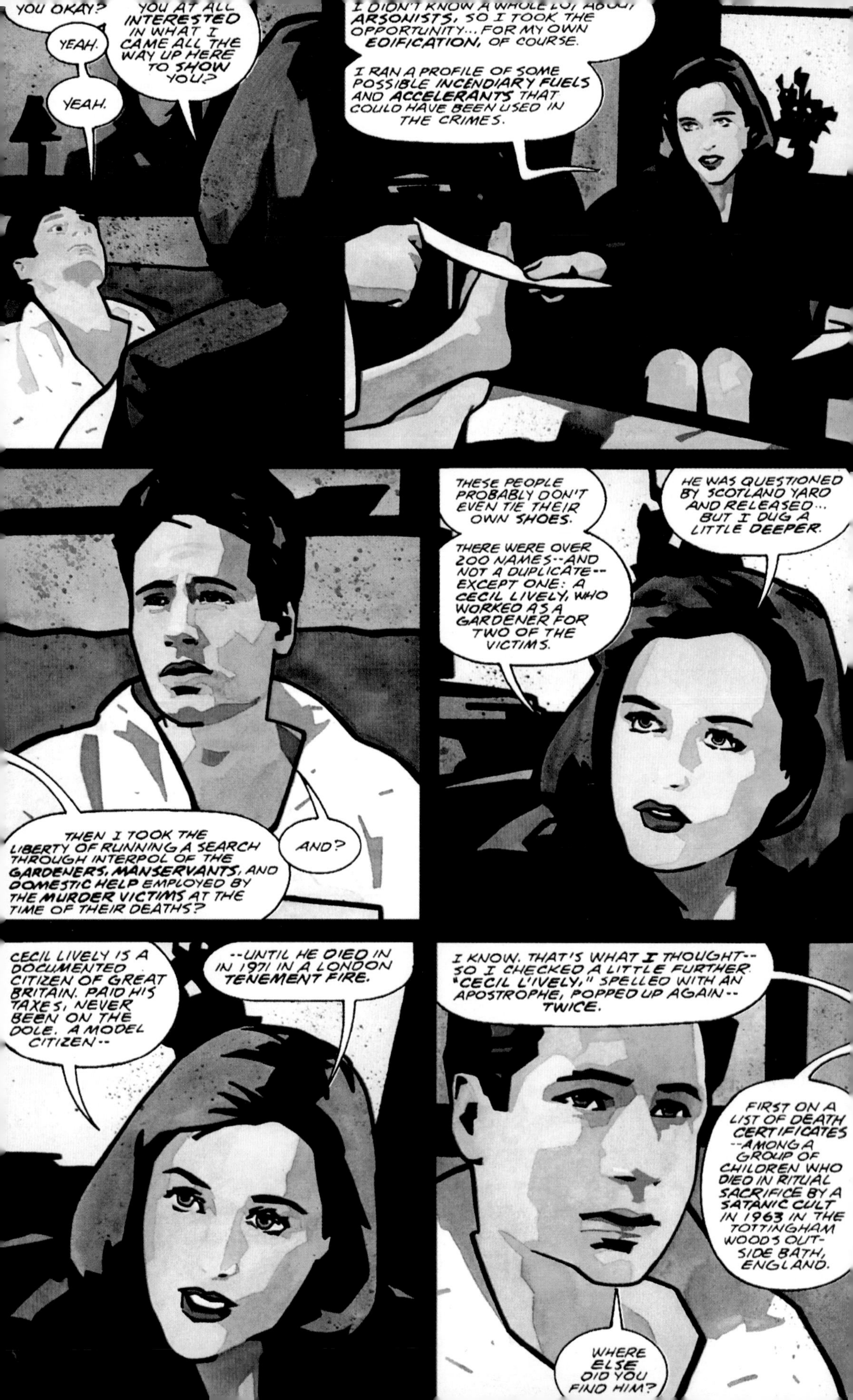
YOU OKAY?
YOU AT ALL INTERESTED IN WHAT I CAME ALL THE WAY UP HERE TO SHOW YOU?
YEAH.
YEAH.
I DIDN'T KNOW A WHOLE LOT ABOUT ARSONISTS, SO I TOOK THE OPPORTUNITY... FOR MY OWN EDIFICATION, OF COURSE.
I RAN A PROFILE OF SOME POSSIBLE INCENDIARY FUELS AND ACCELERANTS THAT COULD HAVE BEEN USED IN THE CRIMES.
THEN I TOOK THE LIBERTY OF RUNNING A SEARCH THROUGH INTERPOL OF THE GARDENERS, MANSERVANTS, AND DOMESTIC HELP EMPLOYED BY THE MURDER VICTIMS AT THE TIME OF THEIR DEATHS?
AND?
THESE PEOPLE PROBABLY DON'T EVEN TIE THEIR OWN SHOES.
THERE WERE OVER 200 NAMES--AND NOT A DUPLICATE--EXCEPT ONE: A CECIL LIVELY, WHO WORKED AS A GARDENER FOR TWO OF THE VICTIMS.
HE WAS QUESTIONED BY SCOTLAND YARD AND RELEASED... BUT I DUG A LITTLE DEEPER.
CECIL LIVELY IS A DOCUMENTED CITIZEN OF GREAT BRITAIN. PAID HIS TAXES, NEVER BEEN ON THE DOLE. A MODEL CITIZEN--
--UNTIL HE DIED IN IN 1971 IN A LONDON TENEMENT FIRE.
I KNOW. THAT'S WHAT I THOUGHT--SO I CHECKED A LITTLE FURTHER. "CECIL L'IVELY," SPELLED WITH AN APOSTROPHE, POPPED UP AGAIN--TWICE.
FIRST ON A LIST OF DEATH CERTIFICATES --AMONG A GROUP OF CHILDREN WHO DIED IN RITUAL SACRIFICE BY A SATANIC CULT IN 1963 IN THE TOTTINGHAM WOODS OUTSIDE BATH, ENGLAND.
WHERE ELSE DID YOU FIND HIM?

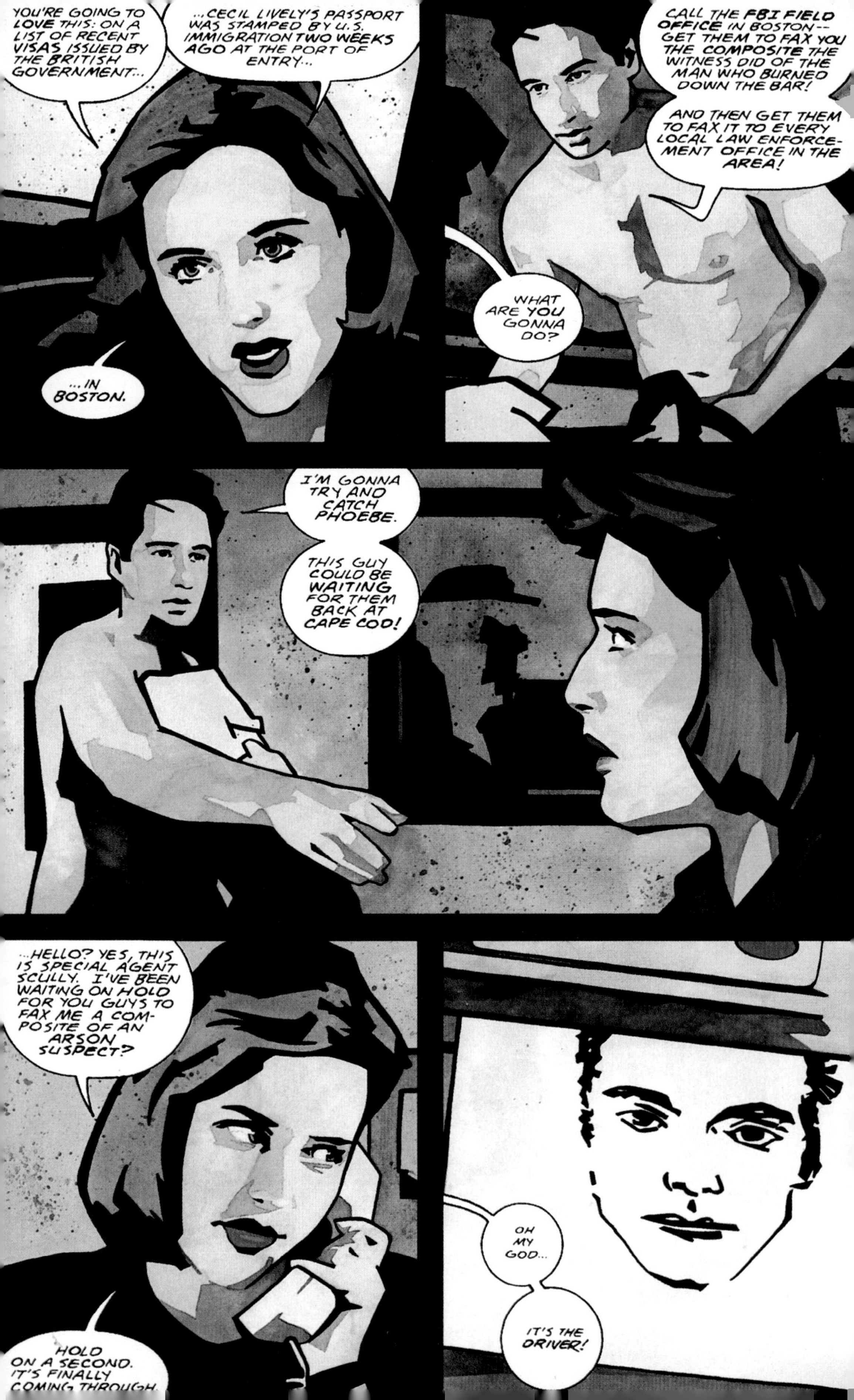
YOU'RE GOING TO LOVE THIS: ON A LIST OF RECENT VISAS ISSUED BY THE BRITISH GOVERNMENT...
...CECIL LIVELY'S PASSPORT WAS STAMPED BY U.S. IMMIGRATION TWO WEEKS AGO AT THE PORT OF ENTRY...
...IN BOSTON.
CALL THE FBI FIELD OFFICE IN BOSTON--GET THEM TO FAX YOU THE COMPOSITE THE WITNESS DID OF THE MAN WHO BURNED DOWN THE BAR!
AND THEN GET THEM TO FAX IT TO EVERY LOCAL LAW ENFORCEMENT OFFICE IN THE AREA!
WHAT ARE YOU GONNA DO?
I'M GONNA TRY AND CATCH PHOEBE.
THIS GUY COULD BE WAITING FOR THEM BACK AT CAPE COD!
...HELLO? YES, THIS IS SPECIAL AGENT SCULLY. I'VE BEEN WAITING ON HOLD FOR YOU GUYS TO FAX ME A COMPOSITE OF AN ARSON SUSPECT?
HOLD ON A SECOND. IT'S FINALLY COMING THROUGH.
OH MY GOD...
IT'S THE DRIVER!

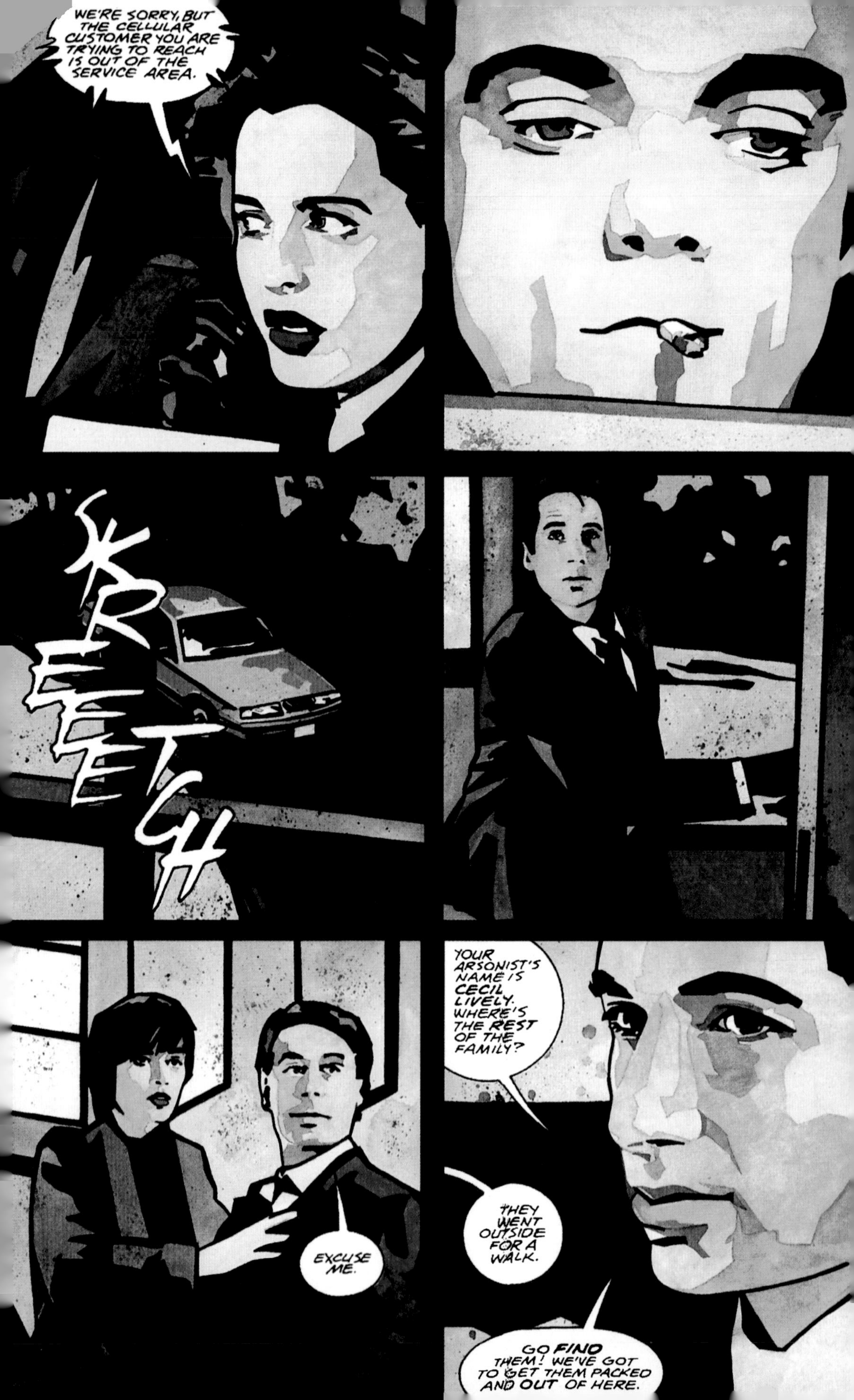
WE'RE SORRY, BUT THE CELLULAR CUSTOMER YOU ARE TRYING TO REACH IS OUT OF THE SERVICE AREA.
SKREEETCH
EXCUSE ME.
YOUR ARSONIST'S NAME IS CECIL LIVELY. WHERE'S THE REST OF THE FAMILY?
THEY WENT OUTSIDE FOR A WALK.
GO FIND THEM! WE'VE GOT TO GET THEM PACKED AND OUT OF HERE.

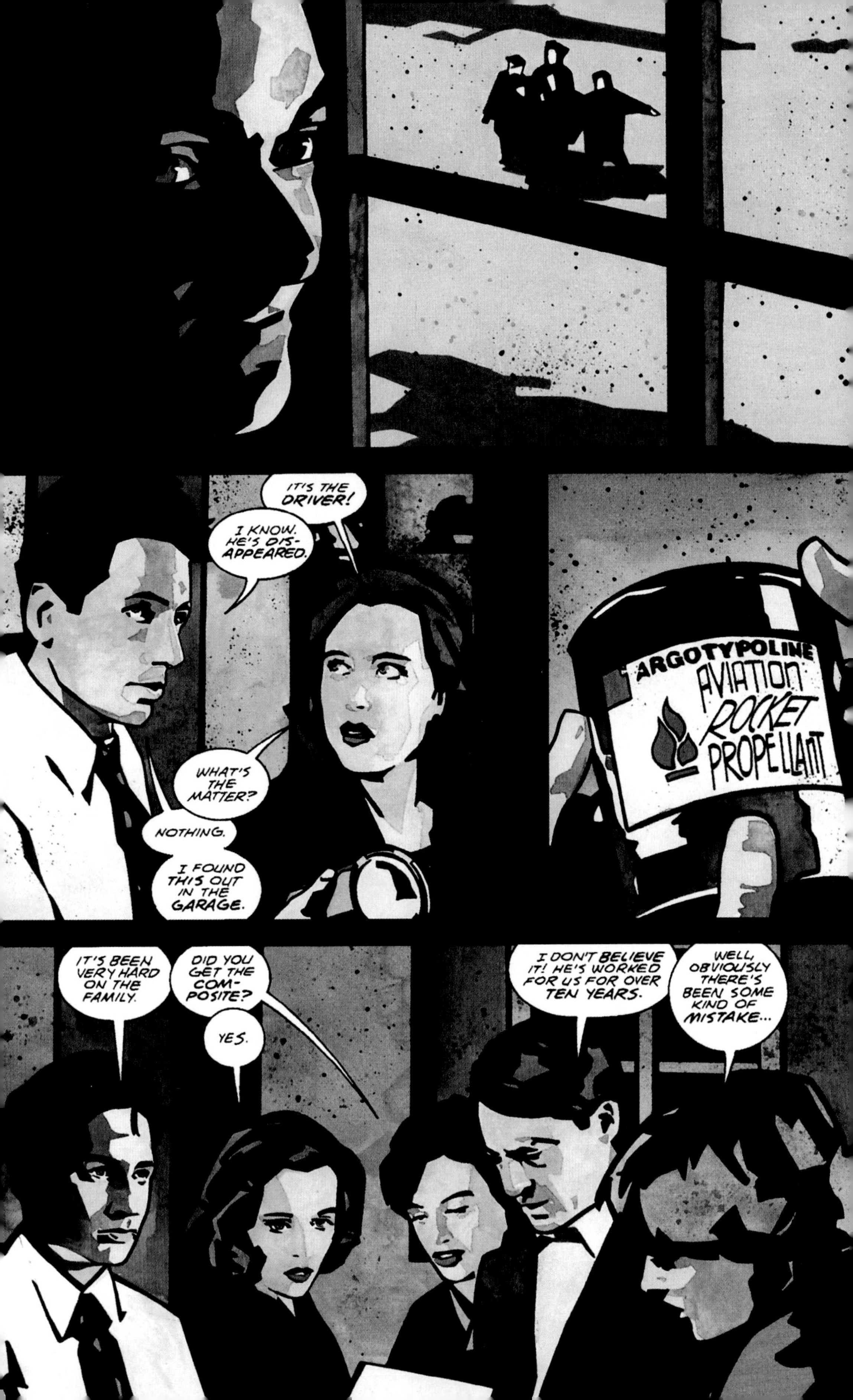
IT'S THE DRIVER!
I KNOW. HE'S DIS-APPEARED.
WHAT'S THE MATTER?
NOTHING.
I FOUND THIS OUT IN THE GARAGE.
ARGOTYPOLINE AVIATION ROCKET PROPELLANT
IT'S BEEN VERY HARD ON THE FAMILY.
DID YOU GET THE COM-POSITE?
YES.
I DON'T BELIEVE IT! HE'S WORKED FOR US FOR OVER TEN YEARS.
WELL, OBVIOUSLY THERE'S BEEN SOME KIND OF MISTAKE...

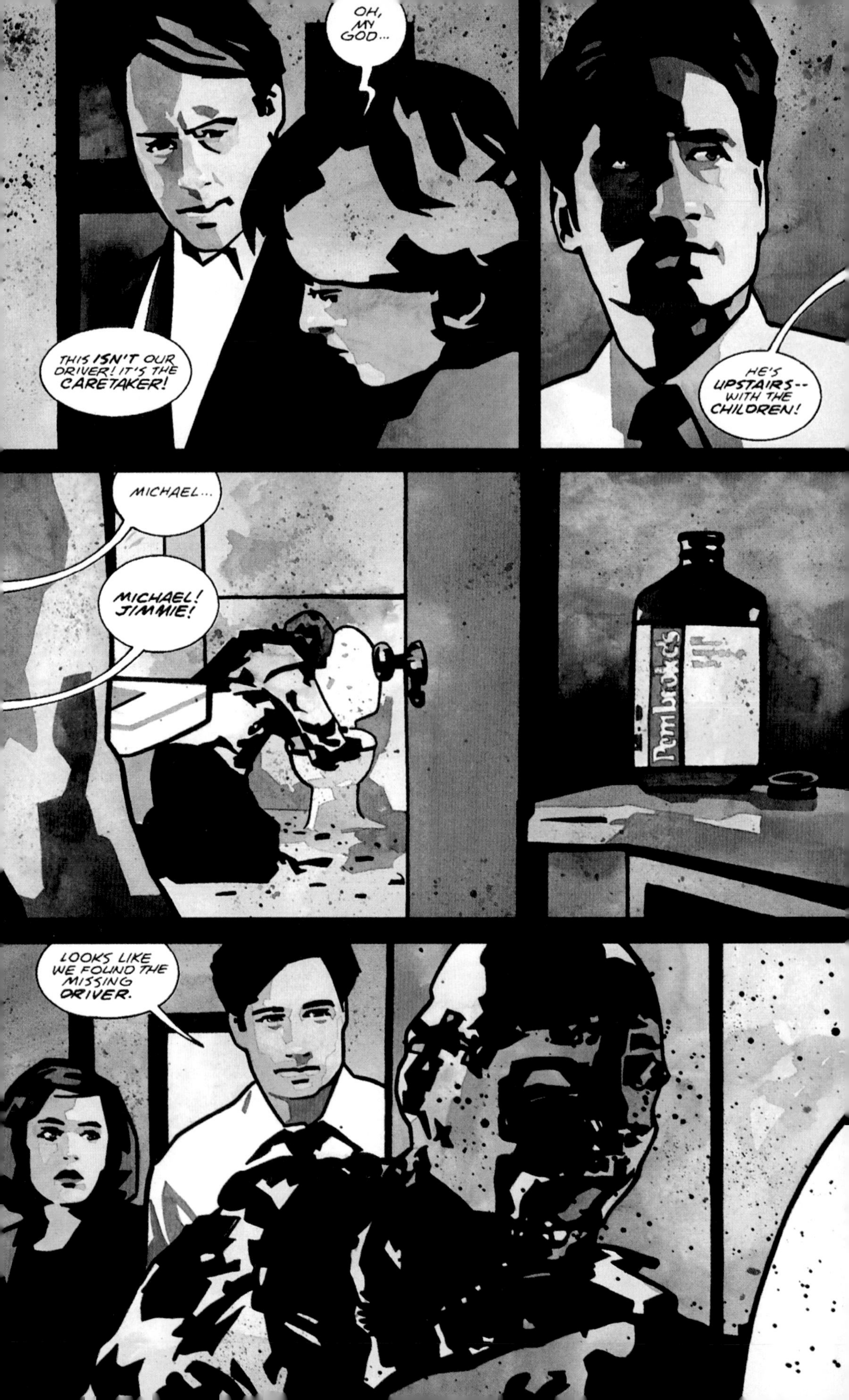
OH, MY GOD...
THIS ISN'T OUR DRIVER! IT'S THE CARETAKER!
HE'S UPSTAIRS-- WITH THE CHILDREN!
MICHAEL...
MICHAEL! JIMMIE!
Pembroke's
LOOKS LIKE WE FOUND THE MISSING DRIVER.

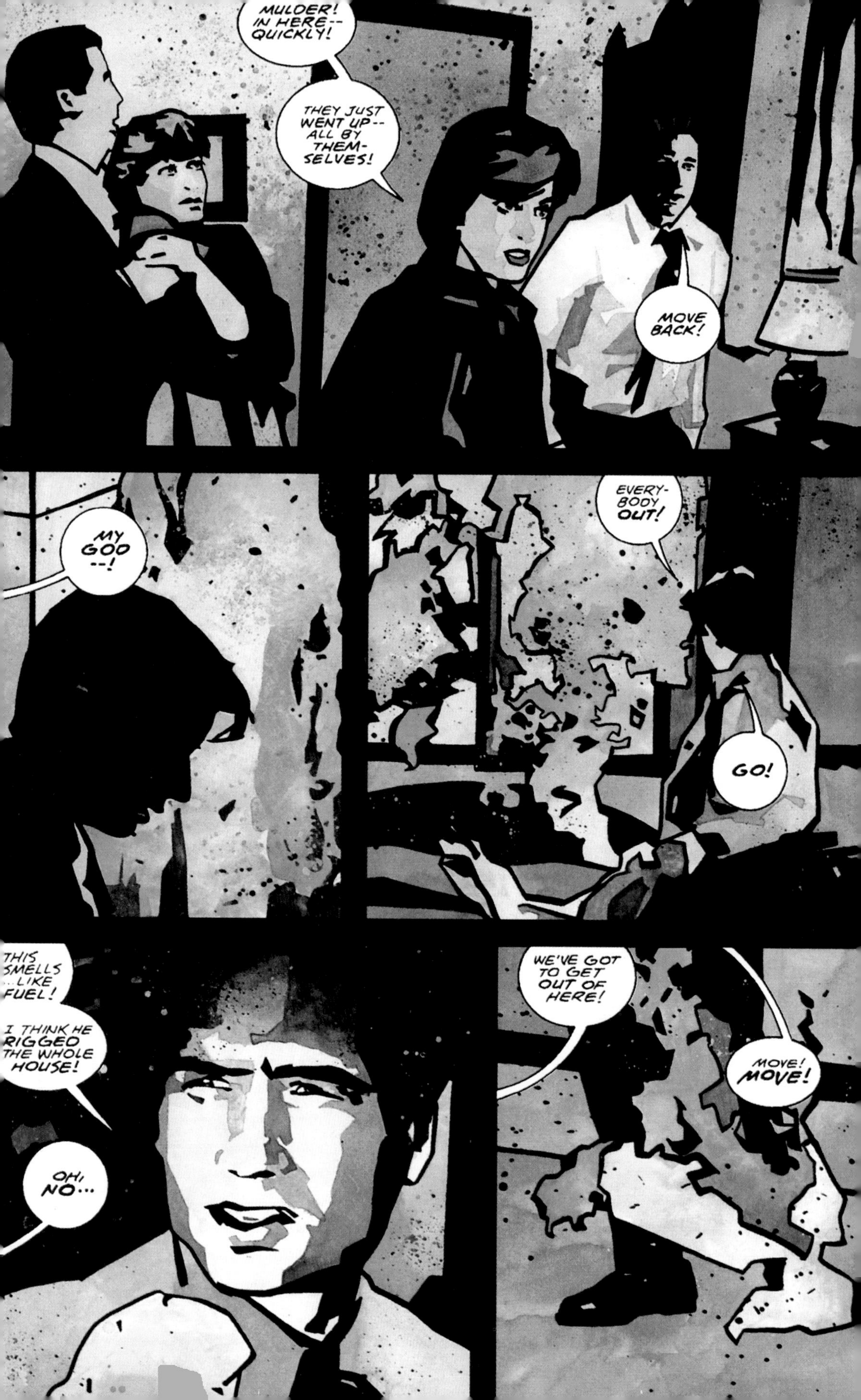

MULDER! IN HERE-- QUICKLY!
THEY JUST WENT UP-- ALL BY THEM-SELVES!
MOVE BACK!
MY GOO --!
EVERY-BODY OUT!
GO!
THIS SMELLS ...LIKE FUEL!
I THINK HE RIGGED THE WHOLE HOUSE!
OH, NO...
WE'VE GOT TO GET OUT OF HERE!
MOVE! MOVE!

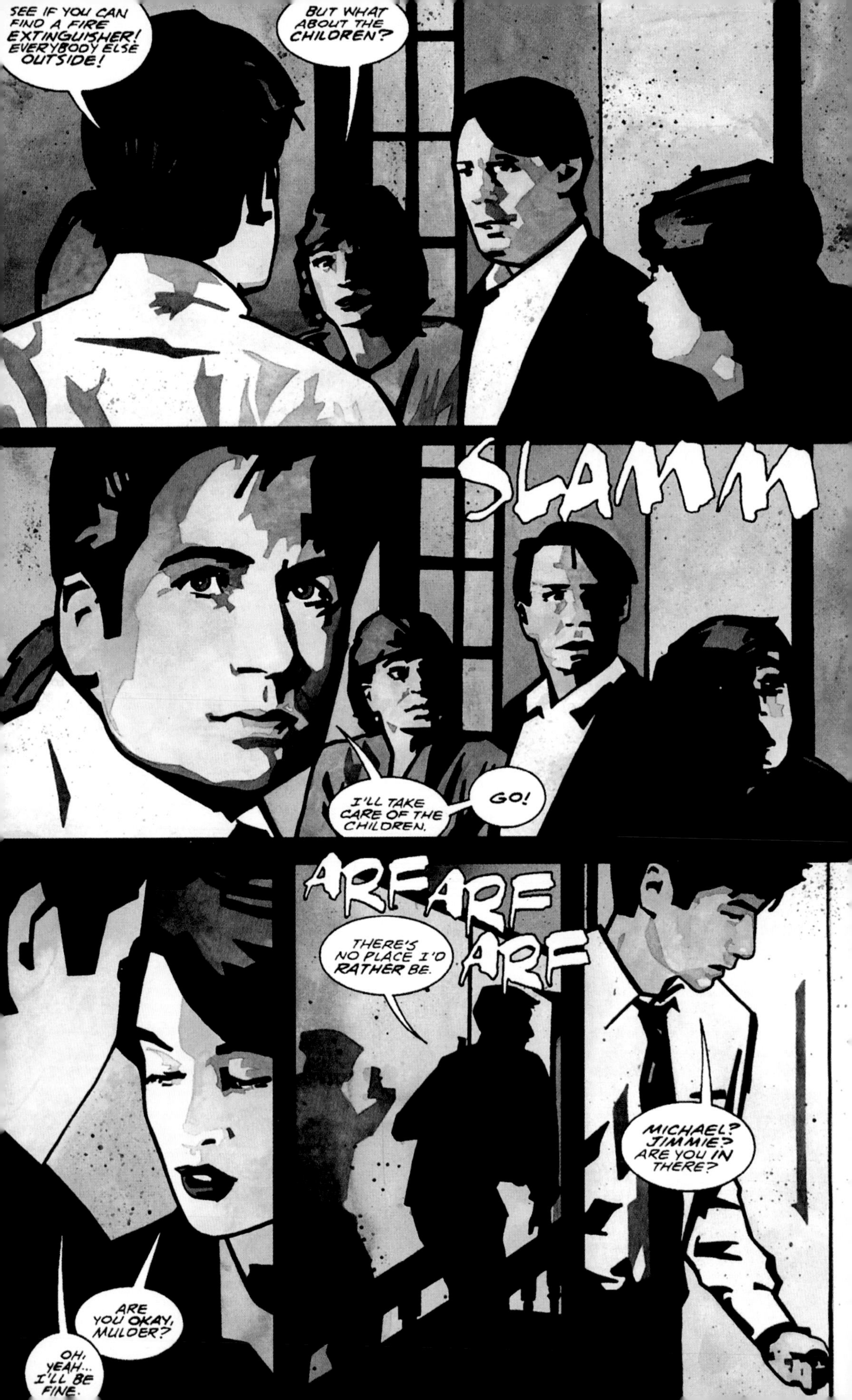
SEE IF YOU CAN FIND A FIRE EXTINGUISHER! EVERYBODY ELSE OUTSIDE!
BUT WHAT ABOUT THE CHILDREN?
SLAMM
I'LL TAKE CARE OF THE CHILDREN.
GO!
ARFARF
ARF
THERE'S NO PLACE I'D RATHER BE.
MICHAEL? JIMMIE? ARE YOU IN THERE?
ARE YOU OKAY, MULDER?
OH, YEAH... I'LL BE FINE.

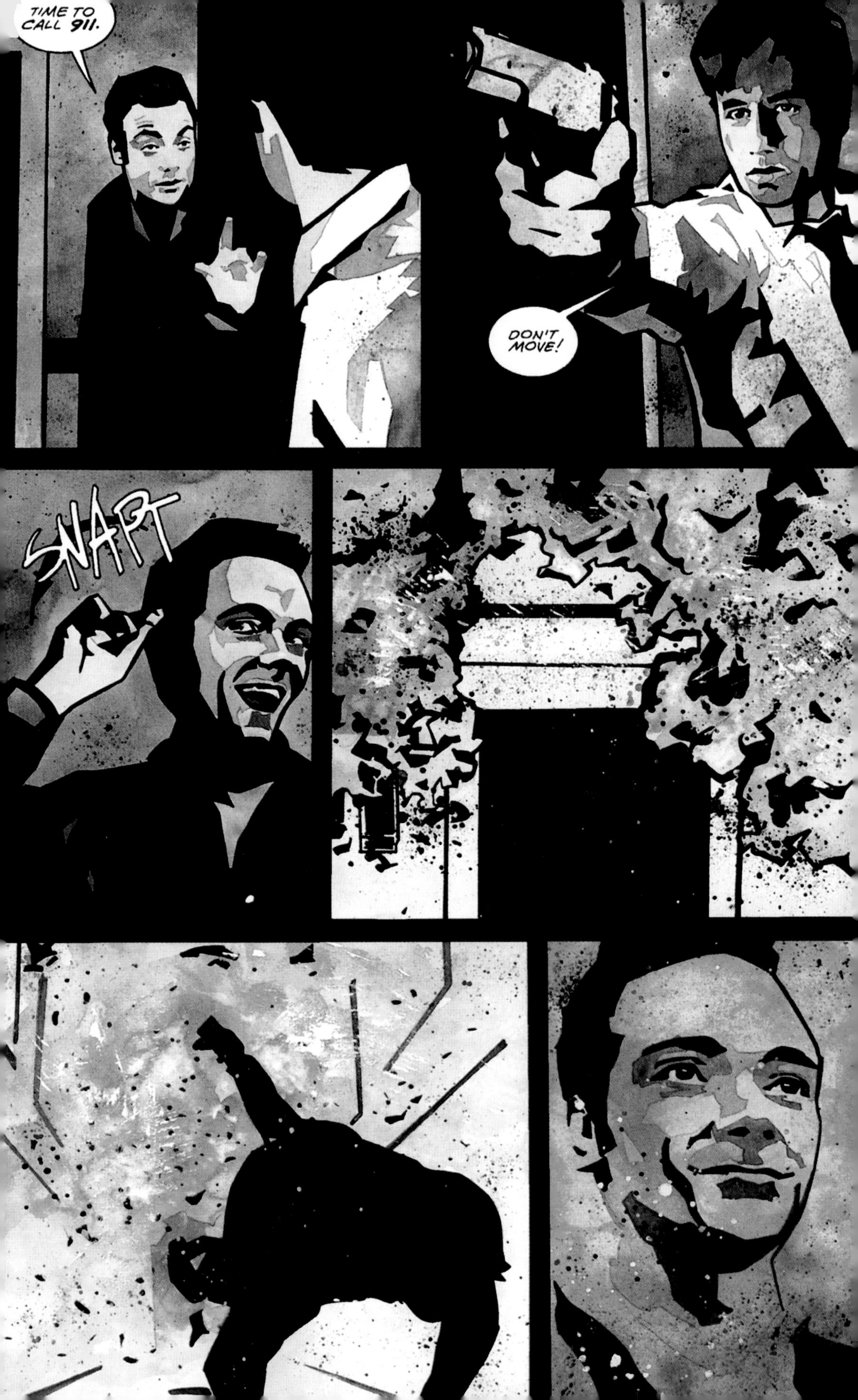
TIME TO CALL 911.
DON'T MOVE!
SNAP!

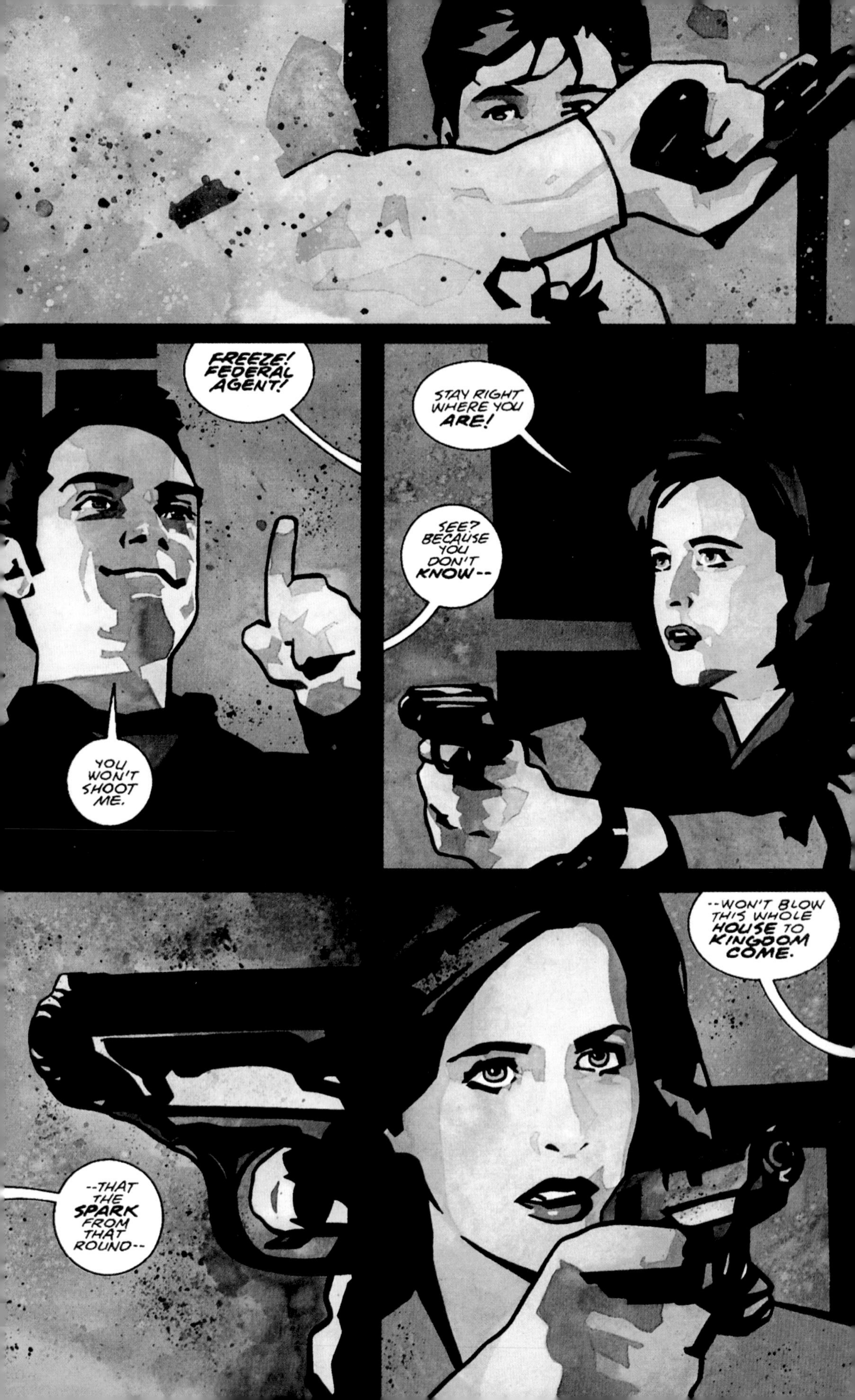
FREEZE! FEDERAL AGENT!
YOU WON'T SHOOT ME.
STAY RIGHT WHERE YOU ARE!
SEE? BECAUSE YOU DON'T KNOW--
--THAT THE SPARK FROM THAT ROUND--
--WON'T BLOW THIS WHOLE HOUSE TO KINGDOM COME.

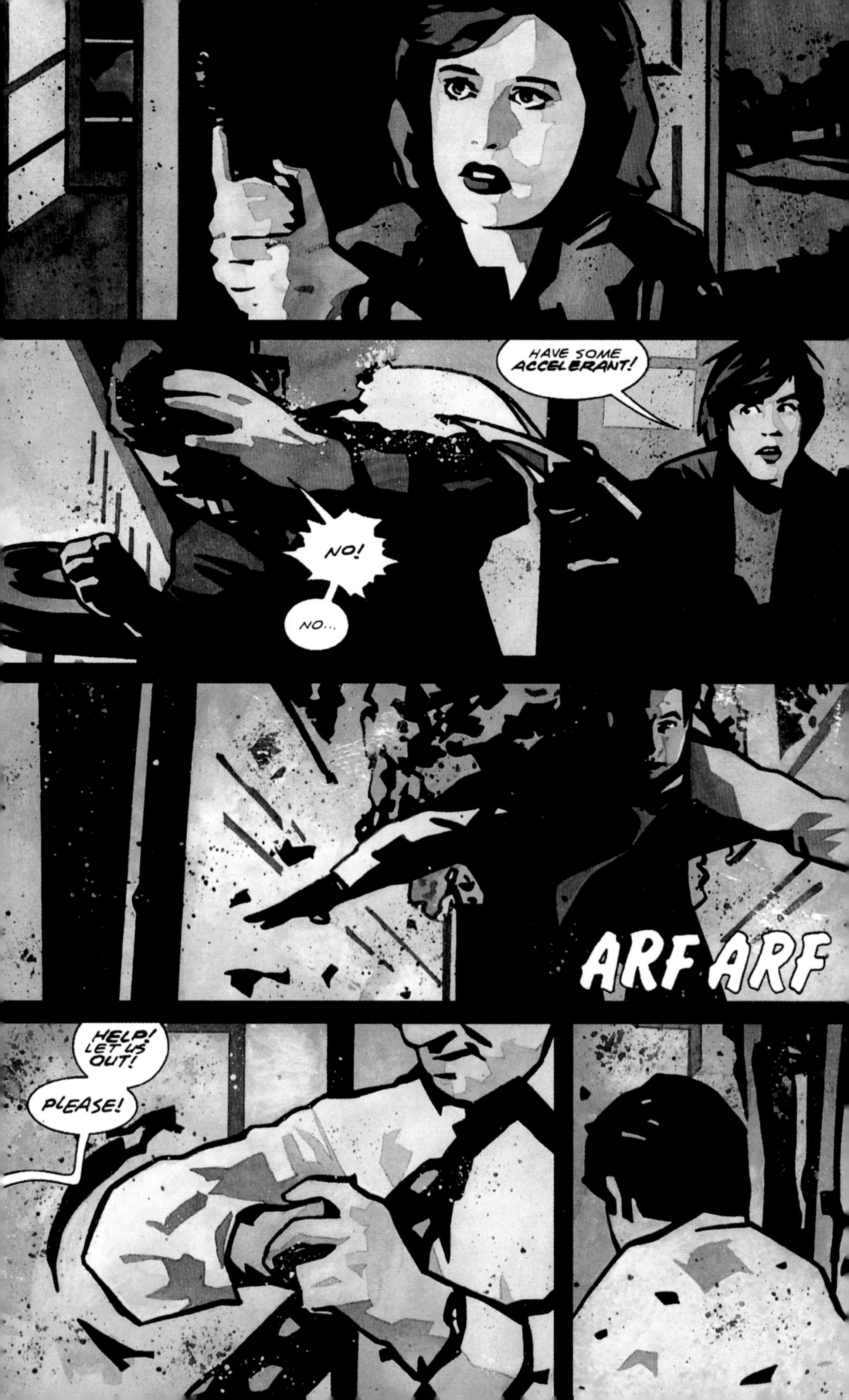
HAVE SOME ACCELERANT!
NO!
NO...
ARF ARF
HELP! LET US OUT!
PLEASE!

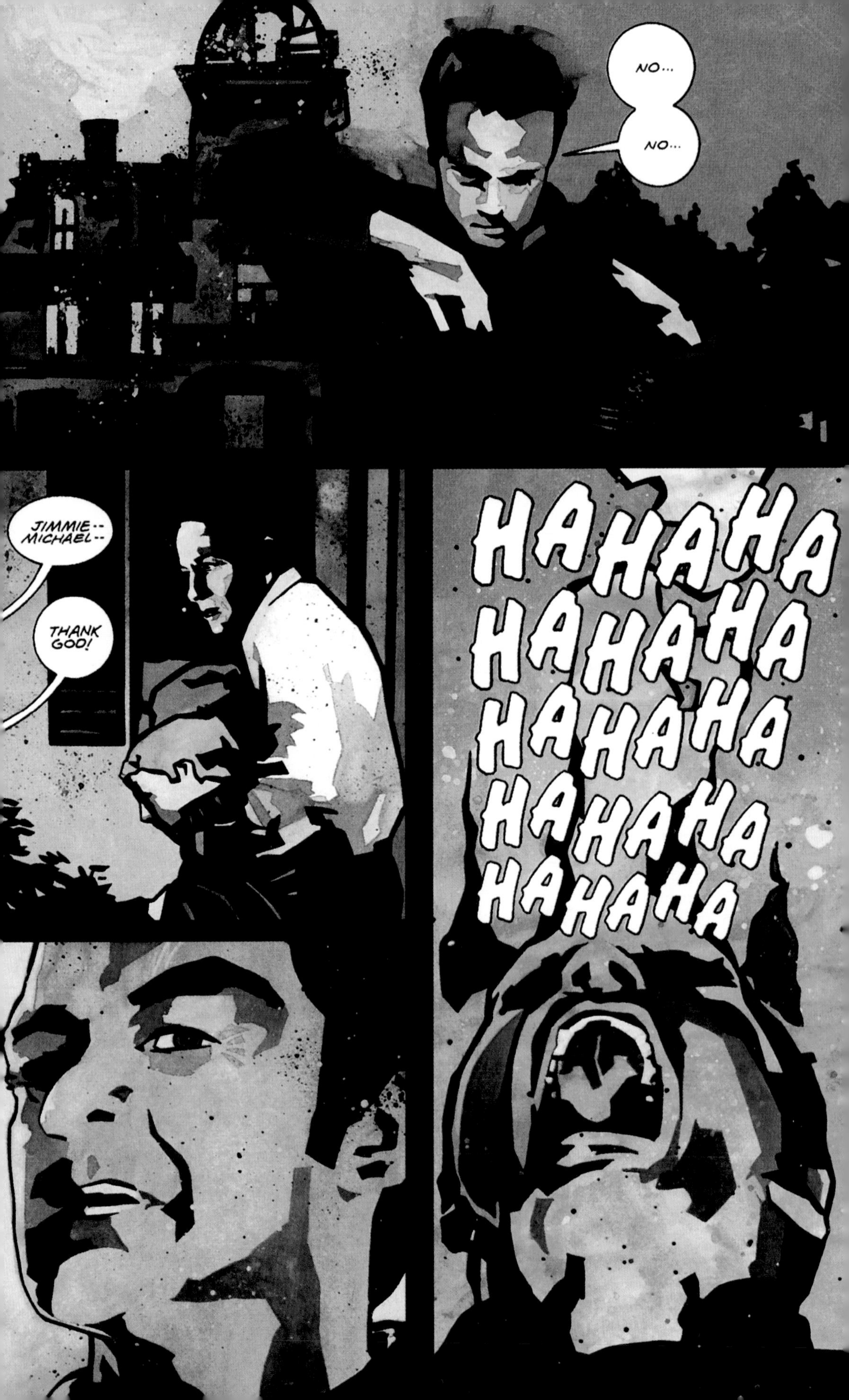
NO...
NO...
JIMMIE--
MICHAEL--
THANK GOD!
HAHAHA
HAHAHA
HAHAHA
HAHAHA
HAHAHA

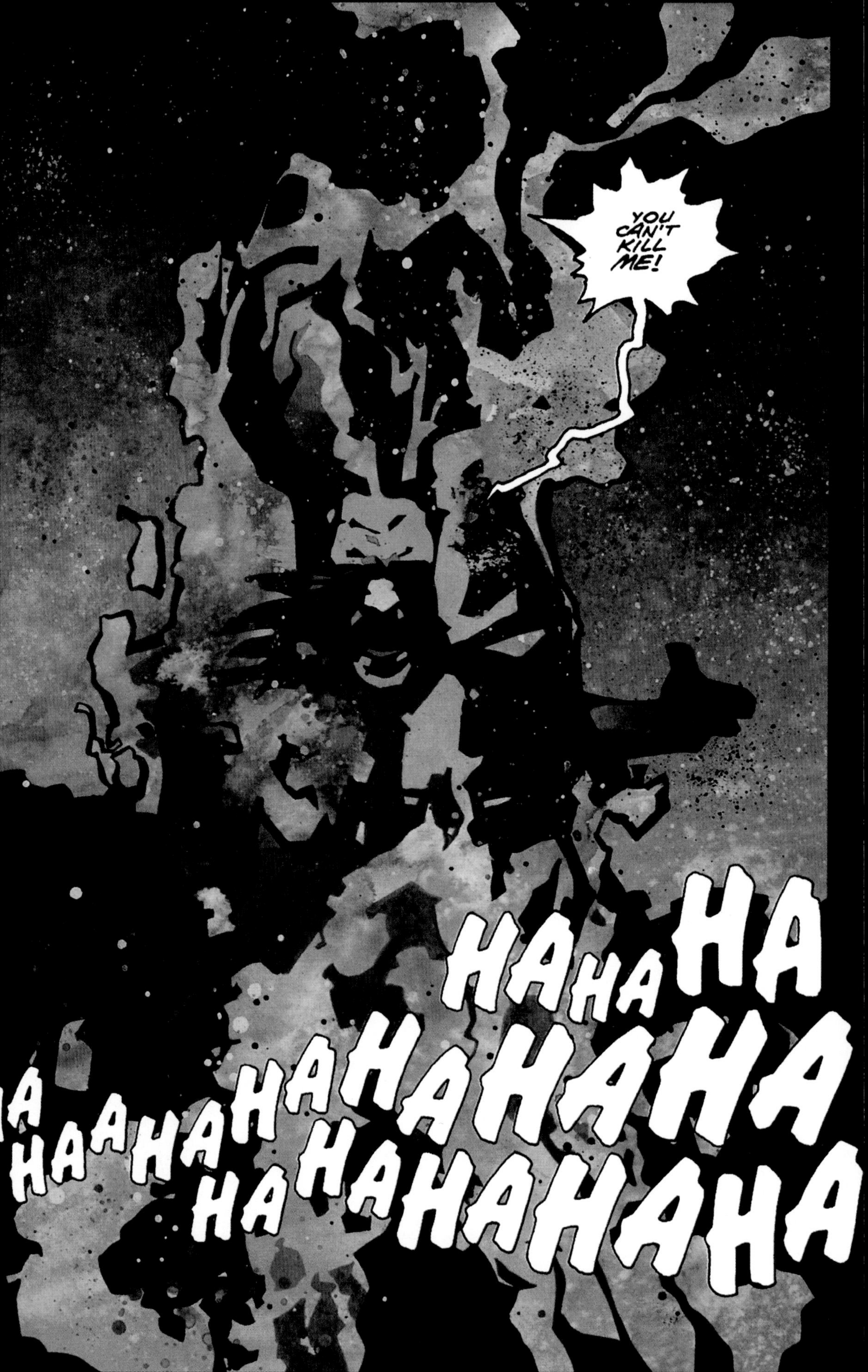
YOU CAN'T KILL ME!
HAHAHAHA
HAHAHAHAHA
HAHAHA
HA HAHAHAHAHA

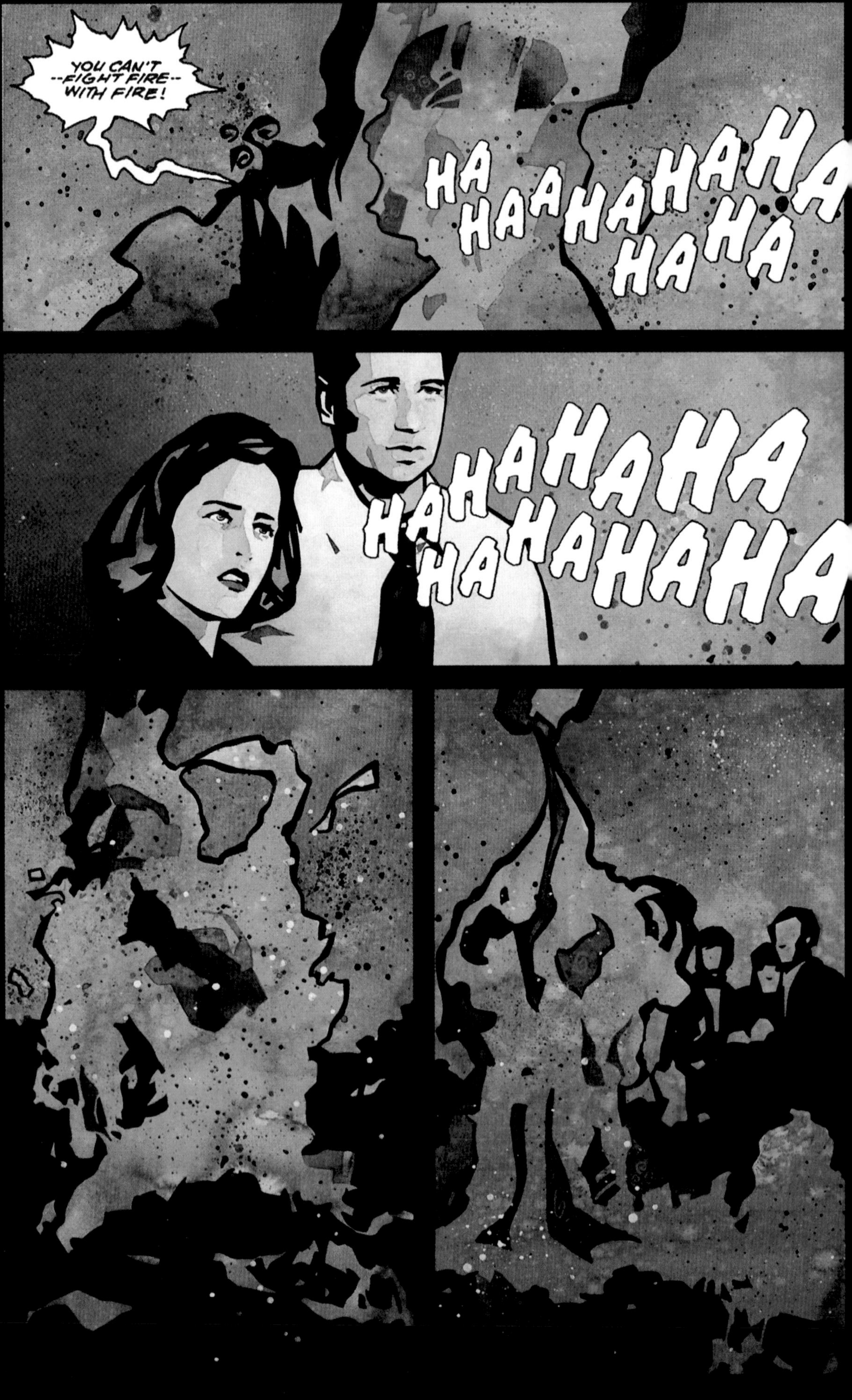
YOU CAN'T --FIGHT FIRE-- WITH FIRE!
HA HAHAHAHAHA HAHA
HAHAHAHA HAHAHAHAHA

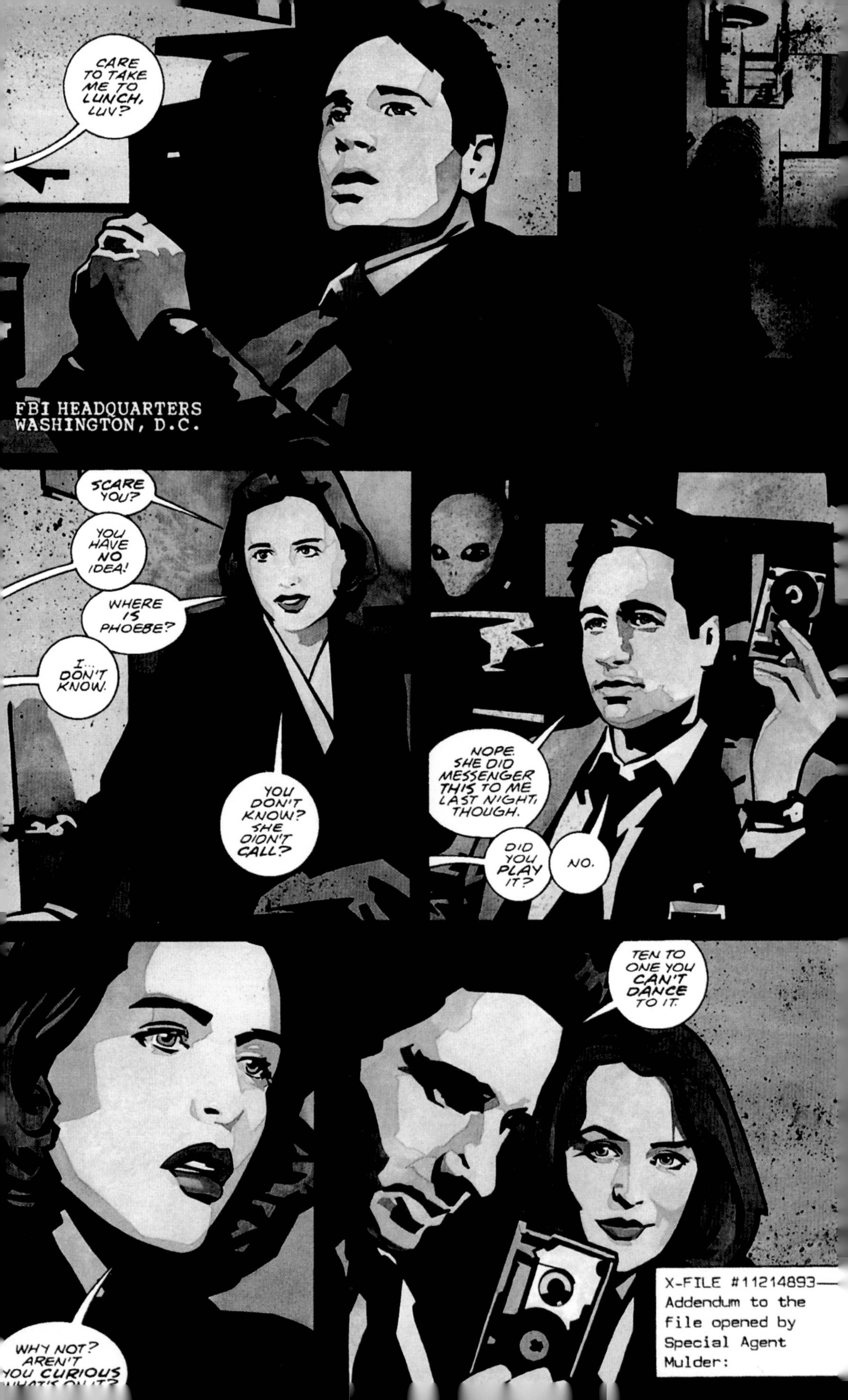
CARE TO TAKE ME TO LUNCH, LUV?
FBI HEADQUARTERS WASHINGTON, D.C.
SCARE YOU?
YOU HAVE NO IDEA!
WHERE IS PHOEBE?
I... DON'T KNOW.
YOU DON'T KNOW? SHE DIDN'T CALL?
NOPE. SHE DID MESSENGER THIS TO ME LAST NIGHT, THOUGH.
DID YOU PLAY IT?
NO.
WHY NOT? AREN'T YOU CURIOUS
TEN TO ONE YOU CAN'T DANCE TO IT.
X-FILE #11214893— Addendum to the file opened by Special Agent Mulder:

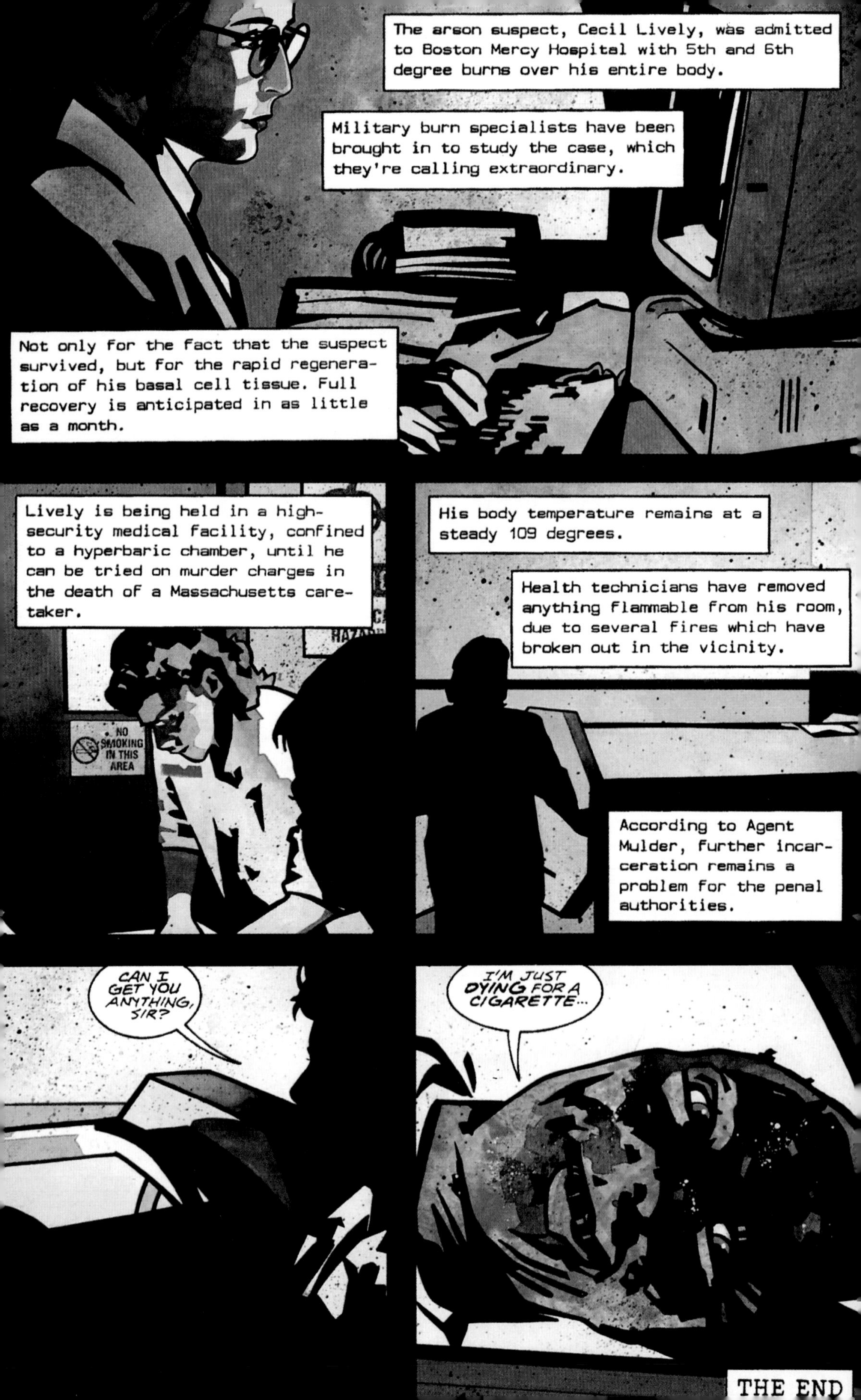
The arson suspect, Cecil Lively, was admitted to Boston Mercy Hospital with 5th and 6th degree burns over his entire body.
Military burn specialists have been brought in to study the case, which they're calling extraordinary.
Not only for the fact that the suspect survived, but for the rapid regeneration of his basal cell tissue. Full recovery is anticipated in as little as a month.
Lively is being held in a high-security medical facility, confined to a hyperbaric chamber, until he can be tried on murder charges in the death of a Massachusetts caretaker.
NO SMOKING IN THIS AREA
His body temperature remains at a steady 109 degrees.
Health technicians have removed anything flammable from his room, due to several fires which have broken out in the vicinity.
According to Agent Mulder, further incarceration remains a problem for the penal authorities.
CAN I GET YOU ANYTHING, SIR?
I'M JUST DYING FOR A CIGARETTE...
THE END

CHAPTER 6

# ICE

STORY: Roy Thomas
ART: John Van Fleet

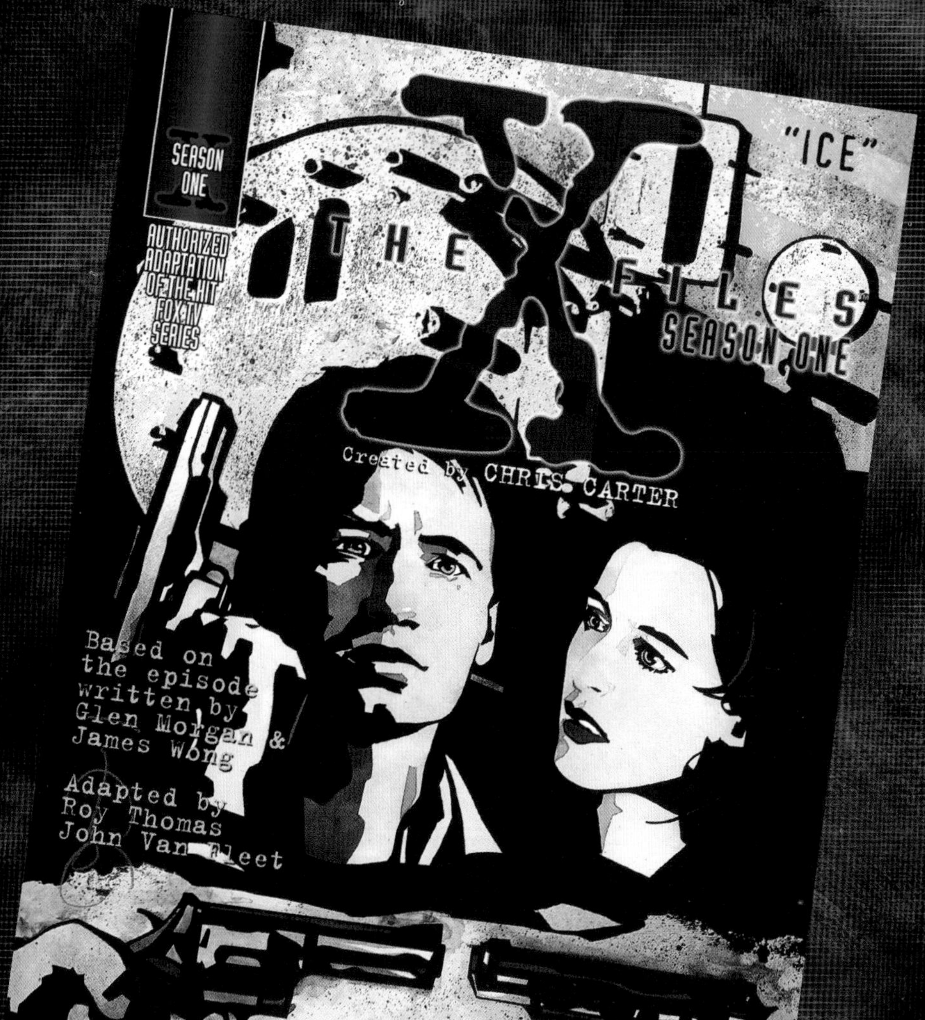
SEASON ONE
AUTHORIZED ADAPTATION OF THE HIT FOX TV SERIES
"ICE"
THE X FILES SEASON ONE
Created by CHRIS CARTER
Based on the episode written by Glen Morgan & James Wong
Adapted by Roy Thomas John Van Fleet
$4.95 U.S. / $6.95 CANADA

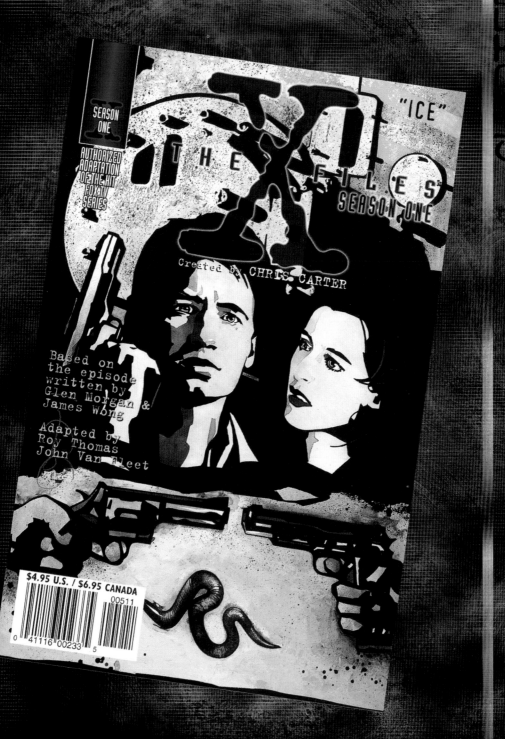

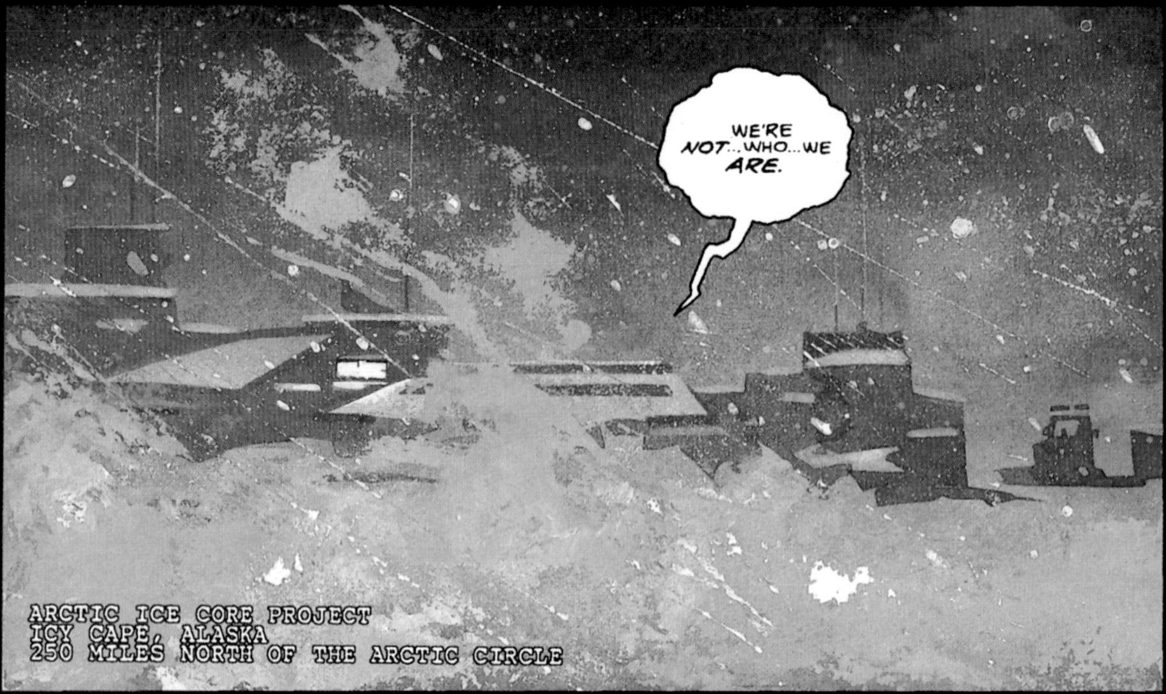
WE'RE NOT...WHO...WE ARE.
ARCTIC ICE CORE PROJECT
ICY CAPE, ALASKA
250 MILES NORTH OF THE ARCTIC CIRCLE

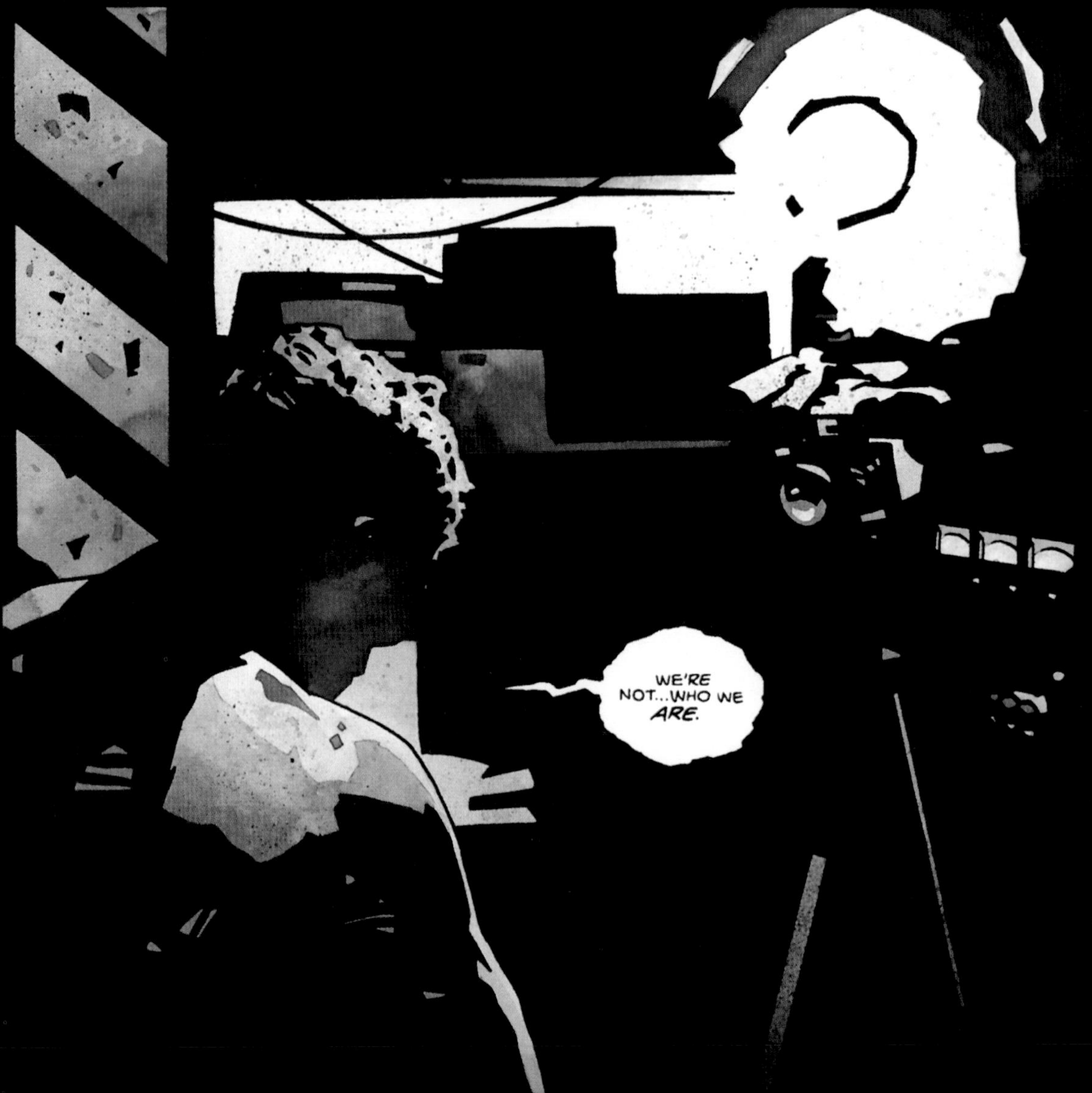
WE'RE NOT...WHO WE ARE.

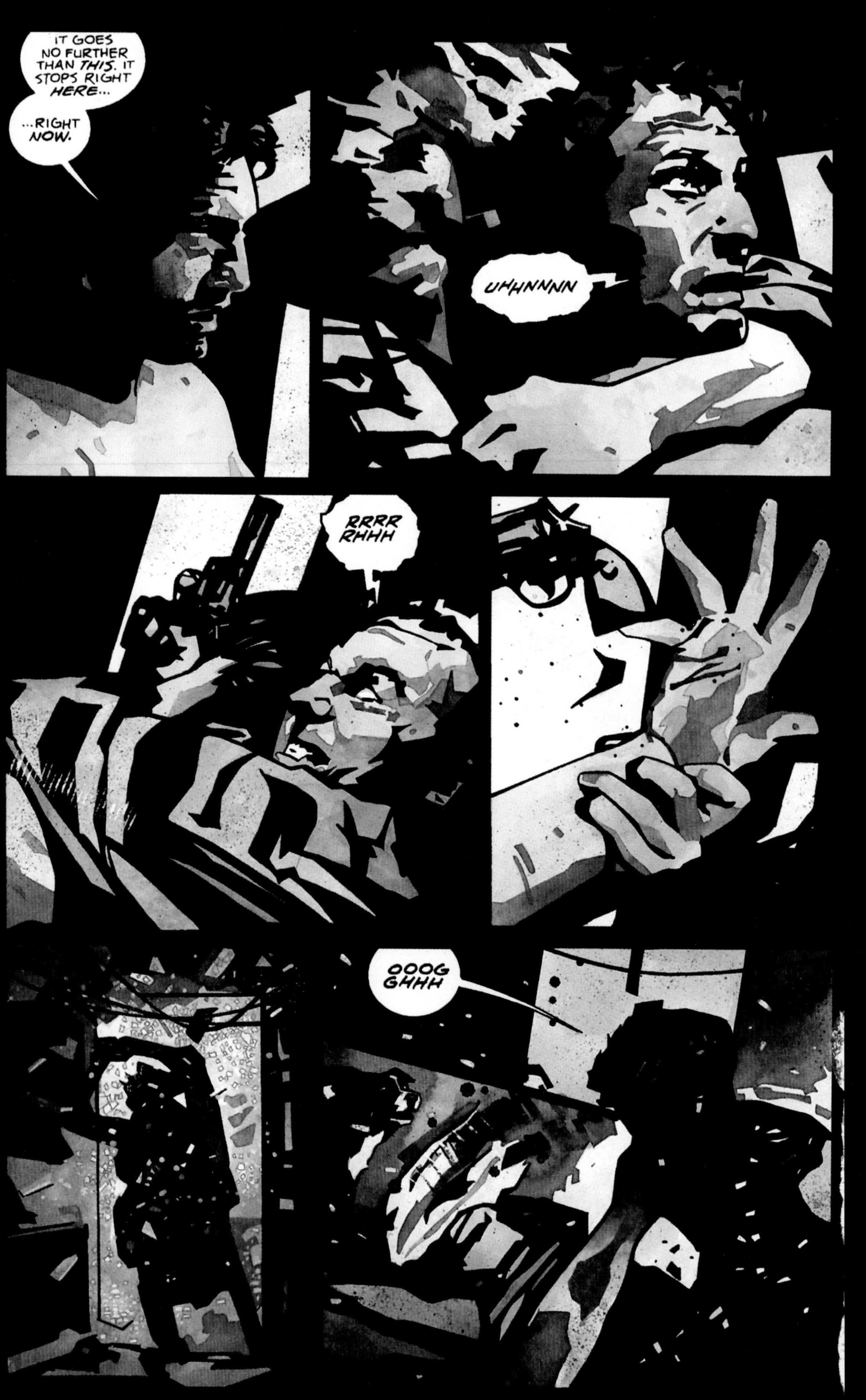
IT GOES NO FURTHER THAN THIS. IT STOPS RIGHT HERE...
...RIGHT NOW.
UHHNNNN
RRRR RHHH
OOOG GHHH

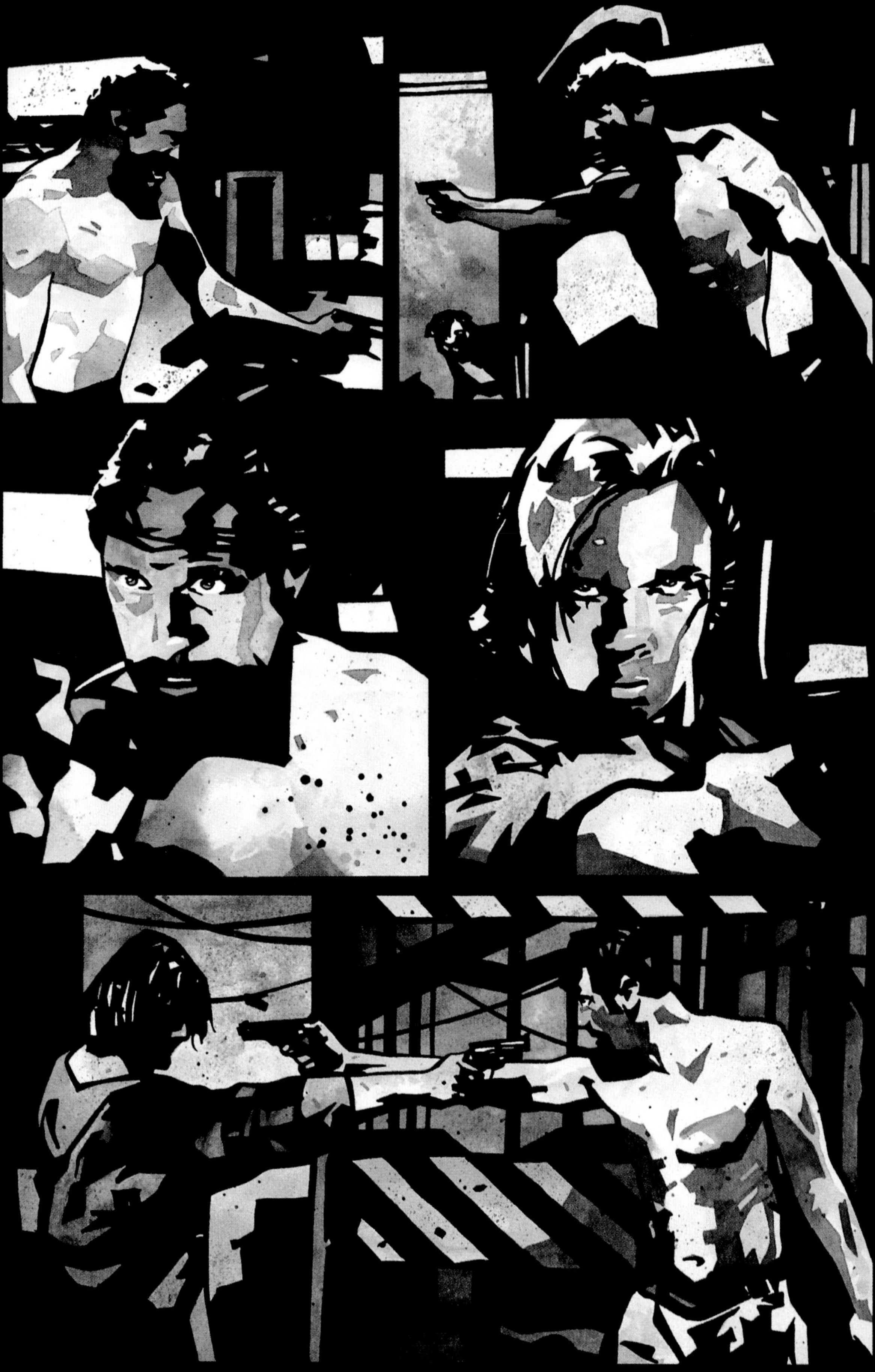

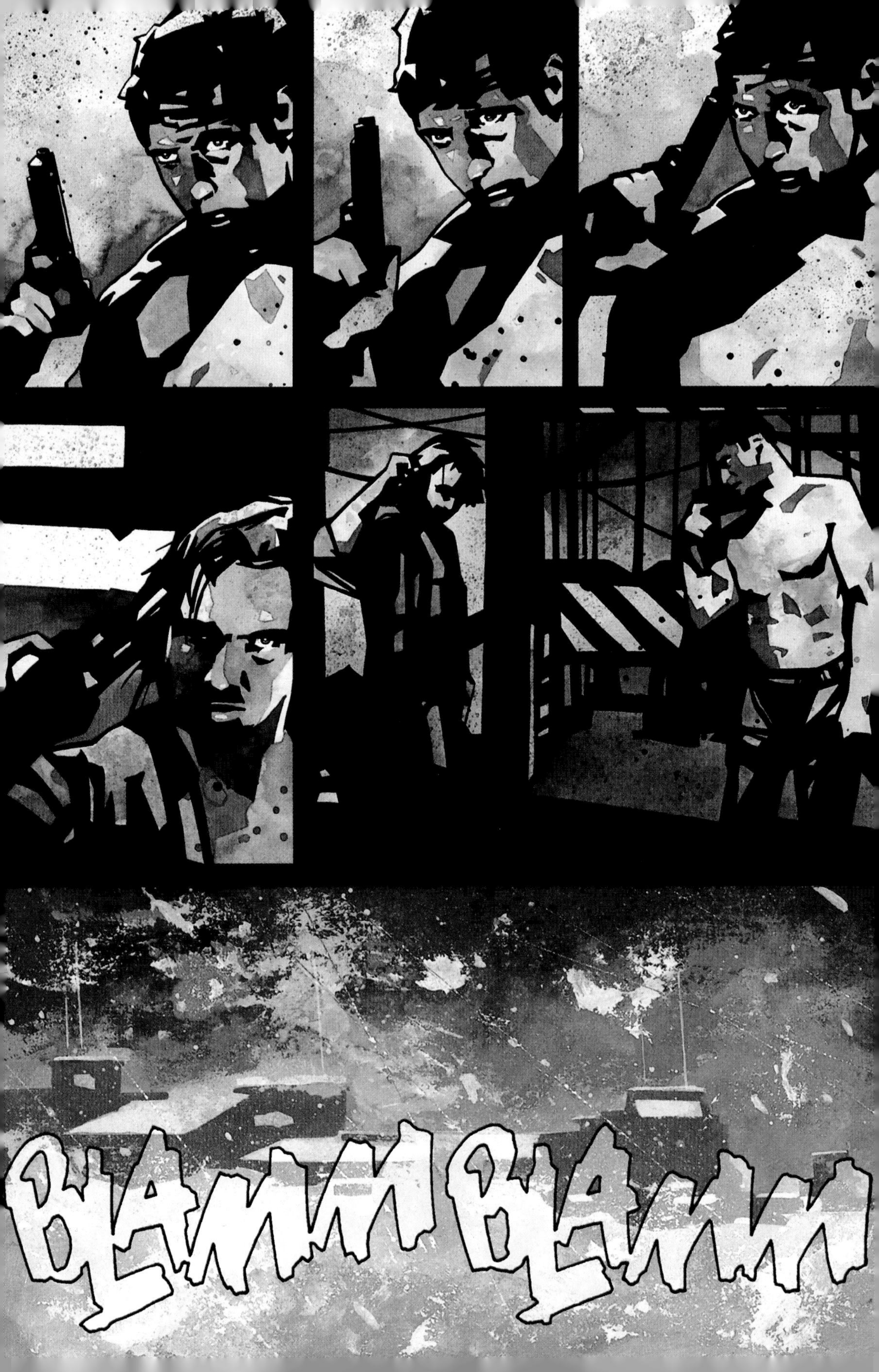
BLAMM BLAMM

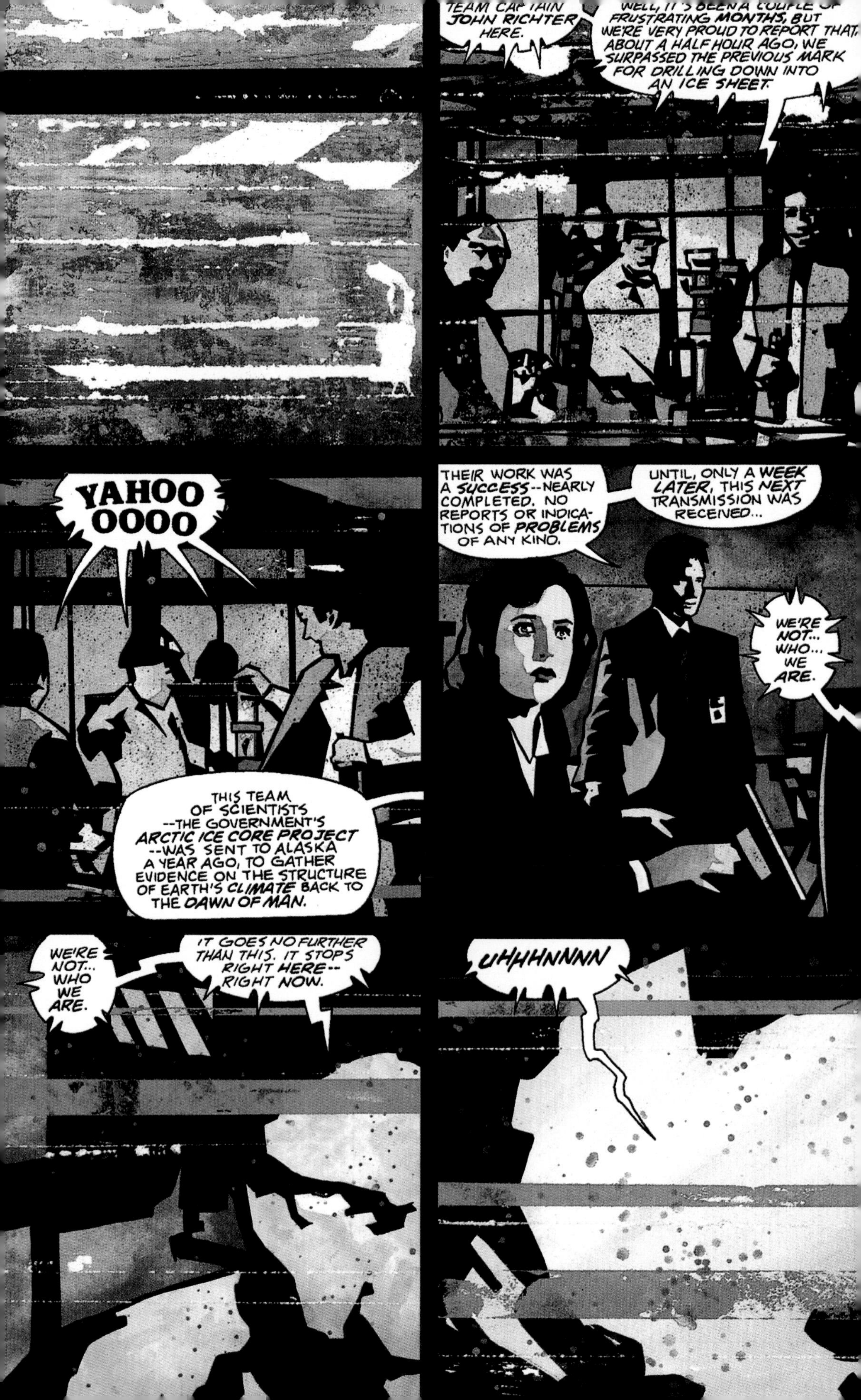

TEAM CAPTAIN JOHN RICHTER HERE.
WELL, IT'S BEEN A COUPLE OF FRUSTRATING MONTHS, BUT WE'RE VERY PROUD TO REPORT THAT ABOUT A HALF HOUR AGO, WE SURPASSED THE PREVIOUS MARK FOR DRILLING DOWN INTO AN ICE SHEET.
YAHOOOOOO
THIS TEAM OF SCIENTISTS --THE GOVERNMENT'S ARCTIC ICE CORE PROJECT --WAS SENT TO ALASKA A YEAR AGO, TO GATHER EVIDENCE ON THE STRUCTURE OF EARTH'S CLIMATE BACK TO THE DAWN OF MAN.
THEIR WORK WAS A SUCCESS--NEARLY COMPLETED. NO REPORTS OR INDICATIONS OF PROBLEMS OF ANY KIND.
UNTIL, ONLY A WEEK LATER, THIS NEXT TRANSMISSION WAS RECEIVED...
WE'RE NOT... WHO... WE ARE.
WE'RE NOT... WHO WE ARE.
IT GOES NO FURTHER THAN THIS. IT STOPS RIGHT HERE-- RIGHT NOW.
UHHHNNNN

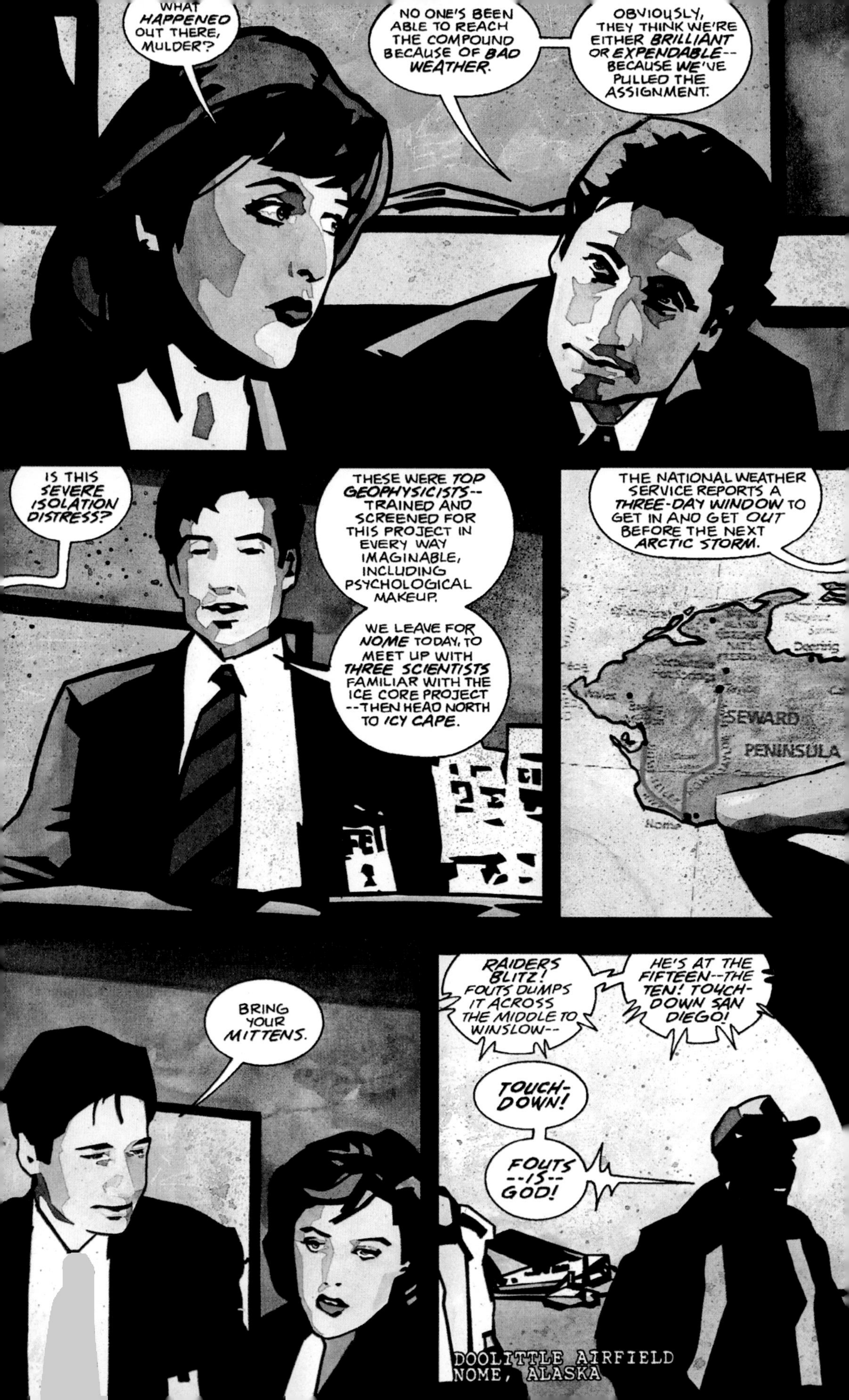
WHAT HAPPENED OUT THERE, MULDER?
NO ONE'S BEEN ABLE TO REACH THE COMPOUND BECAUSE OF BAD WEATHER.
OBVIOUSLY, THEY THINK WE'RE EITHER BRILLIANT OR EXPENDABLE-- BECAUSE WE'VE PULLED THE ASSIGNMENT.
IS THIS SEVERE ISOLATION DISTRESS?
THESE WERE TOP GEOPHYSICISTS-- TRAINED AND SCREENED FOR THIS PROJECT IN EVERY WAY IMAGINABLE, INCLUDING PSYCHOLOGICAL MAKEUP.
WE LEAVE FOR NOME TODAY, TO MEET UP WITH THREE SCIENTISTS FAMILIAR WITH THE ICE CORE PROJECT --THEN HEAD NORTH TO ICY CAPE.
THE NATIONAL WEATHER SERVICE REPORTS A THREE-DAY WINDOW TO GET IN AND GET OUT BEFORE THE NEXT ARCTIC STORM.
SEWARD PENINSULA
BRING YOUR MITTENS.
RAIDERS BLITZ! FOUTS DUMPS IT ACROSS THE MIDDLE TO WINSLOW--
HE'S AT THE FIFTEEN--THE TEN! TOUCH-DOWN SAN DIEGO!
TOUCH-DOWN!
FOUTS --IS-- GOD!
DOOLITTLE AIRFIELD
NOME, ALASKA

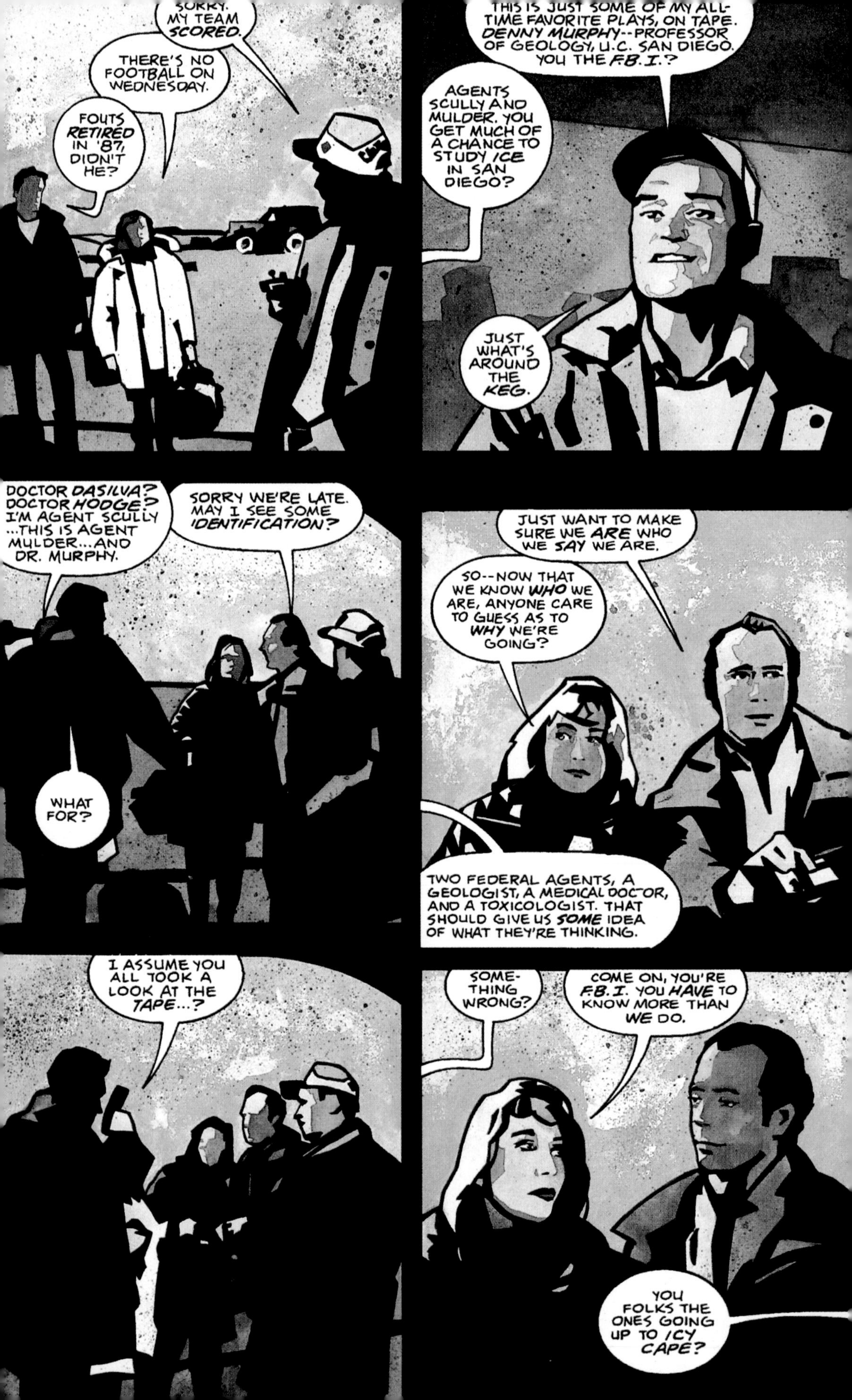
SORRY. MY TEAM SCORED.
THERE'S NO FOOTBALL ON WEDNESDAY.
FOUTS RETIRED IN '87, DIDN'T HE?
THIS IS JUST SOME OF MY ALL-TIME FAVORITE PLAYS, ON TAPE. DENNY MURPHY--PROFESSOR OF GEOLOGY, U.C. SAN DIEGO. YOU THE F.B.I.?
AGENTS SCULLY AND MULDER. YOU GET MUCH OF A CHANCE TO STUDY ICE IN SAN DIEGO?
JUST WHAT'S AROUND THE KEG.
DOCTOR DASILVA? DOCTOR HODGE? I'M AGENT SCULLY ...THIS IS AGENT MULDER...AND DR. MURPHY.
SORRY WE'RE LATE. MAY I SEE SOME IDENTIFICATION?
WHAT FOR?
JUST WANT TO MAKE SURE WE ARE WHO WE SAY WE ARE.
SO--NOW THAT WE KNOW WHO WE ARE, ANYONE CARE TO GUESS AS TO WHY WE'RE GOING?
TWO FEDERAL AGENTS, A GEOLOGIST, A MEDICAL DOCTOR, AND A TOXICOLOGIST. THAT SHOULD GIVE US SOME IDEA OF WHAT THEY'RE THINKING.
I ASSUME YOU ALL TOOK A LOOK AT THE TAPE...?
SOME-THING WRONG?
COME ON, YOU'RE F.B.I. YOU HAVE TO KNOW MORE THAN WE DO.
YOU FOLKS THE ONES GOING UP TO ICY CAPE?

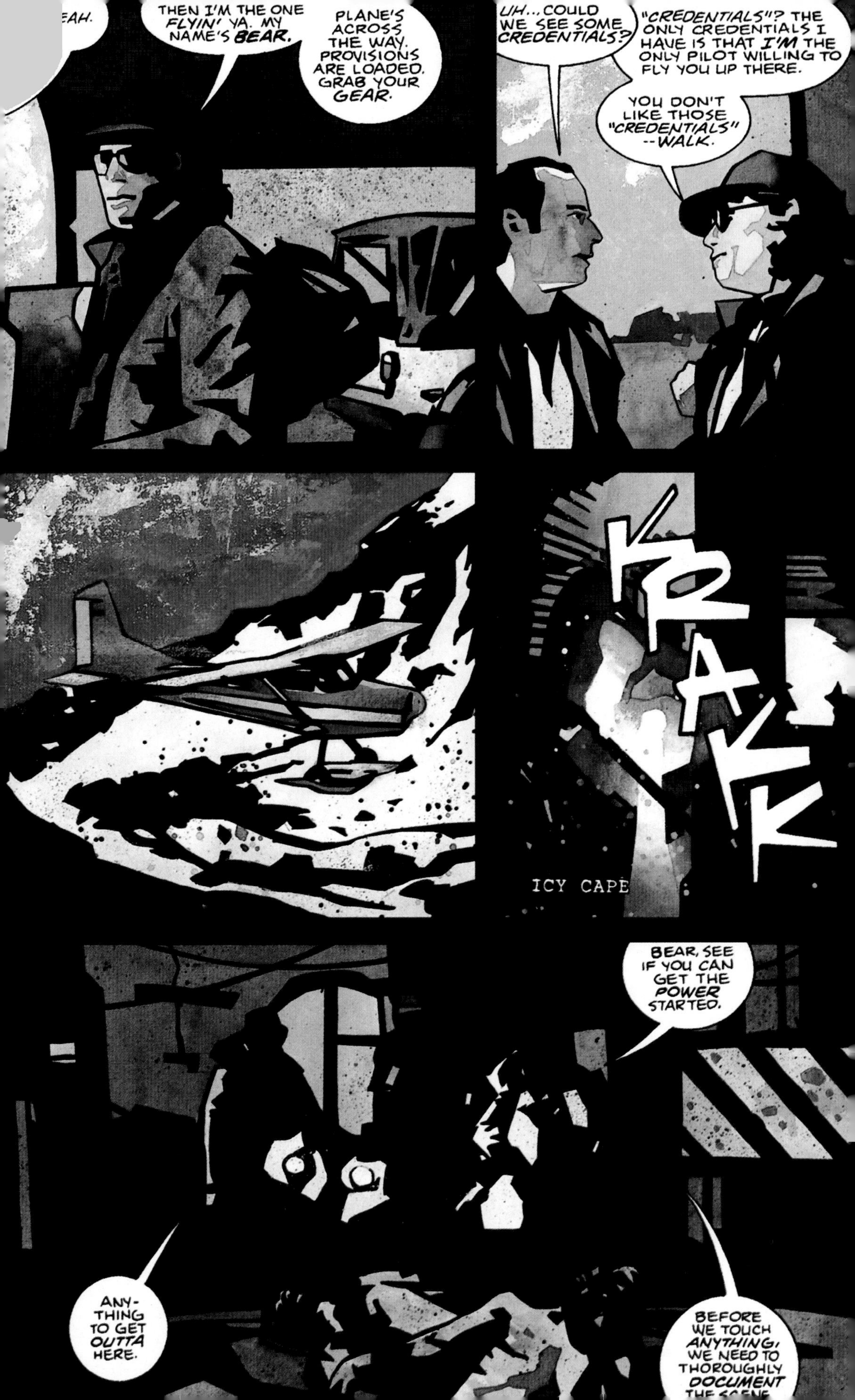
THEN I'M THE ONE FLYIN' YA. MY NAME'S BEAR.
PLANE'S ACROSS THE WAY. PROVISIONS ARE LOADED. GRAB YOUR GEAR.
UH... COULD WE SEE SOME CREDENTIALS?
"CREDENTIALS"? THE ONLY CREDENTIALS I HAVE IS THAT I'M THE ONLY PILOT WILLING TO FLY YOU UP THERE.
YOU DON'T LIKE THOSE "CREDENTIALS" --WALK.
KRAKK
ICY CAPE
BEAR, SEE IF YOU CAN GET THE POWER STARTED.
ANY-THING TO GET OUTTA HERE.
BEFORE WE TOUCH ANYTHING, WE NEED TO THOROUGHLY DOCUMENT

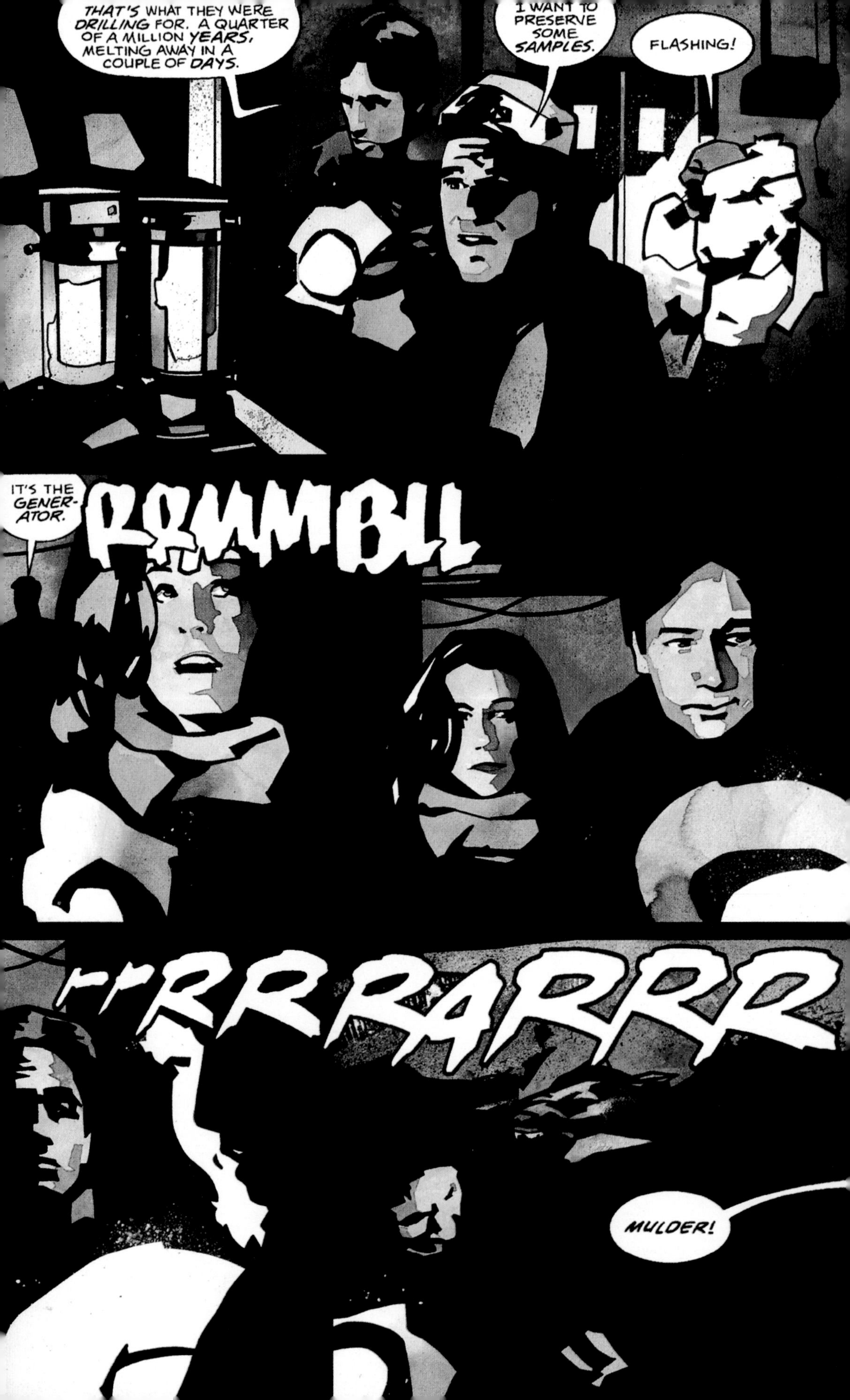
THAT'S WHAT THEY WERE DRILLING FOR. A QUARTER OF A MILLION YEARS, MELTING AWAY IN A COUPLE OF DAYS.
I WANT TO PRESERVE SOME SAMPLES.
FLASHING!
IT'S THE GENERATOR.
RRUMBLL
rrRRRARRR
MULDER!

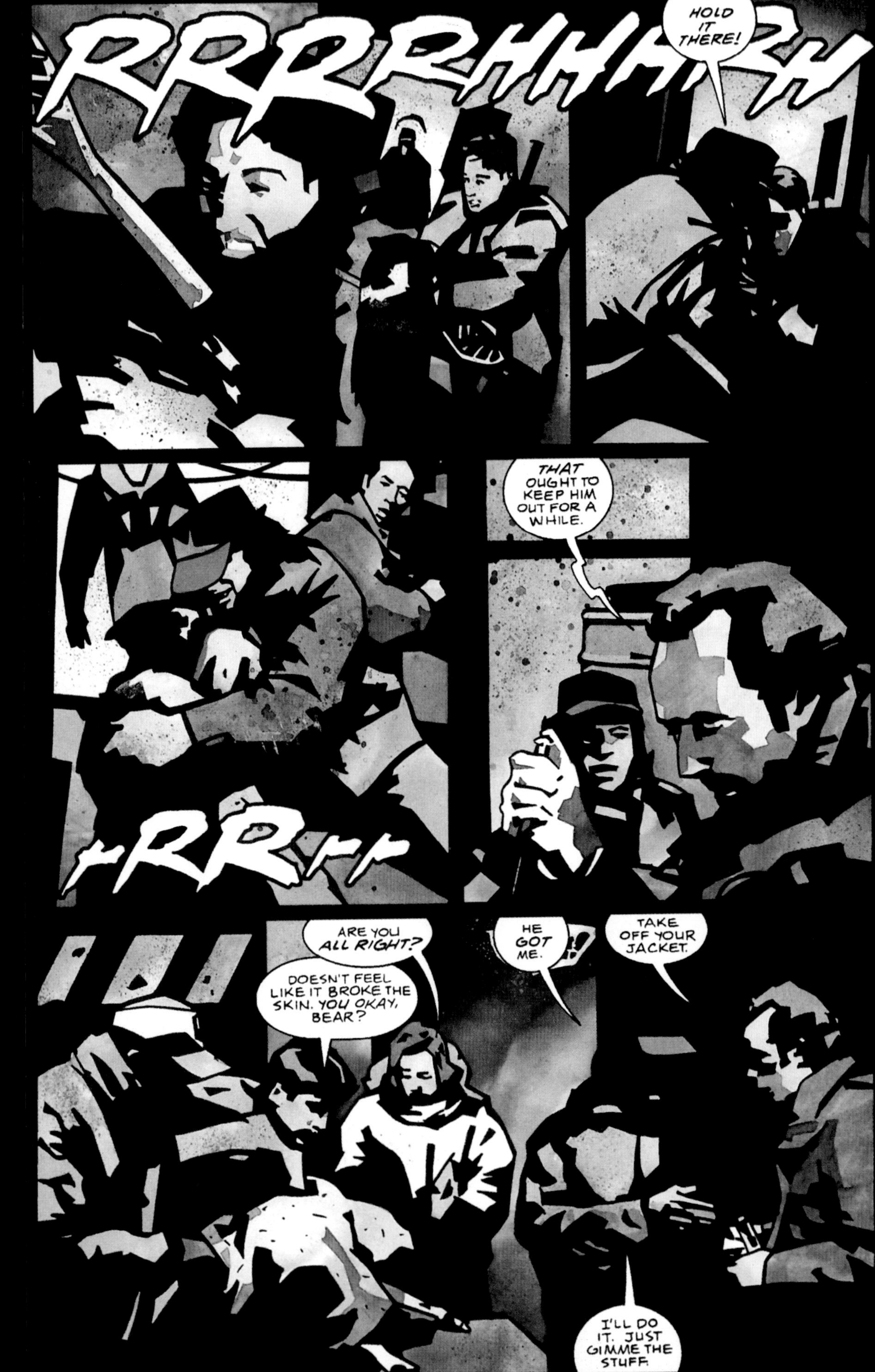
RRRRHHHRRH
HOLD IT THERE!
THAT OUGHT TO KEEP HIM OUT FOR A WHILE.
rRRrr
ARE YOU ALL RIGHT?
DOESN'T FEEL LIKE IT BROKE THE SKIN. YOU OKAY, BEAR?
HE GOT ME.
TAKE OFF YOUR JACKET.
I'LL DO IT. JUST GIMME THE STUFF.

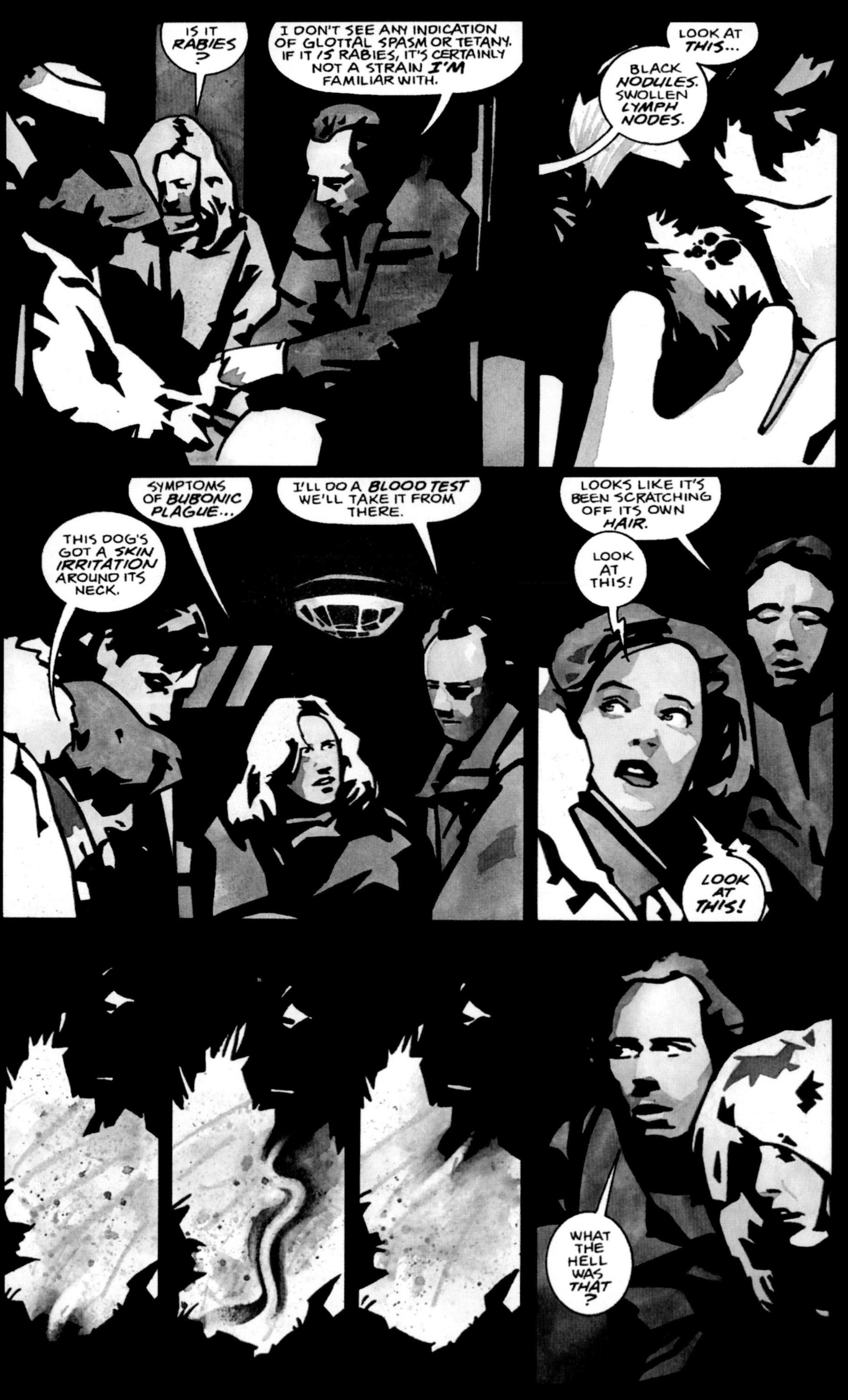

IS IT RABIES?
I DON'T SEE ANY INDICATION OF GLOTTAL SPASM OR TETANY. IF IT IS RABIES, IT'S CERTAINLY NOT A STRAIN I'M FAMILIAR WITH.
LOOK AT THIS...
BLACK NODULES. SWOLLEN LYMPH NODES.
SYMPTOMS OF BUBONIC PLAGUE...
THIS DOG'S GOT A SKIN IRRITATION AROUND ITS NECK.
I'LL DO A BLOOD TEST WE'LL TAKE IT FROM THERE.
LOOKS LIKE IT'S BEEN SCRATCHING OFF ITS OWN HAIR.
LOOK AT THIS!
LOOK AT THIS!
WHAT THE HELL WAS THAT?

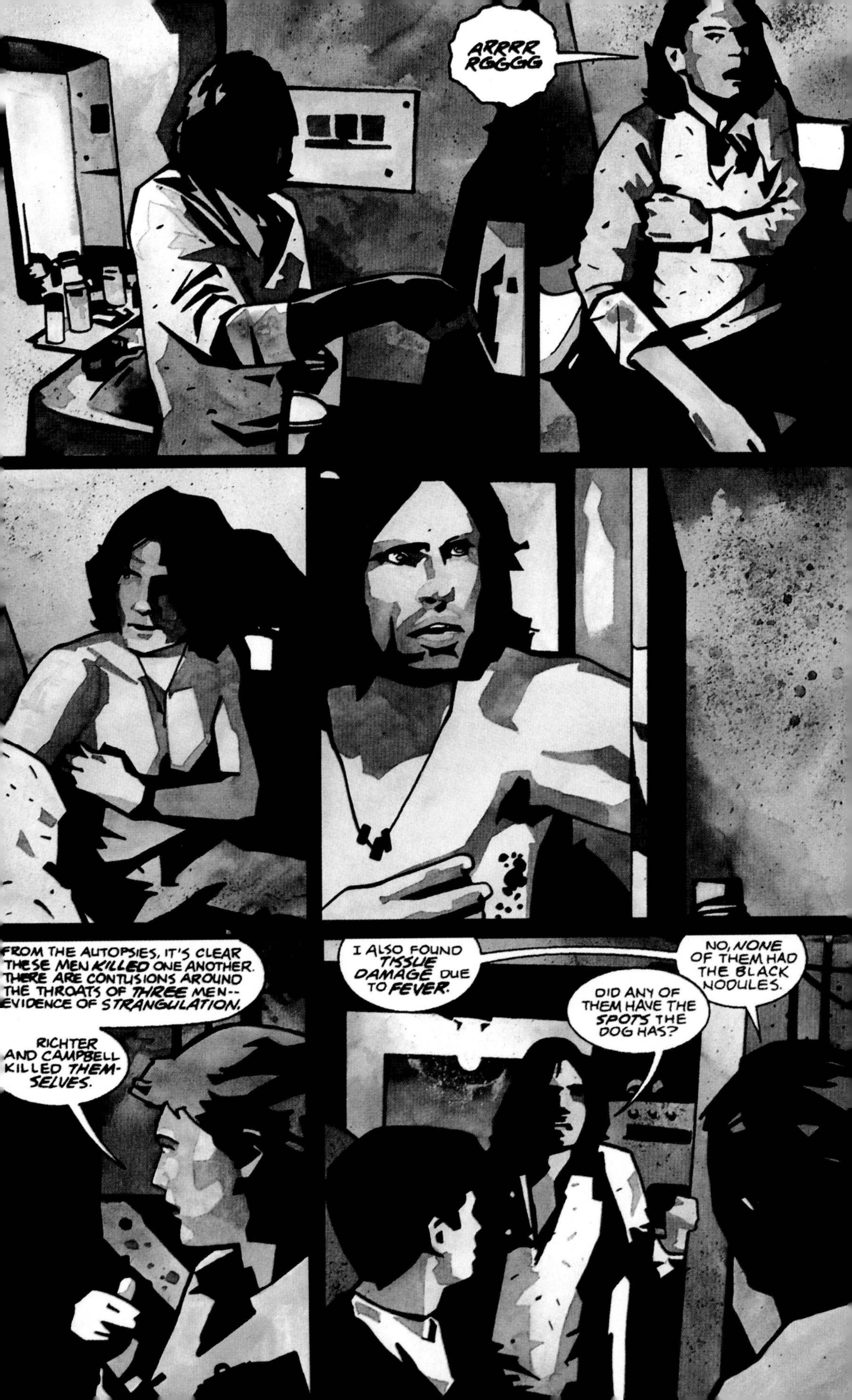
ARRRR RGGGG
FROM THE AUTOPSIES, IT'S CLEAR THESE MEN KILLED ONE ANOTHER. THERE ARE CONTUSIONS AROUND THE THROATS OF THREE MEN--EVIDENCE OF STRANGULATION.
RICHTER AND CAMPBELL KILLED THEMSELVES.
I ALSO FOUND TISSUE DAMAGE DUE TO FEVER.
DID ANY OF THEM HAVE THE SPOTS THE DOG HAS?
NO, NONE OF THEM HAD THE BLACK NODULES.

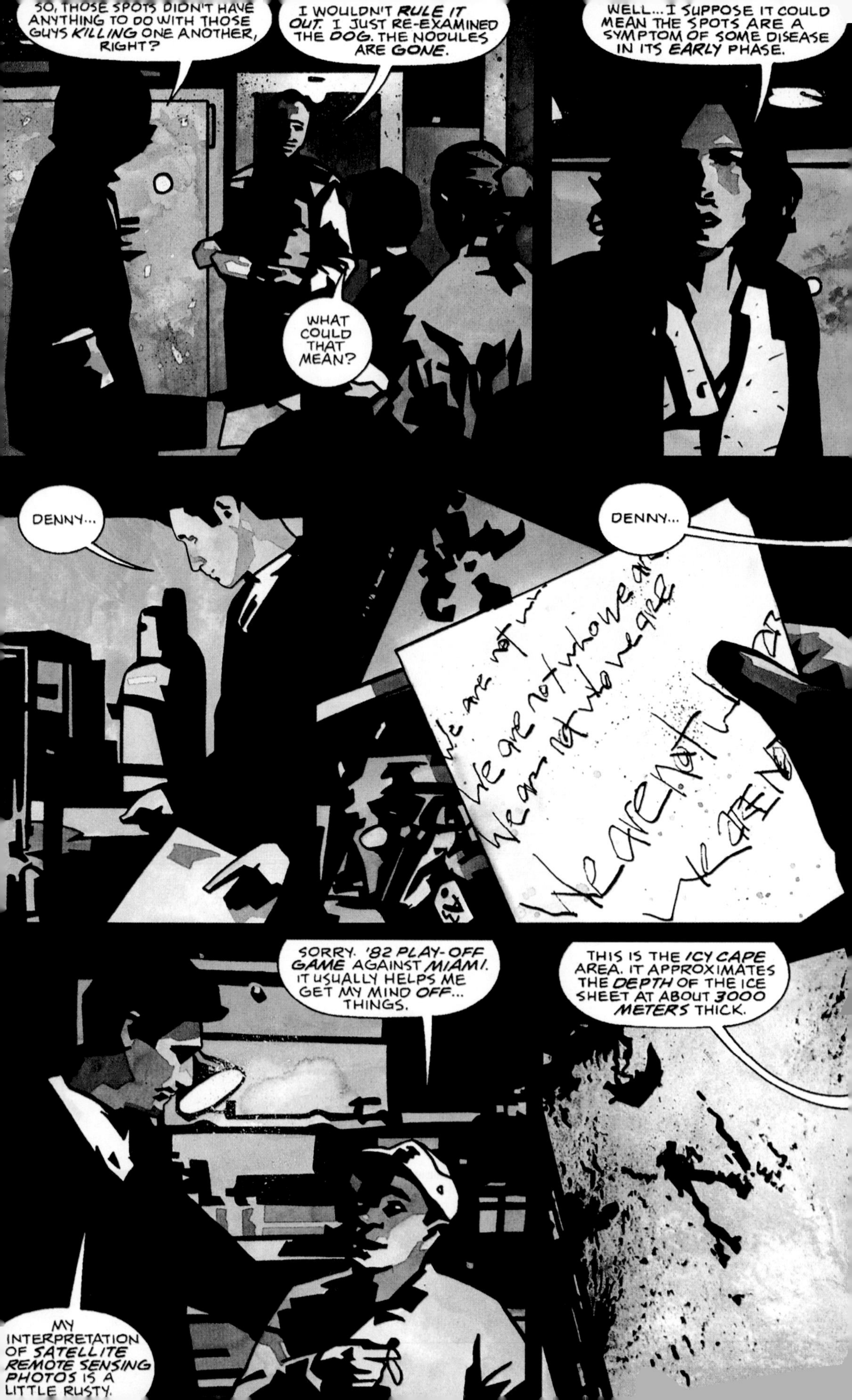

SO, THOSE SPOTS DIDN'T HAVE ANYTHING TO DO WITH THOSE GUYS *KILLING* ONE ANOTHER, RIGHT?
I WOULDN'T *RULE IT OUT.* I JUST RE-EXAMINED THE *DOG*. THE NODULES ARE *GONE*.
WHAT COULD THAT MEAN?
WELL... I SUPPOSE IT COULD MEAN THE SPOTS ARE A SYMPTOM OF SOME DISEASE IN ITS *EARLY* PHASE.
DENNY...
DENNY...
We are not who we are
We are not who we are
SORRY. *'82 PLAY-OFF GAME* AGAINST *MIAMI*. IT USUALLY HELPS ME GET MY MIND *OFF*... THINGS.
THIS IS THE *ICY CAPE* AREA. IT APPROXIMATES THE *DEPTH* OF THE ICE SHEET AT ABOUT *3000 METERS* THICK.
MY INTERPRETATION OF *SATELLITE REMOTE SENSING PHOTOS* IS A LITTLE RUSTY.

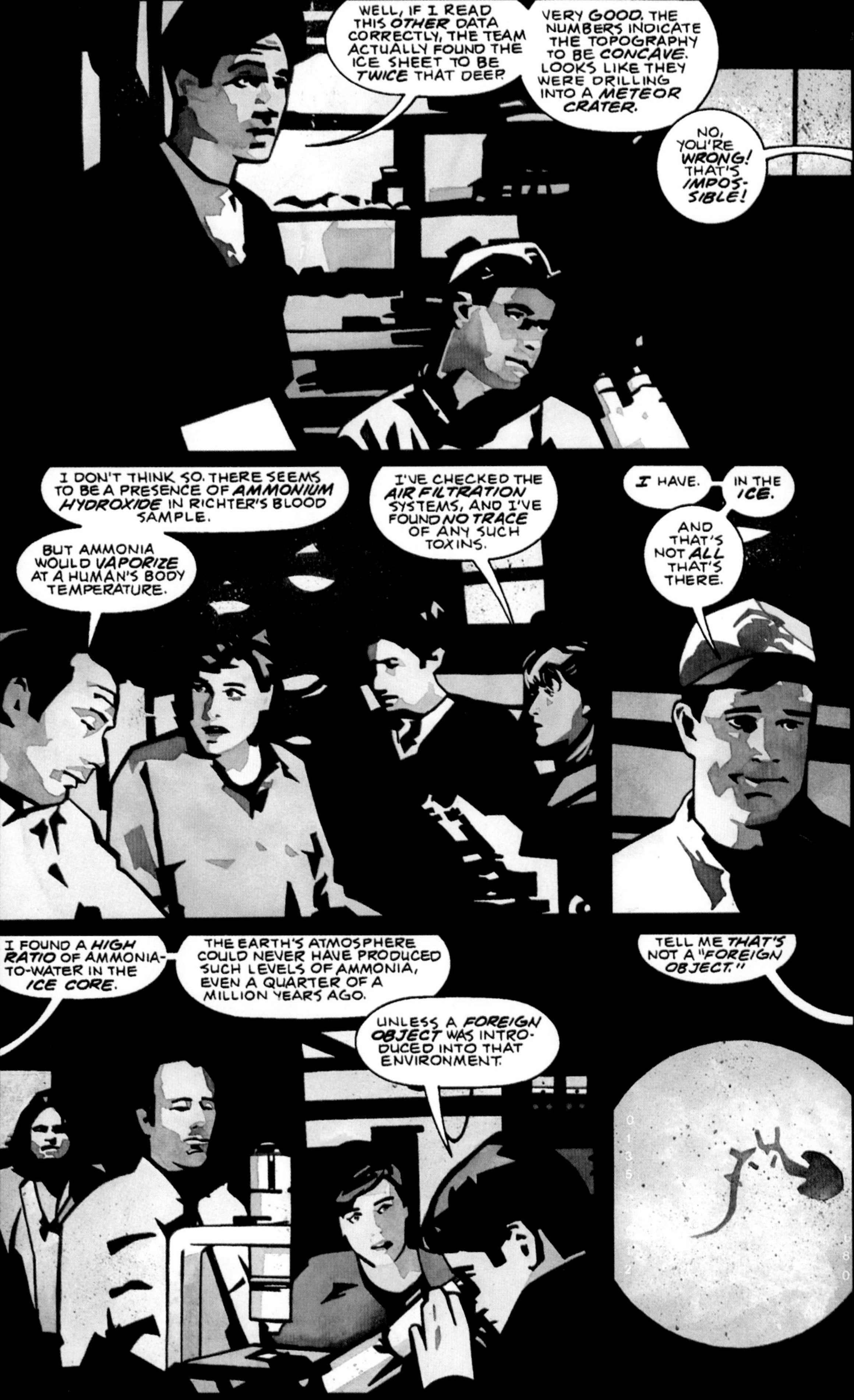
WELL, IF I READ THIS OTHER DATA CORRECTLY, THE TEAM ACTUALLY FOUND THE ICE SHEET TO BE TWICE THAT DEEP.
VERY GOOD. THE NUMBERS INDICATE THE TOPOGRAPHY TO BE CONCAVE. LOOKS LIKE THEY WERE DRILLING INTO A METEOR CRATER.
NO, YOU'RE WRONG! THAT'S IMPOS-SIBLE!
I DON'T THINK SO. THERE SEEMS TO BE A PRESENCE OF AMMONIUM HYDROXIDE IN RICHTER'S BLOOD SAMPLE.
BUT AMMONIA WOULD VAPORIZE AT A HUMAN'S BODY TEMPERATURE.
I'VE CHECKED THE AIR FILTRATION SYSTEMS, AND I'VE FOUND NO TRACE OF ANY SUCH TOXINS.
I HAVE.
IN THE ICE.
AND THAT'S NOT ALL THAT'S THERE.
I FOUND A HIGH RATIO OF AMMONIA-TO-WATER IN THE ICE CORE.
THE EARTH'S ATMOSPHERE COULD NEVER HAVE PRODUCED SUCH LEVELS OF AMMONIA, EVEN A QUARTER OF A MILLION YEARS AGO.
UNLESS A FOREIGN OBJECT WAS INTRO-DUCED INTO THAT ENVIRONMENT.
TELL ME THAT'S NOT A "FOREIGN OBJECT."

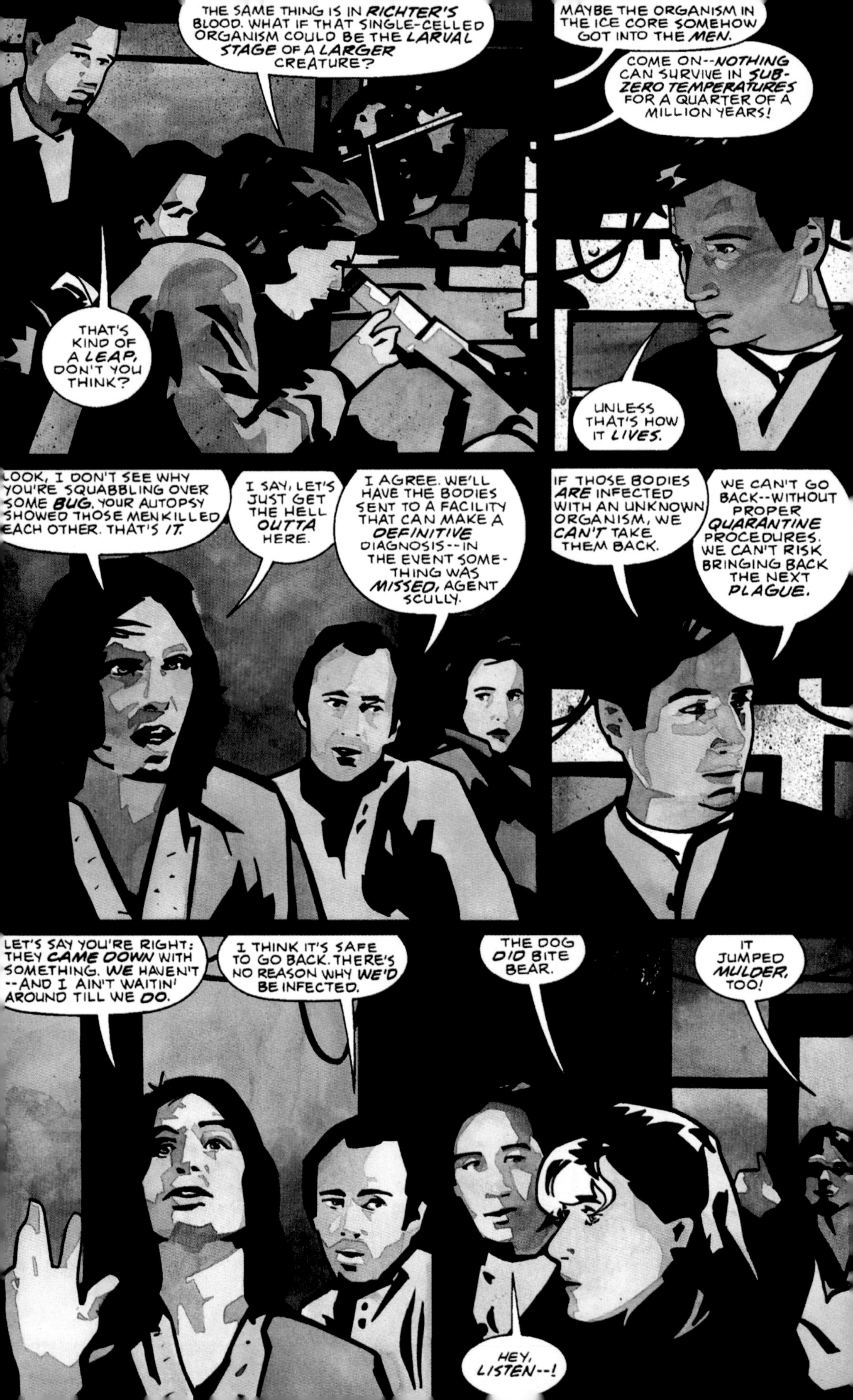
THE SAME THING IS IN RICHTER'S BLOOD. WHAT IF THAT SINGLE-CELLED ORGANISM COULD BE THE LARVAL STAGE OF A LARGER CREATURE?
THAT'S KIND OF A LEAP, DON'T YOU THINK?
MAYBE THE ORGANISM IN THE ICE CORE SOMEHOW GOT INTO THE MEN.
COME ON--NOTHING CAN SURVIVE IN SUB-ZERO TEMPERATURES FOR A QUARTER OF A MILLION YEARS!
UNLESS THAT'S HOW IT LIVES.
LOOK, I DON'T SEE WHY YOU'RE SQUABBLING OVER SOME BUG. YOUR AUTOPSY SHOWED THOSE MEN KILLED EACH OTHER. THAT'S IT.
I SAY, LET'S JUST GET THE HELL OUTTA HERE.
I AGREE. WE'LL HAVE THE BODIES SENT TO A FACILITY THAT CAN MAKE A DEFINITIVE DIAGNOSIS--IN THE EVENT SOMETHING WAS MISSED, AGENT SCULLY.
IF THOSE BODIES ARE INFECTED WITH AN UNKNOWN ORGANISM, WE CAN'T TAKE THEM BACK.
WE CAN'T GO BACK--WITHOUT PROPER QUARANTINE PROCEDURES. WE CAN'T RISK BRINGING BACK THE NEXT PLAGUE.
LET'S SAY YOU'RE RIGHT: THEY CAME DOWN WITH SOMETHING. WE HAVEN'T--AND I AIN'T WAITIN' AROUND TILL WE DO.
I THINK IT'S SAFE TO GO BACK. THERE'S NO REASON WHY WE'D BE INFECTED.
THE DOG DID BITE BEAR.
IT JUMPED MULDER, TOO!
HEY, LISTEN--!

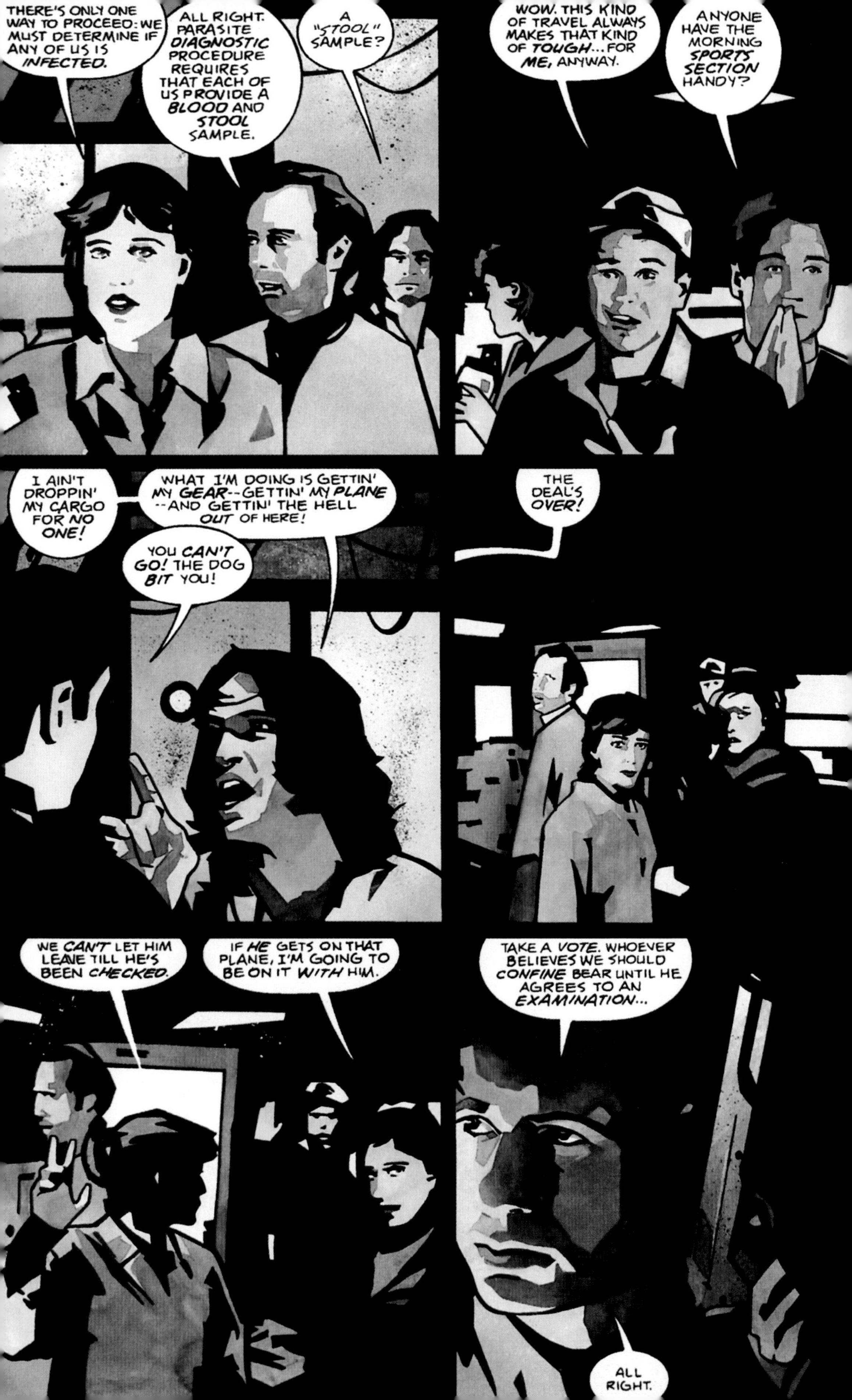
THERE'S ONLY ONE WAY TO PROCEED: WE MUST DETERMINE IF ANY OF US IS INFECTED.
ALL RIGHT. PARASITE DIAGNOSTIC PROCEDURE REQUIRES THAT EACH OF US PROVIDE A BLOOD AND STOOL SAMPLE.
A "STOOL" SAMPLE?
WOW. THIS KIND OF TRAVEL ALWAYS MAKES THAT KIND OF TOUGH... FOR ME, ANYWAY.
ANYONE HAVE THE MORNING SPORTS SECTION HANDY?
I AIN'T DROPPIN' MY CARGO FOR NO ONE!
WHAT I'M DOING IS GETTIN' MY GEAR--GETTIN' MY PLANE --AND GETTIN' THE HELL OUT OF HERE!
YOU CAN'T GO! THE DOG BIT YOU!
THE DEAL'S OVER!
WE CAN'T LET HIM LEAVE TILL HE'S BEEN CHECKED.
IF HE GETS ON THAT PLANE, I'M GOING TO BE ON IT WITH HIM.
TAKE A VOTE. WHOEVER BELIEVES WE SHOULD CONFINE BEAR UNTIL HE AGREES TO AN EXAMINATION...
ALL RIGHT.

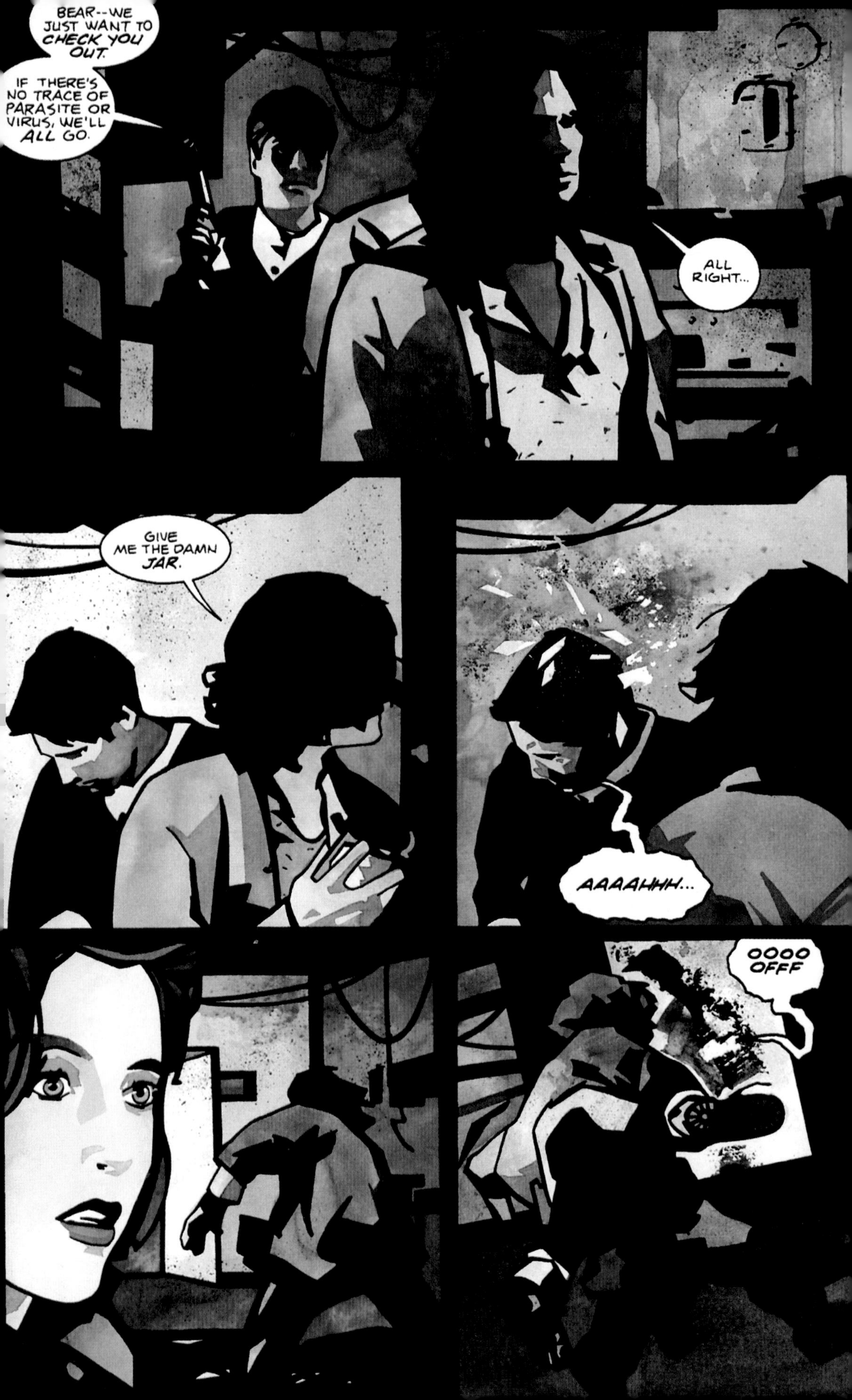
BEAR--WE JUST WANT TO CHECK YOU OUT.
IF THERE'S NO TRACE OF PARASITE OR VIRUS, WE'LL ALL GO.
ALL RIGHT...
GIVE ME THE DAMN JAR.
AAAAHHH...
OOOO OFFF

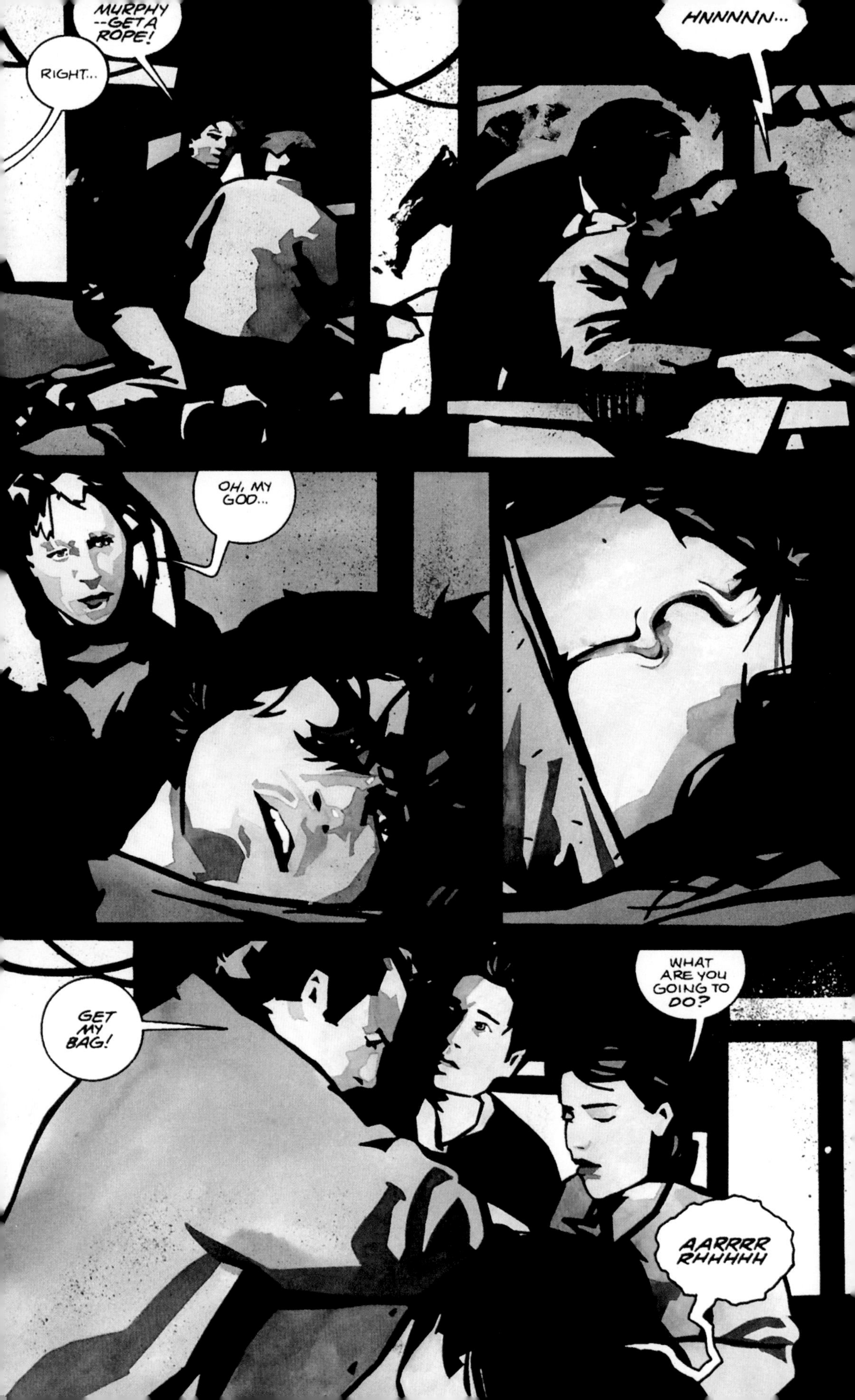
MURPHY --GET A ROPE!
RIGHT...
HNNNNN...
OH, MY GOD...
GET MY BAG!
WHAT ARE YOU GOING TO DO?
AARRRR RHHHHH

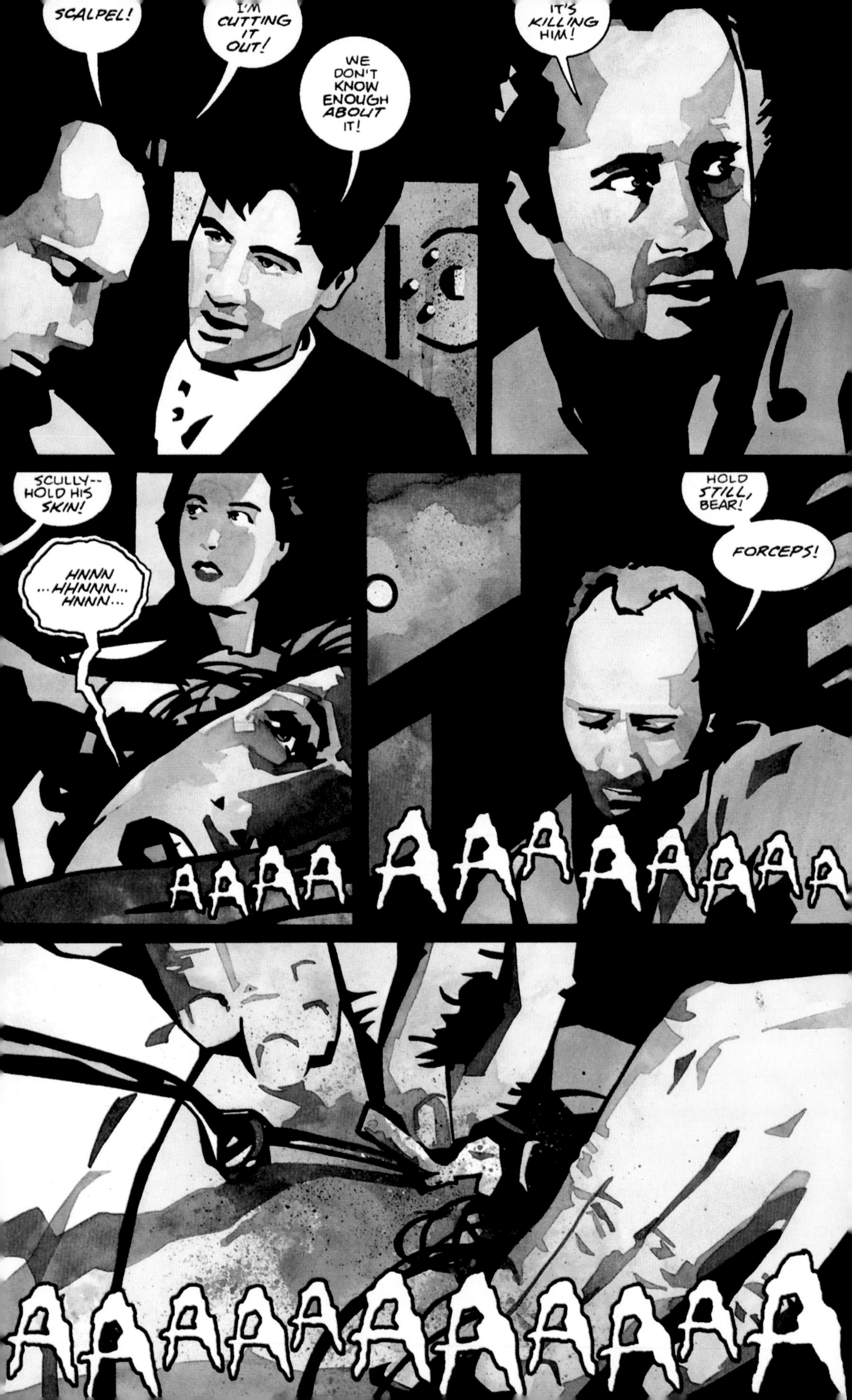
SCALPEL!
I'M CUTTING IT OUT!
WE DON'T KNOW ENOUGH ABOUT IT!
IT'S KILLING HIM!
SCULLY-- HOLD HIS SKIN!
HNNN ...HHNNN... HNNN...
HOLD STILL, BEAR!
FORCEPS!
AAAA AAAAAAAA
AAAAAAAAAAAA

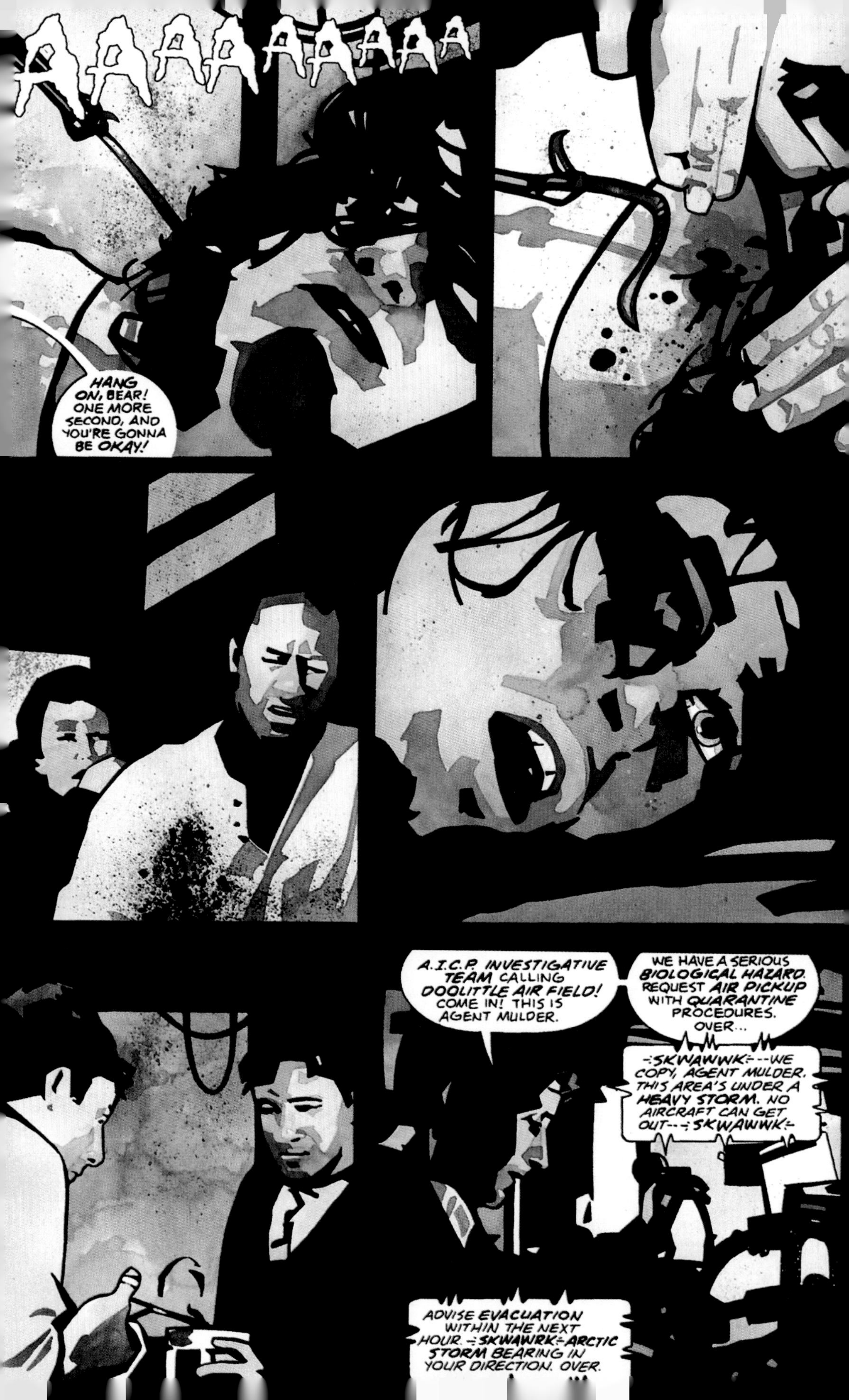
AAAAAAAAA
HANG ON, BEAR! ONE MORE SECOND, AND YOU'RE GONNA BE OKAY!
A.I.C.P. INVESTIGATIVE TEAM CALLING DOOLITTLE AIR FIELD! COME IN! THIS IS AGENT MULDER.
WE HAVE A SERIOUS BIOLOGICAL HAZARD. REQUEST AIR PICKUP WITH QUARANTINE PROCEDURES. OVER...
=SKWAWWK= --WE COPY, AGENT MULDER. THIS AREA'S UNDER A HEAVY STORM. NO AIRCRAFT CAN GET OUT-- =SKWAWWK=
ADVISE EVACUATION WITHIN THE NEXT HOUR. =SKWAWRK= ARCTIC STORM BEARING IN YOUR DIRECTION. OVER.

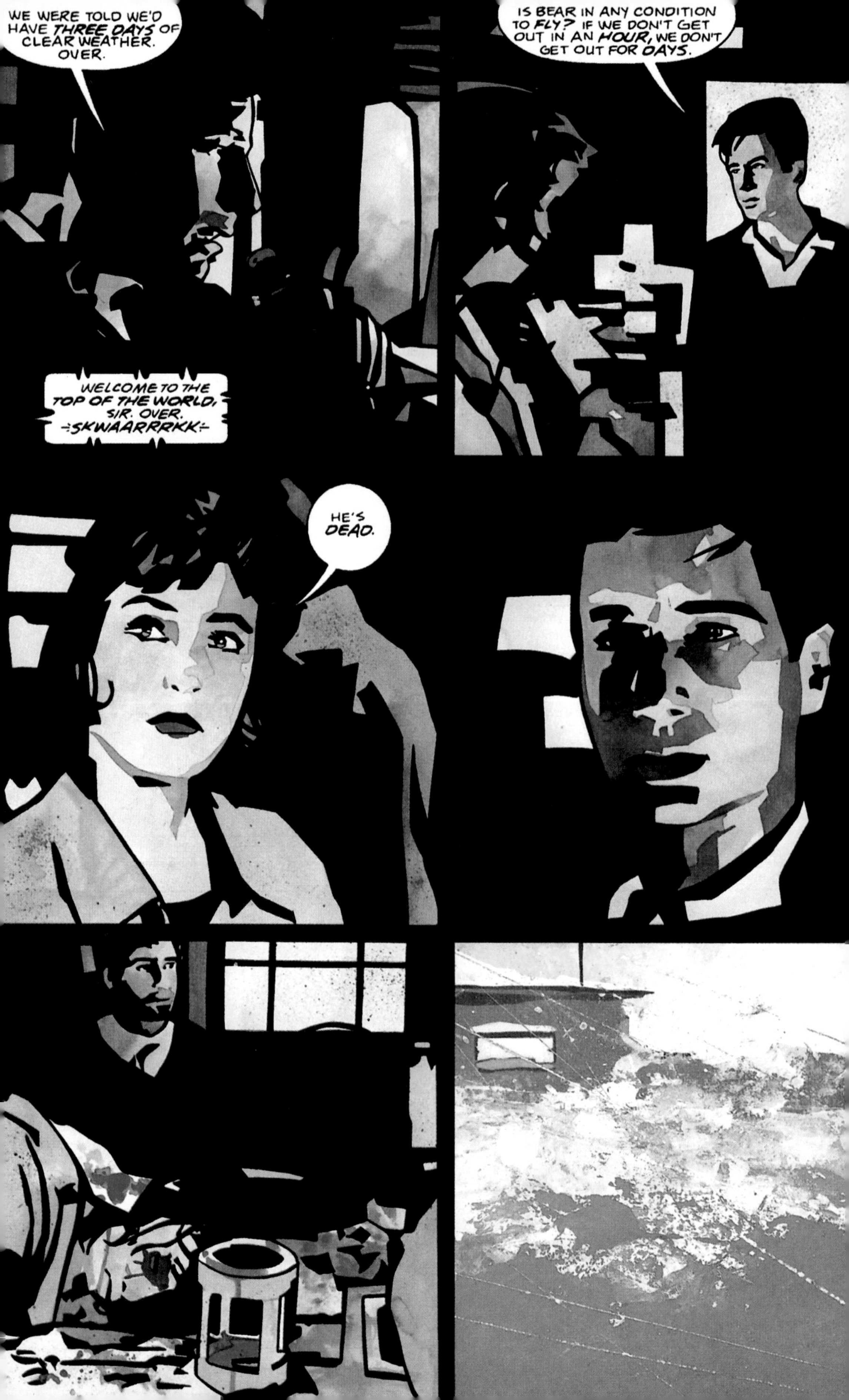
WE WERE TOLD WE'D HAVE THREE DAYS OF CLEAR WEATHER. OVER.
WELCOME TO THE TOP OF THE WORLD, SIR. OVER. -SKWAARRRKK-
IS BEAR IN ANY CONDITION TO FLY? IF WE DON'T GET OUT IN AN HOUR, WE DON'T GET OUT FOR DAYS.
HE'S DEAD.

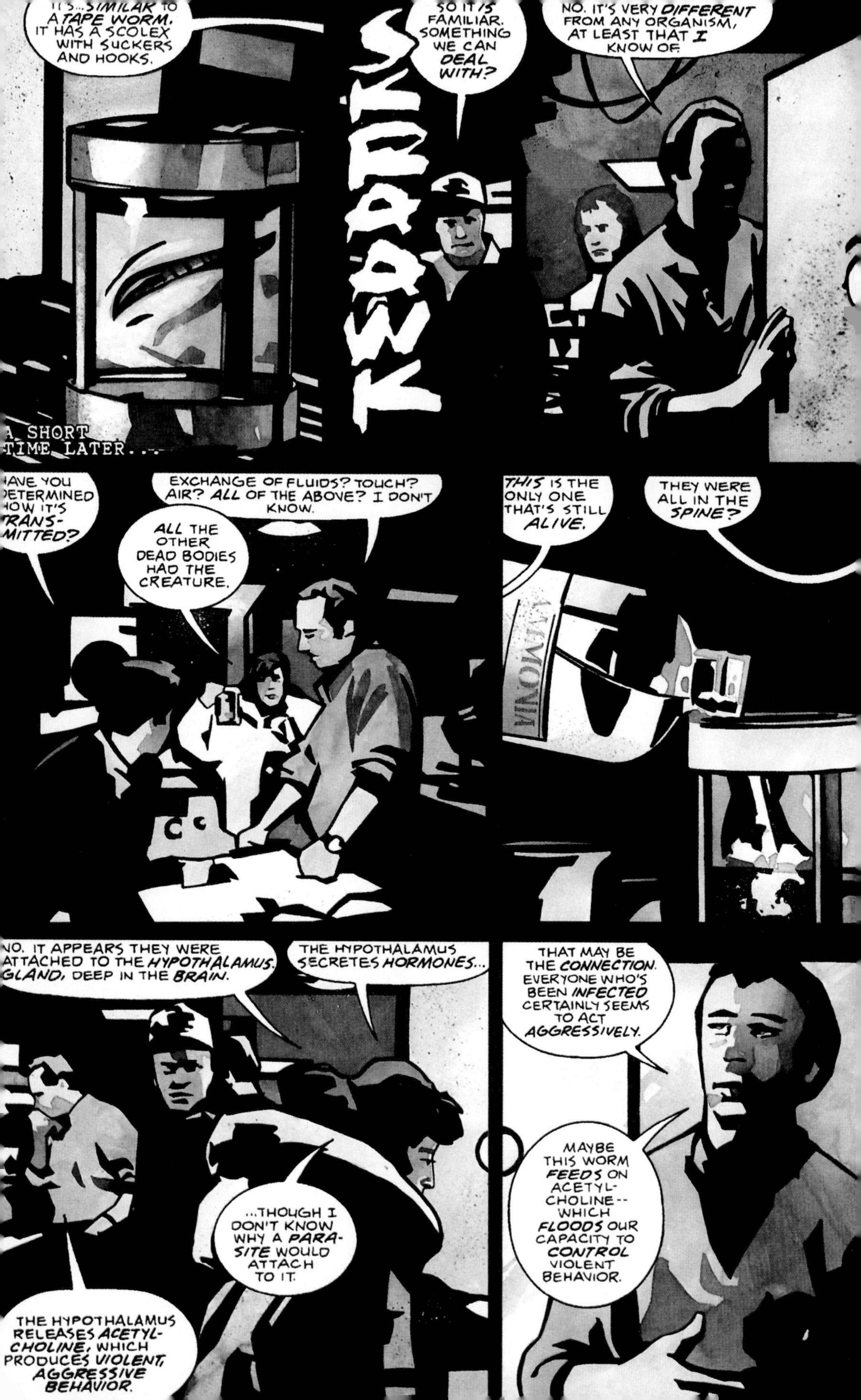
IT'S...SIMILAR TO A TAPE WORM. IT HAS A SCOLEX WITH SUCKERS AND HOOKS.
SO IT IS FAMILIAR. SOMETHING WE CAN DEAL WITH?
NO. IT'S VERY DIFFERENT FROM ANY ORGANISM, AT LEAST THAT I KNOW OF.
A SHORT TIME LATER...
HAVE YOU DETERMINED HOW IT'S TRANSMITTED?
EXCHANGE OF FLUIDS? TOUCH? AIR? ALL OF THE ABOVE? I DON'T KNOW.
ALL THE OTHER DEAD BODIES HAD THE CREATURE.
THIS IS THE ONLY ONE THAT'S STILL ALIVE.
THEY WERE ALL IN THE SPINE?
AMMONIA
NO. IT APPEARS THEY WERE ATTACHED TO THE HYPOTHALAMUS GLAND, DEEP IN THE BRAIN.
THE HYPOTHALAMUS SECRETES HORMONES...
...THOUGH I DON'T KNOW WHY A PARASITE WOULD ATTACH TO IT.
THE HYPOTHALAMUS RELEASES ACETYLCHOLINE, WHICH PRODUCES VIOLENT, AGGRESSIVE BEHAVIOR.
THAT MAY BE THE CONNECTION. EVERYONE WHO'S BEEN INFECTED CERTAINLY SEEMS TO ACT AGGRESSIVELY.
MAYBE THIS WORM FEEDS ON ACETYLCHOLINE-- WHICH FLOODS OUR CAPACITY TO CONTROL VIOLENT BEHAVIOR.

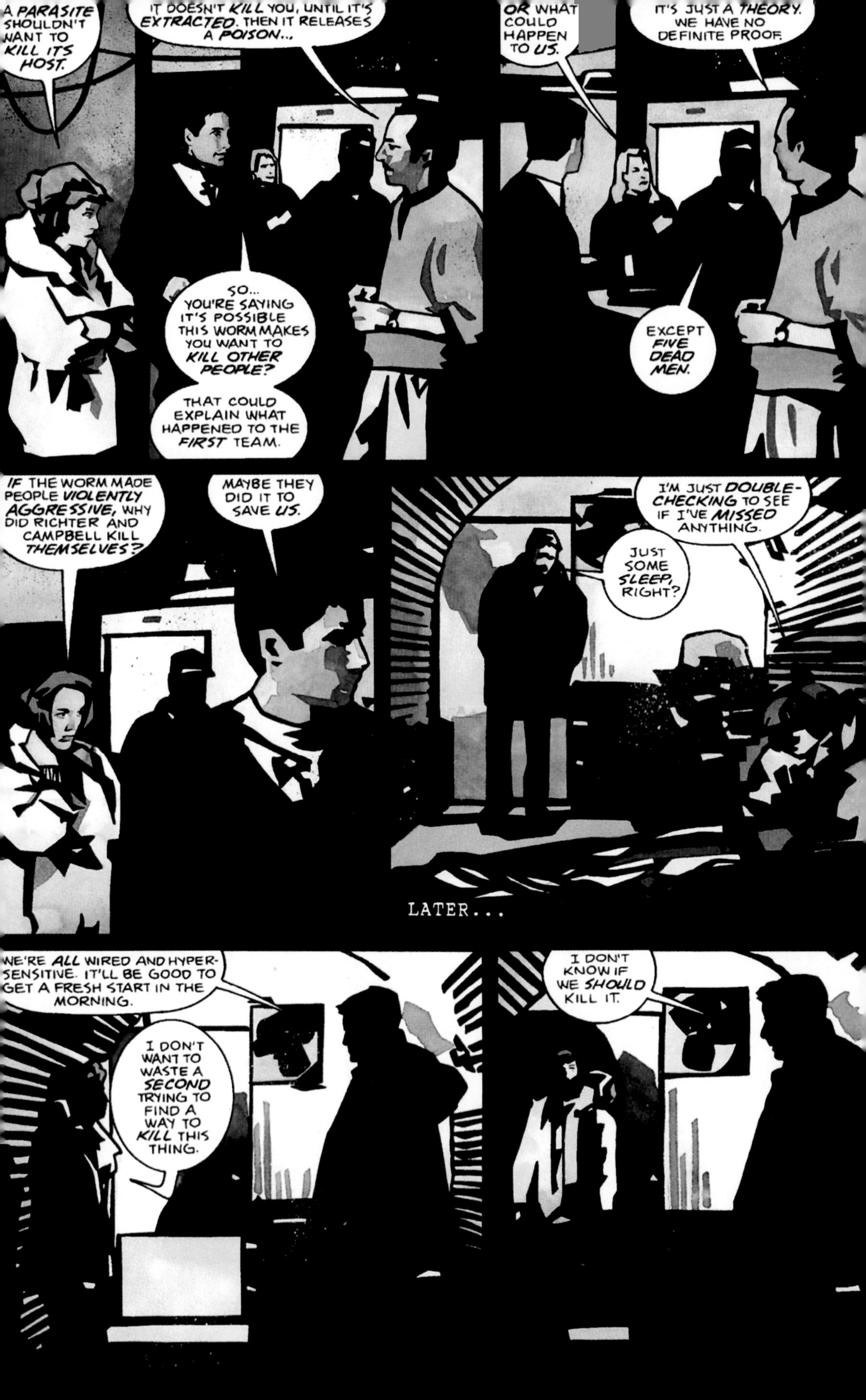

A PARASITE SHOULDN'T WANT TO KILL ITS HOST.
IT DOESN'T KILL YOU, UNTIL IT'S EXTRACTED. THEN IT RELEASES A POISON...
SO... YOU'RE SAYING IT'S POSSIBLE THIS WORM MAKES YOU WANT TO KILL OTHER PEOPLE?
THAT COULD EXPLAIN WHAT HAPPENED TO THE FIRST TEAM.
OR WHAT COULD HAPPEN TO US.
IT'S JUST A THEORY. WE HAVE NO DEFINITE PROOF.
EXCEPT FIVE DEAD MEN.
IF THE WORM MADE PEOPLE VIOLENTLY AGGRESSIVE, WHY DID RICHTER AND CAMPBELL KILL THEMSELVES?
MAYBE THEY DID IT TO SAVE US.
I'M JUST DOUBLE-CHECKING TO SEE IF I'VE MISSED ANYTHING.
JUST SOME SLEEP, RIGHT?
LATER...
WE'RE ALL WIRED AND HYPER-SENSITIVE. IT'LL BE GOOD TO GET A FRESH START IN THE MORNING.
I DON'T WANT TO WASTE A SECOND TRYING TO FIND A WAY TO KILL THIS THING.
I DON'T KNOW IF WE SHOULD KILL IT.

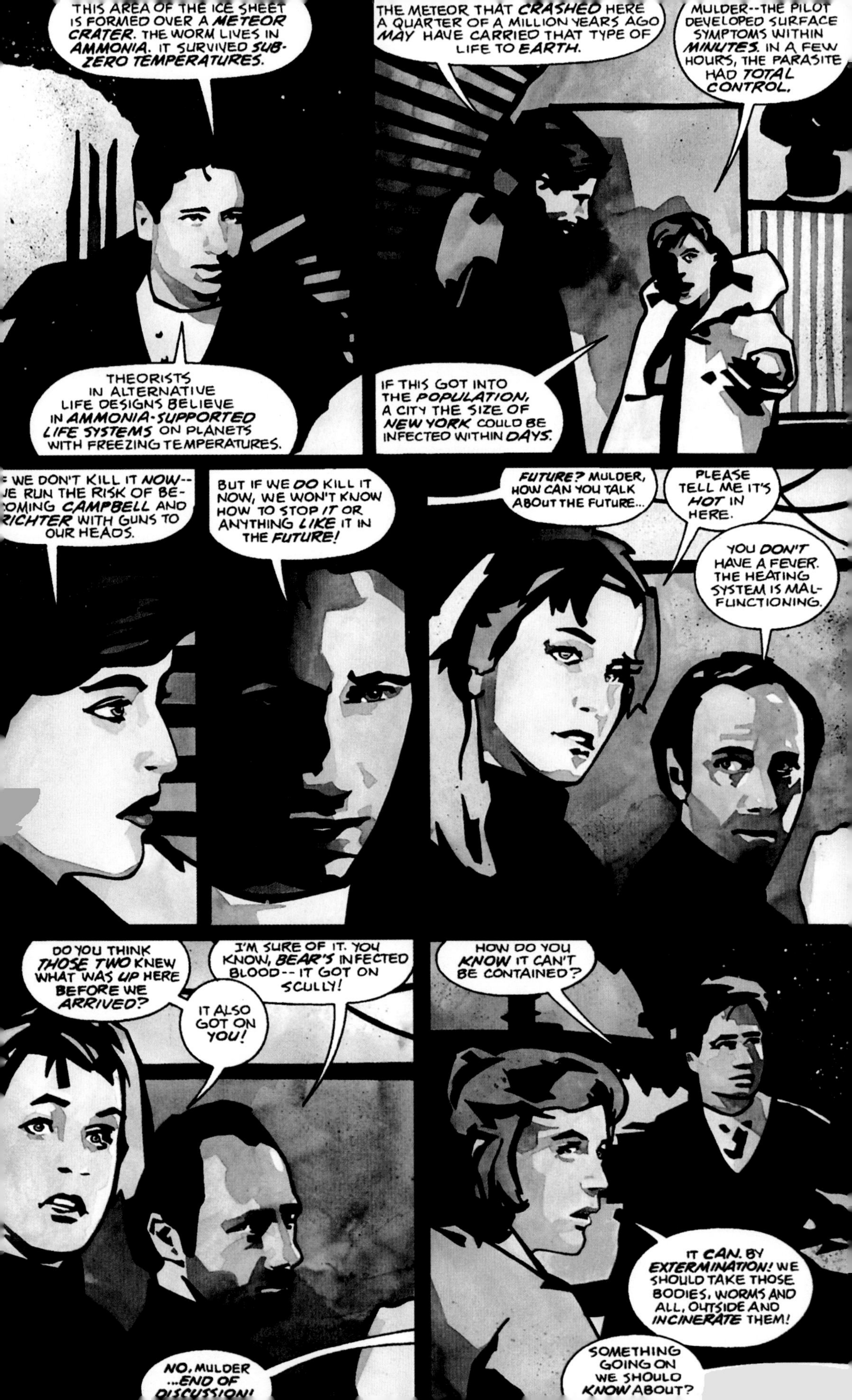
THIS AREA OF THE ICE SHEET IS FORMED OVER A METEOR CRATER. THE WORM LIVES IN AMMONIA. IT SURVIVED SUB-ZERO TEMPERATURES.
THEORISTS IN ALTERNATIVE LIFE DESIGNS BELIEVE IN AMMONIA-SUPPORTED LIFE SYSTEMS ON PLANETS WITH FREEZING TEMPERATURES.
THE METEOR THAT CRASHED HERE A QUARTER OF A MILLION YEARS AGO MAY HAVE CARRIED THAT TYPE OF LIFE TO EARTH.
MULDER--THE PILOT DEVELOPED SURFACE SYMPTOMS WITHIN MINUTES. IN A FEW HOURS, THE PARASITE HAD TOTAL CONTROL.
IF THIS GOT INTO THE POPULATION, A CITY THE SIZE OF NEW YORK COULD BE INFECTED WITHIN DAYS.
F WE DON'T KILL IT NOW-- JE RUN THE RISK OF BE-OMING CAMPBELL AND RICHTER WITH GUNS TO OUR HEADS.
BUT IF WE DO KILL IT NOW, WE WON'T KNOW HOW TO STOP IT OR ANYTHING LIKE IT IN THE FUTURE!
FUTURE? MULDER, HOW CAN YOU TALK ABOUT THE FUTURE...
PLEASE TELL ME IT'S HOT IN HERE.
YOU DON'T HAVE A FEVER. THE HEATING SYSTEM IS MAL-FUNCTIONING.
DO YOU THINK THOSE TWO KNEW WHAT WAS UP HERE BEFORE WE ARRIVED?
I'M SURE OF IT. YOU KNOW, BEAR'S INFECTED BLOOD-- IT GOT ON SCULLY!
IT ALSO GOT ON YOU!
NO, MULDER ...END OF DISCUSSION!
HOW DO YOU KNOW IT CAN'T BE CONTAINED?
IT CAN. BY EXTERMINATION! WE SHOULD TAKE THOSE BODIES, WORMS AND ALL, OUTSIDE AND INCINERATE THEM!
SOMETHING GOING ON WE SHOULD KNOW ABOUT?

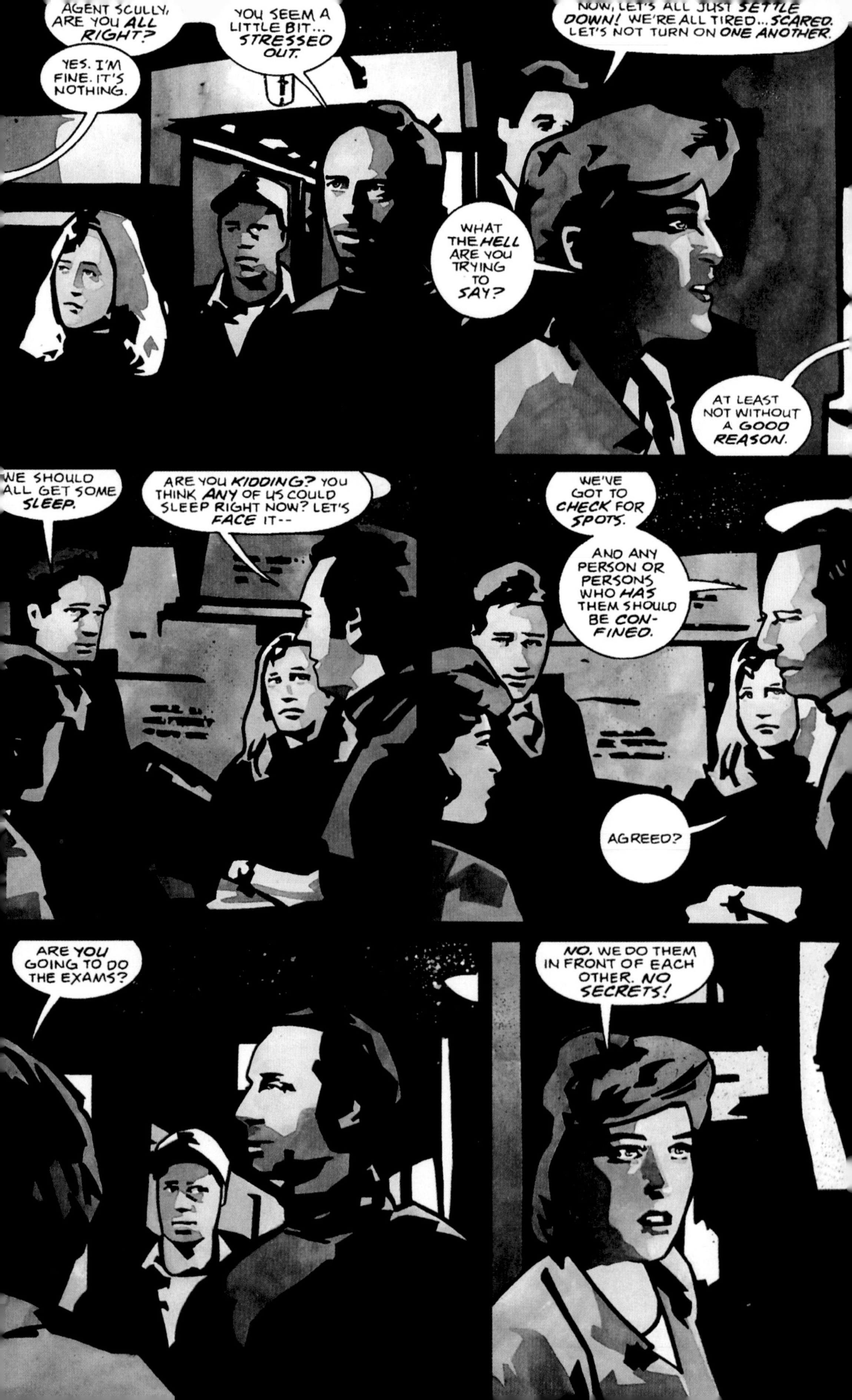
AGENT SCULLY, ARE YOU ALL RIGHT?
YES. I'M FINE. IT'S NOTHING.
YOU SEEM A LITTLE BIT... STRESSED OUT.
NOW, LET'S ALL JUST SETTLE DOWN! WE'RE ALL TIRED... SCARED. LET'S NOT TURN ON ONE ANOTHER.
WHAT THE HELL ARE YOU TRYING TO SAY?
AT LEAST NOT WITHOUT A GOOD REASON.
WE SHOULD ALL GET SOME SLEEP.
ARE YOU KIDDING? YOU THINK ANY OF US COULD SLEEP RIGHT NOW? LET'S FACE IT--
WE'VE GOT TO CHECK FOR SPOTS.
AND ANY PERSON OR PERSONS WHO HAS THEM SHOULD BE CON-FINED.
AGREED?
ARE YOU GOING TO DO THE EXAMS?
NO. WE DO THEM IN FRONT OF EACH OTHER. NO SECRETS!

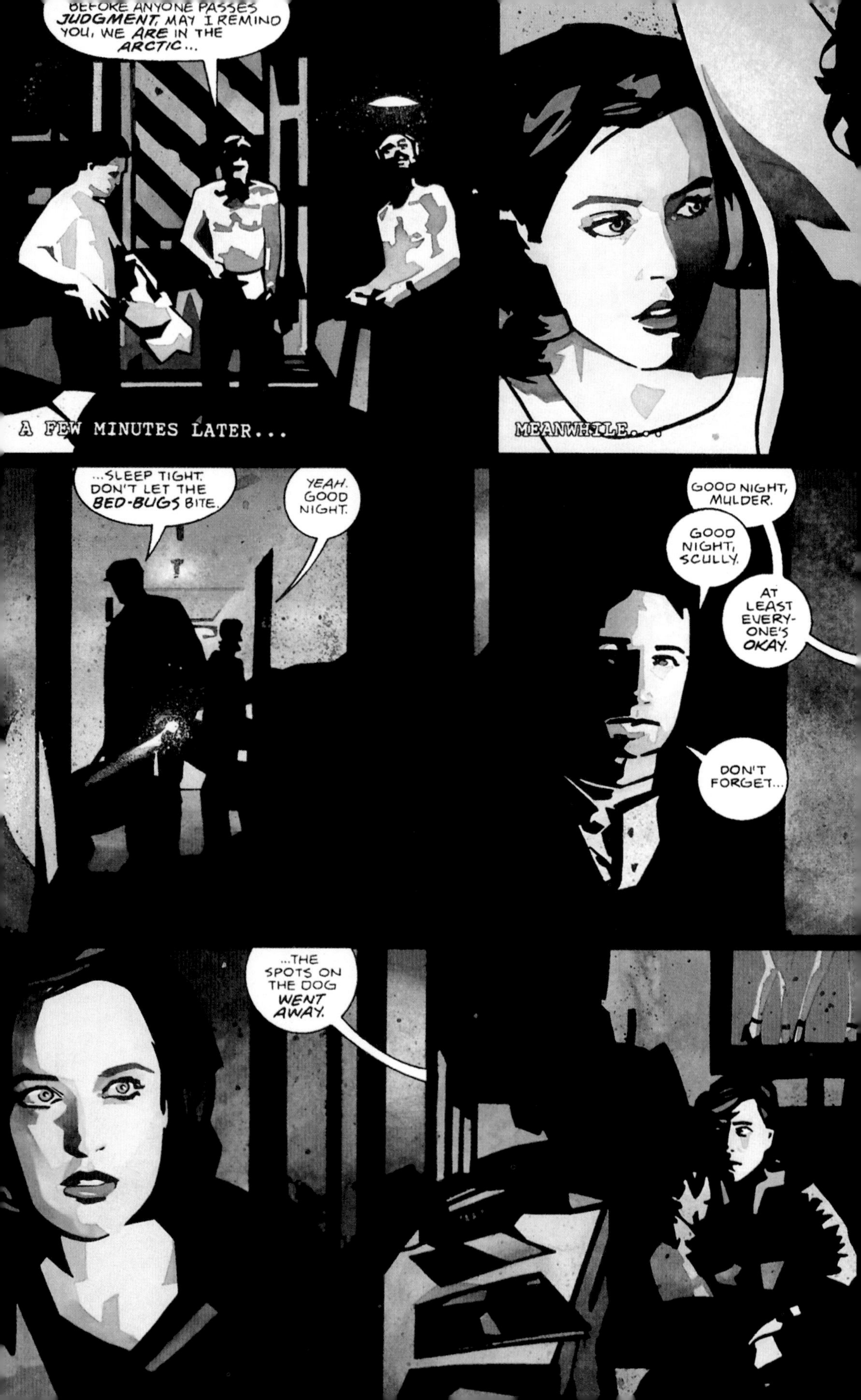
BEFORE ANYONE PASSES JUDGMENT, MAY I REMIND YOU, WE ARE IN THE ARCTIC...
A FEW MINUTES LATER...
MEANWHILE...
...SLEEP TIGHT. DON'T LET THE BED-BUGS BITE.
YEAH. GOOD NIGHT.
GOOD NIGHT, MULDER.
GOOD NIGHT, SCULLY.
AT LEAST EVERY-ONE'S OKAY.
DON'T FORGET...
...THE SPOTS ON THE DOG WENT AWAY.

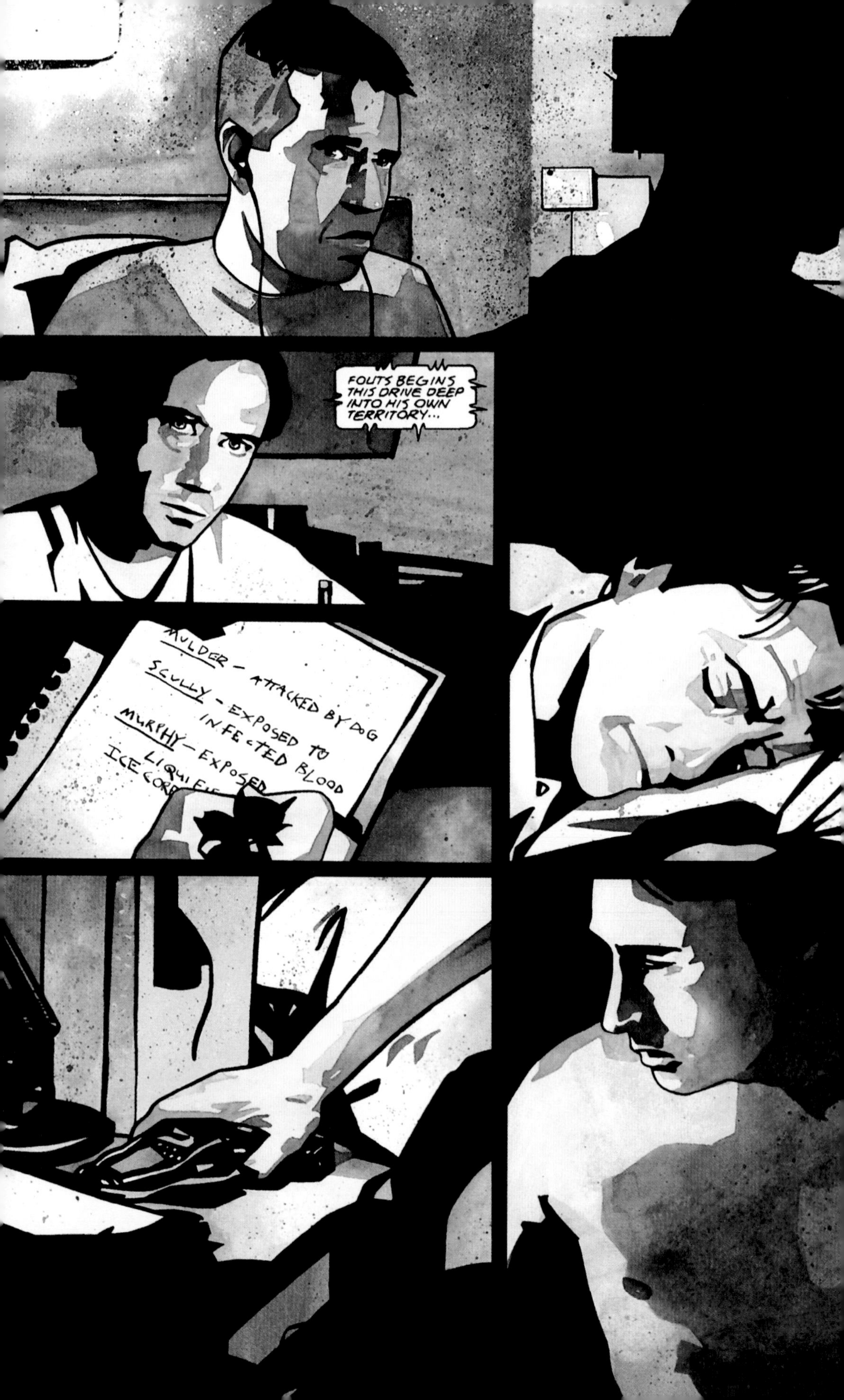
FOUTS BEGINS THIS DRIVE DEEP INTO HIS OWN TERRITORY...
MULDER – ATTACKED BY DOG
SCULLY – EXPOSED TO INFECTED BLOOD
MURPHY – EXPOSED

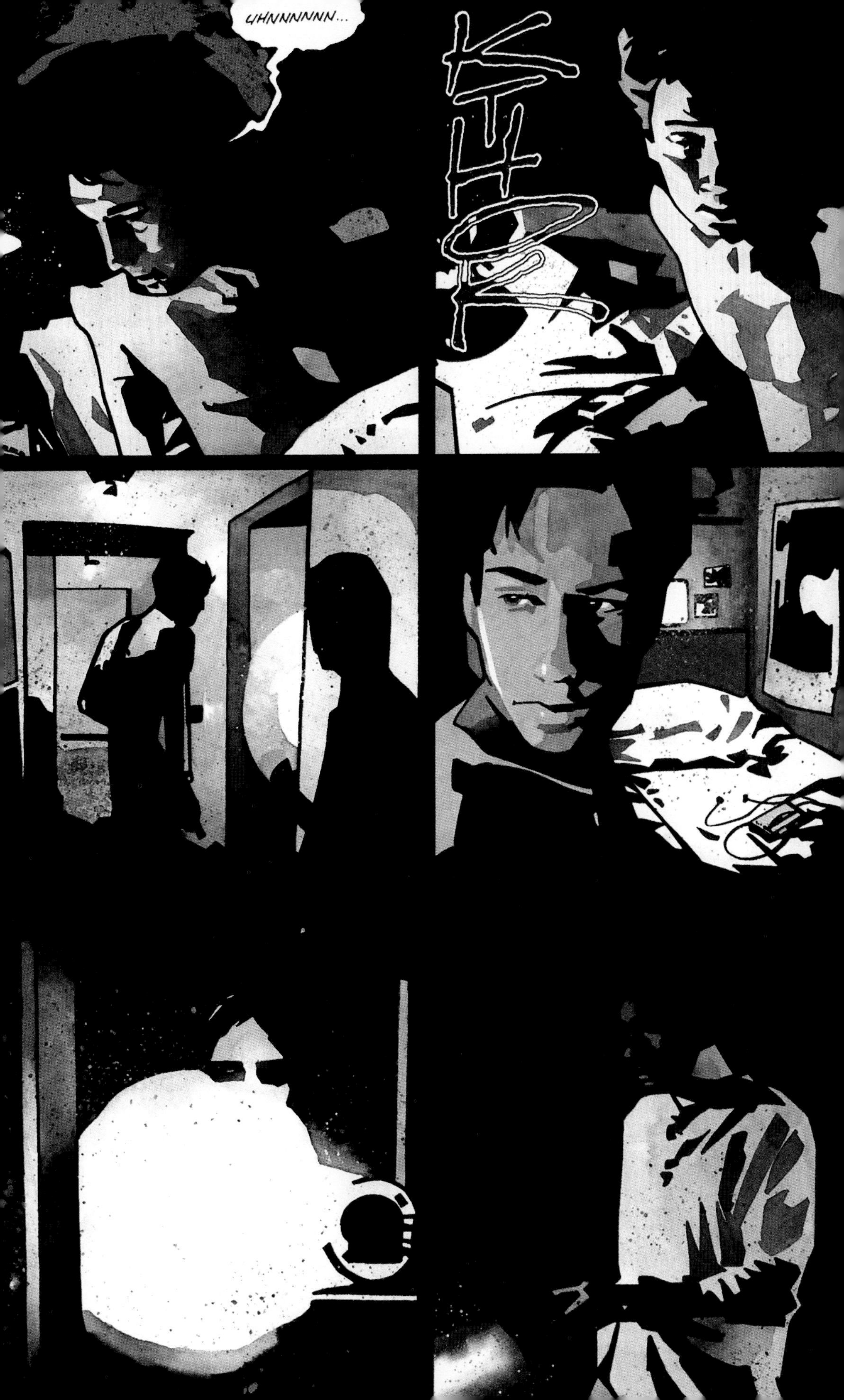
UHNNNNNN...
KTHR

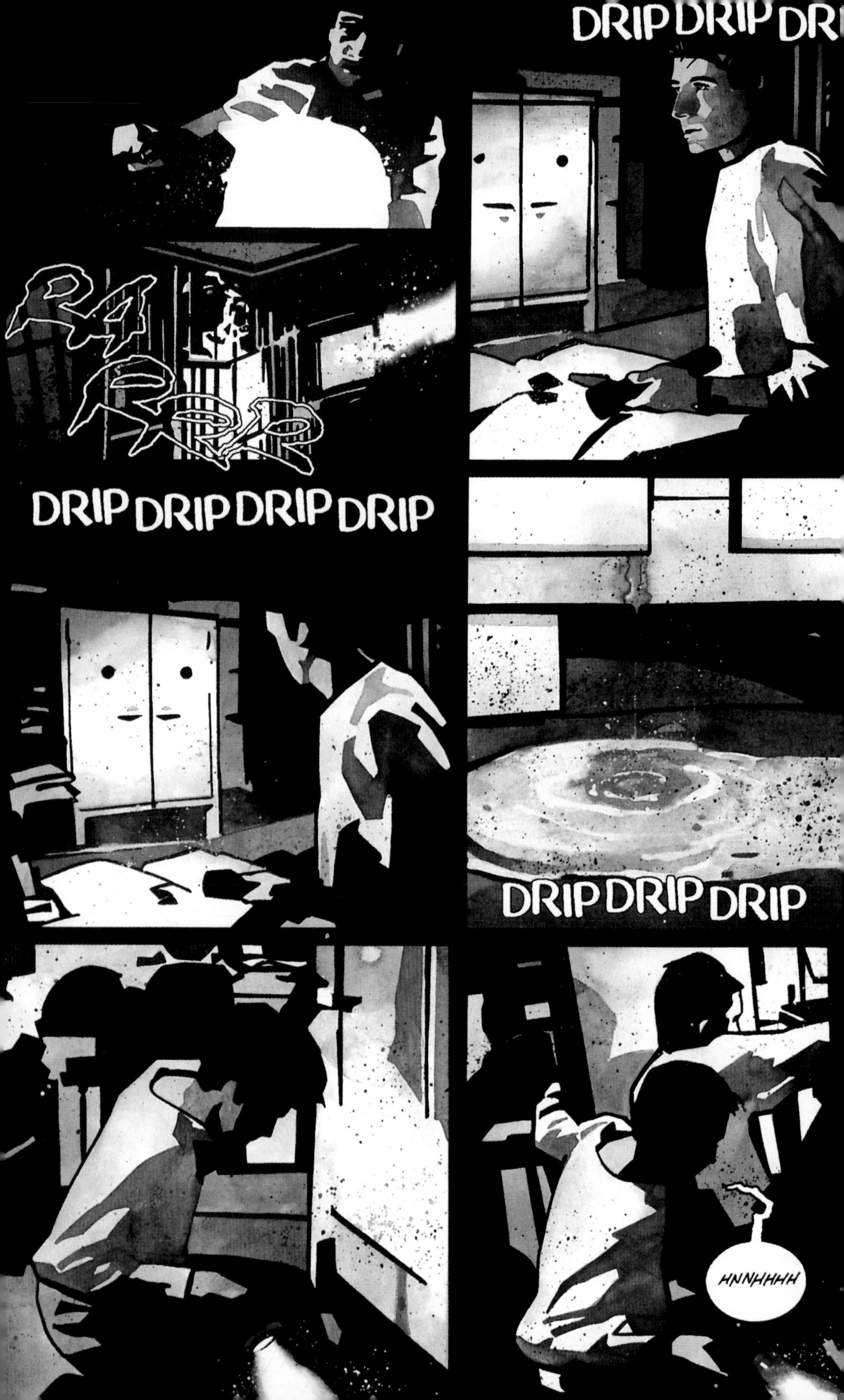
DRIP DRIP DRI
DRIP DRIP DRIP DRIP
DRIP DRIP DRIP
HNNHHHH

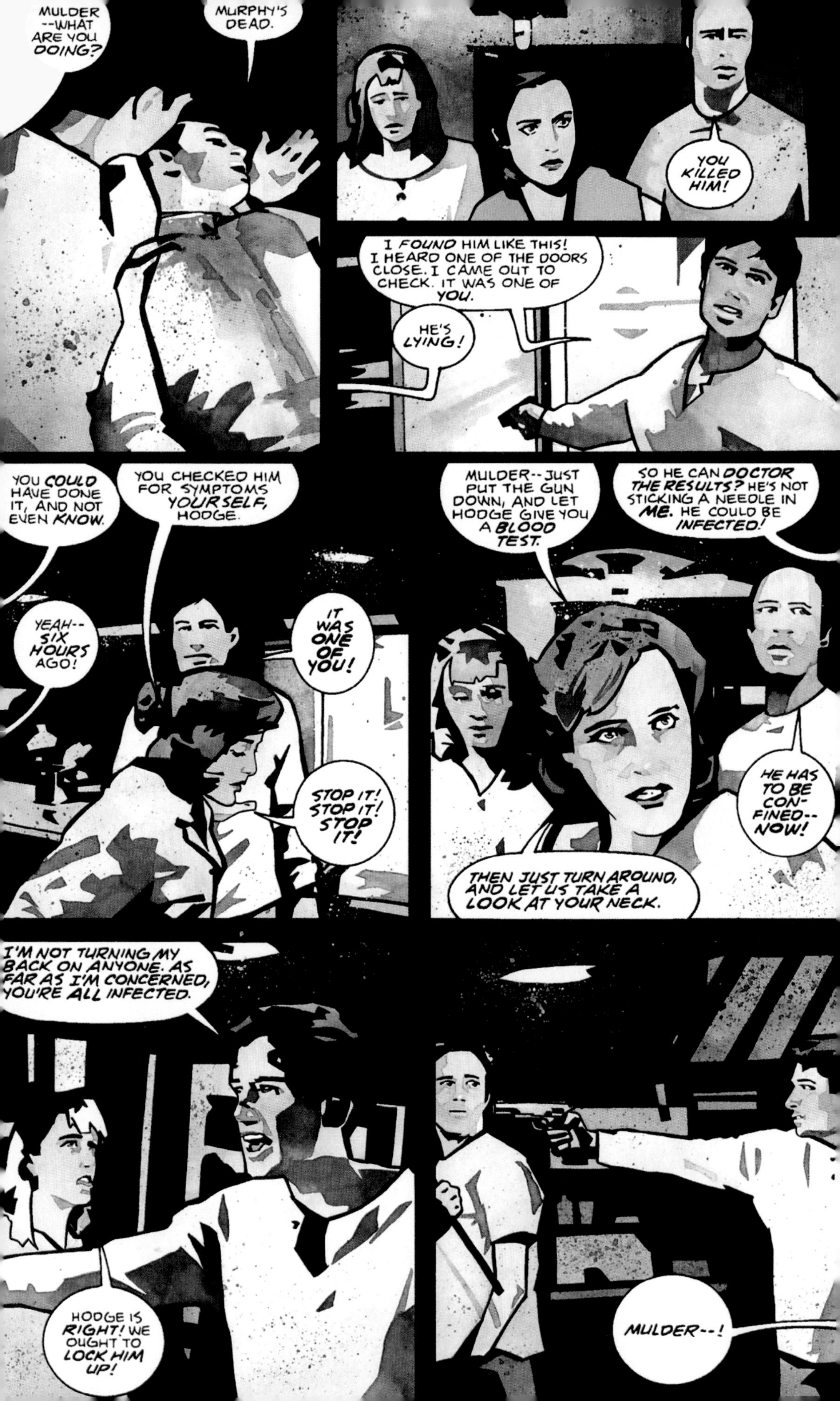
MULDER --WHAT ARE YOU DOING?
MURPHY'S DEAD.
YOU KILLED HIM!
I FOUND HIM LIKE THIS! I HEARD ONE OF THE DOORS CLOSE. I CAME OUT TO CHECK. IT WAS ONE OF YOU.
HE'S LYING!
YOU COULD HAVE DONE IT, AND NOT EVEN KNOW.
YOU CHECKED HIM FOR SYMPTOMS YOURSELF, HODGE.
YEAH-- SIX HOURS AGO!
IT WAS ONE OF YOU!
STOP IT! STOP IT! STOP IT!
MULDER-- JUST PUT THE GUN DOWN, AND LET HODGE GIVE YOU A BLOOD TEST.
SO HE CAN DOCTOR THE RESULTS? HE'S NOT STICKING A NEEDLE IN ME. HE COULD BE INFECTED!
HE HAS TO BE CON-FINED-- NOW!
THEN JUST TURN AROUND, AND LET US TAKE A LOOK AT YOUR NECK.
I'M NOT TURNING MY BACK ON ANYONE. AS FAR AS I'M CONCERNED, YOU'RE ALL INFECTED.
HODGE IS RIGHT! WE OUGHT TO LOCK HIM UP!
MULDER--!

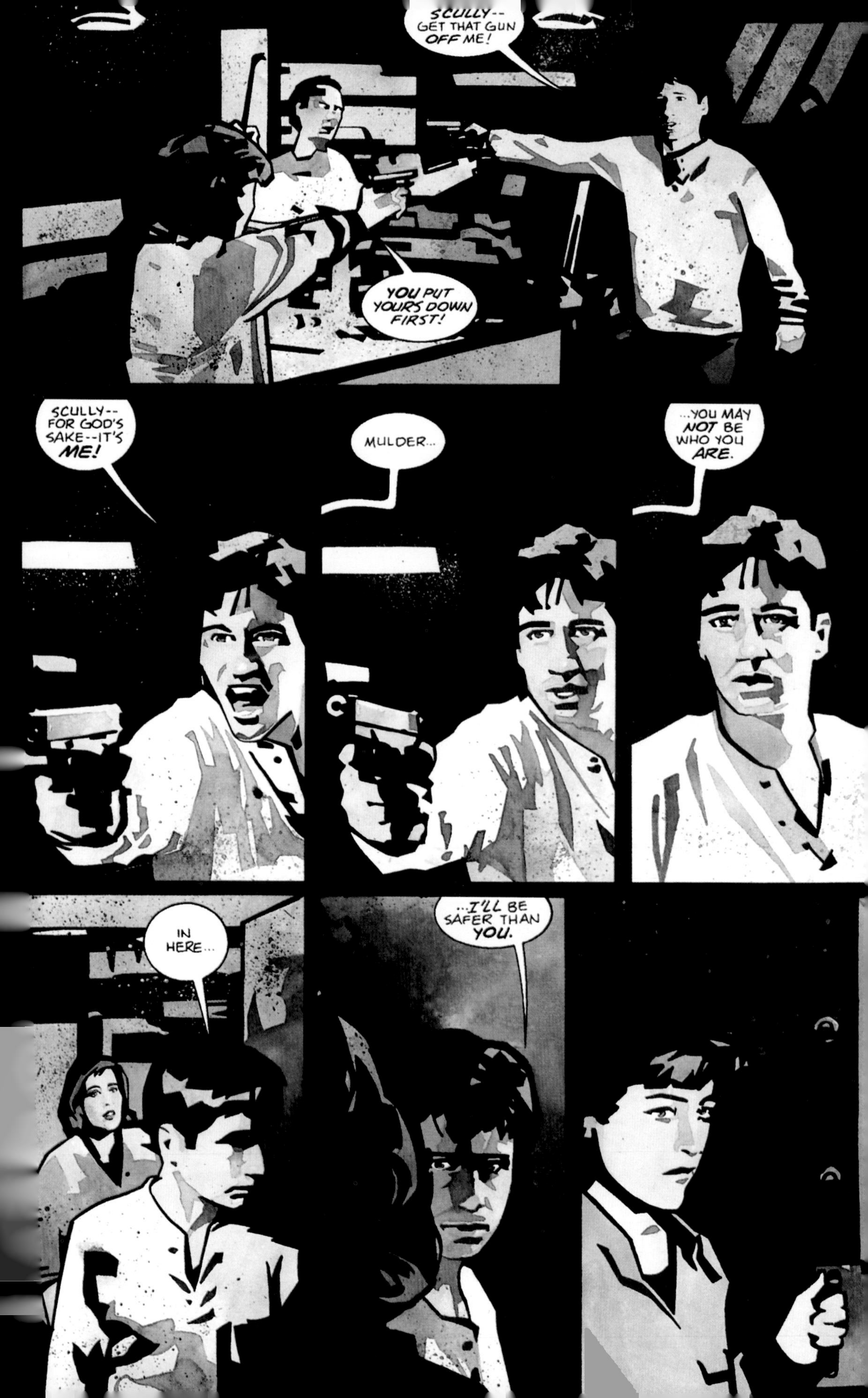

SCULLY--
GET THAT GUN
OFF ME!
YOU PUT
YOURS DOWN
FIRST!
SCULLY--
FOR GOD'S
SAKE--IT'S
ME!
MULDER...
...YOU MAY
NOT BE
WHO YOU
ARE.
IN
HERE...
...I'LL BE
SAFER THAN
YOU.

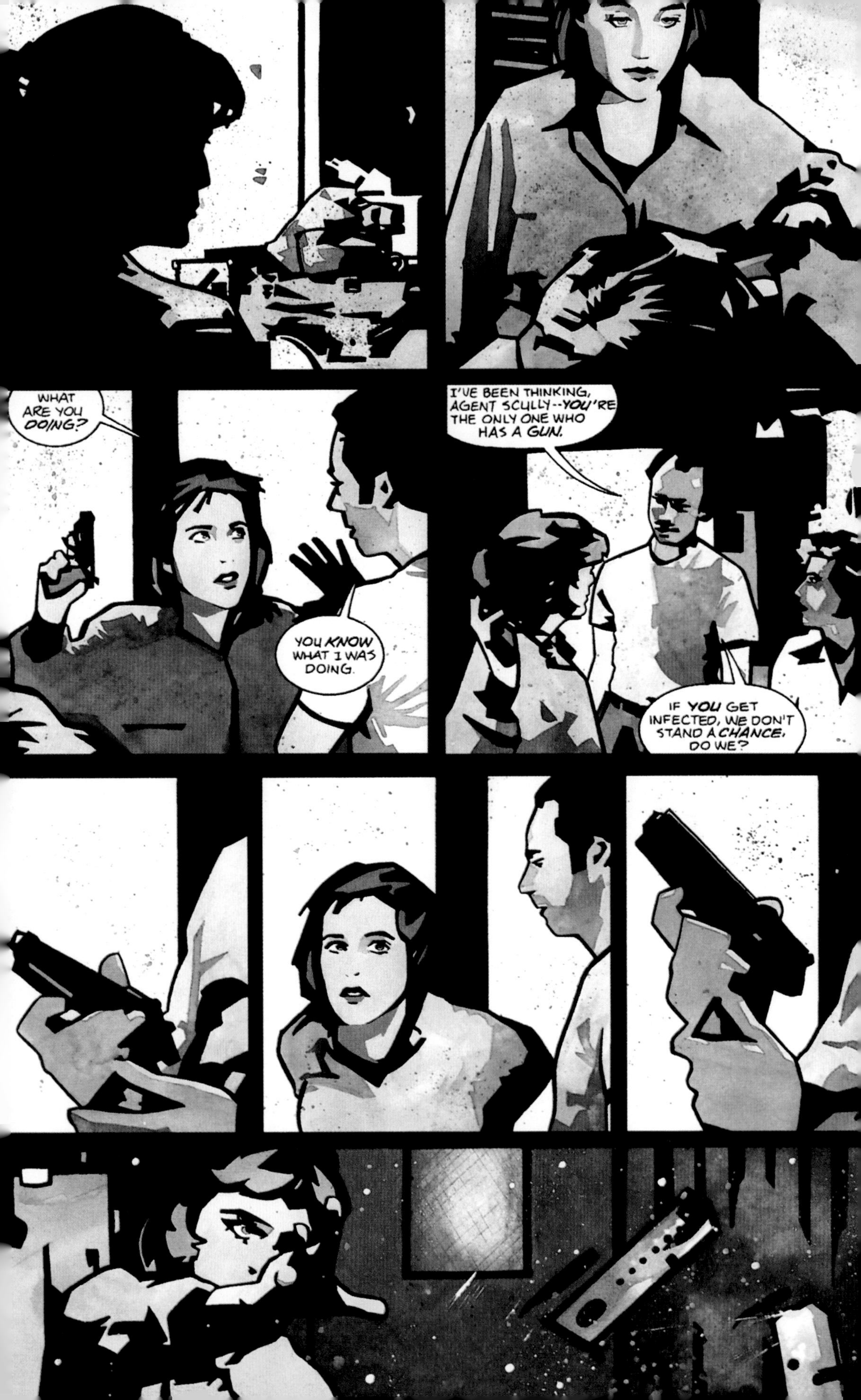
WHAT ARE YOU DOING?
YOU KNOW WHAT I WAS DOING.
I'VE BEEN THINKING, AGENT SCULLY--YOU'RE THE ONLY ONE WHO HAS A GUN.
IF YOU GET INFECTED, WE DON'T STAND A CHANCE, DO WE?

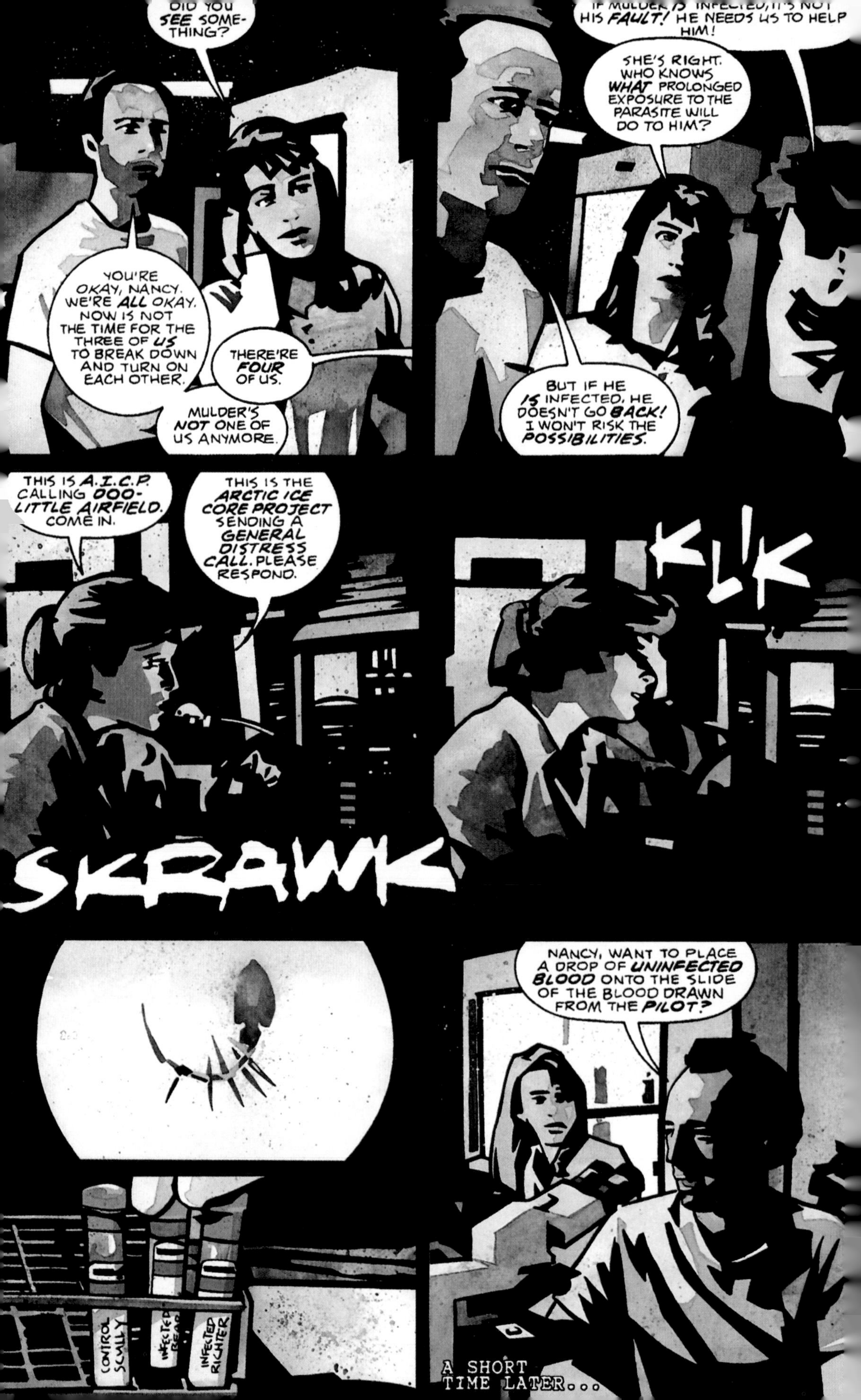
DID YOU SEE SOME-THING?
YOU'RE OKAY, NANCY. WE'RE ALL OKAY. NOW IS NOT THE TIME FOR THE THREE OF US TO BREAK DOWN AND TURN ON EACH OTHER.
THERE'RE FOUR OF US.
MULDER'S NOT ONE OF US ANYMORE.
IF MULDER IS INFECTED, IT'S NOT HIS FAULT! HE NEEDS US TO HELP HIM!
SHE'S RIGHT. WHO KNOWS WHAT PROLONGED EXPOSURE TO THE PARASITE WILL DO TO HIM?
BUT IF HE IS INFECTED, HE DOESN'T GO BACK! I WON'T RISK THE POSSIBILITIES.
THIS IS A.I.C.P. CALLING DOO-LITTLE AIRFIELD. COME IN.
THIS IS THE ARCTIC ICE CORE PROJECT SENDING A GENERAL DISTRESS CALL. PLEASE RESPOND.
SKRAWK
KLIK
A SHORT TIME LATER...
CONTROL SCULLY
INFECTED BEAR
INFECTED RICHTER
NANCY, WANT TO PLACE A DROP OF UNINFECTED BLOOD ONTO THE SLIDE OF THE BLOOD DRAWN FROM THE PILOT?

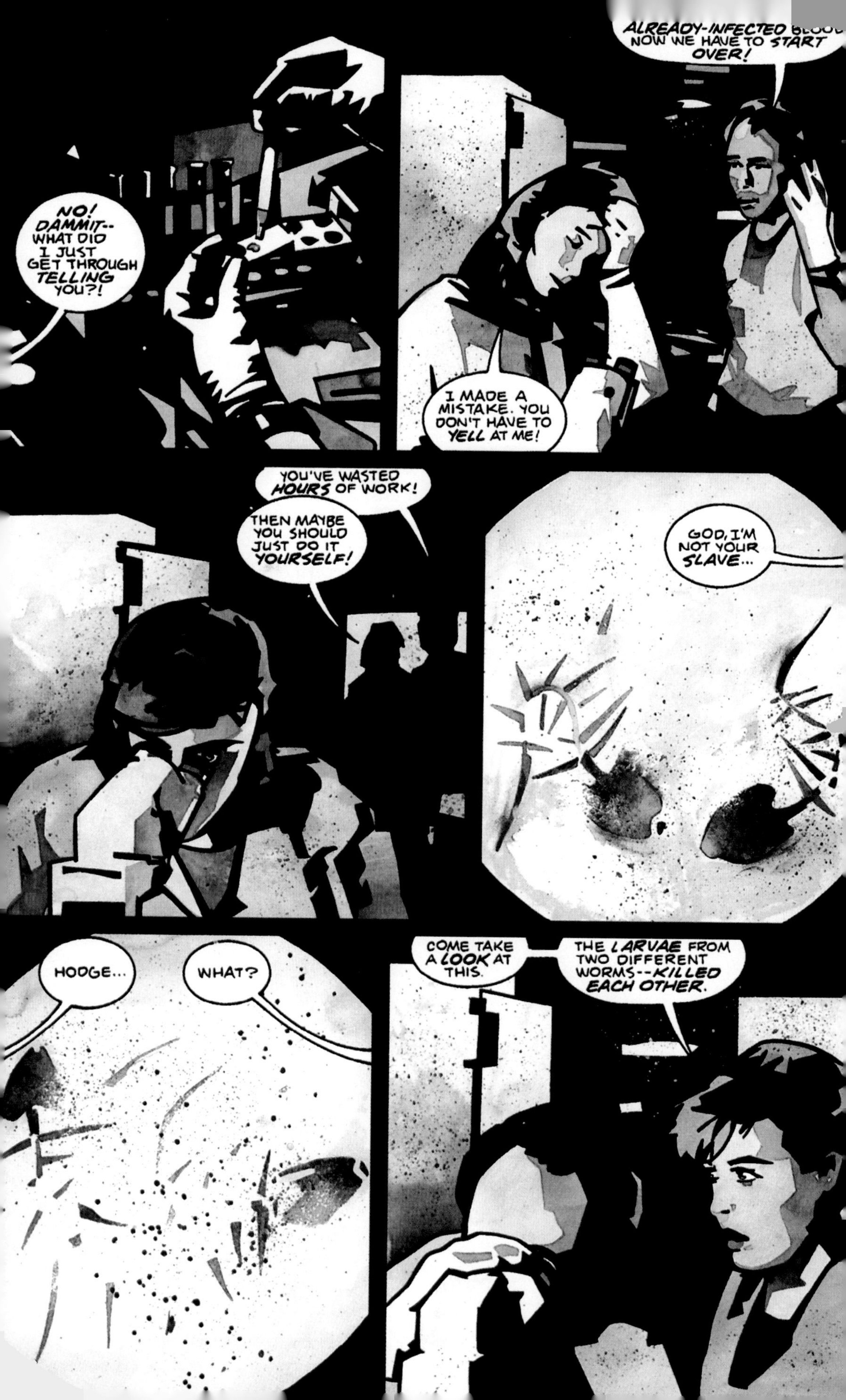
ALREADY-INFECTED BLOOD NOW WE HAVE TO START OVER!
NO! DAMMIT-- WHAT DID I JUST GET THROUGH TELLING YOU?!
I MADE A MISTAKE. YOU DON'T HAVE TO YELL AT ME!
YOU'VE WASTED HOURS OF WORK!
THEN MAYBE YOU SHOULD JUST DO IT YOURSELF!
GOD, I'M NOT YOUR SLAVE...
HODGE...
WHAT?
COME TAKE A LOOK AT THIS.
THE LARVAE FROM TWO DIFFERENT WORMS--KILLED EACH OTHER.

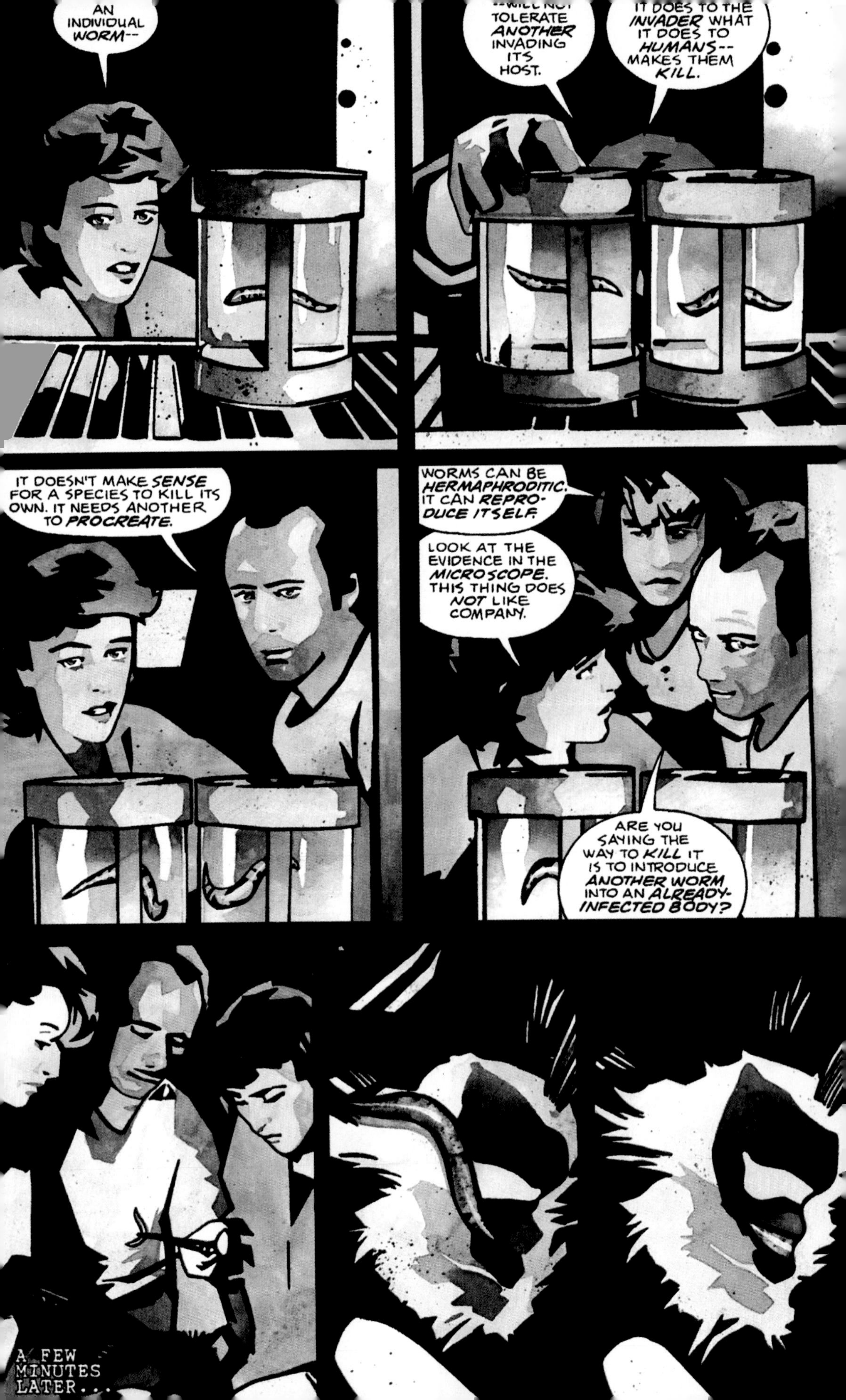
AN INDIVIDUAL WORM--
--WILL NOT TOLERATE ANOTHER INVADING ITS HOST.
IT DOES TO THE INVADER WHAT IT DOES TO HUMANS-- MAKES THEM KILL.
IT DOESN'T MAKE SENSE FOR A SPECIES TO KILL ITS OWN. IT NEEDS ANOTHER TO PROCREATE.
WORMS CAN BE HERMAPHRODITIC. IT CAN REPRODUCE ITSELF.
LOOK AT THE EVIDENCE IN THE MICROSCOPE. THIS THING DOES NOT LIKE COMPANY.
ARE YOU SAYING THE WAY TO KILL IT IS TO INTRODUCE ANOTHER WORM INTO AN ALREADY-INFECTED BODY?
A FEW MINUTES LATER...

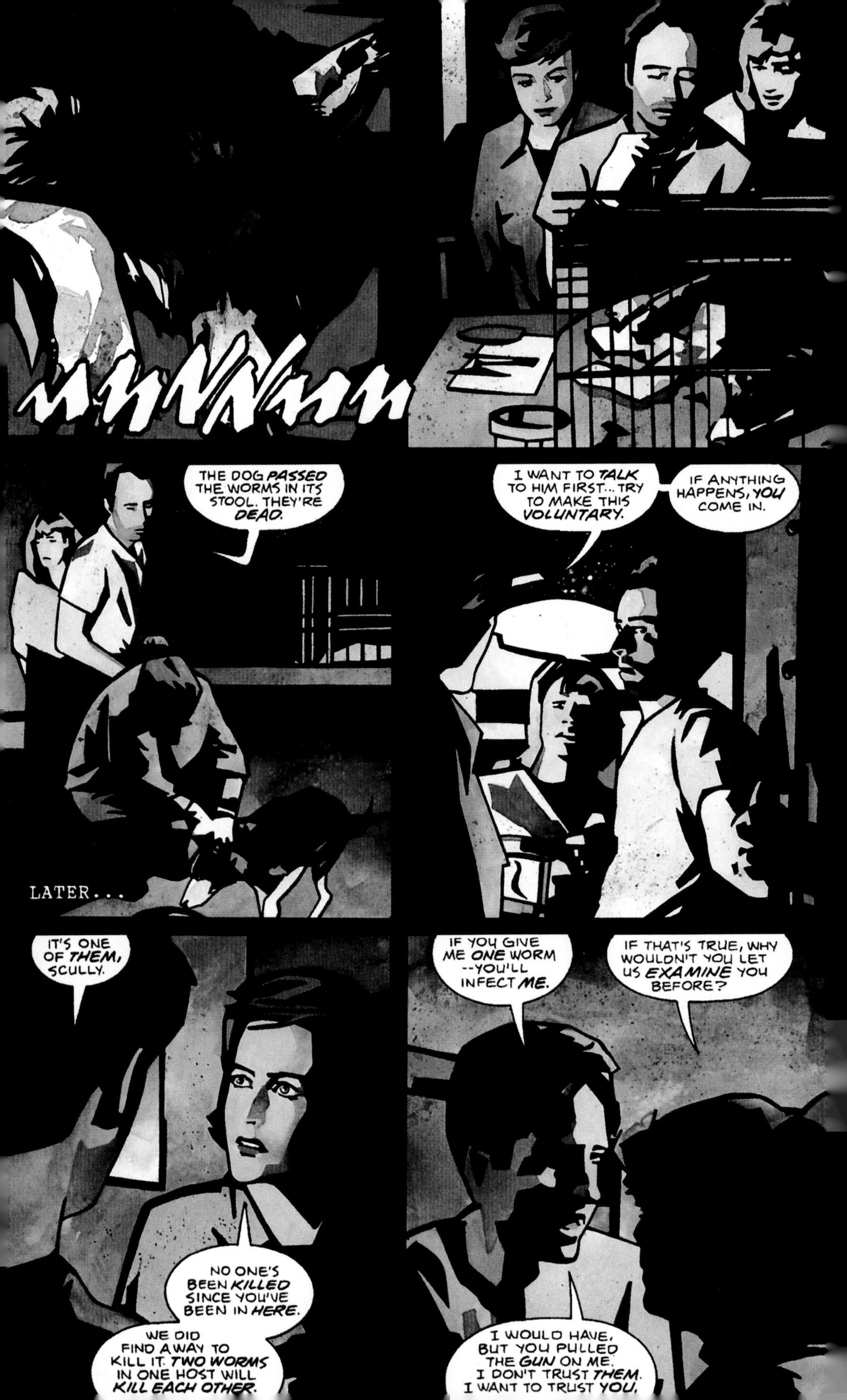
MMMMMMMM
THE DOG PASSED THE WORMS IN ITS STOOL. THEY'RE DEAD.
LATER...
I WANT TO TALK TO HIM FIRST... TRY TO MAKE THIS VOLUNTARY.
IF ANYTHING HAPPENS, YOU COME IN.
IT'S ONE OF THEM, SCULLY.
NO ONE'S BEEN KILLED SINCE YOU'VE BEEN IN HERE.
WE DID FIND A WAY TO KILL IT. TWO WORMS IN ONE HOST WILL KILL EACH OTHER.
IF YOU GIVE ME ONE WORM --YOU'LL INFECT ME.
IF THAT'S TRUE, WHY WOULDN'T YOU LET US EXAMINE YOU BEFORE?
I WOULD HAVE, BUT YOU PULLED THE GUN ON ME. I DON'T TRUST THEM. I WANT TO TRUST YOU.

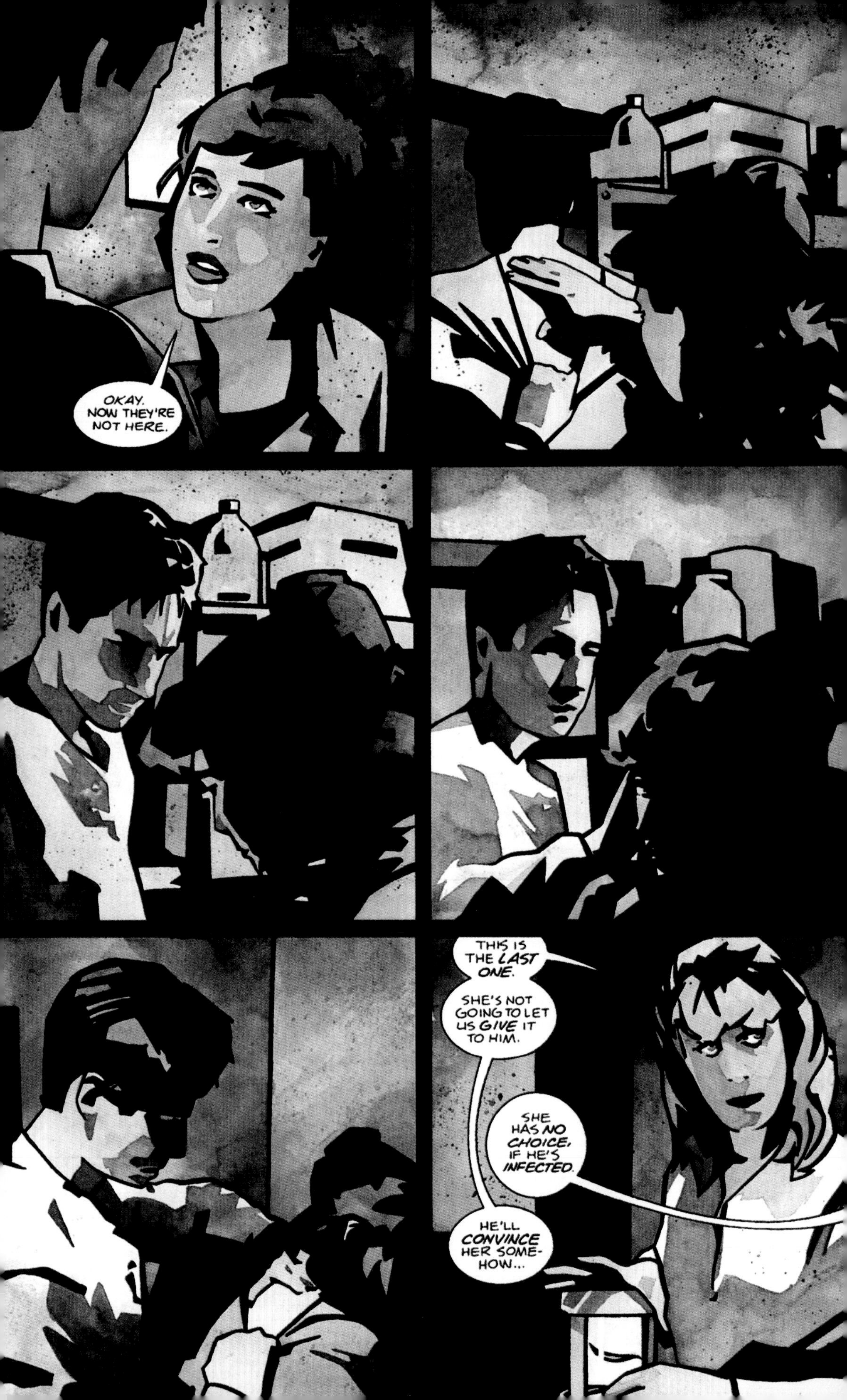
OKAY. NOW THEY'RE NOT HERE.
THIS IS THE LAST ONE.
SHE'S NOT GOING TO LET US GIVE IT TO HIM.
SHE HAS NO CHOICE, IF HE'S INFECTED.
HE'LL CONVINCE HER SOME-HOW...

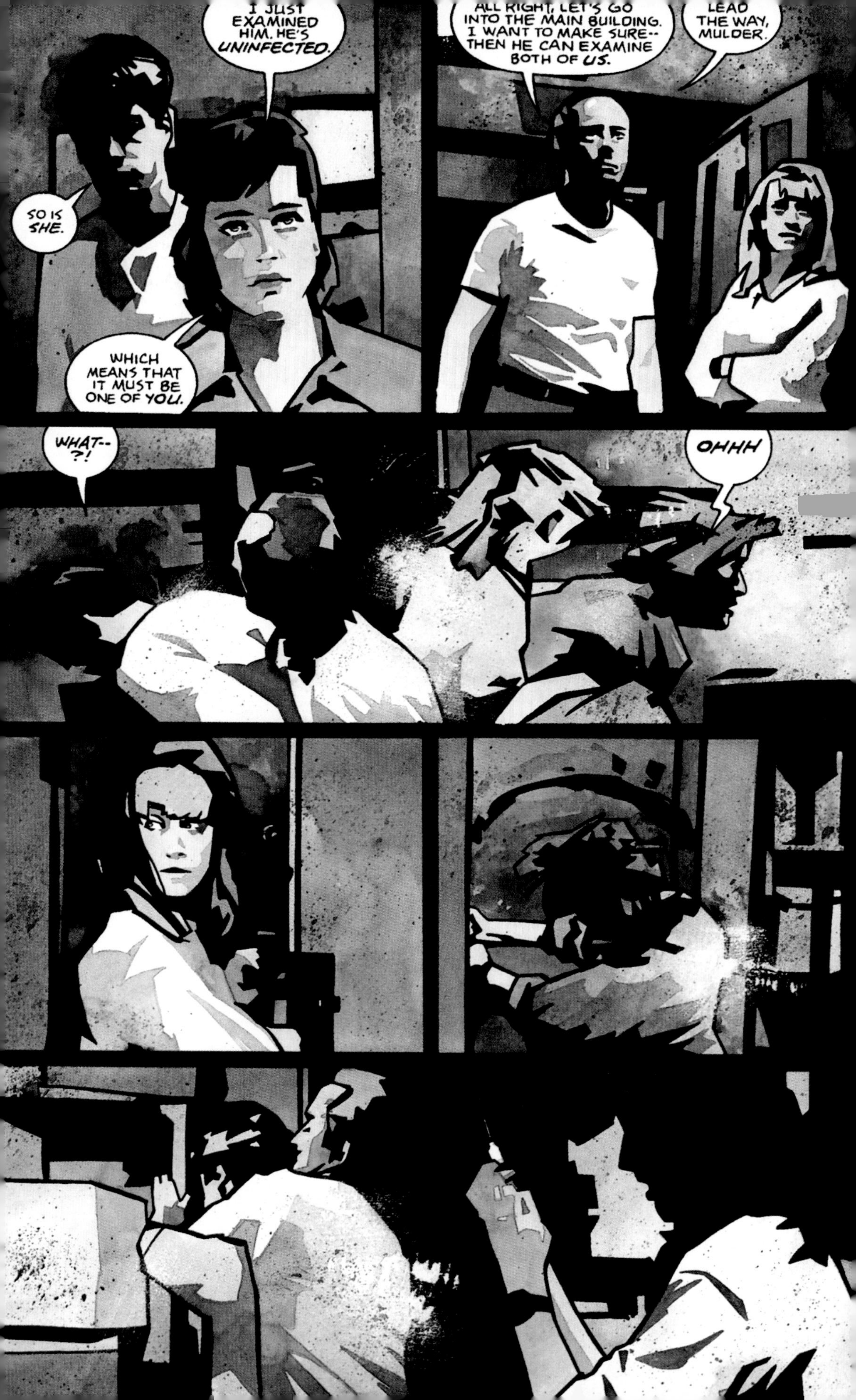

I JUST EXAMINED HIM. HE'S UNINFECTED.
SO IS SHE.
WHICH MEANS THAT IT MUST BE ONE OF YOU.
ALL RIGHT, LET'S GO INTO THE MAIN BUILDING. I WANT TO MAKE SURE-- THEN HE CAN EXAMINE BOTH OF US.
LEAD THE WAY, MULDER.
WHAT-- ?!
OHHH

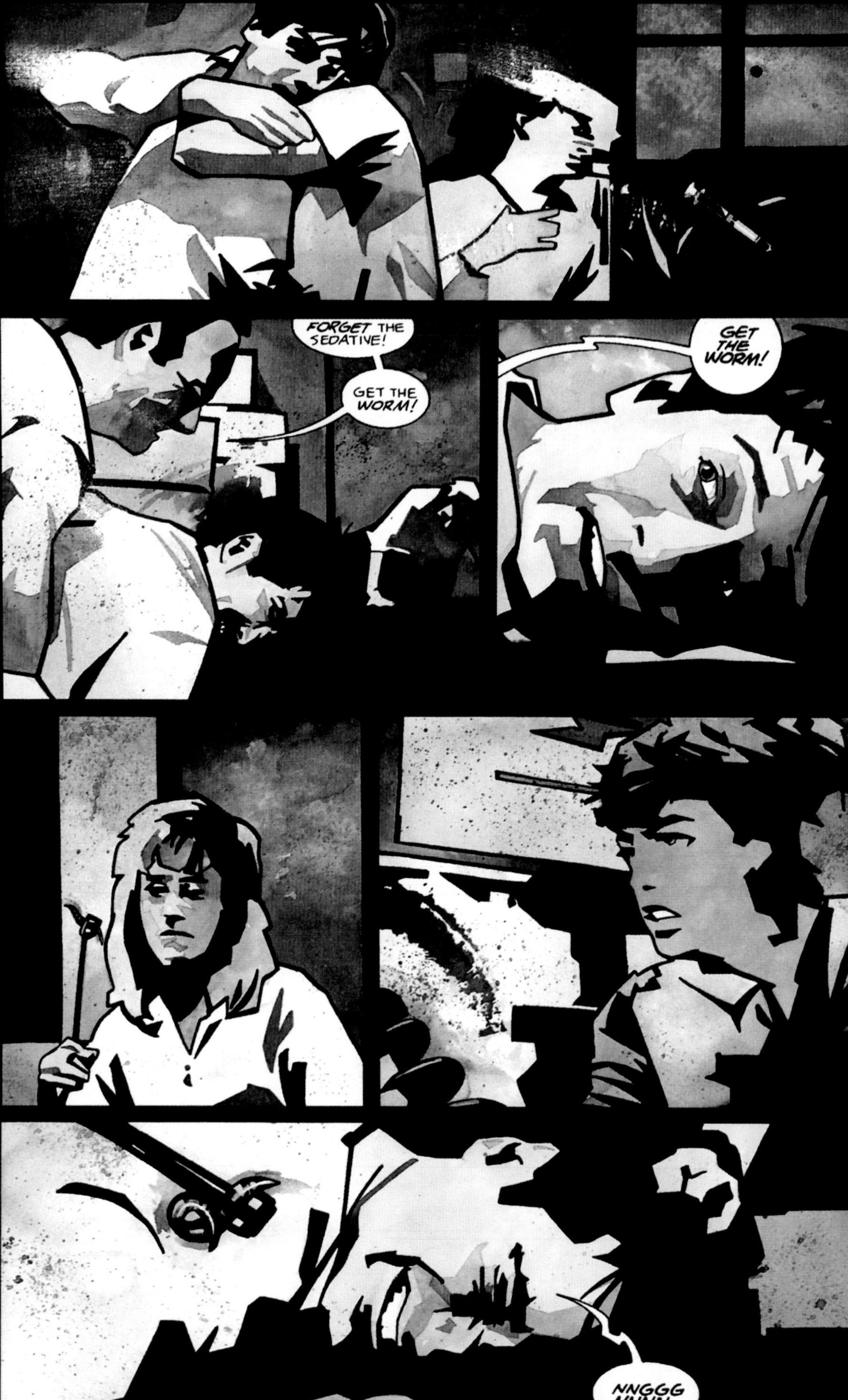
FORGET THE SEDATIVE!
GET THE WORM!
GET THE WORM!
NNGGG NNNN

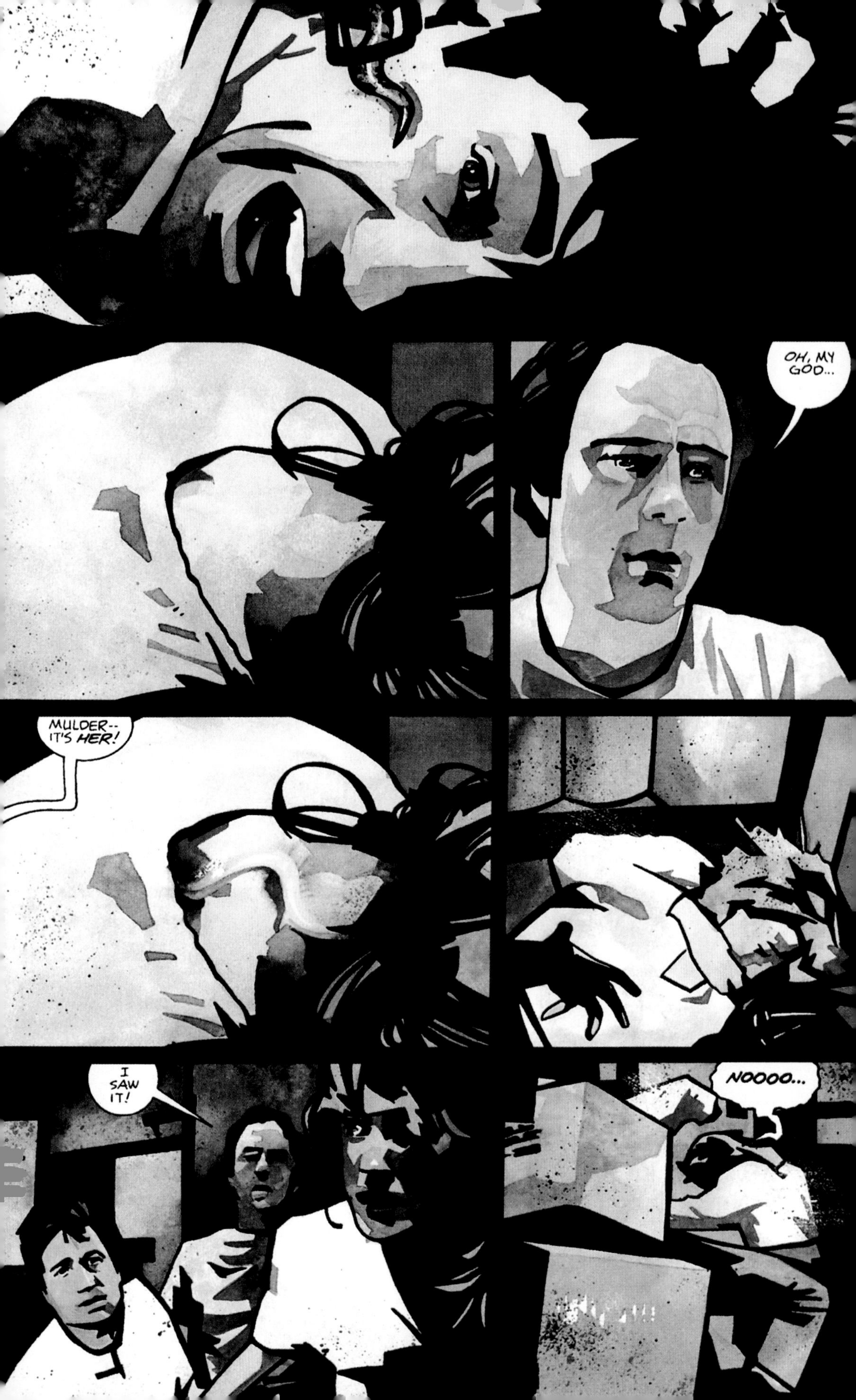
OH, MY GOD...
MULDER-- IT'S HER!
I SAW IT!
NOOOO...

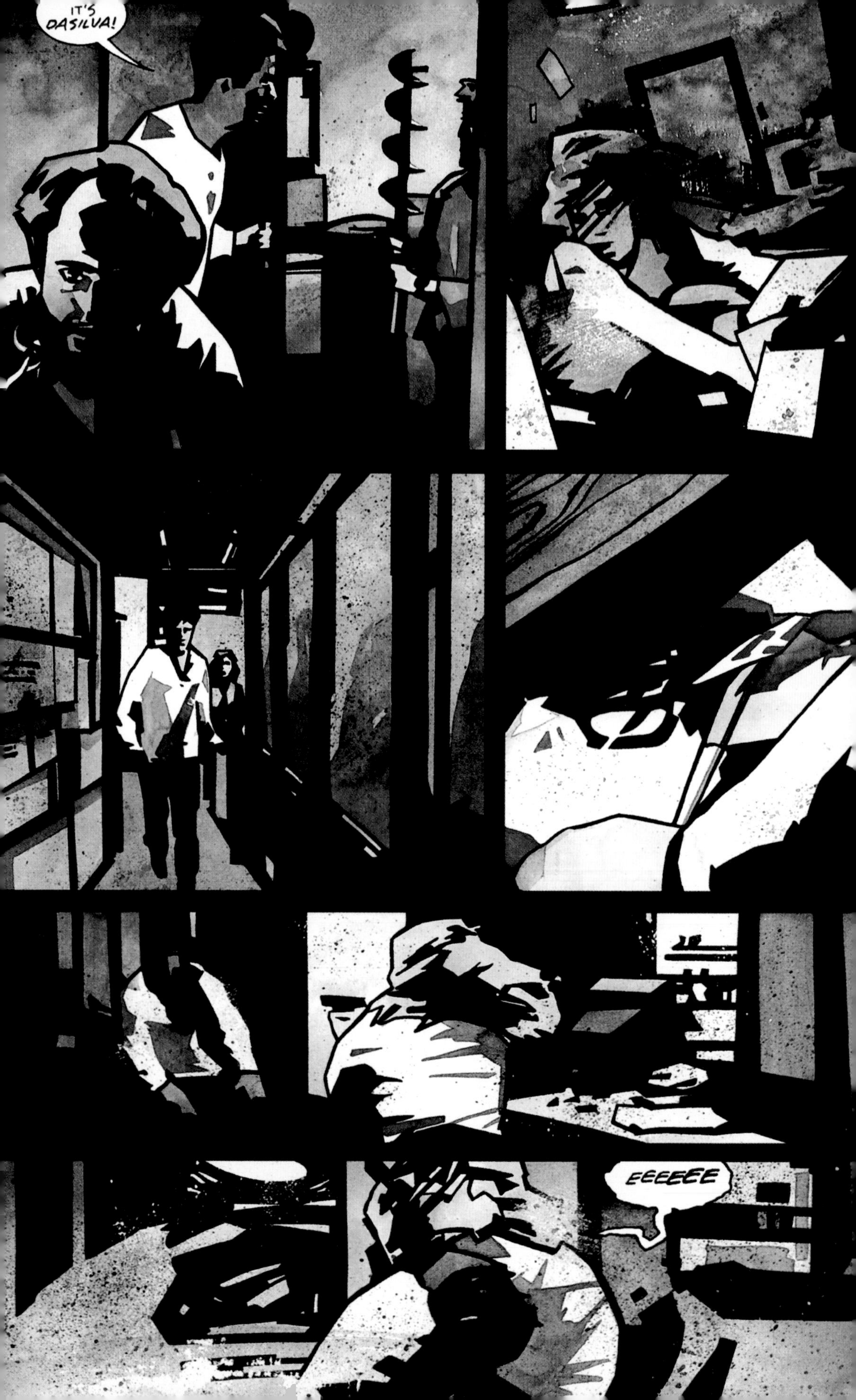
IT'S DASILVA!
EEEEEE

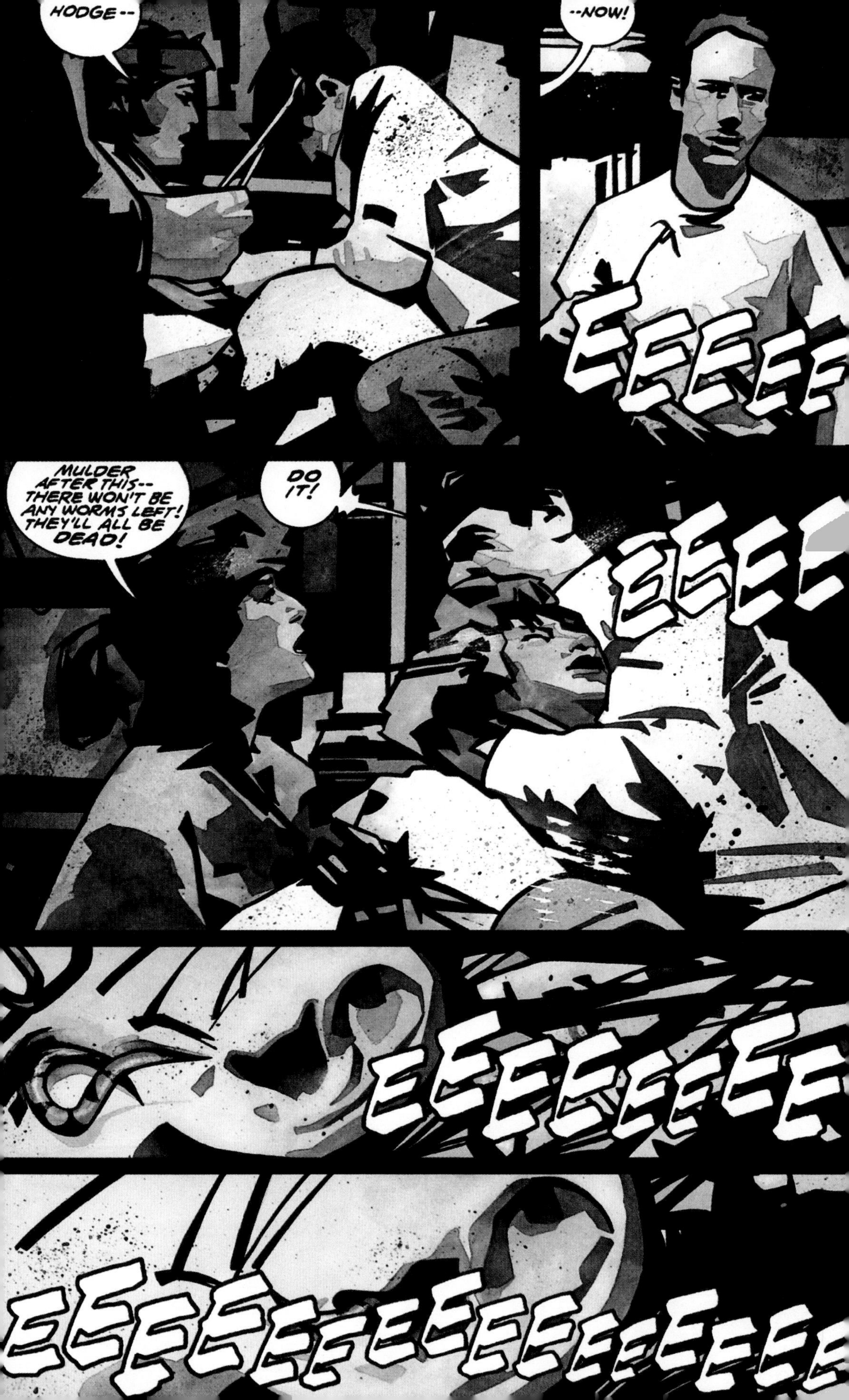
HODGE--
--NOW!
EEEEE
MULDER AFTER THIS--THERE WON'T BE ANY WORMS LEFT! THEY'LL ALL BE DEAD!
DO IT!
EEEEE
EEEEEEEEEEE
EEEEEEEEEEEEEEEEEE

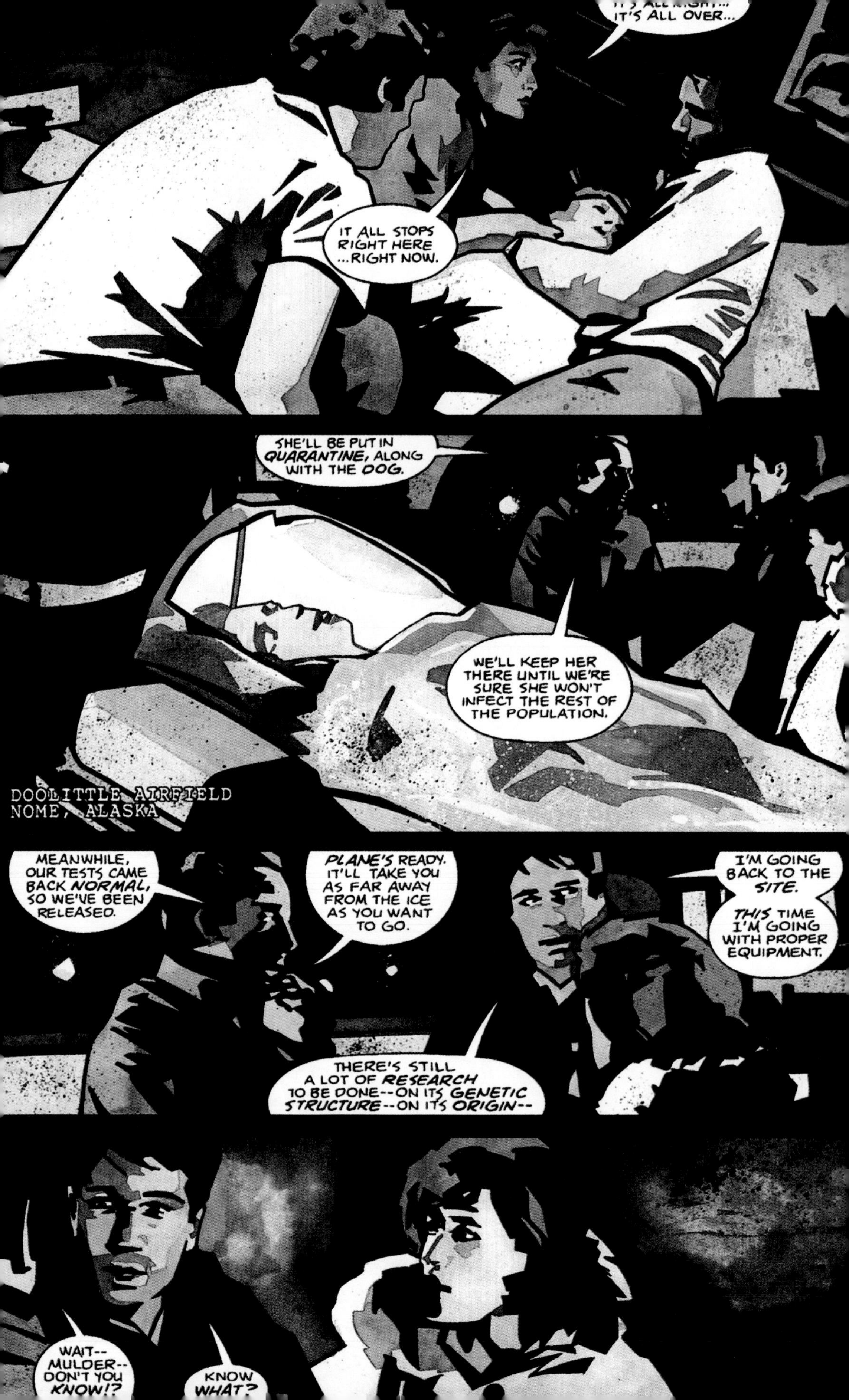
IT'S ALL OVER...
IT ALL STOPS RIGHT HERE ...RIGHT NOW.
SHE'LL BE PUT IN QUARANTINE, ALONG WITH THE DOG.
WE'LL KEEP HER THERE UNTIL WE'RE SURE SHE WON'T INFECT THE REST OF THE POPULATION.
DOOLITTLE AIRFIELD
NOME, ALASKA
MEANWHILE, OUR TESTS CAME BACK NORMAL, SO WE'VE BEEN RELEASED.
PLANE'S READY. IT'LL TAKE YOU AS FAR AWAY FROM THE ICE AS YOU WANT TO GO.
I'M GOING BACK TO THE SITE.
THIS TIME I'M GOING WITH PROPER EQUIPMENT.
THERE'S STILL A LOT OF RESEARCH TO BE DONE--ON ITS GENETIC STRUCTURE--ON ITS ORIGIN--
WAIT-- MULDER-- DON'T YOU KNOW!?
KNOW WHAT?

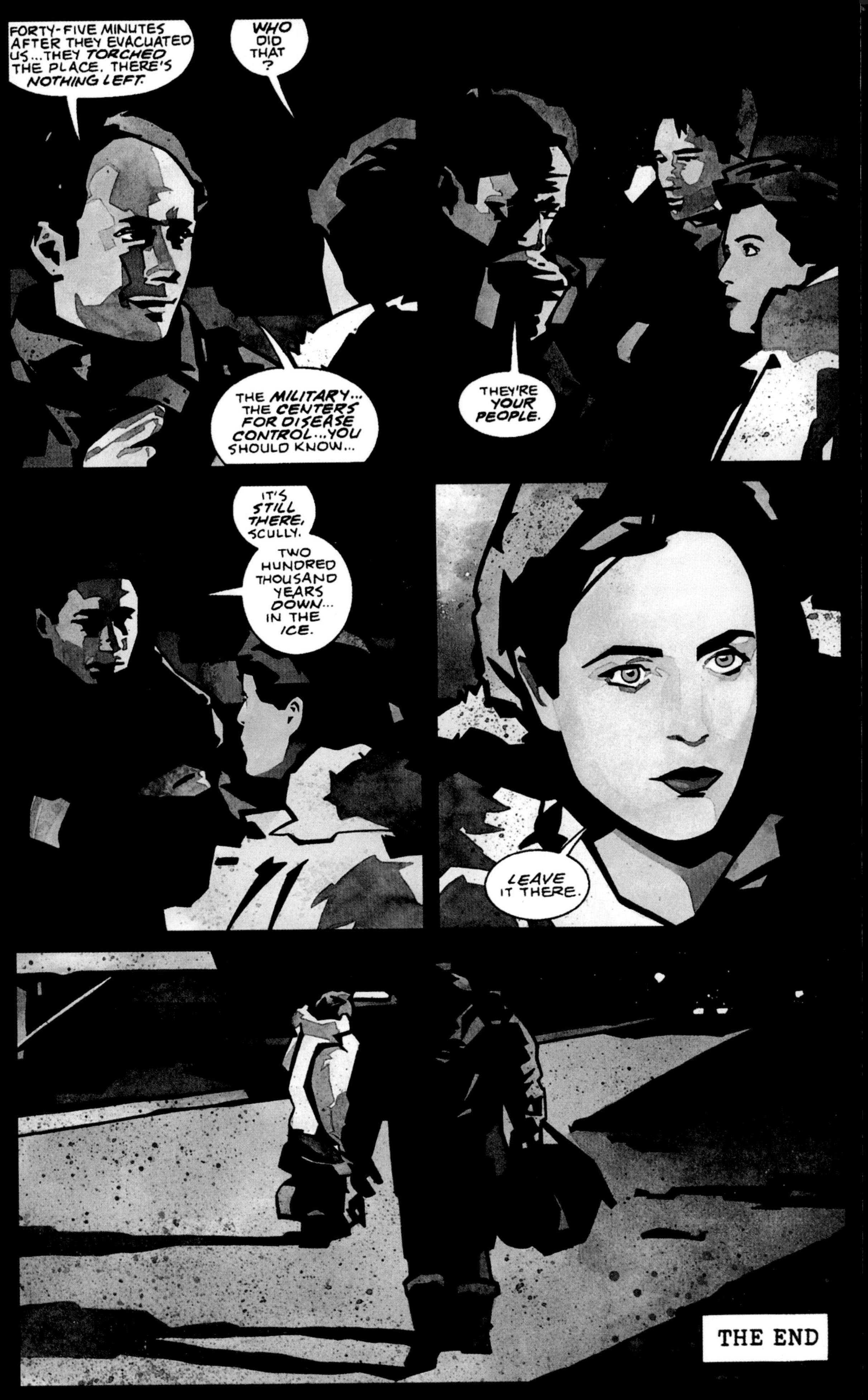

FORTY-FIVE MINUTES AFTER THEY EVACUATED US... THEY TORCHED THE PLACE. THERE'S NOTHING LEFT.
WHO DID THAT?
THE MILITARY... THE CENTERS FOR DISEASE CONTROL... YOU SHOULD KNOW...
THEY'RE YOUR PEOPLE.
IT'S STILL THERE, SCULLY.
TWO HUNDRED THOUSAND YEARS DOWN... IN THE ICE.
LEAVE IT THERE.
THE END

CHAPTER 7

# TRICK OF THE LIGHT

STORY: Stefan Petrucha
ART: Charles Adlard

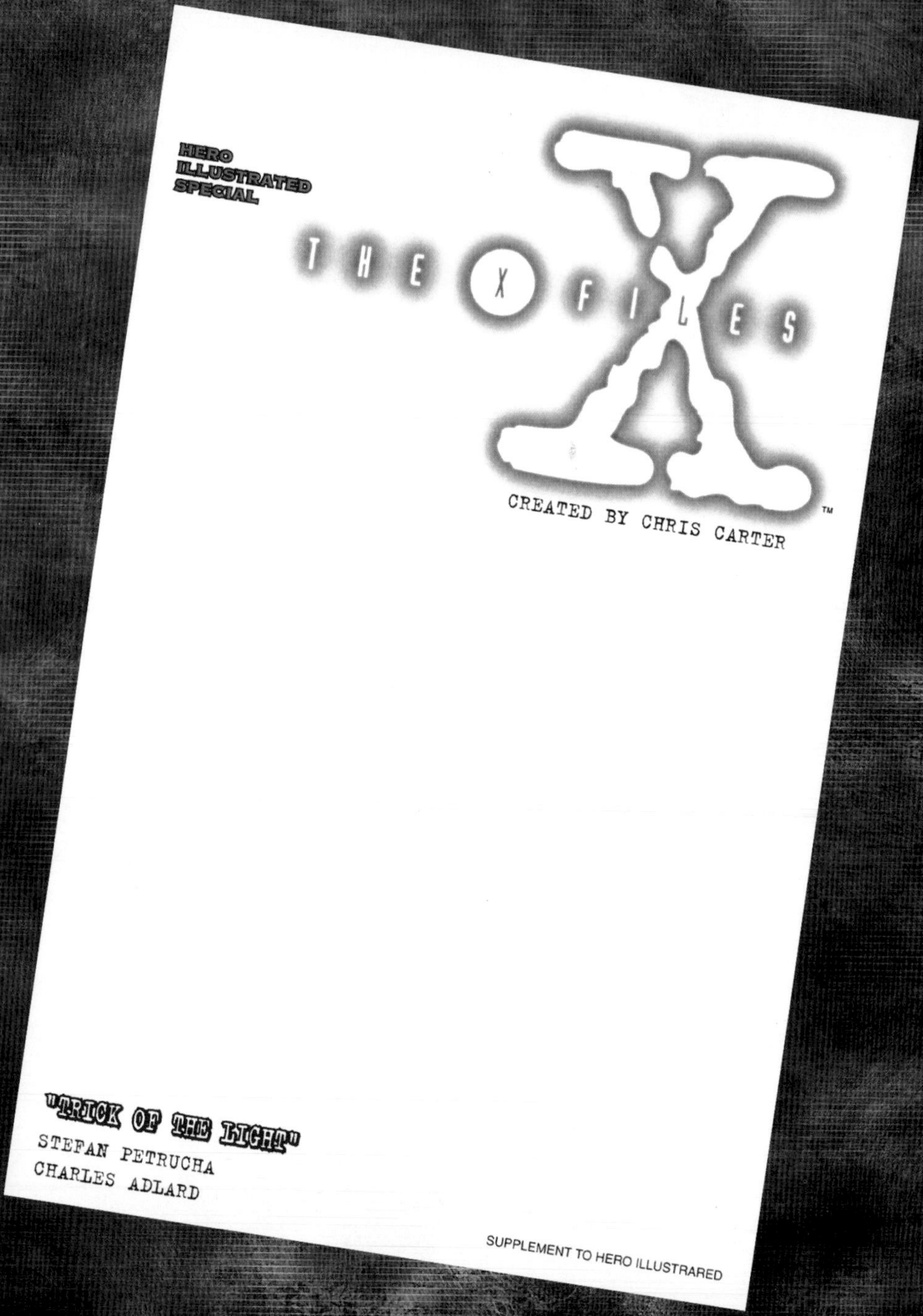
HERO ILLUSTRATED SPECIAL
THE X FILES
CREATED BY CHRIS CARTER™
"TRICK OF THE LIGHT"
STEFAN PETRUCHA
CHARLES ADLARD
SUPPLEMENT TO HERO ILLUSTRARED

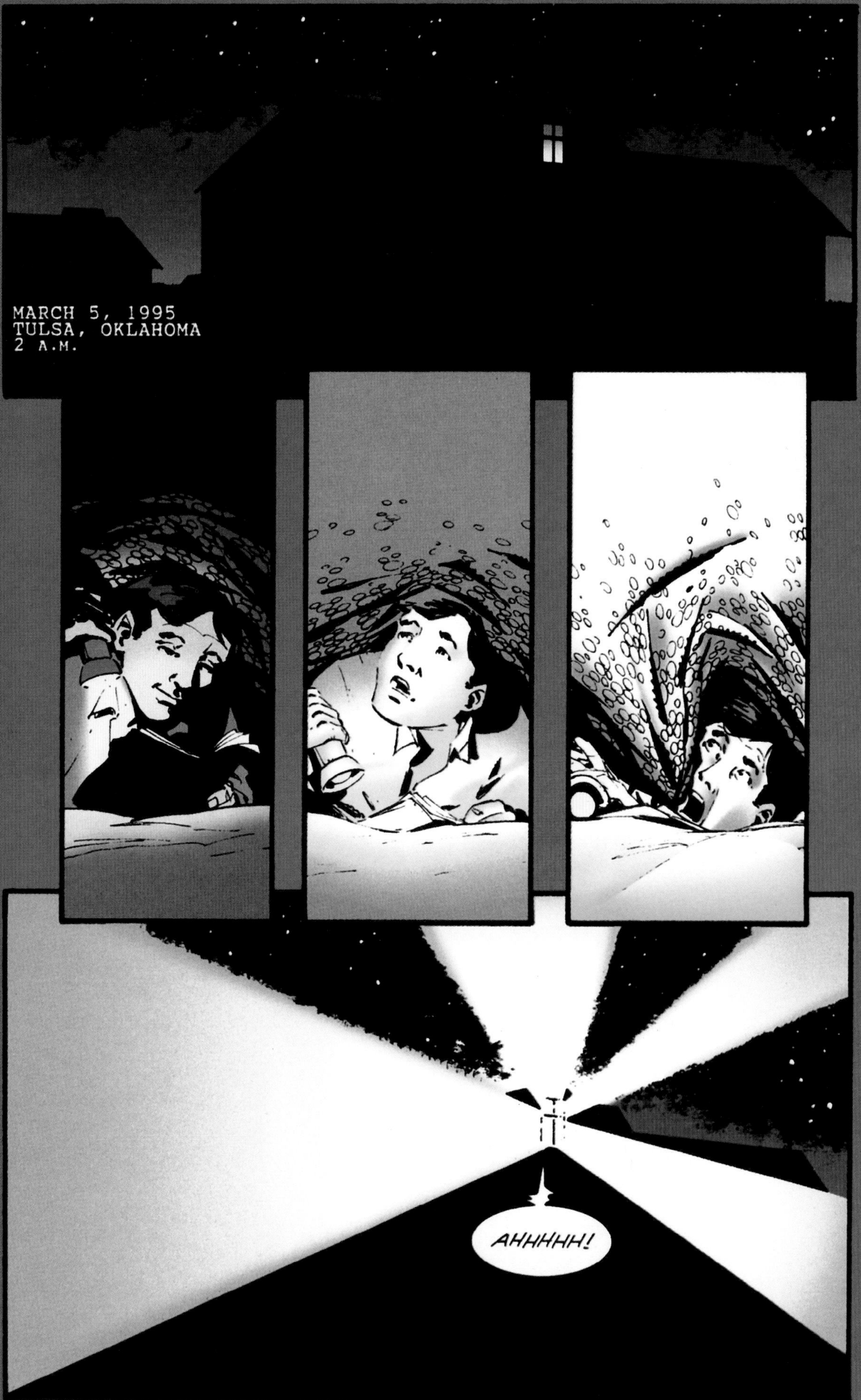
MARCH 5, 1995
TULSA, OKLAHOMA
2 A.M.
AHHHHH!

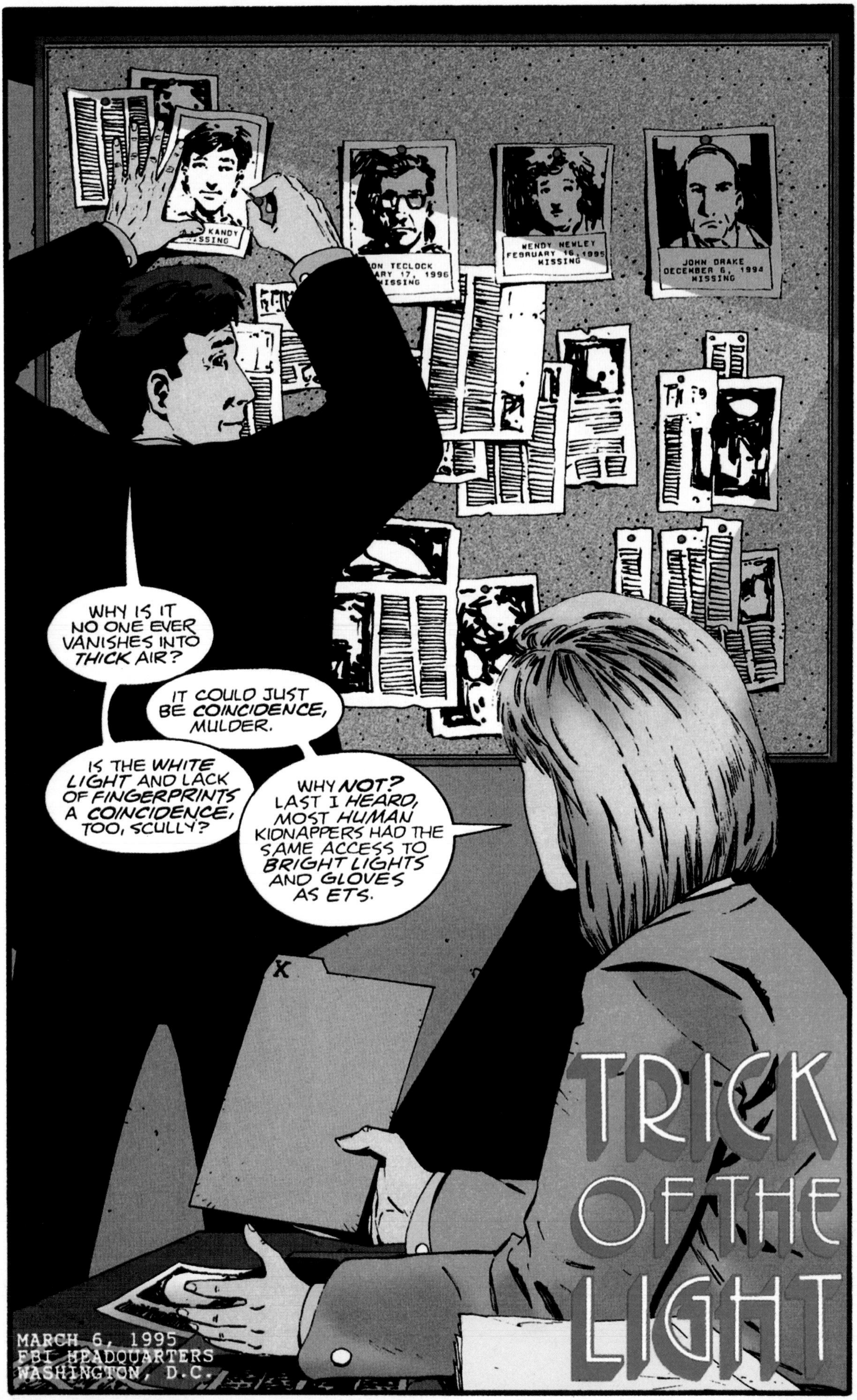
WENDY NEWLEY FEBRUARY 16, 1995 MISSING
JOHN DRAKE DECEMBER 6, 1994 MISSING
WHY IS IT NO ONE EVER VANISHES INTO THICK AIR?
IT COULD JUST BE COINCIDENCE, MULDER.
IS THE WHITE LIGHT AND LACK OF FINGERPRINTS A COINCIDENCE, TOO, SCULLY?
WHY NOT? LAST I HEARD, MOST HUMAN KIDNAPPERS HAD THE SAME ACCESS TO BRIGHT LIGHTS AND GLOVES AS ETS.
TRICK OF THE LIGHT
MARCH 6, 1995
FBI HEADQUARTERS
WASHINGTON, D.C.

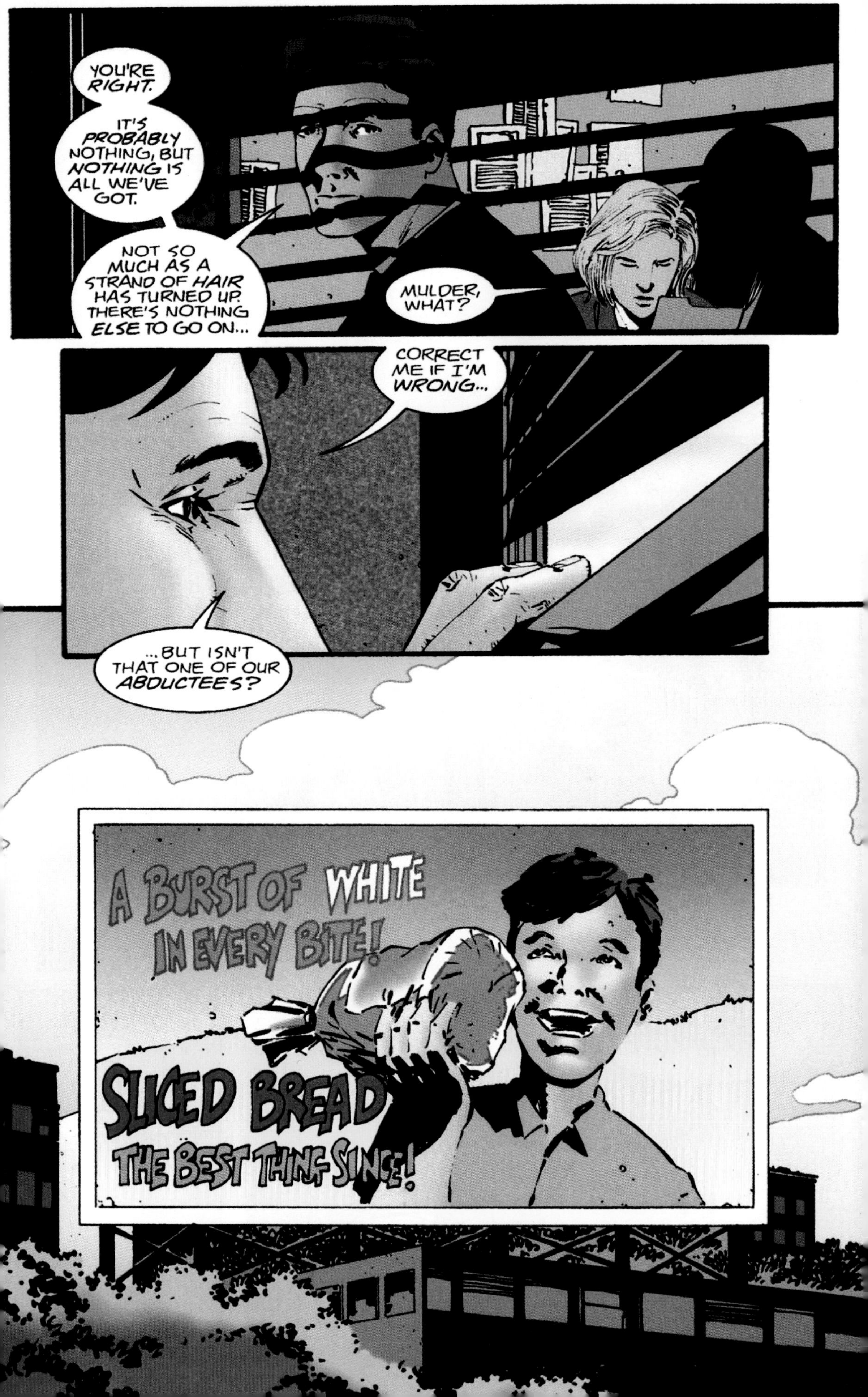
YOU'RE RIGHT.
IT'S PROBABLY NOTHING, BUT NOTHING IS ALL WE'VE GOT.
NOT SO MUCH AS A STRAND OF HAIR HAS TURNED UP. THERE'S NOTHING ELSE TO GO ON...
MULDER, WHAT?
CORRECT ME IF I'M WRONG...
...BUT ISN'T THAT ONE OF OUR ABDUCTEES?
A BURST OF WHITE IN EVERY BITE!
SLICED BREAD
THE BEST THING SINCE!

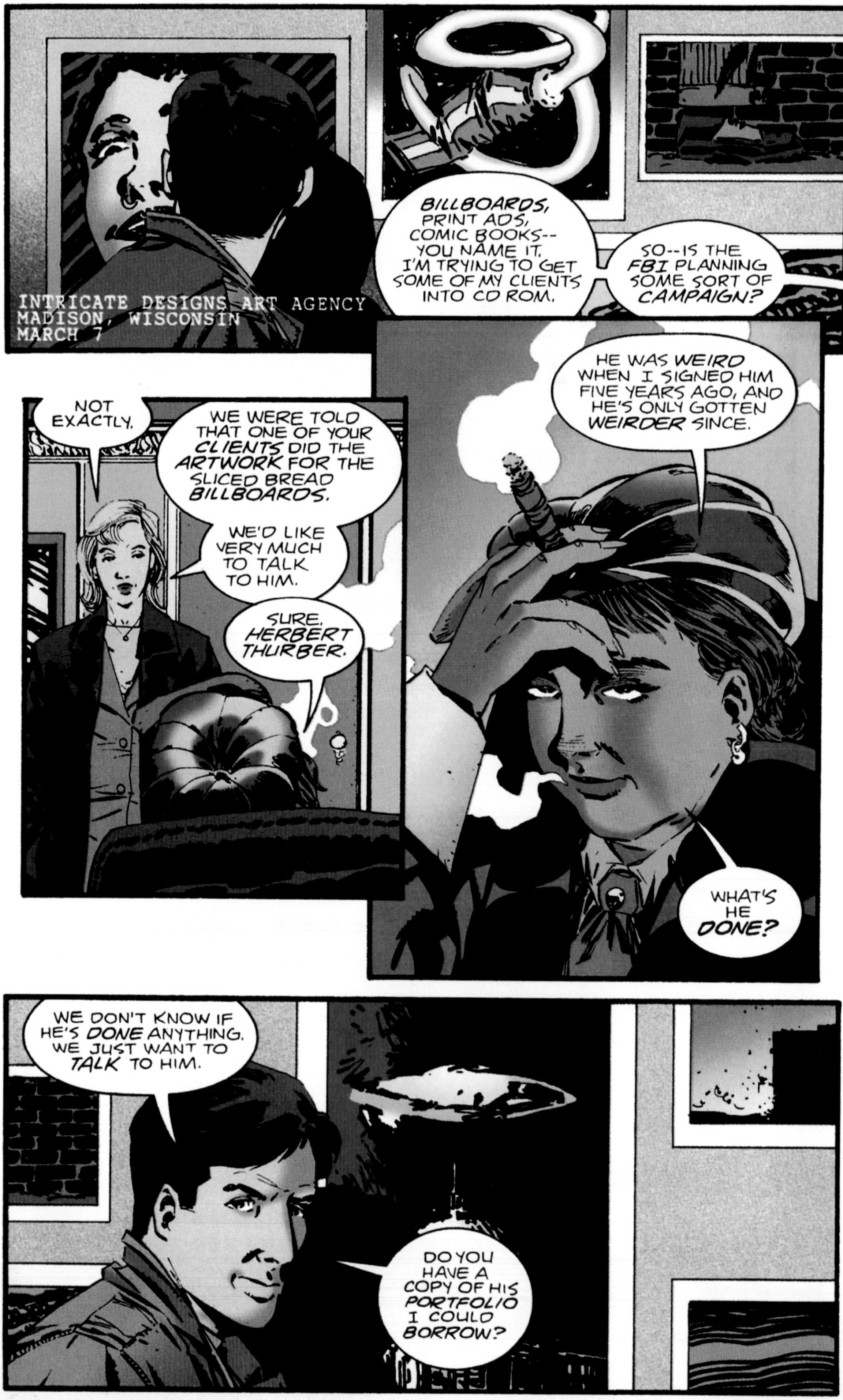
INTRICATE DESIGNS ART AGENCY
MADISON, WISCONSIN
MARCH 7
BILLBOARDS, PRINT ADS, COMIC BOOKS-- YOU NAME IT. I'M TRYING TO GET SOME OF MY CLIENTS INTO CD ROM.
SO--IS THE FBI PLANNING SOME SORT OF CAMPAIGN?
NOT EXACTLY.
WE WERE TOLD THAT ONE OF YOUR CLIENTS DID THE ARTWORK FOR THE SLICED BREAD BILLBOARDS.
WE'D LIKE VERY MUCH TO TALK TO HIM.
SURE. HERBERT THURBER.
HE WAS WEIRD WHEN I SIGNED HIM FIVE YEARS AGO, AND HE'S ONLY GOTTEN WEIRDER SINCE.
WHAT'S HE DONE?
WE DON'T KNOW IF HE'S DONE ANYTHING. WE JUST WANT TO TALK TO HIM.
DO YOU HAVE A COPY OF HIS PORTFOLIO I COULD BORROW?

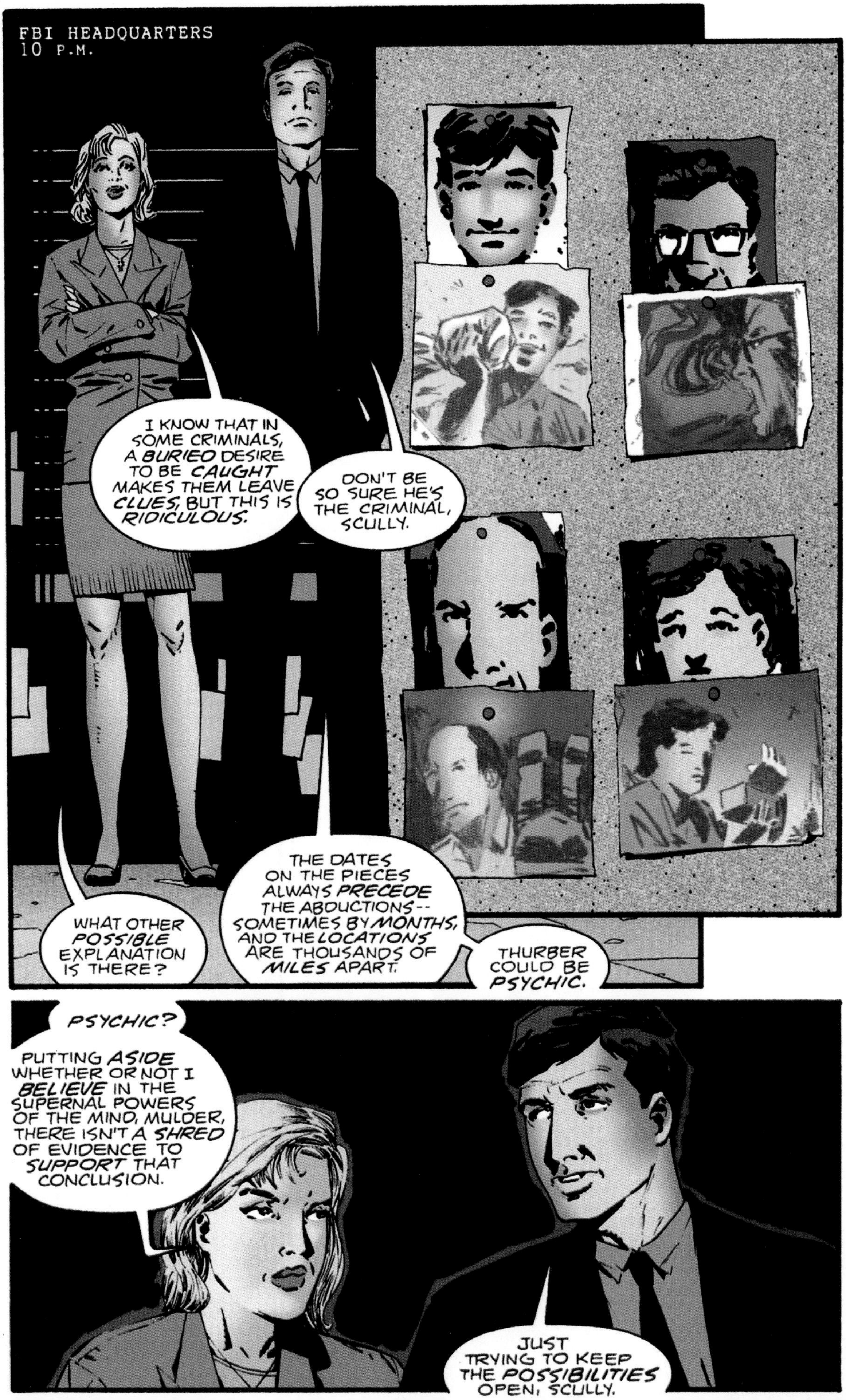
FBI HEADQUARTERS
10 P.M.
I KNOW THAT IN SOME CRIMINALS, A BURIED DESIRE TO BE CAUGHT MAKES THEM LEAVE CLUES, BUT THIS IS RIDICULOUS.
DON'T BE SO SURE HE'S THE CRIMINAL, SCULLY.
WHAT OTHER POSSIBLE EXPLANATION IS THERE?
THE DATES ON THE PIECES ALWAYS PRECEDE THE ABDUCTIONS--SOMETIMES BY MONTHS, AND THE LOCATIONS ARE THOUSANDS OF MILES APART.
THURBER COULD BE PSYCHIC.
PSYCHIC?
PUTTING ASIDE WHETHER OR NOT I BELIEVE IN THE SUPERNAL POWERS OF THE MIND, MULDER, THERE ISN'T A SHRED OF EVIDENCE TO SUPPORT THAT CONCLUSION.
JUST TRYING TO KEEP THE POSSIBILITIES OPEN, SCULLY.

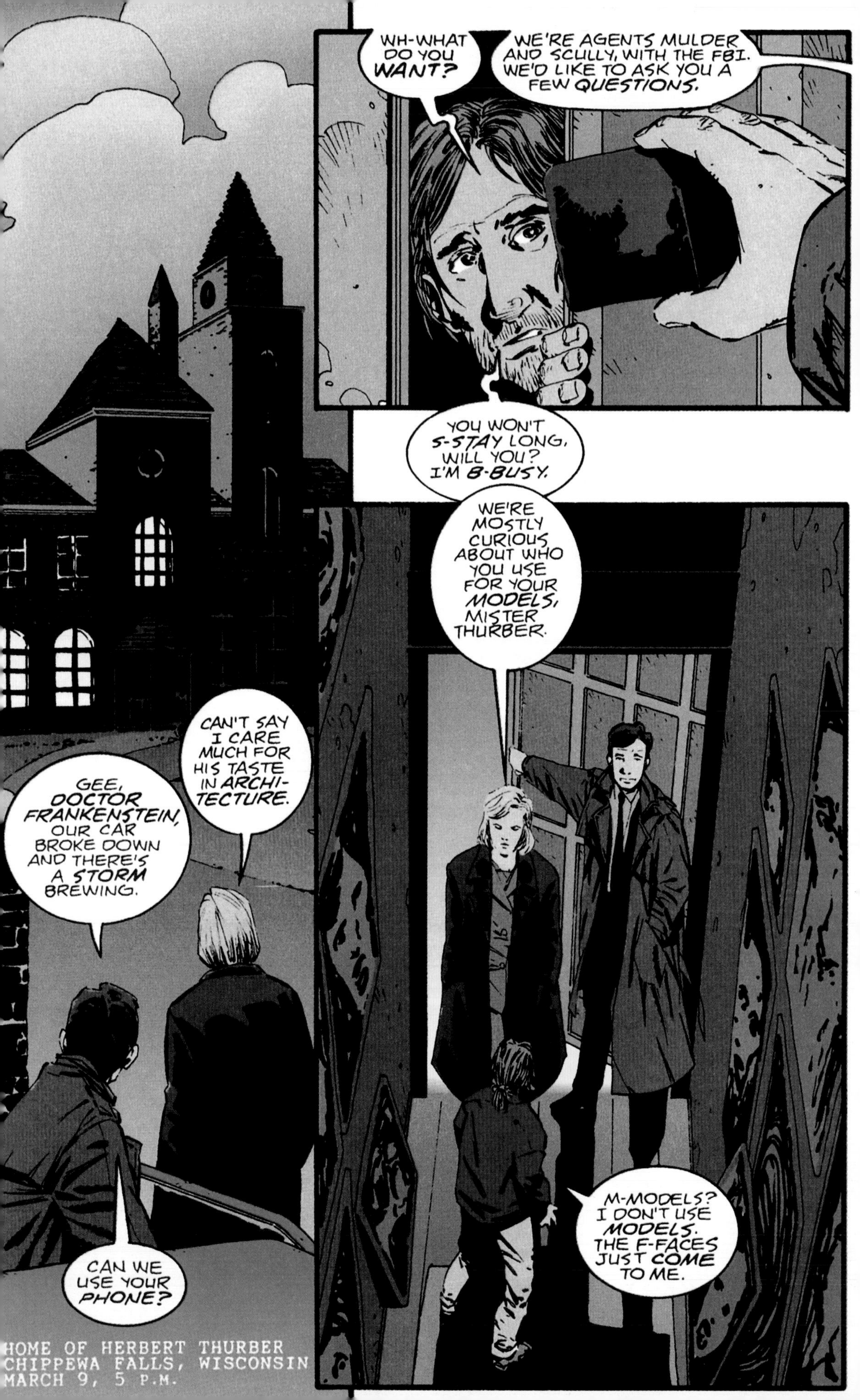
HOME OF HERBERT THURBER
CHIPPEWA FALLS, WISCONSIN
MARCH 9, 5 P.M.
GEE, DOCTOR FRANKENSTEIN, OUR CAR BROKE DOWN AND THERE'S A STORM BREWING.
CAN'T SAY I CARE MUCH FOR HIS TASTE IN ARCHI-TECTURE.
CAN WE USE YOUR PHONE?
WH-WHAT DO YOU WANT?
WE'RE AGENTS MULDER AND SCULLY, WITH THE FBI. WE'D LIKE TO ASK YOU A FEW QUESTIONS.
YOU WON'T S-STAY LONG, WILL YOU? I'M B-BUSY.
WE'RE MOSTLY CURIOUS ABOUT WHO YOU USE FOR YOUR MODELS, MISTER THURBER.
M-MODELS? I DON'T USE MODELS. THE F-FACES JUST COME TO ME.

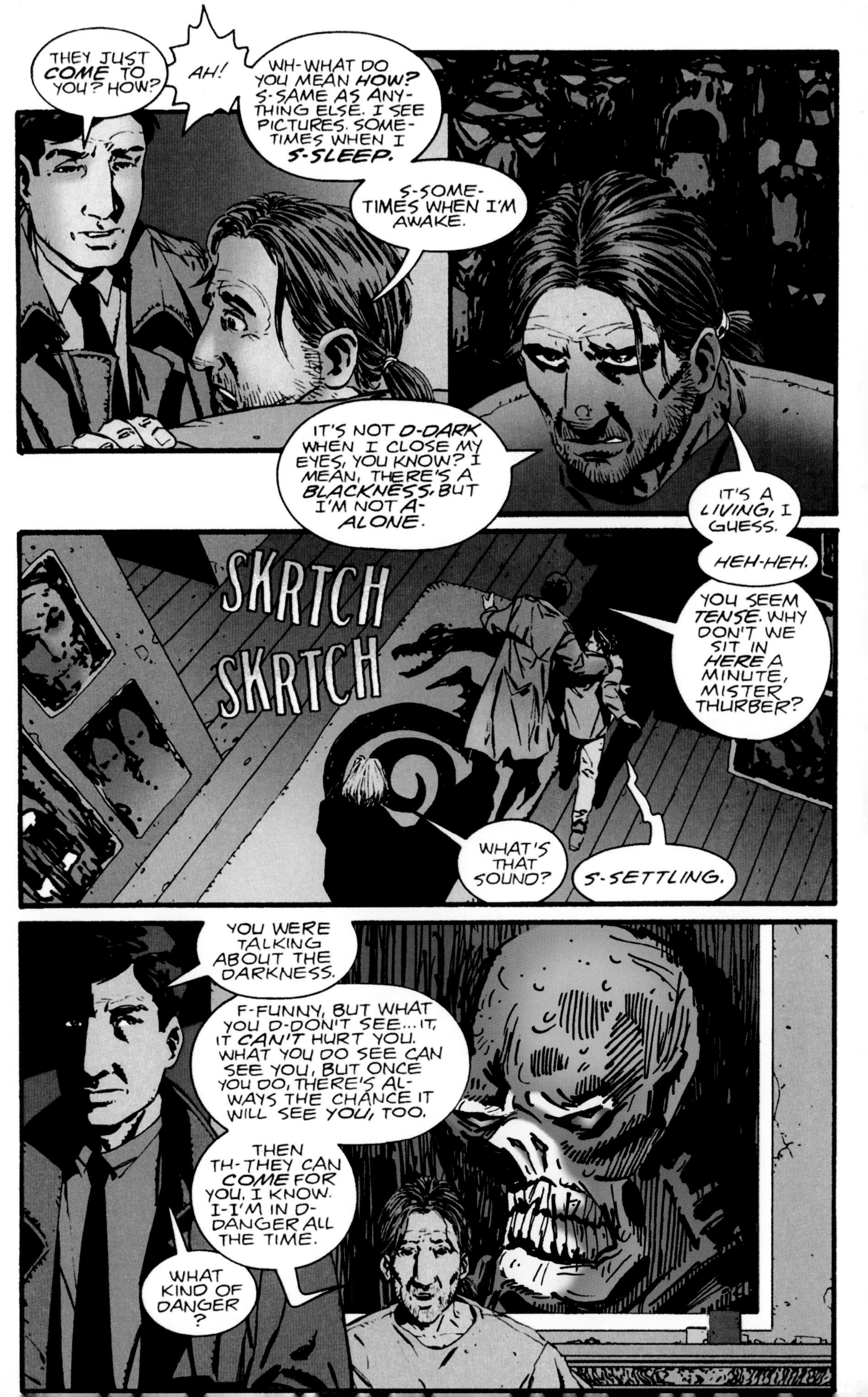
THEY JUST COME TO YOU? HOW?
AH!
WH-WHAT DO YOU MEAN HOW? S-SAME AS ANYTHING ELSE. I SEE PICTURES. SOMETIMES WHEN I S-SLEEP.
S-SOMETIMES WHEN I'M AWAKE.
IT'S NOT D-DARK WHEN I CLOSE MY EYES, YOU KNOW? I MEAN, THERE'S A BLACKNESS, BUT I'M NOT A-ALONE.
IT'S A LIVING, I GUESS.
HEH-HEH.
YOU SEEM TENSE. WHY DON'T WE SIT IN HERE A MINUTE, MISTER THURBER?
SKRTCH SKRTCH
WHAT'S THAT SOUND?
S-SETTLING.
YOU WERE TALKING ABOUT THE DARKNESS.
F-FUNNY, BUT WHAT YOU D-DON'T SEE... IT, IT CAN'T HURT YOU. WHAT YOU DO SEE CAN SEE YOU, BUT ONCE YOU DO, THERE'S ALWAYS THE CHANCE IT WILL SEE YOU, TOO.
THEN TH-THEY CAN COME FOR YOU, I KNOW. I-I'M IN D-DANGER ALL THE TIME.
WHAT KIND OF DANGER?

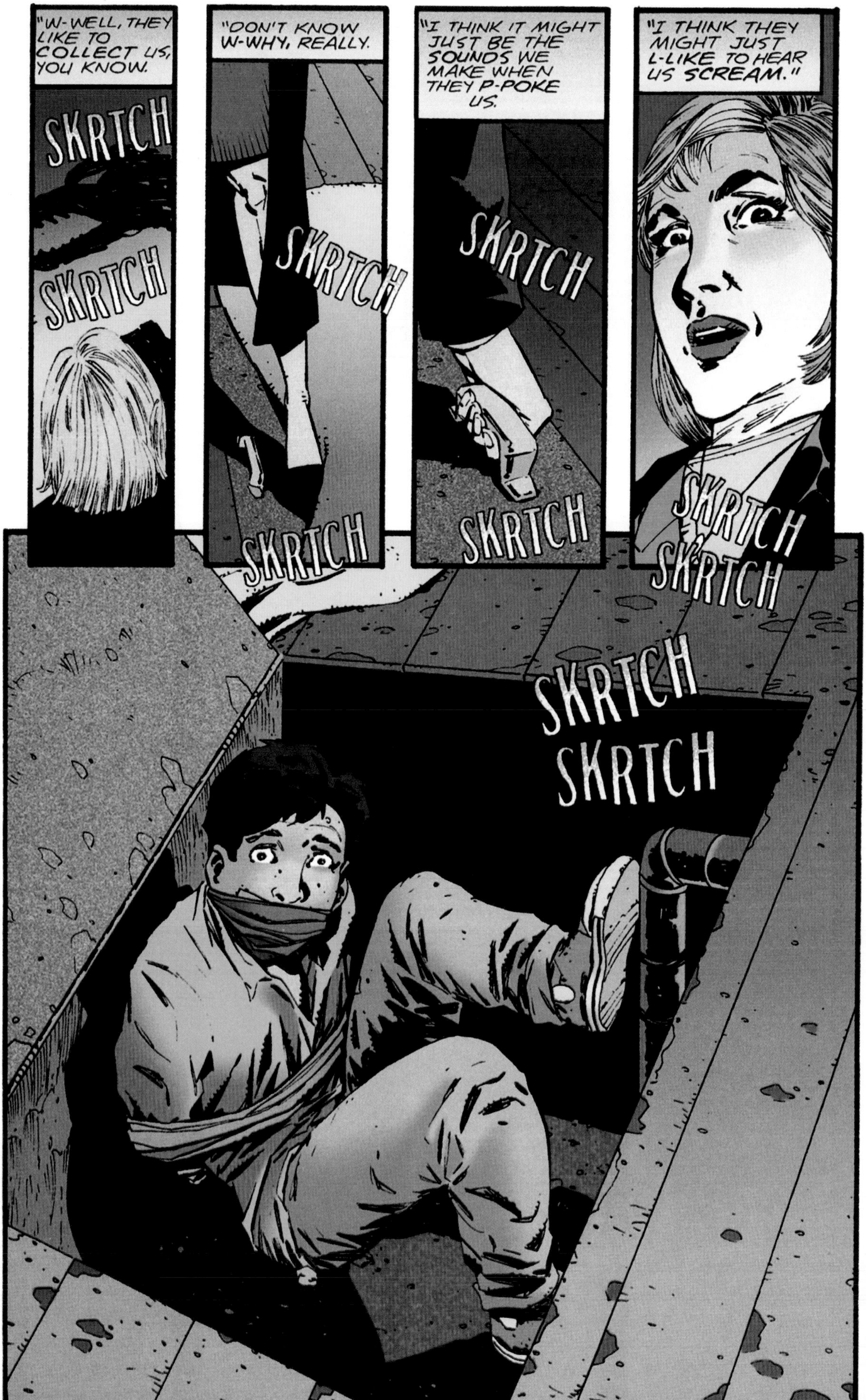
"W-WELL, THEY LIKE TO COLLECT US, YOU KNOW.
SKRTCH
SKRTCH
"DON'T KNOW W-WHY, REALLY.
SKRTCH
SKRTCH
"I THINK IT MIGHT JUST BE THE SOUNDS WE MAKE WHEN THEY P-POKE US.
SKRTCH
SKRTCH
"I THINK THEY MIGHT JUST L-LIKE TO HEAR US SCREAM."
SKRTCH
SKRTCH
SKRTCH
SKRTCH

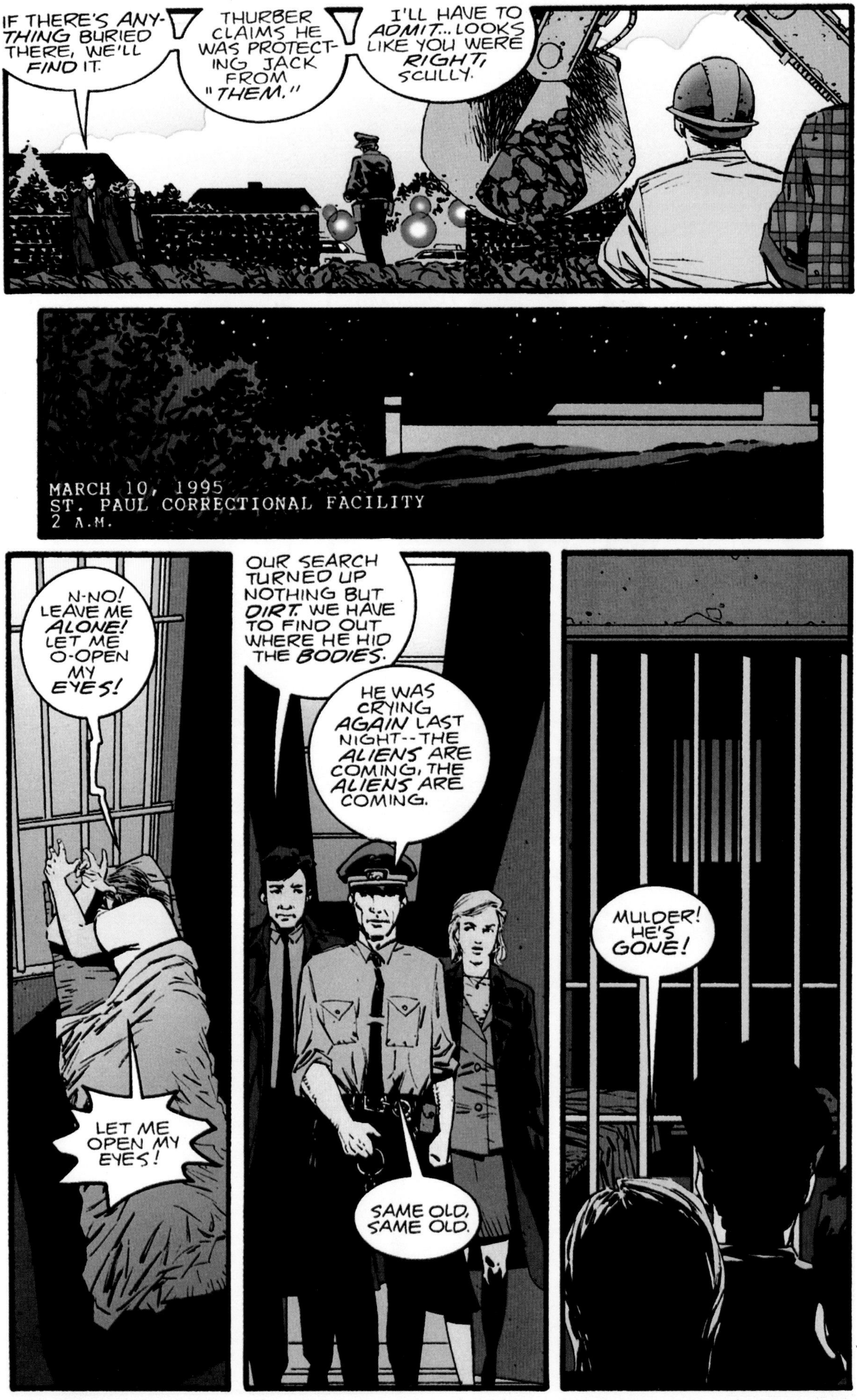
IF THERE'S ANYTHING BURIED THERE, WE'LL FIND IT.
THURBER CLAIMS HE WAS PROTECTING JACK FROM "THEM."
I'LL HAVE TO ADMIT... LOOKS LIKE YOU WERE RIGHT, SCULLY.
MARCH 10, 1995
ST. PAUL CORRECTIONAL FACILITY
2 A.M.
N-NO! LEAVE ME ALONE! LET ME O-OPEN MY EYES!
LET ME OPEN MY EYES!
OUR SEARCH TURNED UP NOTHING BUT DIRT. WE HAVE TO FIND OUT WHERE HE HID THE BODIES.
HE WAS CRYING AGAIN LAST NIGHT--THE ALIENS ARE COMING, THE ALIENS ARE COMING.
SAME OLD, SAME OLD.
MULDER! HE'S GONE!

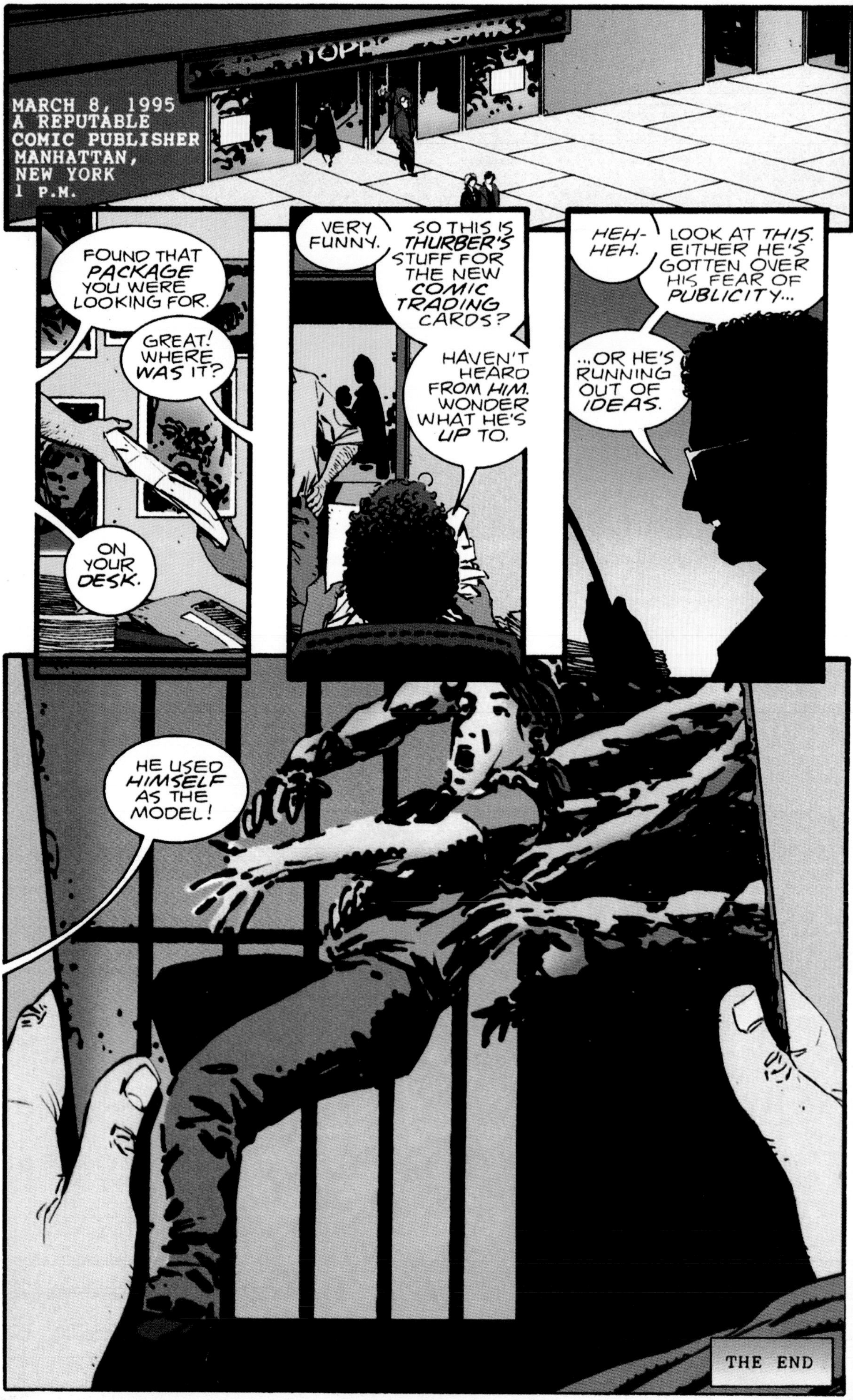
MARCH 8, 1995
A REPUTABLE
COMIC PUBLISHER
MANHATTAN,
NEW YORK
1 P.M.
FOUND THAT PACKAGE YOU WERE LOOKING FOR.
GREAT! WHERE WAS IT?
ON YOUR DESK.
VERY FUNNY.
SO THIS IS THURBER'S STUFF FOR THE NEW COMIC TRADING CARDS?
HAVEN'T HEARD FROM HIM. WONDER WHAT HE'S UP TO.
HEH-HEH.
LOOK AT THIS. EITHER HE'S GOTTEN OVER HIS FEAR OF PUBLICITY...
...OR HE'S RUNNING OUT OF IDEAS.
HE USED HIMSELF AS THE MODEL!
THE END

# ALIEN LEGION

**Alien Legion: Force Nomad**
A premium collection of the first eleven issues of this critically acclaimed comic series about a fighting force a la the French Foreign Legion.

**Alien Legion: Piecemaker**
The follow-up to Force Nomad, the Alien Legion resumes duty in a series of far-flung combat zones.

**Alien Legion: Footsloggers**
Collects the first six comics from the original incarnation of the series in 1984.

Brought to you by

**checker**
BOOK PUBLISHING GROUP

**www.checkerbpg.com**

Alien Legion: Force Nomad
ISBN: 0-9710249-0-1

Alien Legion: Piecemaker
ISBN: 0-9710249-4-4

Alien Legion: Footsloggers
ISBN: 0-9753808-7-7

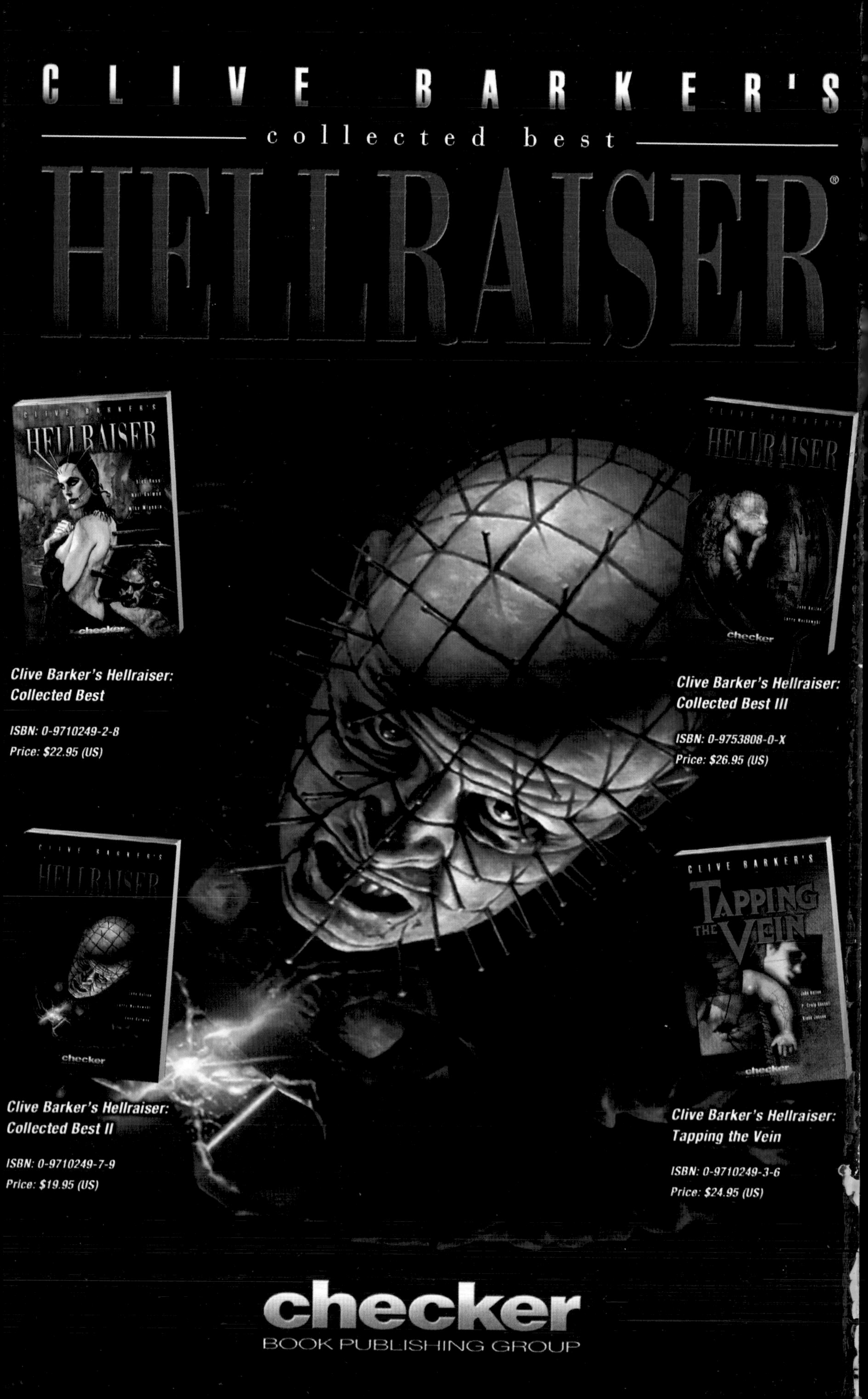
CLIVE BARKER'S
collected best
HELLRAISER®
Clive Barker's Hellraiser: Collected Best
ISBN: 0-9710249-2-8
Price: $22.95 (US)
Clive Barker's Hellraiser: Collected Best III
ISBN: 0-9753808-0-X
Price: $26.95 (US)
Clive Barker's Hellraiser: Collected Best II
ISBN: 0-9710249-7-9
Price: $19.95 (US)
Clive Barker's Hellraiser: Tapping the Vein
ISBN: 0-9710249-3-6
Price: $24.95 (US)
checker
BOOK PUBLISHING GROUP